HAMAN

Haman

A BIOGRAPHY

ADAM J. SILVERSTEIN

PRINCETON UNIVERSITY PRESS
PRINCETON & OXFORD

Published by Princeton University Press
41 William Street, Princeton, New Jersey 08540
99 Banbury Road, Oxford OX2 6JX

press.princeton.edu

GPSR Authorized Representative: Easy Access System Europe - Mustamäe tee 50, 10621 Tallinn, Estonia, gpsr.requests@easproject.com

ISBN 9780691203607
ISBN (e-book) 9780691276304

British Library Cataloging-in-Publication Data is available

Editorial: Fred Appel and Tara Dugan
Production Editorial: Ali Parrington
Production: Erin Suydam
Publicity: William Pagdatoon
Jacket image: ilbusca / iStock

This book has been composed in Minion Pro

Printed in the United States of America

10 9 8 7 6 5 4 3 2 1

MIX
Paper
FSC FSC® C183721

CONTENTS

ACKNOWLEDGEMENTS

ALTHOUGH THIS is a book about villains, I would like to begin it by thanking some heroes. The following people have helped me in numerous ways throughout this book's very long gestation.

Reuven Amitai, Patricia Crone, Robert Hoyland, Aaron Koller, Shari Lowin, Zeev Maghen, David Powers, Gabriel Reynolds, Michael Roaf, Nicolai Sinai, Joseph Witztum, and Shaul Shaked, all either read drafts of some of the book's contents, answered my queries, engaged me in thought-provoking discussions, or some combination of these things. Much of what is good in this book is to their credit. Much of what is bad in this book is Haman's fault.

I first contacted Fred Appel about writing a biography of Haman so long ago that the proposal was probably sent by pigeon-post. Since then, Fred has been incredibly helpful and endlessly patient in seeing the book through the various stages of publication, for which I am very grateful.

My wife Sophie, and my children Ella, Zara, Theo, and Amalia, have reminded me many times and in their many ways what it is in life that really matters (it turns out that the answer is not "footnotes"). For keeping me on my toes, forcing me to improve myself as a person, laughing at my dad-jokes, pretending to be amazed by my magic tricks, and convincingly feigning interest in Haman and in my other projects, they are, for me, super-heroes.

As we will see in the following pages, Haman managed to annoy many people. Had he been fortunate enough to meet my remarkable grandmother, Lila Silverstein (1922–2020), she would have told him that, "you attract more flies with honey than with vinegar," amongst many other pieces of wisdom that she was famous for dispensing. This book is dedicated to her memory.

HAMAN

Introduction

THIS BOOK is about a character by the name of Haman, who is considered a villain in virtually all varieties of Judaism, Christianity, and Islam. As the book is labeled a "biography," I will dutifully describe Haman's life—including his background, family, career, and death. Readers who are acquainted with Haman from scripture and wish to discover more about him are invited to go straight to Part III ("Haman's Life"), where they will (hopefully) find what they are looking for.

However, outside of the Bible and the Qur'ān (and the commentaries on these texts that their interpreters authored), there is very slim evidence for Haman's existence as a historical figure. What we possess, instead, is an abundance of material concerning what those who read the Bible and the Qur'ān have thought about Haman. And although we will explore such evidence as there is for the historical Haman, it will become clear throughout this book that his biography has been repeatedly overlaid by exegetical expansions that make it nigh impossible to recover a historical Haman with any degree of confidence.

In practice, this means two things: First, this book is primarily about Haman as a literary character, whose depictions reflect the perspectives of the religious traditions and scholars that produced our sources. Second, these sources come from diverse regions, periods, and civilizations, a diversity reflected in the multitude of Hamans whom we will encounter. In Part II ("Haman in History"), we examine the various contexts in which Jews, Christians, and Muslims developed Haman's character (Chapter 6) and deployed it polemically (Chapter 7).

Haman's importance in the Abrahamic religions originates in his appearances in scriptures. Although these are limited to a single book of the Hebrew Bible and six verses of the Qur'ān, Haman's descriptions in versions of these texts (and in the commentaries that they spawned) evolved in fascinating ways that will be analyzed in Part I ("Haman in Scripture"). Moreover, as we will see throughout the book, despite Haman's limited coverage in the Bible and the Qur'ān, his impact over the past two millennia has been enormous, making him one of history's great overachievers.

To the best of my knowledge, this book is the first biography of Haman, and—more generally—the first book-length attempt to trace a biblical character both backwards and forwards in time. In addition to the expected Jewish and Christian treatments of Haman, we will explore his prebiblical origins in the ancient Near East and his reception in Islamic cultures. Along the way, we will encounter ancient Iranian history and culture, Hellenism's impact on Second Temple Judaism, Abrahamic transformations in late antiquity, the development of classical Islamic civilization, and various episodes of medieval and early modern European history. We will consider Haman's refraction through the lenses of varieties of Judaism, Christianity, and Islam, as well as the interactions of these religious traditions with Zoroastrianism, Samaritanism, and ancient Near Eastern pantheons. And we will process Haman's roles in scriptures, inter- and intracommunal relations, religious theater, history, and historiography, in varieties of Near Eastern literatures that do not usually feature in discussions of the Abrahamic religions, and in social media.[1]

Clearly, I have bitten off more of the Abrahamic pie than one person can reasonably be expected to chew, and a reader looking for weaknesses, shortcomings, faults, and deficiencies of whatever nature will probably have no problem finding them in this book.[2] And yet, I believe that a comparative study of this sort is justifiable, despite the clear pitfalls, for three reasons.

First, there is merit in adopting a comparative approach to Near Eastern studies in general—by drawing on sources and materials from across a wide spectrum of cultures, languages, and religious traditions—rather than carving up the field along geographical, linguistic, or religious lines so as to produce discrete and largely independent areas of research. The broad, comparative approach envisaged here was instinctive to Orientalists in the nineteenth century (for instance) but is no longer common, for mostly practical reasons. Max Müller (d. 1900), a pioneer in the academic study of religions, once remarked that "to know one [religion] is to know none."[3] Accordingly, limiting ourself to a single community's Haman means not knowing about even that particular manifestation of the character. My aim, therefore, is to chart and analyze the various ways in which Haman's character evolved across time and space, which will allow us to draw broad conclusions about the communities and traditions that produced their own Hamans.[4]

Second, the study of biblical reception history has traditionally privileged the biblical context in which a character first appears as the "original" one, from which subsequent texts diverged. By considering Haman's prebiblical origins (Chapter 8), we are accepting the possibility that the book of *Esther* was receiving Haman and reconfiguring him for its author's purposes no less than did later versions of *Esther* or the Qur'ān. Similarly, the study of "biblical" characters in the Qur'ān has traditionally focused on the pre-Qur'ānic origins of a character. Here, by contrast, we trace Haman's evolution along a chronological spectrum that culminates in the Qur'ān's adaptation of the character to his new scriptural surroundings, allowing us to highlight the Qur'ānic Haman's *originality* rather than his *origins*.

Third, adopting a broad, comparative approach to Haman affords us a panoramic view of Near Eastern or Abrahamic civilization that is rarely seen nowadays, for it has become a casualty of the hyper-specialization that pervades most corners of Near and Middle Eastern studies. In charting Haman's path through history we will see that he was a divisive figure both within religions (on account of stirring debates about his status), and between religions (as his name was used polemically, to denigrate rivals). But we will also see ways in which Haman served as a unifier for competing communities where, for example, celebrations of his demise were attended by Jews, Christians, and Muslims alike.

Bearing the above in mind, this book is less a Haman encyclopedia and more an exploration of Near Eastern history and religious culture through the example of Haman, who is, for some, one of the most evil characters who ever existed, and for others, one of the most maligned characters who never existed.

PART I

Haman in Scripture

Introduction

Describing Haman as he features in the Bible should be a simple task. After all, he figures in only a single book, the book of Esther (hereafter: *Esther*), and that book relates a Cinderella story of the sort that people in most parts of the world have heard since childhood. A disadvantaged orphan girl rises against all odds to become the queen of the greatest empire in the world, a villain plots to destroy "the good guys," and the good guys are victorious in a happy ending that has been commemorated annually ever since in a frivolous, carnival-like holiday. In fact, of all the Hebrew Bible's stories, the one related in *Esther* is surely among the best known to children in the Jewish world (including those who are barely affiliated with the religion and otherwise of limited biblical literacy), precisely because it is so accessible, relatable, and fun. Perhaps no less important for the book's popularity is the fact that the story contains neither complicated theologies, nor esoteric Temple rituals, nor obscure prophetic visions.

Readers who wish to retain this simple, uncomplicated understanding of *Esther* and of Haman's role within it are discouraged from reading the rest of this chapter (and there is good reason to suspect that such readers will not enjoy the book as a whole). For, as we will discover, *Esther* is in reality incredibly complicated, a fact that has been acknowledged both directly and indirectly for over two millennia.

Before pursuing Haman's course through scripture, we must consider the concept of scripture in the Abrahamic religions generally. We begin, predictably enough, with the Bible, about which there are a surprising number of questions. Our first question is: What *is* the Bible? Is it best categorized as a book, an anthology, a series of interrelated books, or perhaps a bookshelf or even a library?

Assuming that we are dealing with a selection of books—as suggested by the phrase "the five books of Moses," which refers to the Torah/*Pent*ateuch (the Hebrew *Ḥumash* also relates to "five")—which books are included? A community of ancient Jews whose library is commonly known as the *Dead Sea Scrolls* had a list of books that differs from the lists of many other Jews who lived before or after them. And even when a particular book was agreed upon, there were various versions of it from which to choose: the Samaritan Pentateuch, to cite but one example, differs from the Jewish one.

Furthermore, once a certain collection of books was accepted by a particular community as their Bible, the language in which it was written also served to distinguish groups of Bible-readers from each other. From ancient times, the Hebrew Bible (hereafter: HB) was available in such languages as Greek, Aramaic, and Latin (and, from late antiquity onwards, in a host of other languages, too).

And as is well known, once the New Testament was produced (after centuries of deliberations similar to the ones we are describing here), the world of Bible-readers was further divided between those who included its contents within the Bible and those who did not.

This may sound like unnecessary philosophizing, but we will see in the following chapters just how relevant these questions are to our understanding of Haman in scripture. The community at Qumran that produced the *Dead Sea Scrolls*, for instance, appears to have known the *Esther* story (as *Esther*'s language shaped some of their writings), but they chose not to include the book in their Bible. The Samaritans at around the same time likely had not even known of the story, while Jews who did include *Esther* in their Bible could choose from a variety of Greek and Hebrew versions of the story, each unique in significant ways.

To this list of primary questions, we may add subordinate ones. Even Jews who read *Esther* in the Hebrew version commonly known as the Masoretic Text (hereafter: MT) and considered it to be a biblical book, were divided on such issues as the book's authorship. Was it written by Mordecai, Esther, the Great Assembly of Jewish Sages, or someone else?[1] Was its purpose straightforward history, to tell a moralizing tale, or something else? What is its relationship to other biblical narratives? And finally, where does the text of *Esther* that one is required to hear on Purim actually begin,[2] and in what language(s) might it be written or read out publicly?[3] We will see that these questions have produced numerous answers over the past two millennia.

Furthermore, most Bible-readers in history were *not* "Jews who read *Esther* in the Hebrew version known as the MT." They read versions of *Esther* that were distinguished from the MT in a variety of ways, including even the identity of the ruling king, the epithets (or even names) of the leading characters, and the concerns, behavior, and portrayal of these characters. Crucially for us, it is Haman's portrayal that varies most between these different versions of the story. And once Christian exegetes turned their attentions to *Esther*, new strategies of interpretation were introduced, which allowed *Esther* (regardless of the scriptural version being used) to be read and interpreted in yet a wider range of ways.

Thus, even a question as simple-sounding as "How is Haman portrayed in scripture?" will have been answered differently by different people. (And we have not yet even mentioned the Qur'ān, which, for Muslims, is the only existing scripture that counts, and which has its own portrayal of Haman.)

This diversity can be perceived negatively: It spoils the simple rags-to-riches narrative that appeals even to children, and it can leave us with a picture of Haman that is complicated, confused, and even contradictory. In my view, however, this diversity of *Esther*s and Hamans may be seen as a plus, for it allows us to appreciate the rich variety of thought about *Esther*, the Bible, scripture, and the Abrahamic religions generally. (It is also the reason this book exists.)

With this in mind as we chart Haman's journey through scripture, we will seek to extract significance from passing details that will allow us, at the end of the book, to draw general conclusions about the Abrahamic religions in history, through the case-study of a single multi-faceted and multi-faced villain, Haman.

1

Haman in the Hebrew Bible

THERE ARE some books of the HB whose relevance to it and scriptural status within it were never in question. *Esther* is not one of them. And although nowadays all Bible-readers (with the exception of the Samaritans) accept some version of *Esther* as part of their scripture, the book's path to acceptance was not smooth—indeed, the founding figures of virtually every community that now accepts *Esther* once questioned its status, relevance, and legitimacy. In some cases, ancient readers of *Esther*, both Jewish and Christian, shared their reservations about the book in their writings. In other cases, we must deduce what it was about *Esther* that bothered them by analyzing the solutions proposed by a new version or a new interpretation of the book. And rather exceptionally, the question of *Esther*'s biblical status was reopened even centuries after a particular community had accepted it, as some Protestant Christians (from the sixteenth century) and Reform Jews (from the nineteenth century) openly questioned the book's message and enduring relevance.

Before seeking to understand why *Esther* has raised questions (and eyebrows) among its readers for centuries, we must familiarize ourselves with the story and Haman's role within it.

MT *Esther*: A Summary[1]

In its simplest outline, *Esther* relates events that occurred during the reign of Xerxes I (Hebrew: *Ahashwerosh* r. 486–465 BCE), specifically events that concerned the fortunes of the Jewish people living under his rule. The king held an enormous banquet during which he requested that his queen, Vashti, display her beauty before him and his guests. Vashti refused to do so and the king held an empire-wide beauty contest in order to find a new queen who would replace her. An orphaned Jewess by the name of Esther, who had been raised by her cousin

Mordecai, was eventually chosen to be the new queen of Persia, but she concealed the fact that she was Jewish. In the meantime, Mordecai, who was a functionary in the royal administration, helped foil an assassination attempt against the king.

Following this, the king decided to promote one "Haman the Agagite" to be his viceroy and ordered that all royal functionaries prostrate themselves before him. All agreed to do so except for Mordecai, which enraged Haman. As Mordecai justified his refusal to bow on the basis of his Jewish identity, Haman sought to have all Jews in the empire killed and he cast lots (Akkadian: *pūr*; with the Hebrew plural, *pūrīm*) to determine the date on which the massacre would take place. The king approved Haman's plan, and edicts were circulated throughout the empire announcing the coming annihilation of the Jewish people, which was to take place towards the end of the year, on the thirteenth of Adar.

Mordecai convinced Esther to intervene on the Jewish people's behalf, at which point the story split into two parallel narratives: In the first, Esther approaches the king and (after a series of banquets) pleads with him to spare her people. She explains that she is a Jewess and that her people were under threat due to Haman's plot. In the second narrative, on his way to one of Esther's banquets, Haman is disrespected by Mordecai once again and his advisors suggest that he hang Mordecai from a tall gallows. Haman sets off to the royal palace to secure permission to hang Mordecai and reaches the palace courtyard just as the insomniac king was having his diaries read to him. By chance, the diaries are opened to the record of Mordecai's foiling the assassination attempt, for which the king decides to reward him. The king then summons whoever happens to be in his courtyard—in this case Haman—and consults him about how to honor someone publicly. Thinking that the king was referring to himself, Haman suggests that the honoree be feted with a regal procession. The king then ordered that Haman execute this plan, albeit in celebration of Mordecai, which he does.

At this point, the two narratives link up, with Esther implicating Haman in the conspiracy against the Jews, and the king—misinterpreting Haman's pleading with Esther as an inappropriate advance against her—ordering that Haman be killed and hanged from the very gallows from which he had planned to hang Mordecai. The king then allows Esther and Mordecai to issue an empire-wide edict, which allows all Jews to defend themselves against their enemies on the thirteenth of Adar. Along with Haman, his ten sons were also killed, as were over 75,000 non-Jews. The annual festival of Purim (recalling the lots that Haman used earlier in the story) was then established, to celebrate the deliverance of the Jews from Haman's plot on the fourteenth or fifteenth of Adar. The story ends with a short chapter describing the reestablishment of stability in the empire and the elevation of Mordecai to the post of second-in-command.

Haman in MT *Esther*

Haman appears as an actor in four of *Esther*'s ten chapters (chs. 3, 5, 6, and 7), and his exploits are referred to in three other chapters (4, 8, and 9). On the one hand, this suggests that he is an important character in the story; on the other, it indicates that MT *Esther* begins and ends without him: Only Ahashwerosh features in the narrative's introduction and epilogue, and only he is mentioned in every chapter in the book (Haman is only introduced in the book's third chapter). On this basis one might conclude that Ahashwerosh is the story's most important character and that Haman, while significant, is secondary to the king (in more ways than one).[2]

However, such a superficial analysis of the story neglects the fact that Haman is the only character who is indispensable to the narrative: not only could Ahashwerosh be replaced by a different king (as he is in LXX *Esther* and versions based on it), but in some retellings of the story (such as the potted version provided in Esth 9:24–26, or in the *ʿĀl ha-Nissīm* prayer, to which we will return), Ahashwerosh is barely mentioned. And whereas Mordecai and Esther are the story's protagonists, a version of *Esther* could be related that did away with one of them. Without Mordecai, one might recount how Haman plotted to destroy Esther's people and how Purim was instituted to celebrate her foiling of the plot; without Esther, one might tell the story of how Mordecai antagonized Haman by refusing to bow to him, for which reason Haman plotted to destroy Mordecai's people, and how Purim was instituted to celebrate his foiling of the plot.[3] Without Haman, however, there is neither plot, nor hero, nor Purim.

When he is introduced in *Esther* (3:1), Haman is described as being three things: the son of one Hammedata, an Agagite and an important functionary whom the king sought to elevate to a status above his other courtiers. While the ensuing events describe how Haman came to be an incorrigible "enemy of all the Jews" (Esth 9:24), it must be admitted that according to the plain meaning of the text, Haman is not portrayed as a villain from the outset: A representative of the Jewish people offends him, so he plans to punish them. And while his actions may seem (again, perhaps only from the Jews' perspective) to be exaggerated—why punish all Jews for the crimes of only one of them?—a precedent for such collective punishment was established in Chapter 1, where it was decided that all women would be punished for Vashti's refusal to comply with the king's order. *Esther* plainly tells us (3:2–3) that in refusing to bow to Haman, Mordecai was offending not Haman but the king himself, as it was the king who had ordered that the courtiers bow before Haman.

Haman then seeks to gain permission from the king to destroy the Jews by two means. He argues that doing so is in the king's and the kingdom's interests, and he offers the king an enormous amount of money. Limiting ourselves to the plain meaning of the text, it appears both that Haman's accusations against the Jews were not inaccurate, and that the king was convinced enough by them to forego the huge sum of money.[4] The accuracy of Haman's accusations is confirmed by data that *Esther* itself supplies. That the Jews are "scattered and dispersed" is confirmed in 9:2 (where the Jews "gathered themselves together in their cities throughout all of the provinces of the king").[5] That their "laws are different from those of other peoples" and that "they do not keep the king's laws" is supported by the fact that Mordecai refused to comply with the king's command to bow to Haman because he was a Jew.[6] As far as the king is concerned, Mordecai and the Jews threaten the imperial order, whereas Haman preserves the order, loyally defending the interests of the kingdom by following precedents established in the Vashti episode.

We next hear of Haman in Chapter 5, where he is honored to be the sole invitee to a royal banquet. Emerging elated from this banquet, Haman is enraged by Mordecai, who again disrespects him, this time by refusing to stand up in his presence.[7] Unlike the king, who acts irrationally when enraged (Esth 1:12ff.), Haman manages to restrain himself (5:10). He then consults with his wife and friends, who suggest that he prepare a gallows from which to hang Mordecai.

Haman's loyalty and emotional restraint are maintained in the following chapter. When the king rewards Mordecai for foiling an assassination plot against him, it is Haman who is commanded to parade Mordecai publicly, thereby bestowing upon his arch-rival precisely the honors that he had wished for himself (Esth 6:6–9). Again, Haman loyally overcomes whatever psychological and emotional anguish that this must have caused him and unflinchingly complies with the order.[8] Only when he returns to the privacy of his home, to the comfort of his friends and family (Esth 6:12), does Haman break down, at which point Haman's wife informs him that he stood no chance against Mordecai to begin with, because Mordecai is a Jew (she does not explain why this is so). In other words, the same wife and friends who recommend that Haman kill Mordecai, then inform him that he will fail to do so. A reader who has been culturally conditioned to side with Mordecai cannot help but celebrate Haman's ill-fortune. An objective reader, however, cannot but empathize with Haman, who loyally executes the king's orders (despite the anguish this causes him) and who is poorly advised by those closest to him.

The final scene in which Haman features is described in the following chapter, where Esther implicates Haman as being the enemy of her people (Esth 7:6). In this case, whereas the king's response is to become enraged (7:7), Haman again responds reasonably (some might even say, laudably), by begging Esther for mercy, even lowering himself physically to do so (7:8), a detail whose full significance is best appreciated when we recall that Mordecai refused to bow before Haman, thereby triggering the genocidal threat against the Jews. It is at this point that the king walks in on Haman and Esther, misinterprets Haman's begging posture as a sexual advance against the queen (7:8), and summarily orders that Haman be executed. Haman is then hanged from the gallows that he had prepared for Mordecai. In other words, Haman has been executed for a crime that he did not commit, and he has suffered the ignominy of being wrongfully executed on a gallows that he himself had constructed, having done so at the suggestion of those to whom he had turned for advice and support. Again, even a reader whose loyalties lie with Mordecai, Esther, and the Jews must surely be able to suspend Schadenfreude and recognize that in this final scene of his life, the author of MT *Esther* seeks to portray Haman as a figure more pathetic than perilous. As villains go, Haman is a tragic one.[9]

Haman, we discover, is depicted in MT *Esther* as a villain, but as one who is not all bad all of the time. This is consistent with the Bible's portrayal of other rogues (such as Esau, Ishmael, and even Nebuchadnezzar), who are portrayed as more complex than the two-dimensional, pantomime-villains that they are now remembered to have been. Consider, also, that in MT *Esther* Haman's death was not the story's happy ending: the anti-Jewish edict was still in effect and it is only in Chapters 8 and 9 that the edict's threats are neutralized. In other words, even from a pro-Jewish perspective, Haman was not "the problem," and his demise was, therefore, not the solution.

In many ways Haman is the character in whose depiction the author of *Esther* has invested most: He is the only character whose family is described—including his father, wife, and ten sons, all of whom are named. He is also the only character whose emotions are described in nuanced terms (the king knows happiness and anger, but Haman can also restrain himself and describe the mixed emotions of elation at his success while at the same time feeling humiliated by Mordecai's indifference to him). And, most curious of all, Haman is the only character whose inner thoughts are revealed. In fact, a first-century CE rabbi adduced the detail that the author of *Esther* knew what was going on in Haman's mind (literally: "heart"; Esth 6:6), as one proof that *Esther* "was written with divine inspiration,"[10] a fact that served to upgrade its status and stabilize its place in the biblical canon. A no less shocking interpretation of the author's access to Haman's inner thoughts is that aspects of the story were being told from Haman's own perspective.[11]

We end this overview of Haman in MT *Esther* where it began, by noting that Haman was introduced as being the son of Hammedata and an Agagite. In Chapter 9 we will have occasion to delve more deeply into members of Haman's family; at this point it is enough to point out that Hammedata is an identifiably Persian name (as are the names of Haman's ten sons, listed in Esth 9:7–9), strongly suggesting that Haman himself was Persian (or at the very least, was from a Persianized family). This is interesting both because from LXX *Esther* onwards, it will be asserted repeatedly that Haman was not a Persian, and because the overwhelming majority of interpreters throughout history have understood "Agagite" to mean a (non-Persian) Amelekite. To appreciate this in detail, we must turn to the relationship between *Esther* and other biblical texts to which *Esther*'s author drew our attention allusively. Placing *Esther* in its scriptural context will help us understand that Haman was, in fact, an actor on a biblical stage much larger than Achaemenid Persia.

Esther in Biblical Context

MT *Esther* can be read (and often is) as an independent, self-contained story. Not only does it have a beginning, middle, and end, but it also lacks many of the references to common biblical themes that could relate it to a broader biblical narrative. That the Jews are in exile is presented as a given (the stage is Ahashwerosh's Persia), and when their representative Mordecai is introduced, the fact of their exiled condition is made explicit (Esth 2:6). Why the Jews were exiled and how they will return to the Holy Land are never mentioned. That the Temple does not exist is also implied (biblical chronology has Ahashwerosh preceding Cyrus, who allowed the exiled Jews to return to Judea and rebuild their Temple), but nowhere is the Temple mentioned, neither its past destruction nor its future rebuilding (despite the fact that MT *Esther* was almost certainly composed at a time when the Second Temple was already standing, *contra* the biblical chronology). The Passover festival and the Exodus similarly go unmentioned (despite the fact that the events described in Esth 4:16 clearly overlap with Passover), as do the Holy Land and Jerusalem (the latter is only mentioned as the city from which Mordecai was exiled). Thus, it is not just that certain biblical themes are missing, but that they are missing from contexts where we would expect to find them. Taking these omissions together, one would be forgiven for assuming that the author of *Esther* specifically sought to dissociate the story from the rest of the biblical narrative. That assumption is incorrect on numerous counts.

To unlock the biblical allusions and intertexts that pervade MT *Esther*, we must recognize that its author consciously chose an allusive rather than a direct means of relating *Esther* to other contexts. Many biblical resonances are dangled in front of us, but it is up to the reader to identify and grab them. Unlike a singer at a concert who occasionally points the microphone at a crowd that dutifully fills in the missing lyrics, the allusive style of *Esther* is playful and subtle—one could read the entire story without noticing the inter-textual resonances (as most children do), and even those who are aware of the inbuilt riddles can never be certain that they have found them all (or, perhaps, that they are not guilty of over-reading biblical allusions into the text). A singer's audience, by contrast, knows when it is up to them to fill in the lyrics and knows precisely what those lyrics are. Therefore, relating MT *Esther* to its wider biblical context is not an exact science. Fortunately for us, the book's audiences have been applying themselves to this task for over two millennia. In this section I will present their findings in three categories: 1) *Esther*'s "genre" in context; 2) *Esther*'s plotline in relation to other biblical stories; and 3) assorted phrases and words that channel biblical intertexts.

In terms of genre, *Esther* is generally taken as an example of a "success at a diaspora court" story, in which a Jew/Israelite/Hebrew manages to achieve professional (and national) success at the court of a non-Jewish/Israelite/Hebrew ruler. Obvious pre-*Esther* examples of this genre are the stories of Joseph (and, to a lesser extent, Moses) in an Egyptian court (Gen 37–50), and the account of Daniel and his three companions in a Babylonian/Persian court (Dan 1–6). Unsurprisingly, ancient exegetes and modern scholars have uncovered multiple parallels between *Esther* and these other "success at a diaspora court" stories, which demonstrate that they shaped the contents and language of *Esther*. Important though this topic may be for understanding MT *Esther*, the Joseph and Daniel stories do not have a clear evil-vizier character who can be seen as the model for Haman's depiction in *Esther*.[12]

More relevant are the biblical plotlines that appear to be on the mind of *Esther*'s author, most notably the story of Saul and Agag related in 1 Sam 15. Here the prophet Samuel anoints Saul as the first king of Israel and demands that he obey God's instructions. In this case, the instruction is to avenge the Amalekites' attack against the Israelites (related in *Exodus* 17) by wiping them out completely—men, women, children, and animals. Saul, however, shows compassion (1 Sam

15:9), opting to spare the Amalekite king Agag and to set aside some of the Amalekites' animals, which would be sacrificed to God (15:21). Despite the positive intentions behind these actions, they are still acts of disobedience against God, for which Saul eventually repents.

Samuel then kills Agag and cuts him up into pieces (15:33). The relevance of this story to *Esther* is apparent in more than one way, and it seems that *Esther* was an opportunity to right the wrongs committed in 1 Sam 15. In the latter context, the people were not meant to take spoils after their victory in the war with the Amalekites, yet they did so (1 Sam 15:19 and 21); in *Esther* the people are specifically allowed to take spoils after their war with the supporters of Haman (Esth 8:11), yet they do not (9:15–16). More importantly, in *Esther* the final scions of Agag are killed, thereby finishing the job begun by Saul, Mordecai's ancestor.[13]

The story of Saul and the Amalekites illuminates Haman's role in MT *Esther* in two ways.[14] First, Haman's "Agagite" epithet is widely taken to refer to the Amalekite king(s) called by that name; thus, *Esther* identifies Haman as an ethnic Amalekite rather than a Persian.[15] Second, it allows us to contextualize Haman's relationship with Mordecai and the Jews within a much broader narrative framework than mere court intrigues in Achaemenid Persia. Already in Num 24:7, Balaam's oracles refer to Agag as the exalted Amalekite king,[16] and the eventual downfall of Amalek is predicted (24:20).[17] The rivalry between Mordecai and Haman is thus the most recent (and final) act in a much grander drama playing out across history, namely the rivalry between the Israelites and the Amalekites. As this rivalry began when the relationship between God and His nation began—in the wake of the Exodus—its ending in *Esther* may have eschatological implications or resonances. It is probably no coincidence that the last four words of MT *Esther* describe Mordecai as "speaking peace to all his seed" (Esth 10:3), these being words used elsewhere in the Bible with reference to the future Messiah (Zech 9:9–10) and to God Himself (Ps 85:9).[18]

The third and final way in which MT *Esther* may relate to biblical intertexts is through phrases and words that the author of *Esther* deploys to tell his story, but which take on added meaning for a biblically literate reader. The point is that when *Esther* was read or heard, the cultural repertoire of its audience was fairly limited—a Jew in the late-Persian period (assuming the book was composed c. 400 BCE), would have been familiar with an assortment of Ancient Near Eastern (hereafter: ANE) and Indo-Iranian myths and folktales, as well as the earlier books of the Bible. A modern, Western-educated author who includes in their work the line "a nose by any other name would smell as sweet," might simply be making a pronouncement about noses and what they smell like, but the echo from Shakespeare's *Romeo and Juliet* would surely be heard by educated readers of the line. At the very least, one might argue that the author was influenced (perhaps subconsciously) by Shakespeare, but such a cautious assessment of the author's intentions would surely be deemed naïve by most readers, and the wordplay (noses, as roses, can also "smell") would be lost. In their defense, such a cautious reader might object that the suggested wordplay is based on an overreading of the line, and that were it the author's intention to suggest that the nose in this statement was its subject (that it is *doing* the smelling rather than *being* smelled, as the statement's object), then an adverb rather than an adjective would have been required ("a nose by any other name would smell as sweet*ly*"). But, as we will see in Chapter 8, the author of MT *Esther* very consciously engaged in wordplay, including sophisticated bilingual punning and the like. And as is often the case in ancient (and even modern) wordplay, philological exactitude—to the extent that it was sought at all—could readily be sacrificed for the sake of a reader's enjoyment or an author's message. To appreciate fully the layers of meaning in MT *Esther* and Haman's portrayal within it, we would do well to open our eyes, ears, and minds to the sort of intertextual allusions for which *Esther*'s author had a penchant.

The list of allusions identified by generations of scholars is long.[19] With particular reference to Haman, the detail that his face was "covered" when he was taken away to be executed (Esth 7:8) echoes other biblical instances in which faces are covered (Jer 14:3–4; Ps 44:16 and 69:8), and in those instances there is a clear association between face-covering and shame. Haman was thus being led away to his death not as a martyr but in disgrace. Moreover, when *Esther* refers to Haman as targeting all Jews as punishment for Mordecai's disobedience, one may detect echoes of earlier descriptions of Esau. The word used in *Esther* (Hebrew: *va-yivvez*; Esth 3:6) is identical to the word used by Esau when he made the (equally misjudged) decision to forego his birthright for lentil pottage (Gen 25:34).[20]

Other examples come from the execution of the two eunuchs who plotted against the king in Esth 2:21–23, and from the execution of Haman and his sons in Esth 7:10 and 9:13, respectively. The language in these passages echoes the language used in Deut 21:22–23, where hanging those who have committed grave sins from a tree is associated with disrespecting God and defiling the land. Likewise, the punishment of the two eunuchs in *Esther* echoes the nearly identical language used in Gen 40:19, where Joseph interprets the baker's dream to mean that he will be hanged from a tree in three days. As noted, the Joseph story has left its fingerprints all over MT *Esther*, and an audience conditioned to hear it might well discern its echoes between the lines of *Esther*.[21]

As stated, generations of exegetes and scholars have identified biblical intertexts in the book of *Esther*, some of which shed light on the particular exegete's view of Haman. In Chapter 6, we will encounter late antique rabbinic attempts to connect Haman with Esau (and the Edomites more generally), on the basis of allusive vocabulary that links the two biblical antagonists. Later on, Saadiah Gaon (d. 942) suggested that "this wicked Haman" (Esth 7:6) was an echo of Ps 140:2–4, where a "wicked" man is described as violent, ill-intentioned, warmongering, sharp-tongued, and like a snake.[22] Rhabanus Maurus (d. 856) suggested more generally that Haman's career reflected the verse in Prov 26:27, which states that whoever digs a pit shall fall into it and whoever rolls a stone will see it return to him.[23] Modern scholars, too, have seen Haman as the embodiment of earlier biblical characters or characteristics: Talmon, for instance, has seen in Haman the proverbial "fool" or "scorner" (Hebrew: *leṣ*) mentioned repeatedly in *Proverbs* (9:7–8, 19:25, 21:24, and others).[24]

How do these biblical intertexts in *Esther* contribute to our understanding of Haman's portrayal in the book? First, it must be appreciated that describing Haman in MT *Esther* without taking note of the numerous resonances that the author intended for his readers (as attempted earlier in this chapter) produces a character whose villainy is less than perfectly clear. His rivalry with a particular Jew and, by extension, with all Jews, appears motivated and strangely reasonable, for it is he who loyally and consistently executes the king's orders, even at great emotional expense, while the Jew(s) refused to do the same. He is the victim of events beyond his control and of more than one miscarriage of justice. Once the range of biblical intertexts comes to light, however, we understand the enormous significance of Haman's rivalry with the Jews, for it proves to be the latest (perhaps even the final) link in a chain of enmity between them and the Amalekites. And while it is true that Haman's death does not neutralize the threat against the Jews in Ahashwerosh's empire, it is important as a long-overdue correction to Saul's mistake in dealing with Agag. In fact, Haman's death may even have eschatological ramifications. The author of MT *Esther* was not telling a story independent of the rest of scripture—on the contrary, it is a story that requires familiarity with the rest of the HB if it is to be understood fully. Children celebrating Purim as an ancient Cinderella tale need not appreciate the wider biblical context and resonances of the story; a more sophisticated reader who seeks to understand Haman's role in *Esther* cannot justifiably remain so blissfully ignorant.

Much as this biblical contextualization of *Esther* solves (or at least diminishes) some of the problems that perturbed ancient readers of the story, there were some readers who required more decisive and explicit solutions. God, the Holy Land, Jewish Law, and other themes missing from MT *Esther* may have been concealed between the lines of the story, but these readers expected them in the lines themselves. For ancient attempts to fix *Esther*'s biblical problems we turn now to the Greek versions of *Esther* and, specifically, to Haman's depiction within them.

2

Greek Versions of *Esther*

The Septuagint (LXX)

The HB was translated into Greek in stages, beginning in the third century BCE. The precise circumstances in which this happened are in some ways clear to us, in others opaque. They are clear because a selection of sources (the oldest of which, *The Letter of Aristeas,* was probably written within a century of the events described) purport to tell us precisely what happened and why; they are opaque because the story that they relate (in various versions) is transparently legendary. The story goes that King Ptolemy II Philadelphus (r. 285–247 BCE, Alexandria) requested that the Torah be translated for him into Greek. Seventy Jewish scholars (or, according to later versions of the tale, seventy-two scholars, six from each of the twelve tribes) produced each their own translation, only to have it emerge that the translations were identical—an outcome that was taken to be miraculous. This translation came to be known as the Septuagint, reflecting the Latin word for seventy (*septuaginta*; most often appearing as "LXX").

Although the story is clearly apocryphal, there are two things that we can learn from it. First, that as the product of a miracle, the translation that emerged had divine sanction. Second, the fact that it needed divine sanction, reflects the unsurprising discomfort, even outright objection, that Jewish tradition had to the idea of translating the Torah into Greek (or any other language). In fact, rabbis in late antiquity stated that one of the reasons why Jews fast in the month of Tebet is to mourn this translation of the Torah into Greek.[1] Their point was that the Hebrew words of the Torah carried spiritual significance beyond the surface meanings that they conveyed in a given biblical text. This was a very ancient idea in the Near East and is a distant relative of the punning and wordplay that we have begun to explore in *Esther*. Important stories such as those related about god(s) may have layers of meaning, only one of which corresponds to the plain words (even letters) in which a text is composed.

Curiously, Talmudic rabbis recount the story of the LXX translation in their discussions of *Esther* and Purim.[2] It is not possible to know precisely what happened to the story as it progressed through different audiences in the years between the MT's composition in Persia (c. 400 BCE) and its arrival in Egypt (c. 100 BCE),[3] but scholars have cleverly pieced together whatever bits of evidence exist to arrive at two conclusions of relevance to this study. First, despite the distance—physical, temporal, and cultural—between the Susa of MT's *Esther* and the Alexandria of the LXX version, the experience of life in the Diaspora and its particular challenges were common to both contexts, and this likely accounts for the story's popularity and relevance in both settings. Second, LXX *Esther* is considerably different from MT *Esther* (even allowing for the minor changes to the text that one finds in virtually all LXX versions of biblical books). In fact, the gap between the Hebrew and Greek versions of *Esther* is greater than that between the Hebrew and Greek versions of any other book of the Bible. For biblicists who use the LXX as an external "control text" in their critical study of the textual history of the HB, this is bad news; for us, however, it is excellent news, as the liberty that the author(s) of LXX *Esther* took in adjusting the story's contents reflects changing attitudes toward Haman.

Before turning to these, there is more good news to share: Yet another Greek translation of *Esther* survives from ancient times, and it is considerably different from both the LXX and MT versions of the story. Commonly referred to now as the "Alpha Text" (hereafter: AT), this version is a fascinating witness to what was possibly an older Hebrew version of *Esther*, which scholars believe circulated at around the same time as the MT (though, confusingly, it survives in a version that probably post-dates the LXX). Importantly for us, the AT portrays Haman in ways that are different from both the MT and LXX and thus represents a third portrayal of Haman in "the Bible."

In the following section, I first survey the general differences between each of the Greek *Esthers* and MT *Esther*, and then analyze Haman's depiction in them.

LXX *Esther*

It appears that the translator of LXX *Esther* had MT *Esther* as his base-text—or perhaps a Hebrew version closely related to it. (While this may seem unsurprising to us, it should be noted that the translator of the AT probably did *not* use the MT.) Knowing that the LXX version was based on the MT allows us to appreciate the specific ways in which its author chose *not* to translate slavishly, but instead to omit material, add material, or otherwise change the text of MT *Esther*.

1) Removals.

In what might have been an attempt at conciseness, the translator removed quite a lot of material: MT *Esther* is peppered with repetitive language, multiple adjectives, and a general wordiness that was trimmed in the LXX. Indeed, most verses of LXX *Esther* attest to editorial decisions that likely aimed at verbal economy. These omissions are, however, of little significance for our understanding of Haman's evolution in this period.

2) Additions.

The LXX's additions to MT *Esther* fall into two categories. In the first, we have occasional insertions of explanatory phrases or religious language into the book's verses that compensate for the lack of references to God/religion in the MT version. Hence, when in the MT version Zeresh tells Haman that he stands no chance in his rivalry with Mordecai as the latter is a Jew (Esth 6:13), there is no explanation as to why Mordecai's Jewishness affords him this advantage. In the LXX, however, Zeresh ("Zosara") is quoted as saying, "If Mardochaios is of the race of the Judeans . . . you will never be able to ward him off, because a living god is with him."[4]

In the second, there are six additions to LXX *Esther* that do not appear in any form in the MT.[5] To complicate matters, these six seem to have been written by different authors (who were probably also different persons from the original translator of LXX *Esther*), and they were made at different times and in different languages: Careful philological study of these passages has determined that Additions B and E were composed last and in Greek, whereas the others were composed in either Hebrew or Aramaic. By the first century CE at the very latest, all six were in circulation as part of the LXX, and—with few, largely negligible, differences—the AT also contains these additions.

The six additions (commonly referred to as Additions A–F) include the following passages:

Addition A: Mordecai's Dream and his uncovering of the eunuchs' plot against the king.
Addition B: The king's anti-Jewish edict, as dictated by Haman.
Addition C: Mordecai's and Esther's prayers.
Addition D: Esther's approaching the king.
Addition E: The king's pro-Jewish edict, as dictated by Mordecai.
Addition F: The interpretation of Mordecai's dream.

The additions may be read as three sets of pairs, with Additions A and F, B and E, and C and D relating to each other in obvious ways, thereby forming a ring structure. We will return to these additions and to their depiction of Haman below.

3) Changes.

The changes that the translator of LXX *Esther* made to MT *Esther* are significant, not only for their contents but for the fact that—unlike in the case of the additions, which did not exist in MT *Esther*—here the translator did have materials and data at his disposal that he chose to replace with other information. Some of the changes are minor and of little consequence for our understanding of Haman in the text.[6] Other changes, while not focusing directly on Haman, change the contours of *Esther*'s narrative significantly and affect our understanding of Haman's role within it.[7]

Three of these stand out as especially significant. First, in the LXX, Haman is described as having been a eunuch.[8] This is stated explicitly in LXX 1:10 (where he is the first of the seven named eunuchs who were charged with summoning Vashti to the king's banquet), and although one might be tempted to explain this inclusion as a mere error on the translator's part (the equivalent name in the MT list of eunuchs is "Mehuman," which shares a consonantal root with "Haman") we will see that AT *Esther* also holds Haman to have been a eunuch, albeit on the basis of other evidence.

Second, when the LXX describes Haman's execution (Esth 7:9–10), it specifies that he was crucified rather than impaled (which is what "to hang from a tree" meant in practice in ancient Persia).[9] This detail will be revisited below, when discussing echoes of *Esther* in the New Testament.

Third, the terms used to describe Haman differ in striking ways. Twice Haman is referred to as *diabolos* (Esth 7:4 and 8:1), a term reserved elsewhere in the LXX and in the NT for Satan (it is from *diabolos* that the English "diabolical" and "devil" are derived). As such, Haman becomes a character associated in the LXX with antagonism towards both God (Job 1) and man (Zech 3:1). Turning Haman into a Satanic figure is significant, but there is an even more consequential change to his characterization in the LXX. Rather than introducing Haman as an Agagite (Esth 3:1), he is described as a "Bougean" (Greek: *bougaios*), a term of uncertain meaning, perhaps related to a Homeric term indicating a "braggart,"[10] and later (Esth 9:23) as a "Macedonian." These changes to Haman's epithet are undeniably intentional, and the intentions behind them are naturally of interest to Haman-watchers like us.

In simple terms, the shift from "Agagite" to "Bougean" and/or "Macedonian" does two things. It dissociates Haman's rivalry with the Jews from the grander narrative of the Israelite-Amalekite rivalry; and it replaces the Amalekite association with other ones, which reflect the political situation of Hellenized Jews at the time and indicate the sort of villain they deemed threatening. To understand the significance of Haman's alternative identity in the LXX, we must consider these epithets together with the portrayal of Haman in the six additions to *Esther* that were an integral part of LXX *Esther* for most of its Jewish and Christian audiences.

Haman in the Additions to *Esther*

As the word implies, the additions were not organic to the *Esther* narrative. Accordingly, Haman's depiction in them almost certainly reflects circumstances different from those which the translator of LXX *Esther* (prior to the additions) lived, and one might reasonably object to considering the Haman of the additions alongside the Haman of LXX *Esther* for this reason. The more important point, however, is that from early Christian times onward, regardless of the precise provenance of the various sections of the LXX, a Greek version based on the MT and supplemented by six significant additions was in circulation among Jews and others. This version was popular, it long influenced depictions of Haman, and would have monumental ramifications for some late antique Christian attitudes towards *Esther* and Purim, and perhaps even for the language of the New Testament (as we will see).

In Addition A, Mordecai dreams of two dragons who, as we learn in Addition F, represent Mordecai and Haman respectively. While the temptation might be to read significance into Haman's portrayal as a dragon,[11] doing so would force us to recognize that Mordecai, too, is a dragon and that whatever is read into this term regarding Haman must therefore apply to Mordecai as well. More significant is the fact that Addition A:16–17 explains the background to Haman's rivalry with Mordecai and with the Jews generally. After Mordecai foils the eunuchs' plot against the king, we are told the following:

> [T]he king ordered Mardochaios to serve in the court and gave to him gifts for these things. But Haman son of Hamadathos, a Bougean, was highly esteemed by the king and he sought to harm Mardochaios and his people because of the two eunuchs of the king.

These verses present both the problem with Haman's depiction in the LXX and its solution. The problem is that Haman, as a Bougean, is not an Agagite, and we therefore cannot pin his antipathy to Mordecai and the Jews on his presumed

Amalekite origins. The solution is provided when the text offers the alternative reason behind Haman's hatred for Mordecai: Haman had supported the eunuchs' plot (which Mordecai foiled). That Haman was a disloyal conspirator against the king is a theme that is established in Addition A and is woven throughout LXX *Esther*.

Addition B provides a tantalizing view of Haman's self-depiction, as imagined by the addition's author. To the extent that the additions (and the LXX more generally) make explicit what is absent from MT *Esther* (God, prayer, Law, and so forth), Addition B:3ff. tells us not only how Haman hoped to be depicted in the anti-Jewish edict circulated throughout the empire, but states specifically that Haman was the second-in-command:

> Haman—who excels among us in sound judgment, and who is distinguished for his unchanging goodwill and steadfast fidelity and has attained the second place in the kingdom . . . who is in charge of the affairs of state and is our second father. . . .[12]

In the final verse of MT *Esther* (10:3), Mordecai is described as holding the position of "second to the king." Seeing as Mordecai was replacing Haman, the implication is that Haman, too, had been second-in-command before his fall. Addition B states this directly.[13]

In Addition C:5, Mordecai refers to Haman as "prideful," while the same word in the AT's version of the Addition (AT 4:15) is instead "uncircumcised."[14] As we will see below, Haman's pride is also mentioned by Josephus, who employs the culturally loaded term *hubris*.[15] Haman's characterization as "uncircumcised" is puzzling and may tie in with yet another difference between the Greek and MT versions of *Esther*. In Esth 8:17, the MT states that the gentile population of the empire "Judaized" out of fear of the ascendant Jews, whereas the LXX tells us that, "many of the nations were circumcised and became Judeans out of fear of the Judeans." We will return to the historical contextualization of this stress on circumcision shortly.

Finally,[16] in Addition E, we hear not only Mordecai's description of Haman (balancing out Haman's self-description in Addition B), but we are also reminded of the implication in Addition A that Haman was behind the eunuchs' plot against the king. E:10–14 (LXX) describes Haman as follows:

> Haman son of Hamadathos—a Macedonian who was in truth a foreigner to the blood of the Persians and quite devoid of our kindness—when he was entertained by us as our guest, obtained the goodwill that we have for every

> nation to such an extent that he was publicly proclaimed our Father and was continually done obeisance to by all as the person second to the royal throne, but being unable to restrain his arrogance, he made it his business to deprive us of our rule and our breath and by the crafty deceit of ruses asked to destroy Mardochaios, our savior and constant benefactor, and Esther, the innocent companion of our kingdom, together with their whole nation. For when by these methods he had caught us undefended he thought that he would transfer the power of the Persians to the Macedonians.

The AT version of Addition E differs from the LXX in two ways. In lieu of "Macedonian," the author of the AT dubs Haman a "Bougean"; and, where the LXX has Haman as "a foreigner to the blood of the Persians," the AT has "a stranger to the *thinking* of the Persians." Although "Macedonian" and "Bougean" certainly have different meanings and resonances (to be explored later), the fact remains that both the LXX and the AT employ these two terms with reference to Haman, albeit at different places in the text.[17] A reader familiar with either the LXX or the AT version of *Esther* would have been aware that Haman was both a Bougean and a Macedonian. Furthermore, in Addition E Haman's disloyalty to the Persian king, hinted at in Addition A, where he was associated with the eunuchs' plot, is made explicit. The distinction between Haman as "a foreigner to the blood of the Persians" on the one hand, and Haman as "a stranger to the thinking of the Persians" on the other, is potentially more interesting: not only does the former speak in ethnic terms and the latter in cultural ones (a revealing distinction in itself), but the insistence that Haman does not think like the Persians appears to reflect an Old Persian pun on Haman's name (either from *vohu-manah*, "good thoughts," or *hamah-manah*, "the same thoughts").[18]

Taken together, the LXX's portrayal of Haman differs significantly from that of the MT. Haman is a prideful eunuch whose aim is to hand the Persian kingdom over to the Macedonians (for he is a Macedonian himself), which he attempts to effect by orchestrating an assassination plot against the king. His schemes are unsuccessful and he is executed through crucifixion. What he is *not* is a Persian and, crucially, not an Amalekite either. The deep-rooted enmity between the Israelites and the Amalekites does not, therefore, underpin the narrative (and the ties between LXX *Esther* and the biblical intertexts relating to the Amalekites are thus severed). But while Haman's rivalry with the Jews is somewhat downgraded in LXX *Esther*, his enmity towards the Persian king and his empire is enhanced. The historical forces that guided the narrative in these directions will be analyzed in Chapter 6. For now, it is to the tantalizing case of the AT and its portrayal of Haman that we turn.

AT *Esther*

Published by Paul de Lagarde in 1883, the AT is by far the most recent of the versions of *Esther* to come to the attention of modern scholars. Once these scholars had studied the AT's contents, however, they came to realize that it probably reflected the *oldest* version of the *Esther* story to come to light.[19] In the form in which the AT has reached us, in which the six additions are integrated into the text rather than gauchely appended to an existing narrative (as they are in the LXX),[20] the AT does appear to post-date the LXX. And yet, removing the additions and making some further, relatively minor adjustments to it, we are left with a Greek text that is manifestly based on a Hebrew version of *Esther* different from the MT, and probably older than it.[21]

The AT's relative concision is not due to the author's more economical style (for while in some cases the text is terse in comparison to the MT and LXX,[22] in others it is wordier), but rather to the absence of certain key moments that appear in the MT and LXX, absences that change the narrative itself in pivotal ways. For instance, in the AT Mordecai does not tell Esther to conceal her identity, and the king—who, as in the MT, is Xerxes (*Assyeros*) rather than the LXX's Artaxerxes—knows that she is Jewish from the outset.[23] Also consequential for the unfolding of the plot in the AT is the fact that there is no notion of Persian law being immutable; there is, therefore, no need to override the original edict against the Jews, and the king simply revokes his original letter (AT 7:16). Moreover, towards the end of the story, Mordecai alone establishes the Purim festival (Greek: *Phouraia*), thus highlighting his role as the sole leader of the Jewish people (with negative implications for Esther's status as the story's co-protagonist).[24]

Regarding Haman, the AT supports the LXX's statement (1:10) that he was a eunuch, by listing Bougaios as the eunuch in charge of the king's harem (AT 2:8; in the MT he is "Hegai," in the LXX "Gai"),[25] and as the eunuch who recommends to the king that he punish all women for Vashti's misbehavior (1:16; in the MT he is Memuchan; in the LXX, Mouchaios). The LXX and AT agree, therefore, that Haman was a eunuch, but demonstrate this in different ways. As noted, "Bougaios" is one of two epithets (together with "Macedonian") that the LXX uses to replace the MT's "Agagite," and it is worth noting not only that the AT also deploys these epithets, but that there are manuscript traditions of the AT that suggest that the epithet "Gogite" was used in lieu of "Bougaios." If this reading is accurate—and some scholars see it as the original epithet that was mistakenly written as "Bougaios"[26]—then Haman's importance is considerably upgraded: Gog in the Bible is a person (or nation) of eschatological significance, who will challenge civilization and will be defeated by the Messiah at the end of times.[27] Referring to Haman as a "Gogite" would thus imply that he was a villain of truly cosmic proportions. If the MT's "Agagite" broadened the stage of Haman's rivalry with the Jews so as to take in the Israelite-Amalekite enmity, and the LXX's (disloyal) "Macedonian" broadened the stage of Haman's rivalry with the Jews of the Persian Empire to take in the entire Persian Empire, then "Gogite" occupies the broadest stage of all. The corollary of this is that his eventual defeat has implications that are not merely political but eschatological.[28]

As with the LXX, what the AT's Haman is not is an Amalekite: his enmity in the immediate, mundane context of the Esther story, is based on the implication of Addition A, that Haman was behind the eunuchs' plot. The AT's version (A:14–18) describes the events as follows:

> Then the king questioned the two eunuchs and found Mardochaios' words true, and when the eunuchs confessed, they were led away. . . . And the king commanded concerning Mardochaios that he serve in the court of the king and conspicuously guard every door. And he assigned to him for these things Haman son of Hamadathos, a Macedonian in the presence of the king. And Haman was seeking to harm Mardochaios and all his people because of what he had said to the king concerning the eunuchs, because they had been executed.

To be sure, Haman eventually would also come to hate Mordecai and his people for refusing to bow to him later on in the story (3:1), but for the AT's audience the refusal to bow was only one more trigger—just as the MT's audience had the Agagite connection to enhance Haman's reaction to Mordecai's refusal to bow. In fact, the AT's description of Haman's reaction to Mordecai's refusal is also worth our attention for two things that it tells us about Haman. The text (AT 3:5–6) reads as follows:

> Now when Haman heard, he was provoked to jealousy against Mardochaios, and rage burned within him. So he was seeking to destroy Mardochaios and all his people on one day. Since Haman was provoked and all his rage was stirred up, he turned red, driving him from his sight. And with a malicious heart he kept speaking evil to the king about Israel.

The first detail of interest is the fact that Haman's emotional reaction to Mordecai's snub was jealousy, which does not occur in the MT, but does feature in the Second Temple era, in the *Life of Adam and Eve.* This ancient midrashic expansion on the early chapters of *Genesis*[29] describes a different refusal-to-bow episode. In the Latin version of the story, we are told that when God created Adam, He commanded the ministering angels to prostrate themselves before him, and all complied except Satan, who explained that it is this episode that accounts for his envy towards Adam and, more generally, the enmity between mankind (Adam's people) and Satan.[30] In the late antique Syriac *Cave of Treasures,* we are told specifically that when Satan witnessed the angels prostrating before Adam, "he was jealous of him from that day, and he did not wish to prostrate himself to him."[31] When the AT describes Haman's reaction as "jealousy," it may be identifying Haman with Satan, whose jealousy towards Adam leads him to target Adam's entire people (just as Haman's jealousy leads him to target all of Mordecai's people), an equation that dovetails nicely with the LXX's reference to Haman as *diabolos.*[32]

The second detail of interest is the reference to Haman turning red, which may simply reflect the extent of Haman's burning rage, but—as we will see in Chapter 8—it may also hint at pre- and post–Esther traditions about Haman's association with the planet Mars and/or with the Edomites.

Haman's accusation against the Jews in the AT also distinguishes this version from the LXX and the MT. In the AT (3:8), Haman describes the Jews as follows:

> There is a people scattered throughout all the kingdoms, a people of war and insubordinate, who have different laws from your laws, O King. They do not pay heed though they are known among all nations because they are evil, and they set aside your commands to undermine your glory.

Earlier, it was argued that Haman's accusation in the MT was, at the very least, not unreasonable by *Esther*'s own standards. The AT, by contrast, portrays Haman as more explicitly subjective in making his case: The Jews are "a people of war and insubordinate," they are "evil," and they seek to undermine the king's glory. These differences bring the AT into line with the LXX's depiction of Haman as disloyal to the king and acting (in Macedonian interests) to undermine Persian rule. In accordance with the theme of reversals that permeates all versions of *Esther,* Haman's accusation against the Jews may be seen as the AT's way of describing Haman himself (hence, Haman's characterization of the Jews as "evil" anticipates Esther's description of Haman in AT 7:8/MT 7:6).[33] The yardstick of virtue in the Greek versions of *Esther* is political loyalty to the Persian king and kingdom, something that is at most implied in the MT.[34]

Finally, in the AT Haman is described in terms not found in other versions. When the king asks Esther who it is who is threatening her people, she replies: "Haman, your friend, is this liar, this evil man!" (7:8). By contrast, the LXX and MT (7:6) refer to him as "A man who is an enemy! Haman is this wicked one."[35] By calling Haman the king's "friend," the AT thus implicates the ruler himself. Such a negative judgment of the king—while not explicit in either the MT or the LXX—is shared with ancient Jewish midrashim on *Esther*, some of which remember Ahashwerosh as having been no less of a villain than Haman himself.[36]

This overlap between the AT and ancient Jewish interpretations of *Esther* is particularly interesting in light of the other examples of such overlap that we have encountered in passing. There is little evidence (if any) that the AT or its *Vorlage* circulated among Jewish commentators, while there is overwhelming evidence that by the early Christian era it was the MT version that had been adopted and canonized by the rabbis. Moreover, the evidence for Jewish awareness of the additions to *Esther* indicates that it is the traditions of the LXX (or a version based on it) that reached the rabbis.[37] And yet, there are three details that occur in the AT that are not shared with other versions of *Esther* but do appear in early rabbinic midrashim.[38] The first, as noted, is the idea that Ahashwerosh was evil rather than an ineffectual buffoon. The second is the reference to Memuchan, the eunuch in 1:16 who advises the king to dispatch anti-women edicts throughout the empire in response to Vashti's behavior, as Bougaios. The identification of Memuchan with Haman (Bougaios) is found in a variety of early midrashim.[39] The third concerns the reaction of the non-Jewish peoples to the Jews' ascendancy following Haman's demise. The MT (8:17) tells us that the gentiles of the empire "Judaized," which, as noted, the LXX renders as "were circumcised and became Judeans." The AT, however, tells us that it was the Jews themselves who, upon surviving Haman's plot, were circumcised (AT 7:41). The implication is that until this reversal in fortunes the Jews were not allowed to practise circumcision, a prohibition that presumably originated with Haman (for the prohibition ended when Haman's life ended). The idea that Haman prohibited circumcision features in rabbinic sources,[40] and while these probably reflect the sort of anti-Jewish legislation that is associated with various persecutors in ancient Jewish history,[41] taken together with the other two points of overlap with the AT, it contributes to the impression that there were more points of contact between the AT and the rabbis than previously thought.

To summarize: The AT is clearly an important witness to ancient views of the book of *Esther* and of Haman within it, one that appears to represent independent, and divergent, traditions about the story. And although the current form of the

AT reflects the text's relatively late composition, it is very likely that the Hebrew *Vorlage* of the AT is older than the LXX and perhaps even than the MT itself. Which aspects of Haman's depiction belong to the earliest forms of the text and which are later interpolations or editorial emendations are questions whose answers are probably beyond us. And while this probably should not matter much, for the AT was not nearly as popular among Jews and Christians as the MT and LXX *Esthers*, there is evidence that its details percolated through to early rabbinic authorities by some means.[42]

A reader whose image of Haman was based on AT *Esther* would have had an impression of Haman that in some potentially pivotal ways differed from the Haman described in either the MT or the LXX. The AT's Haman is a eunuch, a Bougean and a Macedonian, who is associated with the assassination plot against the king and a more general conspiracy to transfer the Persian Empire to the Greeks. In Esther's eyes, he is the Persian king's "friend" and a "liar," this latter word being a term of particular significance in ancient Persian religious thought.[43] In Mordecai's eyes, a noteworthy detail is that Haman is uncircumcised, which might be related to the implication (unique to the AT) that Haman prohibited circumcision. Generally speaking, the AT's Haman is an altogether less sympathetic character than the Haman of the MT/LXX: Emotionally, he is less restrained than the other Hamans—he is jealous of Mordecai, his fiery anger turns his face red, and his accusations against the Jews are characterized by name-calling and judgmental subjectivity (unlike the more sober, verisimilar accusations found in the MT/LXX). Moreover, in the AT, Haman induces fear in the king's servants. He is thus quite a different figure from the miserable, tragic villain whose wife and advisors forget to warn him that his plot against Mordecai is doomed until it is too late. And although he is not an Amalekite, the reasonable assumption that his original epithet in the AT was "Gogite" implies that his villainy is of much greater significance than it is in other versions of *Esther*, for Haman the Gogite is no less than an eschatological agent of Chaos.[44] Haman's immediate enemies may be Jews, but it is the wider Persian kingdom and even the world at large that is threatened by him.

Other Ancient Greek Versions of Esther

By now, we may appreciate that Haman's portrayal in "the Bible" is a complex topic. The foregoing demonstrates that the language in which one accessed *Esther* was a crucial variable in determining which Haman they would know. Hebrew readers would encounter MT's image of Haman, Greek readers either LXX's or the AT's depiction of him. The former was more influential than the latter among Greek readers, but it is possible that aspects of the AT's Haman reached the rabbinic corpus of knowledge, thereby gaining enormous influence (albeit indirectly). As there are no other extant ancient versions of *Esther* in either Hebrew or Greek, readers might reasonably expect that it was time to move on—to Haman's evolution within ancient interpretations of scripture. I hope to be forgiven for holding things up and bringing two further ancient Greek versions of Esther into the mix. The catch is that they do not exist in their original forms and must be pieced together from the surviving works that appear to be based on them.

The first is the Greek *Vorlage* of the Old Latin (hereafter: OL) version of *Esther*, the second is the Greek *Vorlage* of the *Esther* that Josephus Flavius (wr. 94 CE) used when summarizing the story in his *Jewish Antiquities*. Each of these has its selling point: The OL's *Vorlage* is now considered to be the oldest Greek version of *Esther*,[45] predating the LXX and thus originating no later than the second century BCE. Josephus's retelling of *Esther* is important not for its imputed antiquity but for its undeniable legacy, especially in Christian cultures. (By contrast, the influence of OL *Esther* fizzled out with the increasing popularity of Jerome's late-fourth century Vulgate, and its eventual adoption by the Catholic Church as the standard version of the Bible in Latin). For us, what these retellings have in common—aside from their unique Greek *Vorlagen*—is that their depictions of Haman contribute pieces to our scriptural puzzle in numerous ways.

OL Esther

A reader of the OL previously acquainted with one of the other versions of *Esther* discussed above cannot fail to notice quite how unique this version is.[46] For instance, while the OL includes the six additions to *Esther* (with occasional, significant changes to some of them), it also includes a seventh addition (Addition H), which contains the text of a communal prayer inserted between Chapters 3 and 4 of the story. In general, the OL enhances the role that the Jewish community plays in the story, and Mordecai's depiction as the communal leader is also upgraded throughout the OL—meaning that Esther's role in the story is suitably downgraded.[47] Moreover, while the importance of the Jewish community is stressed, the OL strikingly minimizes the significance of the non-Jewish communities in the story by removing all references to the large-scale massacres described in Esth 9:1–16. Instead, we are told that "the chief-officials of the satraps and the tyrants of the king and the scribes honored God as well because fear of Mordecai had set in" (OL 9:3). Accordingly, one of the most controversial features of *Esther* throughout history—the theme of violent vengeance—does not feature in OL *Esther*.[48] There are various other differences between the OL and the other versions surveyed, some of which are more interesting than others: That the list of the seven eunuchs of the king (1:10) differs from other lists, and that the seven advisors of the king (1:14) are reduced to five in the OL might not excite much interest. More remarkable is the fact that the advisor who replaces Memuchan and recommends that all women of the empire be punished for Vashti's disobedience is named in the OL as "Mordecai." Bearing in mind that ancient exegetes (and even the AT) held either that Memuchan was actually Haman, or that he was Daniel, the identification of Memuchan here with Mordecai is noteworthy: Was Memuchan a hero or a villain? Interesting though this may be, it is only indirectly relevant to our understanding of the OL's Haman.[49]

Haman himself is introduced in the OL (3:1) without reference to his father or to some culturally loaded epithet. Haman is neither an Amalekite, nor is he a Macedonian, a Bougean, or a Gogite.[50] By the same token, Mordecai is introduced (2:5–6) simply as "a man in Susa Thebari,[51] and his name was Mordecai, from the captivity of Jerusalem, of the captivity which Nebuchadnezzar, king of Babylon, had captured." Similarly, when Haman's wife and friends break the news to him that he stands no chance against Mordecai (6:13), the reason given is not that Mordecai is a Jew/Judean (as in the MT), but rather because "he is a prophet." The ethnic/national rivalry between Haman's people and Mordecai's is, thus, consistently downplayed in the OL.

Haman's accusation against the Jews (3:8) also differs from that in other versions of *Esther*:

> And he spoke with the king with a deceitful heart regarding the people of the Jews and he said: "There is a people scattered throughout the kingdom, incredibly, having strange laws, but not obeying your laws, who are known in every place as a plague and who spurn your commands, lessening your glory."

According to these verses, Haman's accusation was knowingly "deceitful," rather than reasonable from Haman's own perspective. Furthermore, he describes the Jews as being a threat to the king, this being the sort of preliminary detail so important in the various versions of *Esther* for its later reversal (when we discover that Haman represents the threat). Indeed, as in the Greek versions, the OL sees Haman as not only a threat to the Jewish people, but to the Persian king and kingdom, too. In OL 7:6, Esther exposes Haman to the king as the source of her and her nation's troubles: "Now, Esther said: 'A man *hostile to the king*: this man is the evil Haman!'"

In general, the OL clearly distinguishes between Haman, on the one hand, and the Jews and Persian king, on the other: Haman is disloyal (as in the Greek versions), whereas the Jews are loyal (again, as in the Greek versions). The main difference here is that the king is firmly on the Jews' side, rather than being neutral or, in the case of the AT, Haman's friend. Thus, when news of the plot against the Jews is circulated throughout the empire, rather than telling us that "the king and Haman sat down to drink" (MT 3:15), the OL states that "Haman . . . indulged himself in the company of friends." Of Haman's entourage we hear more in the OL than in the other ancient versions of Esther. Following the dinner that Esther had held for him and the king (5:9), we are told that "Haman, however, returned from dinner, and three hundred men with him.[52] And all honored him; Mordecai, however, did not honor him."[53] Later, after having constructed the "wooden pole" for Mordecai (5:14), the OL tells us that "Haman, meanwhile, was sleepless in the palace of the king, and three hundred men were with him."

The OL's treatments of Haman's reaction to disappointment, his downfall, and his demise are also unique to this version of the tale. When Mordecai refused to honor Haman for the second time (5:9), rather than becoming "filled with wrath" but "restraining himself" (as in MT 5:9–10), Haman is simply described as "dejected" (OL 5:10). When he was forced to honor his arch-enemy Mordecai, the OL (6:10) tells us that Haman "suffered because of these words," and shortly thereafter (6:12) we hear that,

> Haman went in disgrace, and Mordecai was highly honored. And God shattered Haman's heart. Mordecai, however, returned to the king's court. But Haman hurried back to his house, suffering and stricken in his heart.

As before (3:8), the author of the OL focuses on Haman's emotions, including his inner feelings, suggesting that we are experiencing the story through Haman's eyes. The statement that Mordecai "was highly honored" can be made on the basis of external observation; statements regarding Haman's "suffering" and being "stricken in his heart" (after God had shattered it, no less) imply access to Haman's inner thoughts and feelings.

Finally, we turn to the OL's description of Haman's demise. The MT describes Haman's execution towards the end of Chapter 7, his ten sons' executions in the middle of Chapter 9, and makes no reference to his wife Zeresh's fate. The OL, by contrast, has the following to say of the family's final moments (7:9–10): "And the king said, 'Let Haman and his wife and his ten children be hung upon it!' And, just as the king had commanded, they were hung upon the wooden pole which he had prepared for Mordecai the Jew in the gates of Susa." Curiously, not only is Zeresh also executed, but this is the first time in the OL that Haman's sons are mentioned at all. In the other ancient versions, one of Haman's declared sources of pride in life is his "multitude of children" (MT 5:11),[54] and the description of their deaths in *Esther* 9 is therefore yet another reversal-bookend in the story. In the OL, by contrast, we first learn that Haman even has sons when we are told that they were executed with him.[55]

To summarize, the OL's Haman—which likely reflects a second-century BCE Greek perspective on him—is both the enemy of the Jews and a dangerous rival of the king and of Persian rule in general. His only epithet in the OL is "the Macedonian" (E:10; and cf. E:14), and even this occurs only in the additions, which were not part of the OL's Greek *Vorlage*.[56] And while Haman is not an Amalekite or a Gogite, he is supported by an impressive entourage. Interestingly, while the broader historical context of the *Esther* story is thus obscured in the OL, the specific community of Jews threatened by Haman and his supporters plays a greater role in this version than in the other ancient *Esther*s. The rivalry reflected in the OL is thus surprisingly local: The Jewish community under the rule of Artaxerxes faces off against Haman and his community, and the outcome of this clash is of very limited historical (let alone cosmic) significance.

A Hellenized Jew or Christian may have known *Esther* from the LXX or AT versions that have survived, or from the even earlier version on which the OL is based. Each of these related a variation of the story and presented a different image of Haman. Taking these versions together with the ancient Hebrew versions that existed centuries before the first Greek translations appeared, we have a handful of different *Esther*s and different Hamans circulating among Jewish and, eventually, Christian audiences. The diversity of versions attests to the malleability of the story itself, which is reflected in word-choice and other points of detail, but also in such basic facts as the relationships between the story's central characters: Were Mordecai and Esther an uncle and his niece, first cousins, a father and his adopted daughter, or a husband and wife? (Each of these answers may be found in one or another ancient version of *Esther*.) Was it under the rule of Xerxes or Artaxerxes that the events narrated in *Esther* took place? Was the ruler benevolent, evil, or an ineffectual buffoon? And, crucially for us, who was Haman? The diversity of answers to the latter question demonstrates that Haman was, arguably, the most malleable of the story's characters and—to the extent that his changing identity generated a commensurate shift in the story's significance—also its most pivotal character.

This malleability also tells us something about the status of *Esther* in antiquity. For canonical scripture tends to be preserved conscientiously (the word of God, or words inspired by Him, demanded faithful transmission through the generations), while folk-tales and popular stories change with retellings. The diversity apparent among the circulating *Esthers* tells us that the book sat somewhere in between these two categories on the scriptural spectrum. Uncertainty regarding *Esther*'s status would continue for centuries after the book was rendered into Greek, with Christians and Jews in late antiquity debating its status long after other scriptural books had secured their place in the Bible. When, as late as the seventh-century CE, Isidore of Seville (d. 636) stated that Esther was the last of the twenty-two books of the HB, he confirmed that for him *Esther* had indeed made the cut. But it is also worth noting that the list was twenty-two books long in order that it correspond to the number of letters in the Hebrew alphabet. In other words, a list of twenty or twenty-one canonical books might well have been "stretched" to accommodate one more, so that *Esther*—like a Hollywood action-hero—was able to roll under the closing garage door of the biblical canon. Isidore may have been influenced by Josephus, writing in the last decade of the first century CE, who also held that there are twenty-two books in the HB,[57] although which precise "Bible" that Josephus used—at least for his treatment of the *Esther* story—is still debated among scholars. For by the time Josephus was writing, an array of *Esthers* and interpretative traditions associated with them were in circulation in the Near East and the Mediterranean. Josephus's retelling of *Esther* is the first really important non-scriptural version of the story that we have, because it reflects the eclectic nature of the traditions available to him, including competing ideas about Haman. As we will now see, Josephus skillfully deployed these traditions to further his very particular aims.

Josephus's *Esther*

Josephus's summary of the *Esther* story in his *Antiquities of the Jews*—a narrative overview of biblical history aimed at a non-Jewish audience—is different enough from the versions of *Esther* surveyed above to raise the possibility that yet another Greek version of the story was at his disposal.[58] As both a possible witness to this lost Greek *Esther* and a highly influential author (especially for premodern Christian audiences), Josephus and his depiction of Haman deserve our attention here.[59]

Josephus's *Esther* defies simple comparisons with the ancient versions covered thus far: tell-tale clues that should allow us to relate Josephus's account to a particular source, such as the identity of the king during whose reign the story took place, Haman's epithet, the relationship between Mordecai and Esther, or the status of the additions—actually point to the heterogenous nature of his source(s).[60] In Josephus's account, the king is Artaxerxes[61] (as in the LXX and OL, *contra* the MT and AT, which have "Ahashwerosh"), but Haman is an Amalekite (as in the MT, *contra* the AT, LXX, and OL). And while Mordecai and Esther are cousins in the MT, AT, and LXX (but also married in the LXX), Josephus describes Mordecai as Esther's uncle. Moreover, some of the eunuchs' names in Josephus echo those found in the MT,[62] while others do not.[63]

There are, moreover, numerous points in Josephus's account that most closely resemble OL *Esther*. Some of these are relatively minor: In both Josephus and the OL, the eunuch who mediates between Esther and Mordecai in Esth 4 retains his role until the end of their communication (*contra* all other versions); and in both Josephus and the OL, during the events recorded in *Esther* 6, Haman loses the ability to speak. More significant than the details shared by the two versions is the fact that in both of them the relationships between each of the Jews, the king, and the empire's non-Jewish population are similar—and distinctly so from other versions of the story.

Both sources stress the Jews' loyalty to the king and his kingdom and downplay the hostility between the Jews and the empire's gentiles. As noted, the OL omits reference to the widescale killings recorded in Esth 9, whereas Josephus—despite integrating four of the additions to *Esther* in his narrative—omits Additions A and F (Mordecai's dream and its interpretation), as these additions describe a world divided between the Jews and others.[64] Similarly, the king in Josephus is portrayed favorably (as he is in the OL, but *contra* the AT and later traditions that characterize him as evil), and the Jews are unequivocally his allies. This realigning of the political relationships between the Jews, the gentiles, and the kingdom is typical of Josephus's rewriting of the scriptures, as his goal is to present the Jewish people in a favorable light to an educated, Hellenized audience. Even the Jews' God is Hellenized in Josephus's *Esther* story: When Haman is executed on the gallows (Greek: *stauros*, "cross," as in the LXX) that he had prepared for Mordecai, Josephus approvingly states:

> And from hence I cannot forbear to admire God, and to learn hence his wisdom and his justice, not only in punishing the wickedness of Haman, but in so disposing it, that he should undergo the very same punishment which he

had contrived for another; as also because thereby he teaches others this lesson, that what mischiefs any one prepares against another, he, without knowing of it, first contrives it against himself.

It is interesting to observe how Josephus managed to neutralize the one detail of the story inherited from his source(s) that might reflect negatively on his Roman patrons and readership, namely, that Haman was an Amalekite. For their role in destroying the Second Temple, the Romans came to be associated with the Amalekites in the first century CE, so that describing Haman as an Amalekite would align the Romans with the story's villain. Josephus's solution was to preempt such problematic comparisons by equating the Amalekites with the Idumeans, Arab nomads who were challenging both the Romans (militarily) and the Jews (by virtue of being Edomites).[65] That the Romans would be equated with the Edomites before too long (if they had not already been equated with them in certain circles) is beside the point: what matters is that the Jews and Romans shared an Amalekite-Idumean enemy and were thus allies. Unsurprisingly, Josephus's portrayal of Haman also reflects his unique perspective, sources, and aims. Perhaps more than anything else, in his *Antiquities of the Jews*, Josephus was concerned with refuting the charge that Jews were misanthropic and intolerant of other religions.[66] Haman's accusations are perhaps the most direct such charge against the Jews in the HB, and the *Esther* story was, therefore, of particular importance for Josephus.[67] Moreover, as Feldman has argued,[68] one of Josephus's aims in rewriting the biblical stories for a Greco-Roman audience was to de-emphasize God's role in the events. The *Esther* story, at least in its MT version, is the HB's outstanding specimen of this.[69] Thus, in the words of Feldman, ". . . in terms of the sheer amount of space that Josephus devotes to the Esther pericope, it is clearly one of the greatest importance for him."[70]

As was his practice, Josephus Hellenized the story to resonate with his audience. Hence, while Mordecai is "wise," Josephus's Haman is criticized for his *hubris*,[71] and, when forced to parade Mordecai publicly, he lacks the restraint with which he is credited in other versions of the story. In Josephus's version, Haman "was confounded in his mind and knew not what to do," before at last complying with the king's orders. Moreover, Josephus's Haman "could not bear his good fortune, nor govern the magnitude of his prosperity with sound reason," whereas the other versions of Addition E (in which this statement appears) merely have Haman "unable to restrain his arrogance." And when the king discovers Haman begging for Esther's mercy in Josephus's paraphrase of Esth 7:8, Josephus has the king describe Haman as a "wretch" and "the vilest of mankind" (nothing of the sort is found in the other versions). This echoes Mordecai's initial reaction to Haman's parading of him publicly: Because Mordecai thought that this was done in mockery (and not in fulfilment of a royal order), Mordecai chastised Haman, saying, "O thou wretch, the vilest of all mankind, do you thus laugh at our calamities?" Josephus's placing of similar descriptions of Haman in the mouths of both Mordecai and the king serves to align them against Haman and, in passing, describes Haman in unequivocally unflattering terms.

The association of Haman with *hubris* is particularly significant, as the term implies a godlike self-estimation: Josephus does not include ancient traditions that have Haman presenting himself as a god (or wearing an idol on his chest, which would make prostration before him an act of idolatry). And yet, by associating Haman with *hubris*, Josephus hints at the sort of self-divination that is associated with Pharaoh and, elsewhere in his *Antiquities* (I.113), with Nimrod.[72] Moreover, *hubris*, excessive pride, is the opposite of *sophrosyne*, or self-restraint. In the MT (5:10) Haman possesses self-restraint (despite Mordecai's repeated dishonoring of him), whereas Josephus conveniently omits this detail in his retelling of the story.

Josephus also offers unique perspectives on Haman's antipathy towards the Jews. To begin with, when Mordecai refused to bow to Haman, the latter could not fathom why "the Persians, who were free men, worshipped him, [whereas] this man, who was no better than a slave" refused to do so. The reference to Mordecai as "no better than a slave" brings to mind the traditions about Haman being made Mordecai's slave in Addition A (which, as noted, Josephus omits), but implies that Haman saw the relationship inversely, with Mordecai accorded servile status. Thereafter, in deciding to annihilate the entire Jewish nation (rather than merely punishing Mordecai), Josephus tells us that Haman was "determined to abolish the whole nation, for he was naturally an enemy to the Jews, because the nation of the Amalekites, of which he was, had been destroyed by them." At first glance, this statement appears simply to confirm the MT's association between Haman and the Amalekites, which we have already noted as part of Josephus's account. There is, however, significant novelty in it. In Josephus's account, Haman's Amalekite identity is not related to the Jews' unfinished business with his forebears (as per 1 Sam 15), but has precisely the opposite meaning: Haman wishes to exact revenge from the Jewish people for having killed his own ancestors.[73] Once again, the curious implication is that the story reflects Haman's perspective and interests more than it does those of the Jewish protagonists.

Unlike the versions of *Esther* encountered earlier, Josephus did not recount the *Esther* story as though he were rewriting scripture. This is true of his coverage of all biblical materials in his *Antiquities*, but he nonetheless appears to have taken more liberties with *Esther* than he did with other biblical accounts. One can only suppose that this signals some combination of circumstances coincident with this particular writing: the diversity of information at his disposal, the unstable status of *Esther* as a biblical book, and the uniquely important role that this story might play in presenting biblical lore to a Hellenized audience. In this story, he who has accused the Jews of misanthropy, peculiar behavior, and disloyalty to gentile rulers, is himself the personification of *hubris*, is disloyal to the king, and is able neither to "bear his good fortune, nor [to] govern the magnitude of his prosperity with sound reason." Josephus tells us that, like Bigthan and Teresh, Haman was hanged upon a cross (Greek: *stauros*), a detail that reflects well the composite nature of Josephus's sources: He shares the eunuchs' names with the MT, but the mode of their punishment with the LXX. The complexity, even contradictions, inherent in Josephus's account remind us of the complexities and contradictions in Josephus's own identity, for he was both a traitor to his nation (on the battlefield) and their staunchest supporter (on the battlefield of ideas).

Josephus's retelling of *Esther* demonstrates something that may be obvious but is worth stating nonetheless, namely that ancient audiences of *Esther* (and, perhaps, of the Bible generally) were not necessarily limited to a single narrative or text. Whatever "Bible" one happened to know (be it the MT, the AT's *Vorlage*, or one of the Greek versions) was the starting point for one's familiarity with the story, but it was not the end-point, for the story accrued (and shed) details and traditions as it was retold over time. Josephus's version shows us what this process looked like in 94 CE.

This textual flexibility tells us something about the book's shaky scriptural credentials, but it also testifies to its enormous popularity. The story was retold and reimagined time and time again, far more than most biblical narratives, and this despite its lacking the scriptural legitimacy enjoyed by the rest of the HB books by Josephus's time. This paradoxical blend of popular strength with scriptural weakness was solved in the Greek versions in ways we have already seen. The rabbis, however, generally used the MT, and produced their own solutions to the *Esther* paradox, even though there is some evidence that they were aware of traditions found in other versions of the story. They produced midrashic elaborations on *Esther*, many of which would be absorbed within mainstream lore about the narrative, including details that disagreed with the text of the MT.[74] Later on, we will return to the rabbis and other exponents of authoritative exegesis, for as we shall see, their interpretations of scripture also came to acquire near-scriptural authority. But first, we will look at a particularly momentous development within Judaism, one that presents us with new interpretations of Jewish scripture on the one hand, and a new movement with entirely new scriptures on the other. We turn now to the New Testament to uncover the extent of Haman's wiles on the next stop of his scriptural journey.

3

Haman in Christian Scripture

AT THE outset of this chapter, it is worth stressing a point that is as obvious as it is overlooked, namely that Christian scripture *includes* Jewish scripture—commonly referred to as "the Old Testament" (hereafter: OT). When the ways of Judaism and early Christianity parted, the latter added two things to the OT: 1) a "New" Testament; and 2) new readings of the OT. With the exception, most famously, of the early Christian theologian Marcion (d. 160) and his followers, who rejected the divine origins of the OT and its relevance to Christianity, virtually all Christians since ancient times have accepted the contents of the OT as scripture, not least because Jesus was seen as a fulfilment of promises and prophecies found within it. Among the numerous OT proof-texts on which one might draw, Jer 31:30–32 summarizes the complex interaction between the OT and the new religion especially well:

> Behold, the days come, says the Lord, that I will make a new covenant with the house of Israel, and with the house of Judah; not according to the covenant that I made with their fathers in the day that I took them by the hand to bring them out of the land of Egypt; forasmuch as they broke My covenant, although I was a lord over them, says the Lord. But this is the covenant that I will make with the house of Israel after those days, says the Lord, I will put My law in their inward parts, and in their heart I will write it; and I will be their God, and they shall be my people.

On the one hand, from a Christian perspective, Jesus was fulfilling this prophecy, a fact that confers significance not only on Jesus but on the prophecy and its scriptural context as well. On the other hand, the prophecy clearly states that when it is eventually fulfilled, things will change: There will be a *new* covenant, the Law (Hebrew: *Torah*) will be internalized in some way, and it is those who hold by this new covenant who will be God's people. Thus, *Esther*—as a book of the OT—will remain part of Christian scripture, but it will have to undergo a process of reinterpretation. Whereas the ancient Jews who produced the Greek *Esthers* felt the need to rewrite the book, ancient Christians felt the need to re-read it. These ancient Christian rereadings will be discussed later on. For now, we will focus on the New Testament and Haman's portrayal in it.

Esther—and Haman—in the New Testament

Any reader familiar with the question of *Esther* and the New Testament (hereafter: NT), would probably expect this section to be short, for the consensus has long been that *Esther* has left almost no mark on the NT. As one scholar put it, "Esther is the only Old Testament book which is not quoted in the New Testament."[1] The only verse in the NT thought to suggest acquaintance with *Esther* is Mark 6:23,[2] where Herod II's daughter Salome danced before him and his guests at his birthday celebration, for which he offered to reward her with "whatever you ask me . . . up to half my kingdom," a phrase that echoes Esth 5:3, 6, and 7:2.[3]

The assumption has been that the NT's authors intentionally omitted references to *Esther* on account of what the book included, on the one hand, and what it excluded, on the other. What it excluded is any reference to either God, theology, spirituality, morality, or to the sort of OT themes that were deemed attractive or even relevant by NT authors and their audiences. What it included were ideas that actively contradicted the messages imparted in the NT, namely notions of vengeance and ethnocentricity. In the Sermon on the Mount, Jesus famously told his followers, "Do not resist the one who is evil. But if anyone slaps you on the right check, turn to him the other also. And if anyone would sue you and take your tunic, let him have your cloak too (Matt 5:38–40)." In the Sermon on the Plain, Jesus stated, "Love your enemies, do good to those who hate you, bless those who curse you, pray for those who abuse you. . . . (Luke 6:27–28)." MT *Esther*, by contrast, tells us that the Jews killed 75,810 of their enemies, even after Haman and his anti-Jewish edict had been neutralized (9:1–16). Similarly, whereas *Esther* relates how the Jewish nation survived an existential threat, Jesus largely replaced ethnic, familial bonds with spiritual ones (this generalization will be unpacked in Chapter 9).

In other words, early followers of Jesus reading *Esther* are likely to have noticed inconsistencies between its contents and the messages imparted by the Messiah (and to the extent that Jesus was updating the previous covenant, *Esther*'s message became obsolete). Moreover, the carnivalesque festivities that feature at the end of *Esther* are not likely to have resonated with the first generations of Christians.

This disharmony between *Esther* and the Christian scriptural message has generated some strikingly negative verdicts on the book: In 1526, Martin Luther stated regarding *Esther* that, "... [despite] inclusion of it in the canon, it deserves more than all the rest in my judgment to be regarded as non-canonical," and in 1543 he added, "Oh, how fond [Jews] are of the book of Esther, which is so beautifully attuned to their bloodthirsty, vengeful, murderous yearning and hope."[4] More recently, Bush went so far as to state that, "... in the Christian world at large the book of Esther has not found acceptance. It is indeed an *opus non gratum*, an unacceptable work."[5] And, as noted, the community that produced the *Dead Sea Scrolls*, whose worldview overlapped in many ways with that of early Christians, chose to exclude *Esther* from their canon and Purim from their calendar, despite displaying knowledge of the book and its contents.

Why, then, are we even considering Haman here? A first, and easy answer is precisely because the early Christian rejection of *Esther*'s messages tells us how the book (including its villain) was interpreted among certain groups of Bible-readers two thousand years ago. Whatever the merit of such an answer may be, it tells us more about early Christianity than about our subject, Haman. There is, however, another answer, one that is as exciting as the preceding one is evasive. Recent scholarship has shown that *Esther*, and Haman's depiction in the book, had a formative influence on some of the most iconic (so to speak) scenes in the NT.

To understand how centuries of scholarship could have missed Haman's appearance on such an important Christian stage, we must begin with a point about *Esther* in first-century Palestine that has only recently been appreciated. The Jewish groups who came to follow Jesus and to produce the NT are likely to have known a version of *Esther* that included God, prayer, and the other spiritual upgrades that the additions to *Esther* offered. We have already seen how one such first-century CE Jew (Josephus) retold *Esther* using an array of sources and materials that include four of the additions to the story. The gap between MT *Esther* and NT theology is much greater than that between LXX *Esther* and the NT. And, as noted, OL *Esther*, reflecting an ancient Greek *Vorlage*, recounts the story without reference to the problematic theme of violent vengeance. In other words: The authors of the Gospels may have known *Esther* as a story that was neither spiritually nor theologically deficient, nor at odds with Jesus's moral message. None of this detracts from the fact that *Esther* is not mentioned directly in the NT, of course. And yet, we can understand why scholars stopped searching for *Esther* in the NT too soon, if we realize that they (mistakenly) assumed the MT version (rather than a Greek one) to have been the Bible in common use in first-century Palestine.

Where might we find Haman in the NT, and with what ramifications? While there are no direct references to *Esther* in the books that comprise the NT, Lees has identified what he calls "intertextual ripples" of *Esther* in Christian scripture. Focusing on the crucifixion of Haman in Greek versions of *Esther* and on the "Judaizing" of the non-Jews in light of the former's ascendancy (Esth 8:17), Lees has argued that the NT's authors consciously drew on *Esther* in composing their writings. The descriptions of Jesus's Passion and crucifixion are, of course, among the most theologically significant passages in the gospels. Although they largely relate historical events, they do so in a stylized language that echoes biblical texts (which, for the authors of the Gospels, meant some version of the Jewish Bible). Interestingly, whereas in the NT the verb "to crucify" occurs many times, in the LXX it is used only in *Esther* (7:9; and E 18). Hence, as Lees puts it, "To a Jewish audience familiar with LXX *Esther*, the only scriptural reference to crucifixion is the crucifixion of Haman. . . ."[6]

Building on a familiarity with *Esther*, one can read John 19:5–6, where Jesus is described as being paraded "wearing the crown of thorns, and the purple robe" as Pontius Pilate exclaims "Behold the man!," and being also generally mocked and scourged (". . . they cried out, 'Crucify him, crucify him!'"), as a conscious inversion of the victorious presentation of Mordecai (Esth 8:15), who was also paraded while wearing a crown and a purple robe, acclaimed by a herald (Haman), and generally celebrated ("the city of Shushan shouted and was glad").[7] Assuming these echoes of *Esther* in the gospels are real, what do they mean, in general, and what can they tell us about Haman, in particular?

A superficial analysis of the verses describing Jesus's/Mordecai's public procession suggests that both the heroes (Mordecai and Jesus) and the villains (Haman and Pilate) are being compared, a proposition that tallies well with the basic Christian narrative. And just as Mordecai's elevation represents an apex of success and prestige, the inversion of the language when describing Jesus's passion represents a nadir. But what are we to make of the fact that in his crucifixion Jesus in the NT is actually paralleling Haman as he is described in Greek versions of *Esther*? It is worth noting that the crucifixion parallel between Jesus and Haman is not limited to the use of the verb "to crucify" in both cases, but is strengthened by two more parallels between them: Jesus was crucified in lieu of Barabbas, just as Haman was crucified in lieu of Mordecai; and both were executed after having been falsely accused.

Jewish and Christian audiences understandably responded in different ways to these parallels. Predictably, Christians—in the later books of the NT—developed a theological framework within which the Jesus-Haman parallels gained substance. In his *Epistle to the Galatians* (3:13), Paul draws on Deut 21:23 to explain the importance of Jesus's being accursed: "Christ redeemed us from the curse of the law by becoming a curse for us, for it is written: "Cursed is everyone who is hung on a pole."[8] One might also, more simply, interpret the Jesus-Haman parallel theologically by understanding Jesus on the Cross as loaded-up with sins to such an extent that he was comparable to the quintessential character of evil, Haman. As noted, in the LXX Haman is referred to as *ho diabolos*, "the devil,"[9] making him the ideal model for Jesus in his accursed state. Thus, provided one is attuned to early Christian thought, the Jesus-Haman parallel is unproblematic, and—importantly for us—it implies that of all the HB's villains, tyrants, and wretched characters, Haman stood out as particularly accursed.

Equally understandable is the fact that Jewish audiences were not attuned to early Christian thought. Lacking a suitable theological framework for this parallel between Jesus and Haman, Jews could exploit it for their own polemical (and, occasionally, cathartic) needs, and Christians in the first centuries could understand Purim as a Jewish celebration of Jesus's death, which, as we will see in Chapter 6, it sometimes was.[10]

The superficial equivalence between Jesus and Haman was, therefore, inherently controversial, breeding sophisticated theology in later books of the NT on the one hand, and unsophisticated revelry and mockery on the other. Lees detects a third interpretative strategy for this problematic equivalence, one that may predate the previous two responses. In his view, *Matthew*'s description of Judas's betrayal of Jesus (Matt 26–27) is indebted to *Esther* and consciously serves to associate Haman with Judas,[11] thereby dissociating the former from Jesus.[12] For example, in what are the only two episodes in all of the HB and NT in which money is offered to put others to death,[13] Haman offers the king money in exchange for the Jews (*Esther* 3:9) and Judas betrays Jesus for the promise of money (Matt 26:15). One might add, albeit more tentatively, the reference in both Matt 27:46 and Mark 15:34 to Ps 22 in Jesus's "Seven Last Words from the Cross." Jesus is quoted as having cried out, "My God, My God, why have You forsaken me?," a quotation from Ps 22:2 that Rabbi Levi in the Babylonian Talmud attributes to Esther as she approached the king uninvited (Esth 5:1).[14] Although Rabbi Levi lived over a century after the gospels were composed, it is possible that he was influenced by an ancient, pre-Christian tradition about Esther's self-sacrificing approach to the king.[15]

Obviously, the parallel between Haman and Judas is immediately attractive, and it would certainly have been more palatable to an early Christian audience, whose ranks were swelled with Jews, than the association of Jesus with

Haman. We must also assume that complex reinterpretations of scripture of the sort that exploited the Jesus-Haman equivalence theologically, were the preserve of elites,[16] whereas the overwhelming majority of Christians throughout history will have taken more naturally to the Judas-Haman pairing.[17]

Scholars have identified references to *Esther* elsewhere in the NT, some of which are more convincing than others.[18] Wechsler, for instance, has cleverly argued for the existence of conscious parallels between Paul's presentation of Jesus and Greek versions of *Esther*.[19] Combining philology, theology, and the tools of early Christian exegesis, he postulated that Paul depicted Esther as a "type" of Jesus. The coincidence of the fourteenth of Nissan being a turning point in both stories—specifically the three-day event in which Esther's fasting and Jesus's humiliation occur—is supported by the semantic association between fasting and humiliation in biblical Hebrew.[20] Late first-century CE support for this merging of Esther's fast and Jesus's humiliation may also be found in the (apocryphal) *First Epistle of Clement* (55:6), where we read that, "for with fasting and humiliation [Esther] besought the all-seeing Master of the Ages." This helps unlock a statement in Paul's *Epistle to the Philippians* (2:8), in which Esther's three-day fast is paralleled with the three-day period of Jesus's death, as the Greek term for Jesus's "humiliation" in this verse is identical to the word the LXX employed for Esther's "humble days" in the dialogue leading up to her fast (LXX 4:8).[21]

This case-study of *Esther*'s interaction with the NT is important for two reasons: First, it provides us with yet more evidence for *Esther*'s deployment within the NT; and second, it reminds us that early Christians did not only produce a new testament, but also new, theologically useful ways of rereading the old one. What Wechsler is arguing for is a very early example of just such a rereading, whereby Paul is seeing in *Esther*'s story a foreshadowing of Jesus's future story.[22] These strategies for rereading the OT conceive of it as a text that both tells us the story of the pre-Jesus Covenant and discloses the hidden significance of these stories and their characters as "types" of Jesus, who foreshadow him and whose significance is only revealed to us in light of his career.

For this reason, although we have now covered Haman's portrayals in Jewish and Christian scriptures, we cannot yet turn to Muslim scripture: for in the period between the emergences of Christianity and Islam, Jews and Christians developed exegetical tools that aimed to clarify a scriptural text's meaning and message through interpretations that were deemed prestigious and authoritative. In fact, in some cases, they came to be seen as scripture themselves, as we shall now see.

4

Authoritative Exegesis of *Esther*

ON OUR journey from the NT to the Qur'ān, taking a detour through Jewish and Christian authoritative exegetical traditions is justified for two reasons. First, as we will discover, Haman appears in the Qur'ān in a guise that is considerably different from any we have encountered until now. Understanding this extreme makeover between scriptures requires an appreciation of the various Jewish and Christian traditions about him that circulated on the eve of Islam. Second, although until now it has been assumed that scripture for Jews was the HB, in the centuries preceding the rise of Islam, Jewish authorities developed the idea that there was actually a second Torah, which was revealed alongside the written one and complemented it. This point deserves some clarification.

At the beginning of Chapter 1, I asked "What is the Bible?" without providing a satisfactory answer to the question. Instead, I merely observed that the answer to the question is complex for a range of reasons. A further layer of complexity stems from that fact that most readers of scripture in the Abrahamic traditions have not limited themselves to the Jewish Tanakh, the Christian "Bible" (Old and New Testaments) or the Muslim Qur'ān, respectively. For while all sorts of attempts have been made in each of these religions to limit "scripture" to a single volume or collection of holy books (Sadducees and Karaites in Judaism; Protestants in Christianity; Qur'ānists in Islam, to name but a few examples), the average reader of scripture needed help understanding what the words meant, and there were always people who, for whatever reasons and with whatever legitimacy, felt qualified to provide it. In each of the three religions, certain groups of purported authorities acquired such prestige that their explanations of scripture were deemed correct and even divinely sanctioned.

Thus, to know what scripture meant, one needed to know what these people *said* that it meant.[1] The Jewish case is perhaps most instructive in this context for in Judaism these interpretative traditions became another "Torah"; not of the sort transmitted in writing, but rather orally. Some of what scripture came to mean, already in late antiquity (if not earlier), was an entire library of materials that for an observer from outside the tradition did not appear to be scripture at all. The Babylonian Talmud itself (b. ʿEruvin 13b) relates that after three years of intractable debates between the school of Hillel and the school of Shammai, a heavenly voice announced that, "both these and these are the living words of God,[2] [but] the law follows the school of Hillel." From this we learn three things: That the law generally follows the school of Hillel; that the traditions produced and adduced by the rabbis in their debates are actually "the living words of God"; and that despite the first fact, even the losing side is transmitting the words of God. In a sentence, the discussion of scripture was itself deemed to be scripture.[3]

Comparable attitudes are to be found in varieties of Christianity and of Islam, but in different manifestations. Early on, Christians sought to read the OT in new ways, allowing for a diversity of interpretation that we will later encounter. But the NT did not claim for itself the same divine authorship that the Qur'ān has in Islam and the Torah has in the most conservative of Jewish circles (Christians who disagree with this statement simply have not learned enough about the Torah in traditional Judaism or the Qur'ān in Islam),[4] and exegesis of the NT—being another degree of separation away from the text itself—is even less "the living word of God" than the NT is (for it is Jesus himself who is "the Word"). In Islam, by contrast, the authenticated traditions of the Prophet (and, for most Shīʿa Muslims, their Imāms) have the authority that the Oral Torah enjoys in Judaism, albeit without the grandiose label (for there can be no concept of a separate "Oral Qur'ān").[5]

Any discussion of Haman in scripture must therefore include this much broader definition of the term, for the simple reason that most of scripture's readers over the ages have taken for granted that this definition of scripture is the correct one. Haman has been waiting patiently while that point was being made, and we now at last turn to what the rest of scripture has to say about him.

Exegesis through Translation

As we noted with reference to Greek versions of *Esther*, a translation, even one that aims to be literal, almost always reveals to us something about the translator's interpretation of the original text. We have also noted that in the case of ancient translations of *Esther*, there was often little pretense that the translated text was a literal rendering of the original: Six (or seven) additions to *Esther* were composed, which were added to some versions in their entirety and to others in part. Within these same texts, we also saw entire phrases or even sentences added to or removed from the base text of *Esther*. Accordingly, an ancient Jew reading "*Esther*" will have read a very specific version of the story based on the particular language in which she encountered it, and even within each language there were different options (with different Hamans) in play. (Interestingly, such a reader is unlikely to have known that alternatives to her version of the story existed.)

Earlier, we related this flexibility in recounting *Esther*'s story to the book's uncertain status within the biblical canon. By contrast, authoritative interpretations of *Esther* originate in a different context, one in which questions of canonicity have finally been answered for both Jewish and Christian readers. Those (within Christianity) who rejected *Esther*'s scriptural status may still have held that we can learn moral lessons from the book's contents, whereas those (both Jews and Christians) who accepted *Esther* as canonical were elevating interpretations of it from mere retellings of an important ancient Jewish story to divinely sanctioned scriptural exegesis.

One historical variable that contributed to the diversity of interpretations in this period is the exponential expansion of *Esther*'s readers geographically, a process that affected both Jews and Christians (albeit in different ways and for different reasons). In the aftermath of the Second Temple's destruction in 70 CE, and of the unsuccessful Bar Kokhba revolt against the Romans in 132–136, Jews were dispersed widely across the Near East and the Mediterranean world, so that significant communities were to be found under Roman rule in Greater Syria, Egypt, North Africa, and southern Europe; under Persian (Parthian and then Sasanid) rule in Iraq and Iran; as well as pockets living on the Arabian Peninsula (including ancient communities in Teyma to the north and Yemen to the south). What this means in practice is that Jews came to be acquainted with *Esther* in different languages, and rabbis in late antiquity had to ponder whether one might adequately fulfill the commandment of reading *Esther* on Purim in Greek, Coptic, Elamite, or Median.[6]

In the case of Christianity, the early community's evolution (largely through Paul's efforts) from a type of messianic Judaism to the status of a distinct religion with universal relevance and ambitions required that scripture be rendered in languages intelligible to each community. It is not just that the Pauline epistles address communities in such places as Rome, Ephesus, Corinth, Galatia, Philippi, Thessalonica, and Colossae (all but the latter of these are widely regarded as being genuinely Pauline), but that in the centuries between the careers of Jesus and Muḥammad, Christianity continued to spread and develop, generating cultural (and dogmatic) diversity within the religion. We thus find important Christian communities reading scripture in Greek, Latin, Armenian, Ethiopic, Syriac, and other languages. And unlike the Septuagint, these versions could not boast of any miracle that conferred uniformity on the translations; multiple *Esthers* with their multiple Hamans circulated widely.

Haman's Quest for Immortality: Jewish and Christian Canonizations of *Esther*

We have discovered that these multiple *Esthers* could differ significantly from one another, because ancient purveyors of the text took liberties in changing their contents. What enabled this liberty-taking were the question marks that hovered over the *Esther* story, concerning its genre, significance, and authority (among other issues). At some point, readers of scripture had to decide, categorically, what did (and did not) constitute scripture, and when the Greek versions of *Esther* were being formed, it seems that the decision had yet to be taken.

According to a wise saying, a person suffers three deaths: the first is when their body dies; the second is when their body is buried; and the third is when their name is spoken for the last time. With this in mind, the question of canonization, as far as Haman is concerned, was a momentous one: featuring in scripture meant becoming the subject of innumerable commentaries, immeasurable scholarly attention, and enduring cultural importance. The book of *Judith*, comparable in many ways to *Esther* (and consciously so, as we will see in Chapter 6), did not make it into most Bibles, nor did its villains enter into mainstream Jewish or Christian culture. *Esther*, by contrast, was canonized and its villain's legacy has benefited accordingly. Thus, when canonization questions arose, what was at stake for Haman was nothing less than his potential immortality.

The precise process of the HB's canonization is not well-known, and—as is to be expected from a topic with far-reaching religious ramifications—different accounts have been offered, both from within the Jewish and Christian traditions and by modern scholars.[7] What is clear is that *Esther*'s candidacy for canonization was considered more than once, among different groups of Jews and Christians, and that it raised numerous questions: Did *Esther* belong in the Bible? Did the additions to *Esther* belong in the Bible? If so, were they on a par with the rest of *Esther*'s contents (and, thus, deserving to be integrated into the flow of the narrative), or were they on an inferior level of authority (and therefore to be relegated as a group to the end of the book, detached from the story's contents)?

Unsurprisingly, the answers proposed were no less complex than the questions themselves.

Judaism

From the centrality and prominence of Haman's place in Jewish culture, and from its Judeo-centric storyline, one might assume that *Esther* passed the canonization test with flying colors. This assumption is emphatically wrong. The problem was certainly not that *Esther* was unknown or poorly distributed, as there is good evidence that both in the Holy Land and in the Diaspora there were those who knew the book but consciously chose to exclude it. We have seen that the *Dead Sea Scrolls* community did not preserve a single copy of *Esther* in their library (and the absence of Purim from their liturgical calendar demonstrates that *Esther*'s exclusion was intentional). In fact, there were Jews living in the Holy Land during the Second Temple period who attempted to replace *Esther* with books that solved some of the problems they perceived in MT *Esther*.[8] As for the Diaspora, even in Alexandria, where the LXX was produced (or to which LXX *Esther* was sent c. 100 BCE), such a prominent scholar as Philo (d. 50 CE) did not bother to mention it.

In general terms, however, there clearly were differences between *Esther*'s reception in the Holy Land and in the Diaspora, as there were numerous reasons why the book would have been attractive to Diaspora Jews (for its encouraging message that Jews can succeed in exile, even when faced with threats), and unattractive to Holy Land Jews (for its lack of reference to the Land and the Temple, and for its celebration of heroes who were exiles). The fact that *Esther* ends with the message that the Jews lived happily ever after, albeit *outside* of the Land of Israel, might not have endeared the book to residents of the Holy Land.[9]

Wall paintings from the Dura Europos synagogue (mid-third century Syria) testify to the popularity of *Esther* in the cultural consciousness of the Diaspora. One panel, depicting Mordecai's public triumph as described in Esth 6, is positioned immediately to the left of the synagogue's prayer niche, further evidence of *Esther*'s importance.[10] Meanwhile, at around the same time and also under Persian rule, Talmudic sages were debating *Esther*'s status in terms that suggest the story was far from secure in the Jewish canon.[11] Picking up on a Mishnaic statement (m.Yadayim 3:5), according to which all biblical books "defile the hands," the Babylonian rabbis (b.Megillah 7a) considered whether *Esther*, too, "defiled the hands."[12] As part of the discussion another question with implications for the issue of canonization was raised: Was *Esther* written with divine inspiration? Not all agreed that the book satisfied these conditions.[13] As mentioned, one proof supporting divine inspiration was the author's apparent access to Haman's inner thoughts, which an ordinary human author could not access (unless the author was Haman himself!). Other rabbis gave their own proofs for *Esther*'s divine status. The answers are interesting in that they highlight the very existence of the question. Thus, even the Talmudic rabbis who lived in the Persian Empire and presumably felt extra affinity for *Esther*'s subject, grappled with its status as a biblical book.

Regardless of these doubts, it would appear that *Esther* and Purim were widely popular, both in the Diaspora and in the Holy Land. Megillat Ta'anit (a rabbinic text composed in the Holy Land in the mid-first century CE), lists Purim as an important festival, demonstrating that people adopted the holiday even if the rabbis had not (yet) adopted the book, and Koller has argued that the Holy Land rabbis succumbed to popular pressure and came to accept *Esther*, a process that took place during the Herodian period (37 BCE–73 CE).[14]

One final point regarding Jewish canonization is in order, not least because it has practical implications for understanding depictions of Haman in Jewish sources: Despite the fact that LXX *Esther* was the product of ancient Judaism, the *Esther* that the Jewish authorities canonized was the MT version, which did not include the six additions and other religious upgrades that went some way towards remedying the religious deficiencies identified in the text.[15] As it is difficult to date precisely both specific rabbinical statements and each of the six additions, we cannot really know what the LXX *Esther* that the rabbis were rejecting looked like. In any case, it is only with Josippon (writing in tenth-century Italy) that the additions to *Esther* found their way into a popular Jewish text.[16] For this reason, the rabbis in late antiquity had to find their own solutions to the problems posed by the text, and these solutions—recorded in an enormous corpus of midrashim—enjoyed great prestige among many Jews.

We will encounter many of these midrashim throughout this book, but for now, one rabbinic statement from late antiquity is worth our attention: In the Jerusalem Talmud it is stated that in the days of the Messiah, when all the books of the Prophets and the Writings are nullified, only the Torah and *Esther* will remain.[17] The incredible implication of this statement is that *Esther*'s status underwent something of a revolution: having started out on shaky ground, *Esther* would unexpectedly enjoy a rare measure of scriptural stability. It was predicted to outlast every other book of the Prophets and Writings.[18]

Christianity

The question of *Esther*'s canonization was also divisive in early Christian communities.[19] In this case, however, the tension was not between Holy Land and Diaspora, but rather between the Western and Eastern churches. Moreover, seeing as in the Christian case both the MT and the LXX versions (or translations thereof) were in circulation, we might have expected there to be a correlation between the version used and canonization (with the theologically satisfying LXX making the cut more consistently than the theologically deficient MT did), yet no such correlation exists. Haman's quest for immortality among Christians was a protracted, complicated, and altogether suspenseful process. And, as was often the case in his career, just when Haman thought things were going his way, fate conspired against him. There were churches that, having accepted *Esther* for centuries, came to resist *Esther*'s inclusion within the Bible.[20]

As a general rule, *Esther* fared better in the West than in the East. Such Church Fathers as Hilary (d. 367), Ruffinus (d. 410), Augustine (d. 430), and others accepted *Esther* as canonical, as did the councils of Hippo (393) and Carthage (397). Latin translations of the Bible were available early on, to serve Christians in the Roman Empire, but these versions contained numerous variations, leading Pope Damasus in the late-fourth century to commission Jerome (d. 420) to retranslate the Bible into Latin. And although it was only in the late-sixteenth century that Jerome's Vulgate was officially deemed authoritative, it had become the standard Latin version already in late antiquity. And yet, despite *Esther*'s widespread canonicity in the West, it was barely quoted or used in sources. For although Clement of Rome (d. 99) already spoke positively of Esther, referring to her as brave and godly, the first systematic Christian commentary on the book was not written until seven centuries later by Rhabanus Maurus (d. 856), archbishop of Mainz, who published his allegorical commentary on *Esther* in 836.

In the Eastern churches, *Esther* was frequently regarded as non-canonical. Melito, Bishop of Sardis in Asia Minor, excluded *Esther* from the list of biblical books he compiled in 170 CE. And when the famous Mishnaic authority Rabbi Meir travelled in Asia Minor (shortly before Melito compiled his list), he could not find a single copy of *Esther* in Hebrew, for which reason he wrote the entire text down from memory (to read it on Purim).[21] Other Eastern authorities, such as the Church Father Athanasius (Pope of Alexandria, d. 373) regarded *Esther* as uncanonical, while the late-fourth century Coptic *Apostolic Constitutions* considered *Esther* a book for "young persons to learn . . . [in which] is much instruction," while at the same time denying it equal status to the rest of the OT books.[22]

On the other hand, some Eastern churches and authorities did accept *Esther* as canonical, including such esteemed Church Fathers as Origen (d. 253), Cyril of Jerusalem (d. 386), Epiphanius (d. 403), and John of Damascus (d. 745). Similarly, a Syriac list of books written in the second half of the fourth century includes *Esther* as canonical,[23] and both Ephrem the Syrian (d. 373) and Aphrahat, "the Persian sage" (d. 345), accepted *Esther* and referred to it in their writings.

Whether Eastern or Western, the Christians who accepted *Esther* were almost always doing so in translation, and the operative question in assessing their understanding of Haman was whether their translation was based on the MT or the LXX. The OL, the "Coptic" (which is actually written in Sahidic), the Ethiopic, and the Armenian versions of *Esther* were translated from the LXX,[24] and they included all the theological improvements that the Greek version offered. By contrast, the Syriac *Peshitta* (150–220 CE) was based on the MT[25] and, as Wechsler has argued, shows acquaintance in at least one instance (*ad* Esth 9:26) with rabbinic traditions.[26] The Vulgate presented something of a middle path between the options: When commissioned to re-translate the Bible into Latin, Jerome went back to the Hebrew text of the MT and realized that the LXX's additions (found also in the OL) were not organic to the original text, for which reason he relegated them to the end of *Esther* (10:4–16:24, in the Vulgate). Excising the additions from the text removed them from the flow of the narrative and downgraded their importance. Thus, the OL *Esther* that Augustine accepted as canonical,[27] was significantly different from the Vulgate *Esther* that came to be widely accepted in the West. Augustine's Haman was a Bougean and a Macedonian; Jerome's was an Agagite.

The Christian debate over *Esther*'s scriptural status contrasted with the Jewish one in yet another way: Whereas the Jewish canonization process meant including MT *Esther* universally, it also meant excluding the LXX additions universally. In the Christian case, even those who did not canonize *Esther* could accept it as a useful work for some purposes. For Athanasius of Alexandria, who denied *Esther* canonicity, the book was "edifying reading,"[28] and the Coptic *Apostolic Constitutions* saw in the book "instruction" for young people. The curious reality is that *Esther*'s status in late antique Christianity converged towards a range of compromise positions. Western authorities canonized it but otherwise tended not to draw on it in their writings, while Eastern authorities who rejected its canonicity still felt the book had some relevance to readers.

Either way, despite an unpromising start out of the blocks, followed by a rough ride through the skeptical courts of scriptural legitimacy, and despite having to present himself to authorities as an Agagite here or as a Macedonian or Bougean there, Haman eventually rode to immortality on the back of *Esther's* canonization.

Haman in Early Christian Authoritative Interpretation

Once some version of *Esther* made it into a community's biblical canon, both Jews and Christians still had to decide how to read it. Did it belong to the genre of sacred history, theology, spiritual/moral guidance, or some combination of these options? Unsurprisingly, Jews and Christians proposed different answers to this question.

For Christians, *Esther* posed challenges that we have surveyed earlier. A physical threat to an ethnic group—genocidal though the threat may have been—did not ring relevant to Christian readers of the story, for whom ethnic bonds were *passé* and who expected spiritual or Christological messages from the Bible's books. Christians whose Bible included LXX *Esther* were less troubled by the book's literal contents due to the text's relative concern for theology. Hence, Origen, whose *Esther* was the LXX version, could read the text fairly literally and find meaning in it.[29] Relating *Esther* to his own circumstances, he wrote: "Perhaps even now Haman wishes you Mordecais to bow down to him. But you must say, 'I will not set the glory of men above the glory of the God of Israel.'" (Esth Add C:7)." Later, discussing the potency of prayer, he again turned to Addition C: "When the people were about to be destroyed by a single decree because of Haman's plot, the prayer of Mordecai and Esther offered with fasting was heard and engendered in addition to the feasts prescribed by Moses a day of rejoicing given the people by Mordecai."[30]

For most Christian readers of the book, however, even the LXX was not enough on its own, and non-literal readings of the story were proposed. Ephrem, who used the MT-based *Peshitta*, could not refer to Esther's prayer, though he did refer approvingly to her fasting (Esth 4:16) in his hymns "On Fasting," to which he added the non-literal interpretative twist that, "on the Day of Judgment 'the King's bride' [= the Church] will mock Satan just as Esther did Haman."[31] Curiously, Ephrem both equates Haman with Satan and assumes that Esther "mocked" Haman, a reading of *Esther* that tallies well with our depiction of MT Haman as a tragic villain, but flies in the face of most Jewish and Christian readings of the story.

Even less literal were the kinds of typological and allegorical interpretations of *Esther* that came to characterize Christian readings of the story. "Typology" refers to the practice of reading biblical history as *both* factual *and* predictive, with HB characters and events seen as foreshadowing Jesus's future career. "Allegory," by contrast, involves reading it as a sort of extended metaphor that is not to be taken literally at all. Hence, whereas the *Song of Songs* appears to be a love poem, it was widely taken to be an allegory: Jewish and Christian readers could not agree whether it was an allegory for the love between God and His people (Judaism) or between Christ and his bride, the Church (Christianity); but they could agree that a literal reading would be largely meaningless. Neat though this distinction between typology and allegory may be, it is almost certainly a modern one that did not occur to the Church Fathers (the probably exaggerated rivalry between Antiochene and Alexandrian exegetical traditions notwithstanding).

An example of a typological reading of *Esther* may be found in Aphrahat's *Demonstrations*, where he repeatedly draws on Mordecai and Esther as "types" of Jesus, without foregoing the literal, historical meaning of the book. Thus, he explains:

> Because of Mordecai, Esther pleased the king and came in and sat in the place of Vashti who did not do his will. And because of Jesus the Church pleased God and came in to the King in place of the Synagogue, which did not do his will. Mordecai warned Esther and her maids to fast, that they might be saved from the hands of Haman, she and her people; and Jesus warned his Church and her children, that they might be saved from the Wrath, she and her sons.[32]

Here, Aphrahat does two things: He equates Haman not with earthly tyrants or oppressors, but with a more cosmic, eschatological evil—as implied by the identification of Haman with "the Wrath";[33] and he interprets *Esther* in a supersessionist way, with the now-repudiated Jews as the then-repudiated Vashti, replaced by Esther/the Church. For Aphrahat, though, the story itself, at its literal level, retained its historicity.

By contrast, Rhabanus Maurus's commentary tends towards the allegorical, as he explains at the outset of his introduction to *Esther*:[34]

> The Book of Esther . . . contains in the form of mysteries many of the hidden truths of Christ and of the Church—that is, Esther herself, in a prefiguration of the Church, frees the people from danger; and after Haman—whose name is interpreted as wickedness[35]—is killed, she assigns future generations a part in the feast and the festival day.

Unlike Aphrahat, who equates Mordecai with Jesus, Maurus equates the Persian king with Jesus, reigning far and wide. Maurus does, however, share Aphrahat's adoption of replacement theology, which compares Vashti to the Synagogue and Esther to the Church.

Turning to Haman, Maurus curiously offers both earthly and cosmic interpretations of his villainy. On the one hand, he repeatedly refers to Haman as "the spiritual enemy of the people of God," suggesting that Haman did not represent physical adversaries alone. On the other, when Haman is introduced, Maurus sees him as personifying haughty and powerful people:

> [W]hat could the arrogant Haman symbolize if not the haughtiness of the powerful of this world. . . . That is why they wickedly attempt to direct toward themselves the honor and reverence which should properly be paid to God alone; and they persecute with hatred, pursue with torments, and even try to have killed anyone who refuses to do or agree to this.[36]

And although the Jews could hardly be deemed "the powerful of this world" in ninth-century Mainz, Maurus compares Haman to the Jews ("Haman signified the Jews themselves when they were rioting against Christ"). Furthermore, drawing on Josephus's identification of Haman as an Amalekite, Maurus states that Haman "prefigures the bloody people of the Jews who killed their prophets and were not afraid to kill even the Lord of the prophets and his apostles." Finally, and most generally, Maurus explains that Haman "prefigures the enemies of the Church."

These figurative readings of *Esther*, and of Haman's role in the story, remind us that Jews and Christians were not only divided on which books to include in scripture, but also on how to read them. And although Christians using MT *Esther* would have had a very different conception of Haman from those using the LXX, non-literal interpretations of *Esther* transform the meaning of the story and its characters so thoroughly that the distinction between Haman as a Bougean or Haman as an Amalekite would likely have retained little, if any, significance.

Haman in Early Jewish Authoritative Interpretation

In numerous, pivotal ways, Jewish authoritative exegesis on *Esther* differs from its Christian counterpart.[37] The focus on Jewish ethnicity in the text did not pose problems for ancient Jews; there were no admonitions to "turn the other cheek" or "love thine enemy" that ancient Jews had to square with the contents of *Esther*;[38] and there was of course no Christological framework into which *Esther* could be fitted. To be sure, *Esther* posed problems for Jewish readers. The relatively large volume of solutions that midrashic materials offered are evidence to this point. That the midrashim were authored, transmitted, or deployed by the ancient rabbis who constructed rabbinic Judaism imbued their contents with considerable influence. The historical context in which these authors lived shaped the contents of their exegesis, a dynamic to which we will return in Chapter 6, where rabbinic perspectives on Haman will feature. For now, we limit our focus to those exegetical traditions that found their way into pre-Islamic translations of *Esther*, which—for their respective audiences—were the *Esthers* that they knew as scripture.

There is obvious interplay between scripture and midrash in the Aramaic targums to *Esther*, of which there are at least two.[39] A "targum" is literally a translation, but the targums to *Esther* are anything but literal renderings of the MT into Aramaic.[40] Whereas the Christian translation of the MT into Christian Aramaic (the Syriac *Peshitta*) may reflect in one case the influence of a rabbinic midrash (*ad* Esth 9:26, as noted), the authors of the Jewish targums interpreted their task liberally and the translations (especially the second targum, *Targum Sheni*) are interspersed with copious exegetical materials, some of which are only distantly related to the contents of *Esther*.[41] The targums are relevant as scripture because in many Near Eastern Jewish communities, from late antiquity onwards, a targum of *Esther* was read publicly alongside MT *Esther*. The targum thereby made the book accessible to an audience for whom the text was otherwise unintelligible. Thus, the midrashic materials related within these targums were integrated into the *Esther* that audiences understood, and these audiences were not necessarily able to disentangle the text of *Esther* from the midrashim added to it.

To the midrashim imbedded in targums of *Esther* we may add the rabbinic interpretations of *Esther* recorded in the Mishna and Talmuds, which came to be accepted as the "Oral Torah." It is particularly noteworthy that *Esther* is the only biblical book that was the subject of a running commentary in the Babylonian Talmud.[42] The prestige that these commentaries enjoyed guaranteed that their contents would serve as the basis for virtually all Jewish ideas regarding *Esther* and Haman until modern times. In this context, two points about late antique rabbinic midrashim are in order, the first dealing with Christianity and the second with Islam.

The assumption thus far has been that Jewish and Christian exegetical activities occurred in parallel contexts, which were independent from each other. This assumption is not entirely accurate, however, for there was considerable overlap between the two traditions. For example, despite the tendency towards figurative interpretations of *Esther* (and, for that matter, much of the OT) within Christianity, there still were Christians who read *Esther* literally, as part of "sacred" history, but history nonetheless. Sulpicius Severus's (d. 425) *Sacred History*, written at the turn of the fifth century, covered all of history from the Creation to his own times (curiously excepting the events recorded in the NT). Included was a summary of *Esther* (apparently using a version based on the MT)[43] that presents Vashti in terms that stray far from the figurative readings of *Esther* encountered above. He writes:

> There was at that time a certain Vastis (sic) connected with the king in marriage, a woman of marvelous beauty. Being accustomed to extol her loveliness to all, he one day, when he was giving a public entertainment, ordered the queen to attend for the purpose of exhibiting her beauty. But she, more prudent than the foolish king, and being too modest to make a show of her person before the eyes of men, refused compliance with his orders. His savage mind was enraged by this insult, and he drove her forth, both from her condition of marriage with him and from the palace.[44]

Vashti is thus honorable, impressive, and in every way superior to the king, rather than a representative of the repudiated Jews/Synagogue. What aligns Severus's account with the rabbinic one is not his verdict on Vashti (for the rabbis took things in the opposite direction, almost universally vilifying her), but rather his reading of *Esther* literally and as part of sacred history.

Similarly, there are rabbinic midrashim that employ a kind of typology very characteristic of Christian exegesis. In one case, members of his community in Babylonia asked Rabbi Mattanah where in the Torah Moses is referred to before his birth. Once the rabbi supplied an answer, they asked him where Haman is referred to in the Torah. Rabbi Mattanah replied that the verse, "Have you [eaten] of the tree [whose fruits were forbidden to you]?" (Gen 3:11), refers to Haman, explaining that the Hebrew for "Have you [eaten] of" is spelled *ha-min*, which is written in Hebrew with the same consonants as Haman's name. The same question is then asked concerning Esther's and Mordecai's pre-*Esther* appearances in the Torah, and the rabbi manages to deliver equally relevant (or perhaps irrelevant) verses in response, drawing on Deut 31:17–18.[45] The point here is that both sides of the discussion assumed that the characters in *Esther* were prefigured in the earliest books of the Bible.[46]

The relationship between rabbinic midrashim on *Esther* and Islam is no less significant, for Haman appears in the Qur'ān in a guise so different from all biblical versions that we have encountered that the case can (and has) been made that we are not dealing with a manifestation of the biblical Haman at all, but rather with a different character of the same name. It would appear, however, that the biblical and Qur'ānic Hamans were one and the same, and—as we shall now see—it is through recourse to ancient authoritative Jewish exegesis that we may explain Haman's transition from Judeo-Christian to Islamic scriptures.

5

Haman in the Qur'ān

IT COULD reasonably be argued that from a Muslim perspective our discussion of Haman in scripture has been naïvely proceeding in the wrong direction, misguided by an erroneous conception of scriptural chronology. For mainstream Islamic theology held from its very beginning that the Qur'ān was eternal, having forever existed in a "preserved tablet" (Q 85:22). It therefore preceded the Torah, which was one version of the Qur'ān, the text of which (or its interpretation) was at some point corrupted, for which reason it was sent again as *al-Injīl*, a term usually rendered as "the Gospel." The second sending restored the first version. But that, too, was corrupted so that the Qur'ān had to be sent one last time, through Muḥammad, the "Seal of Prophets" (Q 33:40). Accordingly, the thousands of prophets sent before Muḥammad were themselves Muslims, and this book should therefore have started with Haman in the Qur'ān, followed by his subsequent transfigurations in the Jewish and Christian Bibles.

And yet, the Qur'ān as we *now* have it was revealed in the seventh century, transmitted through a historical figure, Muḥammad, whose designation as the "Seal of Prophets" indicates that he came as much to complete a process as to launch it. Thus, the Qur'ān itself repeatedly asserts that in its current form it is confirming the previous (Jewish and Christian) scriptures, rather than preceding them.[1]

If the Qur'ān does not better the HB and NT chronologically, then it certainly does so theologically: For whereas Jewish and Christian scriptures furnish accounts of God's miracles as described in the words of dozens of prophets, according to Islamic theology the Qur'ān itself is a miracle, and its words are God's own words, placed unchanged in Muḥammad's mouth. In fact, the idea emerged fairly early that the Qur'ān was the proof of Islam—an idea with numerous consequences, ranging from a deep-rooted reticence to translate the text into different languages—how does one translate God's words?—to the claim that no inconsistencies, errors, or other imperfections may be detected within the text. What is at stake, then, is not only scripture's integrity but Islam's. We will see in Chapter 7 that Haman's appearances in the Qur'ān generated a centuries-long debate, with one party seeing in them an *error* (thereby disproving Islam), and the other a *miracle* (thereby proving Islam).

A character by the name of Haman (Arabic: *hāmān*) appears six times in the Qur'ān,[2] and in each case he is associated with Pharaoh (Arabic: *fir'awn*). Twice (Q 29:39 and 40:23–24),[3] Pharaoh and Haman are joined by Korah (Arabic: *qārūn*),[4] in two other instances (Q 28:6, 8)[5] they are described as commanding soldiers (Arabic: *junūd*), and in two other instances (Q 28:38 and 40:36–37),[6] Pharaoh orders Haman to build him a lofty tower (Arabic: *ṣarḥ*), from which Pharaoh would survey the God of Moses and prove that Moses is a liar.

Accordingly, although Haman is unmistakably villainous in the Qur'ān, he never appears as a stand-alone villain. There is no positive spin or sympathetic reading of his character, he is not a tragic villain, and—compared to the MT's (and even the LXX's) depictions of him—he comes off as two-dimensional. Most significant, of course, is the difference between the biblical and Qur'ānic historical contexts in which Haman is described as operating. For while the MT and LXX cannot agree on the precise Achaemenid Persian king whom Haman served, they agree on the ancient Persian context generally. The Qur'ān, by contrast, places Haman in Pharaonic Egypt, and Pharaoh's request that Haman build him a tower of bricks baked of clay extending between the heavens and the earth evokes the biblical Tower of Babel (Gen 11:1–9).[7] That the Qur'ānic Haman commands soldiers drives yet another wedge between him and his biblical namesake (who, as vizier, is a "man of the pen" rather than a "man of the sword").

Equally interesting is the fact that the Qur'ān does not mention Mordecai, Esther, Vashti, Zeresh, or any other character from Haman's biblical context. We are thus left feeling that either the Qur'ān knew Haman to have been a biblical villain, but not much else about the *Esther* story, or that we are being duped into the comparison by a mere homonym: the reason the biblical and Qur'ānic Hamans seem so different is that they are different people. The latter interpretation has been preferred in recent decades by many Muslim (and a few Western) scholars.[8]

For now, we will assume that the Qur'ān is indeed referring to the biblical Haman, whose transformation may be explained in a number of ways. The bridges between the "two" Hamans draw mostly on Jewish (rather than Christian) interpretations of *Esther* that circulated in late antiquity, for two reasons. First, the Qur'ān's Haman is a "historical" character rather than a typological or figurative one, this despite the fact that there is evidence of typology in the Qur'ān, with previous prophets being reimagined as ancient Muḥammads and previous scriptures as ancient Qur'āns: The library of writings of which the Jewish or Christian Bibles are comprised is reimagined as a single book (*kitāb*), just as the Qur'ān is a single *kitāb*.[9]

Second, Haman features only rarely in ancient Christian writings (even among those who included Esther in their canon), as we have already seen, and relatively frequently in Jewish midrashim, as we will continue to see. In fact, some of these midrashim are instrumental in bridging the biblical and Qur'ānic portrayals of Haman. The Qur'ān itself (Q 10:94) implores Muḥammad to consult with "those who have recited the scripture before you," should there be any doubt concerning the Qur'ān's contents, thereby justifying the sort of recourse to late antique Jewish traditions that we make in what follows.[10] It should be remembered, however, that the borderlines between Judaism(s) and Christianity(ies) in late antiquity were far more porous than modern readers might imagine, and we have already seen ways in which Jewish and Christian exegetical traditions and techniques could overlap.

How, then, may we account for Haman's transformations in the Qur'ān? The answer relies on a combination of materials and points that, individually, are suggestive at best but cumulatively offer a more convincing case for equating the characters. The first is that pre-Islamic biblical exegetes identified a literary relationship between the portrayal of the Persian court in *Esther* and Pharaoh's court earlier in the Bible. In fact, there is little doubt in the minds of both modern Bible scholars and traditional rabbinic sources that numerous scenes in *Esther* are based on the story of Joseph at the court of Pharaoh, as portrayed in Gen 39–42. Both Joseph and Mordecai are Jews/Israelites who, finding themselves in an unfavorable situation, manage to rise to prominence in the court of a foreign king by using their skill and wisdom, and both are exalted by the ruler in terms that are unmistakably similar.[11] Both use their positions to help their families or people, and there are certain words and phrases employed in both contexts that do not occur elsewhere in the Bible. One might reasonably suppose that the linkages between the two courts' heroes could be paralleled by linkages between their villains.[12] And although the Qur'ān places Haman at the court of Pharaoh during Moses's career rather than Joseph's, parallels between Mordecai and Moses also exist,[13] with some early-Islamic traditions specifically asserting that the same Pharaoh ruled during the careers of Joseph and Moses.[14]

Similarly, late antique Jewish sources make connections between *Esther* and the Pharaoh of Moses's time:[15] One midrashic source tells us that when Haman attempted to persuade Ahashwerosh to eradicate the Jewish people, the king retorted that he knew "what befell Pharaoh for his wicked treatment of the Israelites"; and in another midrash, when Haman tells Zeresh of his plot, she too mentions the fate of Pharaoh as a warning. Similar midrashim from pre- and early-Islamic times abound.[16]

The second point is that the biblical Haman and the Qur'ānic Pharaoh are deemed to have been related through their shared Amalekite genealogy. As noted, the Jewish exegetical tradition almost universally interprets the *Esther* story in terms of the Israelite-Amalekite rivalry, both because Haman's epithet in the MT is "the Agagite," and because various details in *Esther* appear to relate to Saul's rivalry with the Amalekites and their king Agag (1 Sam 15). Even those authors who used LXX *Esther* associated Haman with the Amalekites, despite the fact that the LXX never refers to him as an Agagite.[17] Pharaoh's Amalekite credentials are equally well-known in Islamic tradition, with al-Ṭabarī relating, on the authority of Ibn Isḥāq (d. 767), that "the Pharaohs had inherited rule over Egypt from the Amalekites," while other sources hold that the Pharaohs were Amalekites themselves. Some Qur'ānic exegetes explain that the word *fir'awn* (Pharaoh) was "the permanent title (*laqab*) of Amalekite kings."[18]

The third point relates to Pharaoh's request in the Qur'ān that Haman build a tower (*ṣarḥ*) between the heavens and the earth. This idea would appear to hinder comparisons between the biblical and Qur'ānic Hamans doubly, as there is nothing in *Esther* about Haman building towers,[19] while there is a different context in which a rebellious tower made of bricks of baked clay is described, namely the Tower of Babel (a tower with which Haman has no connection in the Bible). And yet, this detail, too, may help bridge the biblical and Qur'ānic descriptions of Haman.

Comparing theologically significant towers was not uncommon in Abrahamic contexts. To cite one relevant example, the Seleucid general Nicanor—a Second Temple-era villain whose demise the Jews celebrated on the thirteenth of Adar (one day before Purim)—compared Jerusalem to a "tower" (Heb: *migdal*, this being the same word used for the Tower of Babel).[20] Turning to Haman-specific examples, it is interesting to note that Josephus refers both to Haman and to the builders of the Tower of Babel as being possessed of *hubris*,[21] thereby linking the two howsoever loosely. Furthermore, there are ancient exegetical narratives about the Tower of Babel that resurfaced in late antique narratives set at Pharaoh's court.[22] In fact, this fluidity between Egyptian and Mesopotamian contexts is in evidence in the Islamic exegetical traditions that deal with Haman's tower, as many Muslim exegetes casually relate Haman's *ṣarḥ* to the Tower of Babel.[23]

Perhaps most relevant to us is the tale of Aḥiqar the sage, a work that was influential and popular in the Near East, from Achaemenid times until the Middle Ages. The story relates how the childless Aḥiqar, wise advisor of the Assyrian ruler, groomed his nephew ("Nadab" or "Nadan") to be his successor.[24] The ungrateful nephew acted treacherously towards his uncle (and towards the Assyrian ruler). Among other things, the nephew sent a letter to the Egyptian Pharaoh in which he falsely reported that Aḥiqar had been executed. Sensing an opportunity, the Pharaoh challenged the Assyrian king (in a high-stakes wager worth three years of tax revenues) to send him a man who could build for him a tower stretching between the heavens and the earth. As the wise Aḥiqar was believed to be dead, it was Nadab who was expected to take up the challenge. However, it was eventually discovered that Aḥiqar was alive and he was sent to Egypt, where he successfully built the tower (while his villainous nephew was rebuked).[25] The story is referred to in the Second Temple era *Book of Tobit*, where Tobit tells his son, "Remember my son how [H]aman treated Aḥiqar (Greek: "Achiacharus") who exalted him—how out of light he brought him into darkness, and how he rewarded him again; yet Aḥiqar was saved but the other had his reward, for he went down into darkness" (Tob 14:10).[26] There appears to be a scribal error in this text with "Haman" replacing the expected "Nadab." (The reference to Ahashwerosh five verses later, may have led to the confusion.) Be this as it may, the point is that an ancient Jewish text has Pharaoh challenging the Assyrians to send a wise advisor—expected to be Aḥiqar's nephew—to construct a tower between the heavens and the earth, and in some versions of the text this nephew was named Haman.[27]

So far, so complicated. We have echoes of Pharaoh's Egypt permeating MT *Esther*; an Amalekite connection between MT Haman and the Qur'ānic Pharaoh; and a variety of connections between the biblical Haman and the Tower of Babel, *or* between the biblical Haman and Aḥiqar's nephew, whom Pharaoh challenged to build a tower between the heavens and the earth. (I promised we would bridge the two scriptural portrayals of Haman, *not* that doing so would be straightforward).[28]

There is one more loose end that deserves our attention, namely the absence of all other *Esther* characters from the Qur'ān. Many biblical books go unmentioned in Muslim scripture, of course, but *Esther*'s messages were particularly unlikely to resonate with the nascent Muslim community: How was one to square the Qur'ān's messages with a story about success in a foreign court, or with an ethno-centric tale about a hidden God and a human king. If *Esther*'s Haman did in fact make it into the Qur'ān, then he did so as an unaccompanied villain, divorced from his biblical context and re-released into an entirely different historical (and scriptural) one, something that is nigh unprecedented in the Qur'ān's processing of biblical lore.

That said, it may be that by the early-seventh century, Haman had already been dissociated from the rest of *Esther*'s cast and deployed as an independent villain. A possible example of this is the *'Āl ha-Nissīm* ("[Gratitude] for the miracles") text. Two versions of *'Āl ha-Nissīm* exist—one inserted into prayers on Purim, the other on Hanukkah—each of which thanks God for effecting the miracles that save the Jewish people/religion, and summarizes the events in question. The Purim *'Āl ha-Nissīm* synopsizes the *Esther* story as follows:

> [And it came to pass] In the days of Mordecai and Esther, in Susa the capital, when the wicked Haman rose up against them and sought to destroy and annihilate all the Jews, young and old, children and women, on a single day, on the thirteenth of the twelfth month—that is the month of Adar—and to plunder their possessions. But You, in Your abounding mercies foiled his council and frustrated his intention, and caused the evil he planned to recoil on his own head, and they hanged him and his sons upon the gallows.

This summary of the story is clearly indebted to Esth 3:13, to which it adds God's intervention and Haman's demise, but as a homework assignment to "recapitulate the contents of MT *Esther*" it gets a low grade, for two reasons. First, Mordecai and Esther are not part of the plot at all. They are merely mentioned as historical referents that orient the reader chronologically. Second, the vacuum created by the absence of the story's traditional heroes is filled by none other than God, who famously does not feature in MT *Esther*. What the *'Āl ha-Nissīm* epitome tells us is that there was a rivalry between the evil Haman and a benevolent God; the former plotted against the latter,[29] who foiled his schemes.[30] Such a summary is more closely aligned with the Qur'ānic depiction of Haman than the biblical one.[31] I am not arguing here that *'Āl ha-Nissīm* was consciously presenting an alternative version of *Esther*, but rather that its reformulation of the plot as a rivalry between Haman and God (with Esther and Mordecai removed from the narrative) may prefigure the Qur'ān's depiction of just such a rivalry.[32]

There is an alternative explanation for the different biblical and Qur'ānic portrayals of Haman, one that takes us away from MT *Esther* and towards the LXX version.[33] As mentioned, there are good reasons to assume that Haman's appearances in the Qur'ān were mediated through Jewish materials; but should we entertain the alternative and consider that it is LXX *Esther* from which the Qur'ān's

Haman emerged, then a tantalizing option presents itself. As noted, Haman in the LXX is not an Agagite but rather a "Bougean," this being a term of opprobrium whose meaning has stumped scholars for centuries. There is evidence to suggest that in the pre- and early-Islamic Near East, the term "Bougean" was related to the name "Bagoas." A number of characters in ancient Persian court culture went by the name Bagoas, perhaps the most infamous of them being a prominent official who served as the viceroy to Persian kings in the fourth century BCE, beginning with Artaxerxes III (r. 358–338).[34] Among other things, we know that this Bagoas served as an Achaemenid vizier who plotted repeatedly to assassinate the Persian king (succeeding twice, but dying on his third attempt when he was forced to ingest the very poison with which he sought to assassinate Darius III, r. 336–330).

Bagoas is relevant to us in a number of ways: First, he served under Artaxerxes (both III and IV), which is the king's name in LXX *Esther*. Second, he commanded armies and successfully led the Persian troops in their attempt to conquer Egypt (recall that Haman in the Qur'ān possesses *junūd*, "armies"). Third, when Artaxerxes III reconquered Egypt with Bagoas's help, the king took the title Pharaoh, thereby creating the thirty-first Pharaonic dynasty.[35] Later on, we shall see that this Bagoas was presumed to be equivalent to Haman in some early Islamic sources,[36] and should the Qur'ān also have related Haman to him, then we could understand why Haman was said to have served Pharaoh and commanded armies. Against this possibility are the facts that in the Qur'ān it is specifically the Pharaoh of Moses's career with whom Haman is associated;[37] that there is no connection between Bagoas and the building of towers to the heavens; and that the LXX spells Haman without the initial "H," whereas the Qur'ānic name is spelled with the initial "H," suggesting that a Semitic version of *Esther* (such as the MT or the Syriac *Peshitta*) was known in the Arabian Peninsula, and in those versions Haman is an Agagite, not a Bougean.

Whatever the case may be, whether the Qur'ān was acquainted with MT or LXX *Esther* (or, as was the case with Josephus, some combination of these versions), Haman's depiction in Islamic scripture as a leading functionary at Pharaoh's court is now less perplexing than it seemed earlier, largely thanks to materials that bridge the biblical and Qur'ānic contexts chronologically. The Qur'ānic Haman is, therefore, both a terminus and a launch-pad. As a terminus, he demonstrates the transformations that biblical characters may undergo at the hands of ancient and late antique tradents. As a launch-pad, his presence in Islamic scripture ensured that he would enjoy the attention of generations of Muslim exegetes and other scholars.

Haman in Early Islamic Authoritative Exegesis

Haman's appearance in the Qur'ān in the context of Moses's career is particularly interesting given the central role that Moses plays in Islamic scripture. Whereas Muḥammad himself is mentioned by name in the Qur'ān only four times (and, in a fifth instance (Q 61:6), he is called *Aḥmad*), Moses is mentioned 136 times, making him the most frequently referenced character in the Qur'ān (by a considerable margin). Thus, whereas *Esther* had to negotiate a bumpy path into Jewish and Christians scriptures, and Haman's existence in the Bible may—for some of its readers—have an asterisk next to it, Haman was parachuted onto the Qur'ān's center-stage, and no reader of the Qur'ān could justifiably ignore or belittle him. That, for us Haman-watchers, is the good news.

The less-good news is that despite these promising credentials, considerably less exegetical attention has been paid to Haman than we might have expected. As noted, the verses that refer to him never place him at the center of events; he is part of a pair or trio of evil-doers, never a leader.[38] For instance, one authoritative tradition attributed to Muḥammad (Arabic: *ḥadīth*) merely states that those who neglect to perform their daily prayers, "will be deprived of light, proof, and salvation, and will join Korah, Pharaoh, Haman, and Ubayy ibn Khalaf on the Day of Judgment."[39] Haman is unquestionably evil in this tradition, but we knew this already from the Qur'ān's verses themselves. In one verse (Q 28:8), we are told bluntly that "Pharaoh, Haman, and their soldiers were sinful (*khāṭi'īn*);" in another verse, we hear that their main sin was to be arrogant (*istakbarū*; Q 29:39), specifically when responding negatively to Moses's clear proofs for God's existence. Rather than accepting the divine proofs, Pharaoh, Haman, and Korah all deemed Moses to have been "a magician, a liar" (*sāḥir, kadhdhāb*; Q 40:23–24). That Haman will not fare well on the Day of Judgment is, therefore, no big surprise.

And yet, perhaps under the influence of Jewish and Christian traditions about Haman's uniquely evil character, some early exegetes described him as the more reprehensible of the two villains. In one tradition, related on the authority of al-Suddī (d. 745), we are told that when God commanded Moses and Aaron to approach Pharaoh "with gentle words" (*qawlan layyinan*; Q 20:44) so as to persuade him to accept God, Moses offered Pharaoh youthfulness and rulership that would not wane as long as he lived, mundane pleasures, and entry to Paradise when he dies, all this in exchange for accepting Moses's divine message. In response, Pharaoh said

> "Stay where you are until Haman comes." When Haman came, he said to him, "This man came to me." He said, "Who is he?" He said that, although previously [Pharaoh] had only called Moses "the sorcerer," when that day came he did not call him "the sorcerer." Pharaoh said, "Moses." Haman asked, "What did he say to you?" He replied, "He said to me such-and-such." Haman asked, "And what did you reply to him?" He said, "I said, '[Wait] until Haman comes and I take counsel of him.'" Haman found him weak and said: "My opinion of you was better than that. You will become a slave who serves, after having been a master who is served."

Al-Suddī then explains that it was in response to Haman's disparagement that Pharaoh declared himself to his people as "your Lord the Highest!" (Q 79:24).[40] This story brings the Qur'ān's Pharaoh into line with *Esther*'s Ahashwerosh, who could barely take a decision without consulting his advisors, and whose villainy amounted to little more than an unthinking application of his evil vizier's manipulative advice.

Another example of Haman's relative malevolence comes from a tradition attributed to ʿAmr ibn al-ʿĀṣ (d. 664), Muslim conqueror of Egypt in the mid-seventh century. The tradition relates that Pharaoh commissioned Haman to dig the Gulf of Sardūs in Egypt. Haman complied, but he funded the project by extorting large sums of money from the local inhabitants through whose villages the waters passed. When Pharaoh discovered that Haman had acted in this way, he condemned him for his behavior and demanded that he return the monies, which Haman did.[41] These two anecdotes portray Pharaoh differently: In the first, Pharaoh is an ineffectual ruler; in the second, he is reasonable and benign. What the portrayals have in common is that both cast Haman, rather than the ruler, as the villain.

These exceptions notwithstanding, early Muslim exegetes generally deemed Haman to be Pharaoh's sidekick, with the latter representing the tyrannical infamy associated with Haman in *Esther*.[42] Returning to Haman the builder, some exegetes explain that in constructing a tower between heaven and earth (Q 28:38), Haman "was the first to bake the bricks with which to build a tower."[43] That Haman invented brick-built towers may be a curious piece of trivia, but it hardly establishes him as an evil genius of cosmic proportions.[44]

Haman's subservience *vis à vis* Pharaoh is also reflected in the early exegetical idea that when Pharaoh pursued Moses and the Israelites during the Exodus, Haman was at the head of Pharaoh's 1,700,000 horses.[45] By contrast, the Qur'ān itself (28:6, 8) states clearly that Haman had his own troops (independent of

Pharaoh's *junūd*). Haman's diminishment within the shadow of evil that Pharaoh cast is also evidenced in the final source that we will consider here. In a tradition attributed to Bishr b. Muʿādh, we are told that God saved those who followed him, adhered to His Covenant, and were obedient. By contrast,

> He [God] destroyed His enemies and theirs, Pharaoh, Haman, Korah, and the Canaanites, for their disbelief and rebellion against Him, and for their insolence, by drowning some of them, engulfing some of them in the earth, and [slaying] some of them by the sword. He made them examples for those who take warning from them and exhortation for those who are admonished by them. . . .[46]

A scripturally literate reader can easily pair the villains with the descriptions of their demise: Pharaoh was drowned, Korah was swallowed up by the earth, and the Canaanites were slain by the sword (of the Israelite conquerors). But what of Haman? Whether local *Esther* traditions related that Haman had been hanged from a fifty-cubit gallows or crucified was information that did not make it into this text. Haman's specific fate is ignored and is presumably merged with Pharaoh's.[47] Crucially, this list of villains and their demise was intended to serve as a warning for future generations; thus, the absence of a Haman-specific death is particularly significant, demonstrating as it does that Haman was not an independent villain, but rather the subordinate half of the Pharaoh-Haman pair.[48]

Haman's appearance in the Qur'ān in so central a context as the Pharaoh-Moses rivalry is yet another moment of disappointment for our wretched tragic villain. Just as excitement at being plunked down in the center-stage of Muslim scripture welled up within him, he discovered that the scriptural spotlight focused on Pharaoh cast so wide a shadow as to diminish those who stood closest to him. And although dozens of traditions about Haman drawn from Jewish and Christian sources would come to inform Muslim historians, exegetes, geographers, and others who referred to Haman in passing, the trajectory of these (Islamicized) midrashim (Arabic: *Isrā'īliyyāt*, "Israelite [material]s") was opposite to that in Jewish and Christian circles. Having been instrumental in accounting for Haman's transformation in the Qur'ān, with the passing of time, the prestige of these traditions declined, and within a few centuries it was no longer deemed reasonable to draw on extra-Islamic sources to elucidate scripture.[49] It must be recognized, therefore, that many of the Muslim traditions about Haman that we draw on throughout this book will resemble Jewish and Christian ones in their form and content, but not in their authority or cultural context.

Summary and Conclusions

So yes—Jews, Christians, and Muslims are informed by their scriptures, these scriptures do refer to Haman, and they all agree that he was a bad guy. But no—that is not the whole story, as we have seen in some detail in the foregoing chapters.

To begin with, we saw that "scripture" means different things to different people, not only in each community's choice of Holy Book(s) but in the competing versions of the text that circulated, in the competing strategies for reading and interpreting the text, and in the weight given to the various commentaries on it. Thus, Abrahamic, scripture-reading communities have had entirely different conceptions of *Esther* and of Haman's role in it. For Samaritans and the Qumran community's Bible-readers, Haman did not appear in scripture at all. For most Jews and Protestants in history, it was the Haman of the MT who mattered, but even then, many Jews will have had access to the MT's Haman through an Aramaic *targum* that strayed significantly from the text of *Esther.* Catholics and quite a number of Eastern Christians were acquainted with the LXX's Haman (as transformed by the Greek translation of the text) and, especially, by Haman's depiction in the additions to *Esther*. But, even for the latter category of Bible-readers, we can distinguish between some for whom the additions were "organic" and equally legitimate parts of the text, and other readers who recognized that these additions were, as the term indicates, added-on (and, for that reason, less authoritative). Crucially, Haman is perhaps the story's most malleable character, the one whose portrayal changes most between the different versions of *Esther.*

Moreover, it is worth remembering that it was the rare Bible-reader whose conceptions of a biblical character were shaped entirely (or even predominantly) by the literal text of a biblical book. Christian allegorical or spiritualized readings of *Esther* and heavy-handed rabbinic midrashic interpretations of it ensured that scripture was but a point of departure towards a destination so different (in some cases nigh unrecognizable) that its path requires charting. Haman's appearances in the Qur'ān exemplify this dynamic well.

What this means in practice is that whereas various groups of Jews, Christians, and Muslims all thought about Haman, they are likely to have had different images of him in mind: Was Haman a tragic villain or an apocalyptic agent of Chaos? Was he a personal rival of a Jewish courtier, an ethnic rival of the Jewish people, a Macedonian vizier disloyal to the Persian king, or a tower-building enemy of God? Was Haman a domineering, manipulative vizier, or an overshadowed sidekick? Was he a Persian, an Amalekite, or an Egyptian? And, finally, was Haman the ultimate manifestation of the Amalekite rivalry with Israel, hanging ignominiously from a tree, or the precursor to a suffering messianic savior, crucified publicly to atone for the sins of humanity? Different *Esthers*, refracted through different interpretational lenses, produced different Hamans.

Neat textual distinctions notwithstanding, we have also discovered that the boundaries between religious communities, versions of *Esther*, and strategies of scriptural interpretation, were more porous in ancient and late antique times than modern readers might assume. The fact is that even the boundaries between and within the various varieties of Judaisms and Christianities in these periods were relatively fluid.

Arguably, one way in which the Abrahamic religions could be distinguished from one another relatively neatly would be by identifying the specific historical contexts in which particular communities read and interpreted scripture. The roles that Haman played differed in important ways in the various Abrahamic societies. In the broadest of strokes, for Jews the *Esther* story punched well above its weight in their consciousness precisely because its contents resonated with those Jews who throughout the ages had found themselves living in foreign empires, where they could be threatened by villainous viziers, who manipulated unpredictable rulers from whom protection was expected. Against such backdrops, the book of *Esther* and Haman's role within it attracted ever more attention, with the result that Haman's biography was repeatedly reimagined and rewritten.

By contrast, for Christians, the story's relevance was less clear, both because new (and competing) strategies for reading OT books were introduced, and because the book's contents (at least in the MT version) were deemed to be theologically uninspiring and even problematic. Thus, although we will see in the next chapters that there were some choice historical contexts in which Christians retrieved Haman's character (and *Esther* generally) from the bottom of the pile, dusted it off, and deployed it effectively, such contexts were relatively limited as compared to Haman's deployment by Jews. Finally, and somewhat unexpectedly, despite the center-stage that Haman occupied in the Qur'ān, Muslim tradition had disappointingly little to say about Haman as an independent villain. And as the volume of Haman traditions increased within Muslim cultures, their prestige decreased in tandem.

Perhaps it goes without saying—but I shall say it anyway: What generates this diversity is the fact that scriptures are dynamic; not merely due to the random circumstances that dictate which version of *Esther* a reader will encounter, but also to the scholarly interpretations of a text that come to shape an audience's understanding of it, interpretations that can be more influential than the texts themselves. That respected scholars were products of their time and place is obvious, and in the next two chapters we will focus both on the ways in which history shaped interpretations of Haman, and on the ways Haman's character was deployed throughout the ages by those who embraced these interpretations.

PART II

Haman in History

Introduction

The aim of the following two chapters is to trace Haman's development and deployment in history. Although these are two separate subjects, they relate to each other and to the scriptural topics raised in the previous chapters. Regarding Haman's *development*, we will survey ideas about Haman through history and seek to explain the contextual forces that shaped his evolution over time.

As for Haman's *deployment*, we will chart the ways that Jews, Christians, and Muslims have used "Haman" as an abusive label, almost always with reference to rivals, enemies, and oppressors who, for their part, were also scripturally literate. The intriguing fact is that when a Jew called a Christian "Haman" in late antiquity, or when a Protestant referred to a Catholic leader by this label centuries later, the two rivals were likely to have interpreted this insult in very different ways. Whether one knew Haman from the MT, the LXX, the Vulgate, or the Qur'ān made a considerable difference to one's interpretation of the label. In the previous chapters we considered the ways in which these Hamans differ; in the following two chapters, we will explain the historical contexts of such differences, and witness the use of the Haman label in practice.

6

Haman's Historical Development: Four Stages

1) From the Babylonian Exile to the Achaemenid Empire

Later on (in Chapter 8), we will look in detail at the prebiblical sources and contexts that combined to produce the biblical Haman. We will see how religio-political rivalries in the Near East in the first millennium BCE shaped the *Esther* story and its villain, and in that context we will have occasion to describe the interplay between early Achaemenid religio-political developments and *Esther*. For now, let us make a few general points about the Achaemenid backdrop against which *Esther* is set and the Bible's perception of this backdrop. As far as *Esther* is concerned, the story takes place during the Babylonian Exile, which, despite its name, includes the Iran-Iraq region as a whole.

The Babylonian Exile was very significant for ancient Jews and Judaism. For Jews, at least in theory, it was a multi-generational prison sentence: In the Bible God repeatedly promises His chosen people that they will be rewarded with "the Land" should they behave, and punished with exile should they misbehave. Accordingly, the Temple's destruction and the subsequent exile of the Jewish people to the east—a sort of retracing of Abraham's steps back to Mesopotamia—were taken to be signs of God's displeasure. The Bible tells us that the agent of God's vengeance was the Babylonian tyrant Nebuchadnezzar.

Unsurprisingly, Nebuchadnezzar does not enjoy a good press in ancient Abrahamic sources. Scripture contains narratives about his destructive actions, about the challenges of life as a Jew under his rule, and about the future vengeance that God would in time exact from him and his people. Nebuchadnezzar's reputation for evil is captured also in a series of *Daniel*-stories, in which he comes to acknowledge his inferiority to God and, in one case (Dan 4), actually becomes a penitent after being punished by God for seven years. While his repentence may indicate that Nebuchadnezzar could also be something of a role model, (and various Christian ascetics in late antiquity did, indeed, seek to emulate him, particularly in his period of penitence in the wilderness), describing Nebuchadnezzar in this way would be effective precisely because he was considered so evil. *Even* Nebuchadnezzar came to recognize God's superiority over human rulers.[1]

Life in Exile meant life away from home and away from God, whose "house" (cf. Isa 56:7) was in ruins. Just as a felon does prison-time, the Jewish people were doing their exile-time. The problem was that, unlike a prison, Exile was not always all that bad. When the Achaemenids conquered the Babylonians in the mid-sixth century BCE, things improved for the Jews on every level. Life under the dualist Zoroastrian Persians was better than life under the idolatrous Babylonians, and while the Babylonians were the Temple's destroyers, the Achaemenid Cyrus the Great (r. 559–530) allowed the Jews to return to the Holy Land and to build a Second Temple. Facilitating the ingathering of the Exiles and funding the building of the Temple are actions associated with Redemption, a fact that did not escape the author of Isa 45:1, who described Cyrus as "God's Messiah."[2]

Thus, although the Jews in Achaemenid lands were supposedly being punished, it did not always feel that way, for there was much about Achaemenid life that was comfortable and even attractive. It is not for nothing that Cyrus and his famous cylinder are often celebrated as the earliest reflections of modern concepts such as multiculturalism, human rights, and an enlightened emperor. *Esther* itself (1:22 and 3:12) tells us that the Persian king communicated with his subjects in their own languages rather than imposing his culture on them. And one can hardly ignore the ending of MT *Esther*, which not only attests that the Jews survived Haman's genocidal plot, but also tells us that later generations of Achaemenid Jews benefited from royal favor.

This was all good for the Jews, but not so much for the biblical justice equation. What sort of punishment was it to live and flourish in the center of the greatest empire of the day? Returning to Judea meant living in a provincial outpost of the Empire; remaining in the Achaemenid heartlands meant enjoying the benefits of a great metropolis or regional capital. Thus, whereas the Jews were theologically experiencing a sort of prison term, they were culturally experiencing something of an overseas vacation.[3]

In fact, much of what concerns the Bible about Achaemenid life is its alluring attraction for the Jews. Koller has highlighted the "political" dimensions of *Esther*, arguing that its author was consciously proposing answers to questions raised by life in the Diaspora.[4] The passage in *Isaiah* 45 mentioned above nicely captures the threat of Persia's allure.

> Thus said the LORD to His anointed, to Cyrus, whose right hand I have holden, to subdue nations before him, and to loose the loins of kings; to open the doors before him, and that the gates may not be shut: I will go before you, and make the crooked places straight; I will break in pieces the doors of brass, and cut in sunder the bars of iron; And I will give you the treasures of darkness, and hidden riches of secret places, that you may know that I am the LORD, who calls you by your name, even the God of Israel. For the sake of Jacob My servant, and Israel My elect, I have called you by your name, I have surnamed you, though you have not known Me. I am the LORD, and there is none else, beside Me there is no God; I have girded you, though you have not known Me; That they may know from the rising of the sun, and from the west, that there is none beside Me; I am the LORD; and there is none else; I form the light, and create darkness; I make peace, and create evil; I am the LORD, that does all these things.

To understand the significance of this passage, one must understand the basic tenets of Zoroastrianism, Cyrus's religion. Zoroastrians believe in two divine powers, Ahura-Mazda represents all that is good, Ahriman all that is bad. The two powers are equal (which is why the religion is generally characterized as "dualist"), and in constant competition with each other for human souls. Ahura-Mazda, the god of light, urges people to do good, while Ahriman, the god of darkness, seeks to misguide them, leading them into sin. At the end of their life people will be judged to determine whether they were mostly good or mostly bad, which will gain reward or punishment for each person, and points on the scorecard for either Ahura-Mazda or Ahriman.

In *Isaiah* 45, we find that God (mediated through the text's author) engages in an anti-Zoroastrian and anti-Achaemenid polemic: Yes, Cyrus, you are impressive, but do not forget the source of your power. And yes, it would appear that there are two "powers"—good and bad, darkness and light—but do not forget that it is God who created both of them. This polemic references the threat that Achaemenid life posed to Jews living in the Babylonian Exile: The author of *Isaiah* 45 interrupted what he was doing to remind his Jewish audience (for it was surely not Cyrus himself who was the text's intended reader) that their God was even better than Cyrus and his religion. Unlike biblical polemics against other religions, this passage does not argue against the merits of competing cultures/

religions, but rather acknowledges them and—interestingly—augments God's own prestige by crediting Him with them.

We do not know whether or not the polemic was successful, but what seems indisputable is that whatever attempts there may have been to protect Jews and Judaism from Persian influence were not entirely successful. Scholars have long argued for the ancient Persian provenance of such key Jewish (and, eventually, Christian and Muslim) concepts as the afterlife, eschatology, the apocalypse, messianism, and a complex angelology, among others. Most relevant to us here is the introduction of Satan to the Jewish theological lexicon. As noted, Zoroastrianism holds that there are two gods, one entirely good, the other entirely bad. In pre-exilic times, the biblical God was multifaceted: He could be loving, merciful, and protective, but also violent, vengeful, and merciless. Through exposure to Zoroastrian ideas, however, God shed his negative attributes, which were absorbed by a new character, Satan. God still punished—even violently—those deserving punishment, but the God of post-exilic biblical books was largely sanitized, with Satan taking over most of the dirty work. The following examples demonstrate what this process looked like in practice.

The author of 2 Sam 24:1 states: "And the anger of the Lord was kindled against Israel, and He incited David . . . to count the people." Counting the people was a sin in the Bible, and in the pre-exilic 2 *Samuel* God incites David to sin in this way. By contrast, the author of 1 Chr 21:1, writing in the post-exilic period, retells the events as follows: "Satan stood up against Israel and incited David to count the people." Similarly, whereas in the pre-exilic *Genesis* it is God who tests Abraham, calling on him to sacrifice Isaac (22:1), in the post-exilic book of *Jubilees* (17:15–18) it is Satan ("Mastemah") who does so. The evil, negative, or merely unpopular attributes that Satan had accrued in pre-exilic stories continued grow in number into the early Christian period, when he was equated with the serpent of Eden (Rev 12:9 and 20:2), and into the early Islamic period—when Job blamed Satan for his suffering (Q 38:41–44), even though in the biblical account it is God whom Job blamed for the same afflictions (Job 19).

The exposure of Jews to Zoroastrian dualism in the Achaemenid period had considerable effects on the construction and construal of villains in Judaism, and in Christianity and Islam as well. The development of Haman's character, as we will see in this chapter, is thus intertwined with the development of ideas about evil and enmity in Abrahamic communities, no less than it is with the reception and interpretation of *Esther* in a given time or place.

To summarize, the Babylonian Exile was a problematic period for Jewish history, both because it was where Jews were serving their sentence, but also because life in Achaemenid Persia was actually quite enticing. Many Jews chose exile over ingathering to the Holy Land, and their theological vocabulary came to be enriched with Zoroastrian and other Iranian concepts, traces of which may be found in the later books of the HB.[5] One of these new concepts was the figure of "Satan," whose adoption in Abrahamic cultures would affect interpretations of both God and His agents of evil, including characters such as Nebuchadnezzar—as seen above, and Haman—as will be seen below.

2) Hellenism, Parthia and the Second Temple Period: 330 BCE–70 CE

Just as the Achaemenid overthrow of the Babylonians effected momentous changes for Jews, for Judaism, and for the Bible's conception of agents of evil, the Greek conquest of the Achaemenid Empire (c. 330 BCE) unleashed processes of monumental significance for Abrahamic history—and specifically for Haman's development. Initially, Alexander's conquests unified an enormous territory stretching from the Mediterranean to Central Asia, but upon his death in 323 BCE, the empire fragmented into four regions following decades of internal warfare. For our purposes, the focal points will be the Second Temple Period in Egypt and Greater Syria on the one hand, and the Parthian (or Arsacid) Period (247 BCE–224 CE) in the eastern regions of Iran-Iraq, on the other. Although Alexander's heritage affected both of these contexts and although there was meaningful cross-pollination between them, the roles that each played in shaping descriptions of Haman were sufficiently different to justify separate treatment of the two. We will begin with the Parthians.

Parthian Culture and LXX Esther

We have already encountered one point of overlap between *Esther* and the Parthians, namely the Dura Europos synagogue with its fascinating frescos, which appear in their iconograpy to prioritize the *Esther* story over most other biblical subjects.[6] Yet there is much more to the story of *Esther* in Parthian lands than that, and two aspects of Parthian culture deserve our particular attention. The first is that the Parthians had been influenced not only by local Persian and Babylonian cultural traditions, but also by the Hellenism spread throughout the region by Alexander and his immediate successors, the Seleucids (r. 312–248 BCE). We will return to Hellenism's role later in this section. For now, the crucial point is that it was in Parthian lands that the Achaemenid heritage and its memory survived, and it is from Parthian lands that local *Esther*-related traditions were transmitted to the Babylonian rabbis whom we will encounter when discussing Haman in late antiquity.

The second critical aspect is that in the second half of the Parthian period a Persian cultural revival—inspired by memories of Achaemenid grandeur—led to the production of numerous historical novels, some of which survive in Islamic-era Persian works. These novels are relevant to both the MT and LXX versions of *Esther* and to the depiction of Haman within them.[7] Scholars have long argued that *Esther* contains elements of ancient storytelling—regardless of whether it is a historical or fictional story that is being related—and with few exceptions they have made their case on the basis of ancient Greek sources,[8] some of which originate in (far-western) regions of the Achaemenid empire.[9]

Parthian novels offer numerous contributions to our understanding of *Esther*'s literary context, particularly as regards LXX *Esther*, which was composed during this period. From a literary perspective, they relate to *Esther* in two ways. First, they originate in Persian culture. Hence, although they post-date the Achaemenid period by a century or more,[10] they generally reflect local storytelling traditions rather than Greek (or other external) perspectives on life at the ancient Persian court. Second, the historiographical context of these stories is unrelated to that shared by the HB and ancient Greek authors. Whereas the latter refer to Xerxes and the Achaemenid dynasty, the Parthian novels refer to kings such as Bahman and dynasties such as the Pishdadids and Kayanids. What this means in practice is that the Parthian novels are uniquely placed to serve as an objective control for parallels with Persian literary culture: Herodotus and *Esther* may tell similar stories about Xerxes, for instance, but we cannot be certain that Herodotus had not read some early version of *Esther*, or that *Esther*'s author had not read the works of Herodotus, or that both were simply not drawing on the same source(s), which they recast in their own languages for their respective audiences. The Parthian novels, by contrast, belong to a narrative framework entirely unrelated to that of *Esther*, and if these works share attributes with MT or LXX *Esther* it is despite the fact that they were relating different stories.

What, then, do the Parthian novels have in common with ancient versions of *Esther*, and what can we learn about Haman from them? In the broadest of strokes, we may note that *Esther* shares with Persian literature such transcendent themes as *Bazm o Razm* ("Feast and Fight") and *Bakht* ("Fates," the literal meaning given for the word "*purim*" in *Esther*). More important, however, are the plots, subplots, themes and motifs, descriptions of celebration, and name etymologies that *Esther* and the Parthian novels share.[11] For clarity, I will discuss the relevance of these stories for MT *Esther* and LXX *Esther* separately, never losing sight of our main goal: Getting to know Haman better by understanding depictions of his behavior in their literary context.

MT *Esther* and Ancient Persian Storytelling

Any discussion of ancient Persian storytelling must begin with the *ShāhNāma* (Book of Kings), an epic poem that continues to have immense influence on Persian culture.[12] This work presents the legendary history of the world according to the Iranian historiographical tradition, beginning with Creation and ending with the Arab conquest of Iran (which introduced Islam to the region, but put an end to Persian kingship).[13] It is this historical narrative that serves as the backdrop for the various ancient Persian stories that we will encounter here. The *ShāhNāma* shares with MT *Esther* the memory of a king (Bahmān) who married a Jewess (Ḥomāy).[14] One of the *ShāhNāma*'s greatest heroes, Rustam, had a horse named *Rakhsh*, who may be related (if only etymologically) to the *rekhesh* horses used in Ahashwerosh's postal system (*Esther* 8:10).[15] And most important for us, the *ShāhNāma* relates that the Persians' perennial enemy, the Central Asian "Ṭūrānians" (comparable to the Amalekites in biblical-Jewish tradition), had a commander by the name of Hōmān. This Hōmān, who served under the Ṭūrānian ruler Pīrān, advised him to attack the Iranians (advice that the cautious Pīrān rejected). Hōmān fought the *Rakhsh*-riding Rustam, and was eventually killed and beheaded (by another hero, Bīzhan). Again, the absence here of "Esther," "Mordecai," and any of the other names known from the biblical tradition suggests that the authors of *Esther* and the *ShāhNāma* were drawing on a common Iranian storytelling repository, rather than on each other. The famed historian and Qur'ānic exegete al-Ṭabarī (d. 923) was well-acquainted with both the Abrahamic historical narrative and the Iranian one, and when he related the *Esther* story in his universal history, he added the detail that it took place during the reign of Bahmān, who appointed one of his relatives by the name of Ahashwerosh to rule the Iran-Iraq region. In this way, al-Ṭabarī used the *Esther* story to bridge the ancient Iranian and Abrahamic historiographical traditions.[16]

The *ShāhNāma*'s influence on Persian culture generated spin-offs that expand on various figures found within it, taking on somewhat the character of a midrashic exposition on the Persian book. One such spin-off is the *BahmānNāma* (Book of Bahmān), which tells of the marriage of king Bahmān to a foreign princess, who convinces the king to appoint her evil secret lover to the position of vizier. This vizier engineers a coup against Bahmān, who flees to the west, marries (the Jewess) Ḥumāy, and returns to defeat the treacherous vizier. While there are contrasts between this tale and *Esther*, there are also commonalities shared by the latter and the *BahmānNāma*'s frame-story. Again, there is no evidence in this story of familiarity with biblical historiography, although—as we will shortly see—the tale (and others like it) may have influenced changes that the author(s) of the LXX made to MT *Esther*.

The *BahmānNāma* spurned its own midrashic tale, the *DārābNāma* (Book of Dārāb), a biography of Bahmān and Ḥomāy's son, Dārāb. In a rare case of overlap with the Western historiographical tradition, this Dārāb appears to be based on "Darius," the name of multiple Achaemenid rulers, the final one of whom was defeated by Alexander the Great (as was the Dārāb in the *DārābNāma*).[17] Here, the Iranian historiographical framework appears to link up with stories of Alexander's rise. Among other similarities, two details bring to mind MT *Esther*. First, the story includes an evil vizier whose name, Rastīn, means "a man of fine mind," who slandered a competitor at court ("Bīrī") together with the latter's supporters.[18] This may relate to the (proposed) derivation of the name "Haman" from the Avestan *vohu-mana*, also meaning "of fine mind" (or "good thoughts"). Second, the *DārābNāma* contains a sub-plot in which two courtiers seek to assassinate the Persian king, Dārāb, to enable Alexander to overthrow the Persian kingdom.[19] Unfortunately for the courtiers, Alexander regretted his complicity in the regicide and decided to have the two killed and hanged from a gallows. The overlap between this story and the "plot of the eunuchs" in *Esther* is unmistakable.[20]

Another specimen of the Parthian storytelling corpus is *Samak-i 'Ayyār* (Samak the Vagabond), which also contains a "plot of the eunuchs" episode. Unlike that recorded in the *DārābNāma*, however, in this version the plot is foiled by a third courtier, who discloses its details to the targeted king. *Samak-i 'Ayyār* not only contains the version of the "plot of the eunuchs" closest to the one found in *Esther*, but also shares with *Esther* numerous other storytelling details, such as the existence of a vizier by the name of "Hāmān." Interestingly, in *Samak-i 'Ayyār*, Hāmān is a loyal vizier, who interacts positively with members of the vagabond class (*'ayyārs*), who are the story's protagonists (in stark contrast to the *ShāhNāma*'s Hōmān or *Esther*'s Haman). Moreover, this Hāmān displays an open aversion to violence that is uncharacteristic of the biblical Haman. For example, he counsels the king to avoid going to battle against a rival, warning him of many grave dangers: "O king, take care: With 400,000 horsemen opposing each other, the friend would no longer be distinguished from the enemy. A world will be destroyed; 100,000 people will be killed. Do not let this happen because it is not necessary."[21] Despite sharing a name with *Esther*'s villain, this Hāmān is not villainous.

The story *does*, however, include a villainous vizier (Mehrān, vizier to the Chinese ruler, Faqfūr), who seeks to have the entire group of *'ayyār*-vagabonds annihilated, and there are other points of detail that parallel MT *Esther*. Perhaps most instructive of all are the descriptions of celebrations in MT *Esther* and *Samak-i 'Ayyār*: In the latter, we find a week-long wedding celebration (cf. the week-long celebration in Esth 1:5ff, taken by many to have been in celebration of Ahashwerosh's marriage to Vashti),[22] as well as a celebration that involves a tax-exemption (cf. Esth 2:18, where the king celebrates his marriage to Esther by offering "a release" to the provinces, generally understood as a tax-exemption), and an entire *month* of festivities (cf. Esth 9:22), during which treats were distributed throughout the country (cf. the "portions" distributed in Esth 9:19). Moreover, the description of an engagement party in *Samak-i 'Ayyār* includes the detail that wine was had by all, "both great and small,"[23] bringing to mind a grammatically difficult phrase in Esth 1:5, where all in the citadel of Susa celebrated, "from great to small." A final similarity between MT *Esther* and *Samak-i 'Ayyār* is the detail that each story's hero(ine) was reared by a foster-father who was the representative of the targeted group in the story: Mordecai is the representative of the Jews and Esther's foster-father, just as Shughāl Pīl-i Zūr represents the *'ayyār* class and Samak's foster-father.

The tale of *Vīs and Rāmīn* is another work of Persian storytelling that sheds light on the literary context of MT *Esther*. In the frame-story of this novel, the Persian king holds a feast attended by dignitaries from the world over, at which he is publicly rejected by a beautiful queen (cf. *Esther* 1:1–12). The king's evil vizier, Zard, then denounces the entire population to the king, encouraging him to annihilate them. Even minor details link the two stories, such as that in both *Esther* and *Vīs and Rāmīn* the eponymous heroine was raised by a nurse in Susa.[24]

In *Vīs and Rāmīn* (as in *Samak-i 'Ayyār*), descriptions of celebrations resemble those found in *Esther*. In one instance, the heroine Vīs was married to Vīrū on one of "the middling days" (that is to say, either the eighth, fifteenth, or twenty-third) of the month of Ādhār (= Adar). Hence, just as in *Esther* the Purim celebration in Susa took place on the fifteenth of Adar, in *Vīs and Rāmīn* the wedding celebration may have been held on this date. Similarly, the celebrations that followed the wedding lasted for approximately six months, recalling the 180-day banquet that the king held in Esth 1:4.[25] Finally, with regard to another wedding celebration, *Vīs and Rāmīn* mentions that for an entire month "there were no separations of rank or gender. . . . Men, women, peasants, lords hunted as one and drank together when the hunt was done. . . . For one month, men knew neither grief nor care."[26] The month-long celebration, the lack of grief during this period, and the effacement of social hierarchies, bring to mind the Purim celebrations in Adar, "the month that was turned unto them from sorrow to gladness" (Esth 9:22), when established hierarchies were overturned (Esth 9:1).

It is likely then, that the narrative related in MT *Esther* draws many elements of its style from the ancient Persian storytelling toolkit. The very reasonable assumption that the authors of these Persian stories were not acquainted with *Esther* means that the commonalities between these works may be attributed to the shared storytelling cultures on which they drew.[27] Tantalizingly, from among the dozens of names mentioned in MT *Esther*, the only one found in Parthian novels is "Haman"/"Hōmān." But although the Haman of *Samak-i ʿAyyār* is a vizier, he is otherwise unrecognizable to *Esther*'s readers as he is not a genocidal, scheming villain. By contrast, the Hōmān of the *ShāhNāma* brings to mind *Esther*'s Haman: He serves the king directly, is a warmonger, and represents the Iranians' traditional enemy, the Ṭūrānians, just as Haman the Agagite (in MT *Esther*) represents the Jews' traditional enemy, the Amalekites.

Any attempt to contextualize the MT's Haman in literature may benefit from recourse to these Parthian novels. And yet, even assuming a Parthian provenance for the materials surveyed here, these materials post-date MT *Esther* by at least a century. Of more direct relevance to us is the contribution of these novels to our understanding of Haman in the LXX, which was produced to the west of the Parthian Empire, but was contemporaneous with it.

LXX *Esther* and Ancient Persian Storytelling

Although the details of *Esther*'s translation(s) into Greek and of the composition of the six apocryphal additions to *Esther* are unclear, there is little doubt that their composition largely coincided with the production of the sort of Persian stories that we have just encountered. Moreover, as Davis has shown, there is evidence of considerable intellectual exchange between the Persian and Greek worlds in the Parthian period, with Persian materials appearing to have influenced Greek storytelling in pre-Christian times.[28] One example of the transmission of Persian stories to Second Temple Judaism comes from the *Dead Sea Scrolls*, which include fragments that relate three Persian court tales. After a significant amount of scholarly debate, it may now be (tentatively) concluded that these tales are *not* fragments of *Esther* (leaving *Esther* as the only HB book not represented among the Scrolls). And yet, these texts clearly relate in some ways to *Esther*'s genre.

Wechsler has argued that one of them is a sort of "prequel" to *Esther*.[29] We cannot, therefore, be surprised to find that elements of Parthian storytelling that migrated westwards may have contributed to the Greek rendering of *Esther* and to the additions that were made to it.

As we have seen, the week-long wedding celebration in *Samak-i 'Ayyār* may be compared to the week-long feast in Esth 1:5, which some commentators interpret as a celebration of the king's marriage to Vashti. While this is indeed a plausible interpretation of the event, it is not stated explicitly in MT *Esther* that any wedding celebration lasted a week. The Greek versions (both LXX and AT 2:18), however, do state that "the king gave a wine party for all his friends and forces for seven days. He celebrated Esther's wedding feast and gave rest to those under his rule."[30]

Overlap between LXX *Esther* and the Parthian novels may also underpin the idea that Mordecai, Esther, and Ahashwerosh formed a "love triangle," of which the king was unaware and in which the king was an unwanted party. Both the *BahmānNāma* and *Vīs and Rāmīn* relate that the heroes were secretly married at the time when the king wed the story's heroine. MT *Esther* states that Mordecai was Esther's cousin, whom he had adopted (Esth 2:7). The LXX (2:7), by contrast, states that Mordecai, "had a foster child . . . and when her parents died, he trained her for himself as a wife." (The AT does not include this detail). In other words, the LXX, too, portrays Mordecai, Esther, and the king as comprising a love triangle of the sort found in Parthian novels. Interestingly, the second-century CE Rabbi Meir in the Babylonian Talmud[31] and the important eleventh century exegete Rashi (*ad* Esth 2:7, 17 and 4:16) follow the LXX rather than the MT in this regard.[32]

Haman's portrayal in the LXX may also be indebted to ancient Persian storytelling. As noted earlier, in *Vīs and Rāmīn*, the evil vizier Zard denounces an entire population (the inhabitants of Māhābād) to the king Mobad, just as Haman denounces the Jews in Esth 3. Zard's denunciation is particularly reminiscent of Haman's in LXX *Esther*. Zard says of Vīrū's people,

> [They] say that you're his underling,
> That you're his functionary, and he's their king.
> I've told you what I saw and heard; they're filled
> With arrogance, they're stubborn and self-willed.

In Add B:5, Haman tells the king that the Jews are, "all alone in opposition to all humanity, perversely following an estranging manner of life due to their laws, and . . . ill-disposed to our interests, doing the worst harm in order that our kingdom may not attain stability." The problem, according to Haman in Addition B, is not that the Jews are scattered and dispersed widely throughout the empire (which is how Haman begins his accusation in MT 3:8), but that the Jews are enemies of all humanity, and particularly of the Persian kingdom.

Haman's accusation in Addition B is probably a projection of his own vices as they are portrayed in LXX *Esther*. Addition E—the mirror image of Addition B—portrays Haman as disloyal to the king and conspiring to hand over Persian rule to the Macedonians (E 14). Haman's disloyalty to the Persian king is also implied strongly in Addition A, which states that Haman "sought to harm Mordecai and his people because of the two eunuchs of the king" (17). Haman's association with the plot of the eunuchs is not even hinted at in MT *Esther*. If, however, we combine Haman's complicity in the regicidal conspiracy with the LXX's other point about Haman's plot to transfer power to the Macedonians, then the Haman of the LXX fits into events recounted in the *DārābNāma*, where the "plot of the eunuchs" involves the regicide of the last Persian ruler and the transfer of power to Alexander and the Macedonians.[33]

Thus, at least one fundamental aspect of the transformation that Haman underwent between the MT (where he seeks to annihilate the Jews) and the LXX (where he seeks to overthrow the Persian Empire) may be explained by reference to the Parthian storytelling context that influenced the LXX. To understand other aspects of his transformation, we now turn to Hellenism's impact on Second Temple Judaism.

Hellenism and Esther *in the Second Temple Period*

Just as life in Achaemenid Persia was far from unmitigated misery for the exiled Jews, Hellenism also had much to recommend it to the non-Greeks who came under its sway. It could be attractive (and, thus, dangerous) as a civilizational alternative to Judaism. Moreover, it did not necessarily present itself as being in competition with Judaism: Jews could adopt Hellenism as a culture while retaining Judaism as a religion.[34] One only had to Hellenize Judaism. To those Jews who opposed it, Hellenism's threat was thus particularly insidious.

And just as the author of *Isaiah* 45 felt the need to polemicize against the Persian Empire, so the ancient rabbis felt the need to polemicize against Greek culture, precisely because it was so enticing: In one Talmudic passage, a group of rabbis stated, "Cursed is the man who teaches his son Greek wisdom," and they added for good measure that those who did so were comparable to those who raise pigs. In the almost inevitable debate that ensued, the rabbis agreed that the

Greek language was acceptable, but not Greek wisdom.[35] In practice, of course, such a disconnect would be artificial and nigh impossible to implement, while the sentiment was clear: rather than complementing Judaism, Hellenism contaminated it.[36] As was the case with Rabbi Akiba's harsh condemnation of those who read the pseudepigrapha and apocrypha, the stronger the objection, the larger the threat was perceived to have been.

However much Hellenism might insist that it simply complemented or upgraded Judaism, there remained a crucial tension between the two civilizations. In fact, the demands of Hellenistic thought could reshape Scripture itself. A good example is the "Curse of Ham," which served those influenced by the Bible as a justification for the enslavement of Africans.[37] In Gen 9:20–27 we learn that when Noah and his family emerged from the ark following the Flood, he became intoxicated and was "uncovered," at which point his son Ham acted disrespectfully (whereas his brothers Shem and Yefet acted laudably).[38] For acting disrespectfully, Noah punished Ham by cursing the latter's son, Canaan, whose descendants were to be enslaved by those of Shem and Yefet. The following chapter goes on to describe the division of the known world between the three sons, with Ham's progeny receiving what would become the Holy Land.

In the mid-second century BCE, the Hellenized author of *Jubilees* rewrote that story in an effort to bring it into line with Hellenistic sensibilities. Among the various problems that he sought to solve were the uncomfortable facts that Canaan was cursed for something that Ham did, and that God subsequently promised the (Hamitic) Holy Land to (the Semitic) Abraham, even though it was actually called the "Land of Canaan." Thus, in his version of events, the author of *Jubilees* corrected the story to relate that when the post-diluvian world was divided, the Holy Land was apportioned to Shem's descendants, but that Canaan unjustly seized it by force (despite the protestations of his brothers and of his father, Ham). That was why the land came to be known as "Canaan," why Canaan's descendants were cursed, and why it was justifiable to promise the land to Abraham's Semitic descendants.[39]

The point here is twofold. On the one hand, the HB's contents were important enough to make even a Hellenized Jew such as the author of *Jubilees* wish to update them so as to ensure that they retained their relevance and met Hellenism's criteria. On the other hand, at least for some influential Jews of the period, the demands of Hellenism could trump the HB's literal meaning. Whether this says something about the relative importance of Hellenism *vis à vis* scripture for Jews at the time, or about the flexibility of the biblical text in this period more generally, the result is the same: A biblical story could be rewritten without doing harm to its authority (no less than fifteen scrolls of *Jubilees* were found at Qumran, which is more than most other books of the HB).[40]

Broadly speaking, rewriting the Bible in the Second Temple Period took two forms: As with *Jubilees*, an existing text could be adjusted—even significantly—to produce a new text that remained recognizably related to its *Vorlage*. Alternatively, new texts could be written that consciously engaged (usually critically) with an existing biblical text, while presenting themselves as independent of it. For *Esther*, we have both types of rewritten Hellenized versions. To the former category belong the Greek versions of *Esther*, to the latter a selection of Second Temple Jewish writings, such as *1*, *2*, and *3 Maccabees*, and *Judith*, which ostensibly narrate events unrelated to *Esther* but in fact engage with it obliquely. What the authors of both types of rewritten *Esther*s have in common is that they were aware of *Esther* but unhappy with (some of) its contents. Of interest to us, as always, is how the depiction of Haman (or his equivalent characters) in these works relate to the context in which they were written. We begin with Haman's transformation in the Greek *Esther*s.

Haman in the Greek *Esthers*

The authors of the Greek *Esther*s and their additions regarded Haman's portrayal in MT *Esther* as problematic. First, as a failed villain, MT Haman had not actually done anything wrong. Should he reasonably be punished for a crime that he did not commit?[41] As in the case of Canaan's punishment for Ham's guilt in the Noah story, Hellenized Jews expected uncompromising equity from biblical author(s). Thus, in the Greek *Esther*s Haman is an active criminal: In Addition A, he is directly associated with the plot of the eunuchs (an attempt to assassinate the king, for which the would-be assassins were executed), while in Addition E, he is accused of conspiring with the Persians' political enemies, the Macedonians, to overthrow the Empire. On both accounts, he is what might nowadays be called, "a hostile foreign actor."

Second, Hellenism provided Jews with a choice: Embrace it and be laudable, reject it and be barbaric. Bearing this in mind, it is clear that ethnicity was not the basis for friendship and enmity. Both Jews and Amalekites can be good (if Hellenized) or bad (if not). But one does not love or hate based on race or ethnicity and "Amalekite" was not a sufficiently unambiguous epithet for a villain by Hellenism's standards (in theory Haman could have been a Hellenized Amalekite, and Mordecai an un-Hellenized Jew).

In any case, Hellenism's diminished concern with ethnic identity is likely the reason why Haman in the Greek *Esthers* is not an Agagite, but rather a Macedonian (who conspires to hand the Persian Empire over to a rival power), or a Bougean—literally a "braggart," which would associate him with *hubris*, a cardinal sin in Hellenistic thought.[42] Inherited enmity prevents people from making their own decisions about how to lead the ideal life, and just as Canaan should not reasonably have been punished for Ham's sins, Haman should not be held accountable for Agag's. A Macedonian agent at the Persian court, or a braggart bursting with *hubris*, however, is a reprehensible figure by Hellenistic standards.

Third, as seen in Chapter 2, another description of Haman particular to Greek *Esthers* is the reference to him as *diabolos*, or Satan. Equating Haman with Satan may also be clarified with reference to Second Temple Judaism, when the *Life of Adam and Eve* was composed as a midrashic expansion on the creation story in *Genesis*. As discussed, this work contains a refusal-to-bow episode in which it is Satan (rather than Haman) who expects that others will prostrate before him.[43] Whether the Greek *Esthers* influenced the production of the *Life of Adam and Eve* accounts or vice versa is difficult to determine (although other "cosmic" aspects of the *Esther* story—such as the messianic language used regarding Mordecai and the possible Gogite connections to Haman—demonstrate that Haman could fit comfortably within an eschatological framework).[44]

Interesting though Haman's transformation in Greek *Esthers* may be, the translator(s) and author(s) of the additions were constrained by the general contours of the *Esther* tale, which pitted "Jews" against those who plot against them. Therefore, even a conscious adaptation of *Esther* to a Hellenistic context was likely to produce an imperfect representation of contemporary Jewish literature and thought. By contrast, the Second Temple Jewish writings that originate in a context shaped, if not dominated, by Hellenism, portray a much more consistently Hellenistic tension between Jews who chose to adopt Greek ways and those who adhered to un-Hellenized Judaism, even at the risk of great personal and communal danger. When crafting their *Esther*-inspired stories, therefore, they almost uniformly portray the villains as being against Judaism rather than against Jews, as we will now see.[45]

Haman in Second Temple Literature

Authors of the works that we will discuss here were acquainted with *Esther*, but dissatisfied with aspects of the book, as reflected in the conscious narrative decisions that they took in producing their own works. Their dissatisfaction related both to the influence of Hellenism[46] and to the immediate political context in which they were writing. Second Temple Jews were divided politically between Alexander's Ptolemaic heirs (based in Egypt) and his Seleucid heirs (based in Syria), who vied for control over the Holy Land in this period. Some of the rewritten *Esthers* originate in (Ptolemaic) Alexandria, others in the (Seleucid, and then later Hasmonean) Holy Land. These different political contexts are especially interesting to us as works composed in the Holy Land were undoubtedly affected by the Maccabean revolt against the Seleucids (167–141 BCE) and the subsequent reign of the Hasmonean dynasty (140–37 BCE). The relevance of this context to contemporary Jewish interpretations of MT *Esther* may be seen in both the political assertiveness of the period (in which a Jewish polity sought to overthrow gentile rule, and succeeded in doing so), and—related to this—in an author's attitude to life in the Diaspora (*Esther* resonated well with Jews living under foreign rule, but less well for those who lived in the Holy Land under Jewish rulers).

By contrast, authors composing works in Ptolemaic Alexandria had to contend with a unique Egyptian-Hellenistic amalgam of antipathy to Jews and Judaism. Schäfer traces the rise of anti-Semitism as an idea to the early-third-century BCE Egyptian priest Manetho, whose (Greek) description of the Jews perpetuated local and national Egyptian traditions that promoted anti-Semitic ideas about Jewish misanthropy.[47] According to Schäfer, as early as the destruction of the temple at Elephantine (410 BCE), local Egyptian priests had rationalized their antipathy towards Jews on the grounds that they supported the Persian Empire, an occupying power that threatened Egypt's "national" interests. Thus, the priests were accusing the Jews of double-loyalty, a charge that came to be a staple of anti-Semitic thought. Schäfer connects this context with the LXX's version of Haman's accusation, which focuses more on Jewish misanthropy than does the MT version of the accusation. To this insight we may add that such a context allows us to better understand Haman's (false) accusation in LXX *Esther* that Jews were disloyal to the Empire, as well as Addition E's counter-accusation that it was Haman who was secretly acting in the interests of the enemy.

Clearly, despite the purported irrelevance of ethnicity in Hellenistic contexts, even Second Temple works composed from scratch in some cases reflect local anti-Jewish notions, generating a diversity of Hellenistic approaches to the Haman-ic character(s) in different stories. The varied depictions of villains in these works contribute to our understanding of the reception of Haman in the century or so immediately preceding the rise of Christianity. As such, Second Temple rewritten *Esthers* represent an important stage in Haman's historical formation, one that will shed light on the Haman-Judas comparison in the NT, on Haman's transition to Pharaoh's court in the Qur'ān (as discussed above), and on early rabbinic conceptions of Haman (as will be discussed below).

The first work to consider is *2 Maccabees*, a mid-second-century BCE Greek text, written in Ptolemaic Egypt.[48] Unlike other works to be discussed here, it refers directly to Purim ("Mordecai's day," 2 Macc 15:36). It was with this work that Martin Luther paired *Esther* when he said, "I wish they did not exist at all, for they Judaize too greatly and contain much pagan impropriety."[49] As a Diaspora text, *2 Maccabees* is not troubled by *Esther*'s focus on Diaspora life. That said, the story its author relates concerns Antiochus IV's persecution of Jews in the Holy Land, the Maccabean revolt against him, and the heroism of Judah Maccabeus in defeating the Seleucid general Nicanor (in 161 BCE), in honor of which a festival was instituted on the thirteenth of Adar, one day before Mordecai's day. It is thus a Holy Land text written from a Diaspora perspective.[50]

Although the defeat of Nicanor provides the etiology for the new festival, and although Nicanor in other Jewish texts is unquestionably a villainous character,[51] in *2 Maccabees* his portrayal is unexpectedly benign.[52] One Menelaus is the story's Haman-character: He was a Hellenized Jew who bribed his way into the high-priesthood of the Temple, had the deposed high priest killed, looted the Temple's treasures,[53] and accused the residents of Jerusalem of supporting the rival Egyptians (an accusation that led to the execution of numerous Jews). In face of growing threats against the Jewish people, Judah Maccabeus approached Antiochus IV after fasting for three days (cf. Esth 4), and Menelaus was eventually executed and hung on a tower 50 cubits high. Clearly, the depiction of the Maccabean revolt in *2 Maccabees* was heavily influenced by *Esther*,[54] and the depiction of Menelaus was heavily influenced by Haman.[55] What is interesting here is that the Haman character was a Hellenized Jew, who accused the un-Hellenized Jews of disloyalty to the ruler. The "Amalekites" in this text are, therefore, philhellenic Jews. As we will see, throughout history there were Jews who compared other Jews to Haman, and to the extent that one can pinpoint the origins of such a practice, *2 Maccabees* may well be where it began.

The establishment in this text of a festival based on Nicanor's defeat suggests that he was remembered as having been a Haman-like villain,[56] and while this does not come across in *2 Maccabees*, *1 Maccabees* makes his evil character rather clear. Written towards the end of the second century BCE, it also relates the story of Maccabean heroism in defeating Antiochus IV and the Seleucids, culminating with the rededication of the Temple. Unlike *2 Maccabees*, however, this text was written in the Holy Land and in Hebrew (the original text is not extant). Its

Hasmonean context will surely have prejudiced its author against *Esther*'s message of Jewish success in the Diaspora. What interests us here, though, is the portrayal of the text's villain—or, in this case, villains.

In *1 Maccabees*, Antiochus IV plunders the Temple's riches (as Menelaus did in *2 Maccabees*), and in the process he slaughters numerous Jews in Jerusalem. He also outlaws Judaism (forbidding such basic elements of the Law as circumcision and the possession of Torah scrolls) and desecrates the Temple (by holding pagan rites in it). By the end of *1 Maccabees* 4, Antiochus IV's plots have been foiled, the Temple is purified, and Judas (and his brothers) establish the Hanukkah festival to commemorate their victory (4:59). This is not, however, the end of the story, which continues for twelve more chapters in which the Jews confront various other enemies following Antiochus IV's demise. Although Jewish philhellenes joined Antiochus's Hellenization program (and they, too, were targets of the Maccabees), these Jewish Hellenizers are not the story's leading villain(s) (unlike in *2 Maccabees*, where Menelaus played this role). Instead, it is two non-Jews—first Nicanor and then Bacchides—who, in turn, assume the Haman-ic role in the ensuing events.

Nicanor is introduced as one of "the friends of the king" (3:38; cf. Haman in AT 5:14, 7:8). We are told that he "hated and detested Israel" and was the man whom Antiochus V chose "to destroy the people" (7:26). He acted "treacherously" (7:27, 30), mocked Jewish leaders, and spoke arrogantly (7:34), while threatening to destroy the Temple (7:35). The Maccabeans defeated Nicanor and his armies on the thirteenth of Adar. Nicanor was decapitated and his right hand, "which he so arrogantly stretched out," was cut off, and an annual festival was established to commemorate these events (7:43–49).[57]

After Nicanor dies at Judas's hand, which further establishes him as the story's chief villain, Bacchides replaces him as the chief enemy of the Jews and the story's new villain. Like Nicanor before him, Bacchides is "one of the king's friends" (7:8), and under Demetrius I (Antiochus V's successor) he becomes the Jews' main antagonist by leading the army that kills Judas. Bacchides continues to fight against the Jews, led now by Judas's brother, Jonathan, and establishes philhellenic Jews as rulers of Judea (9:25), a combination of crimes that all contribute to confirm his identity as a hated villain.

In the late antique *Megillat Antiochus* (hereafter: MA),[58] Bacchides—known in this text (through a scribal error) as Bagras or Bagrīs—takes on villainous attributes greater than those attributed to Nicanor (who is also portrayed negatively in the text). In MA, Nicanor ("Niqanor") is Antiochus (IV)'s "second in command" (v. 10; cf. Haman in the Greek *Esthers*), and he is charged with executing Antiochus's anti-Jewish plans, including the massacre of numerous Jews and the desecration of the Temple (by introducing an idol and sacrificing a pig in the sanctuary; v. 11). So far, so Haman-ic. It is, however, Bacchides (or Bagras/Bagrīs) who channels *Esther*'s Haman most clearly. Bacchides, as Nicanor before him, is identified as Antiochus's "second in command" (vv. 4, 60), but he alone is characterized as "the wicked" (vv. 29, 32, 36, 43, 48, 59).[59] He is charged by Antiochus with outlawing Jewish practices such as circumcision, celebrating the New Moon, and consecrating the Sabbath (v. 31), and he dutifully executes orders, adding to them a massacre of Jews on his own initiative (v. 33). Unlike Nicanor, who was decapitated, Bacchides was burned to death (v. 59).

The MA version of this Maccabean revolt is particularly interesting for a number of reasons. First, the text is stylistically indebted (almost certainly consciously) to *Esther*. That *Esther*'s influence is discernible despite the fact that MA is an Aramaic text testifies to the depth of *Esther*'s influence on it. Second, Haman's depiction in *Esther* is echoed in MA's depiction of Bacchides, as in the latter case we are told what the villain "thought in his heart" (v. 49), just as in *Esther* we hear what Haman "said in his heart" (Esth 6:6).[60] Finally, although Bacchides and Nicanor served under two different rulers (the former under Demetrius, the latter under Antiochus IV), the author of MA collapses the foreign kings into a single "Antiochus," thereby aligning the villains of the Maccabean story with the contents of *Esther*, in which these events take place under a single ruler. In MA, *Esther*'s Ahashwerosh and Haman become Antiochus and Nicanor/Bacchides respectively.

Historically, MA (in Aramaic, Hebrew, or Arabic)[61] has been read publicly during Hanukkah celebrations, just as *Esther* is read publicly as part of Purim. And although there is nothing in *Esther* to suggest that burning effigies of Haman should feature in Purim festivities (if anything, one would expect the impaling, hanging, or crucifying of effigies of Haman), we will see below that burning effigies of Haman was a recorded custom in late antique Palestine. As noted, Bacchides in MA was burned to death.[62]

The style of MA is, as we have noted, clearly influenced by *Esther*, while its contents depend on *1* and *2 Maccabees*. It was also influenced by the book of *Judith*, another Second Temple work that tells a story of the Maccabean revolt, albeit in a disguised version of the events. Criticizing a reigning ruler was understandably unwise, and from the reign of Antiochus IV, we have a good example in the book of *Daniel* of how a contemporary Jewish author might negotiate the dangers. The author of Dan 7–12, writing at a time when Antiochus's anti-Jewish measures were at their highest pitch, made predictions about the unfolding of political history.[63] Clearly, he did not know that, against all odds, the Jews would manage to withstand Antiochus and defeat the Seleucids; thus, he must have been writing in 164 BCE, before the unexpected dénouement of the story. In recounting the events, *Daniel*'s author refers to Antiochus as "the king of the North" (11:6–15, 40, 44). The Seleucids were indeed based to the north of the Holy Land, but in Dan 7–12 the "north" was not simply a geographical direction. It was from the north that the Assyrians had swept into the Holy Land and destroyed the kingdom of Israel in 722 BCE, and it would be from the north that the End of Times chaos agents Gog (and Magog) would one day descend upon civilization (Ezek 38:15).[64] That Antiochus IV in Dan 11 was associated with the apocalyptic Gog in the mid-second-century BCE is particularly interesting in light of the fact that some versions of AT *Esther* identify Haman as a Gogite, as we saw earlier.

With this example in mind, we may return to *Judith*, a Second Temple Jewish text probably written in Greek, perhaps half a century after the Maccabean revolt. This text does not mention Antiochus IV at all: Instead, the events described are set in the reign of Nebuchadnezzar "king of Assyria" (sic!). The king is supported by Holofernes and Bagoas, Persian functionaries who are known to have served under Artaxerxes III (r. 359–338 BCE). For these and numerous other reasons, the extant text is historically inaccurate. It has generated much scholarly debate, but one thing is not debatable, and that is the story's debt to *Esther*, for *Esther* shaped its contents both directly and indirectly. The author of *Judith* disputed elements of the *Esther* story and sought to correct them,[65] and, as noted, MA was influenced not only by *1* and *2 Maccabees* but also by *Judith*. The text, therefore, serves as a bridge between Purim and Hanukkah, and in the early medieval Jewish versions of the story (read in some communities on the Sabbath preceding Hanukkah) the disguises are removed: Antiochus replaces Nebuchadnezzar and Nicanor replaces Holofernes.

What, then, does this Second Temple rewriting of *Esther* tell us about the story's villain? It should come as little surprise that there are not one but two villains here, the evil Nebuchadnezzar and the general Holofernes. *Judith* relates that Nebuchadnezzar fought against the Median king Arphaxad and was gravely disappointed by the failure of several local nations to offer support during this campaign. He therefore set out to exact revenge, conquering numerous regions and peoples, including the Jews in the Holy Land. Whereas most of the defeated submitted to Nebuchadnezzar's rule, the Jews did not, whereupon Holofernes, the general chosen by the king to execute his tour of revenge, threatened not only to conquer the Holy Land and destroy the Temple, but also (on his own initiative) demanded that the Jews worship Nebuchadnezzar as God (cf. Dan 3). The heroine Judith (lit. "the Jewess"; cf. Mordecai "the Jew" in *Esther*)[66] used guile to gain access to Holofernes, beheaded him,[67] and the Assyrians were routed.

As the foil to the story's heroine, Holofernes is clearly the Haman-character here.[68] He is the king's second-in-command (Greek: archistrátēgos, "commander-in-chief"),[69] and he is characterized as "haughty"—a loaded term of opprobrium for a Hellenistic readership, as was noted with reference to Haman's pride in Add C:5, and to his *hubris* in Josephus's narrative. Moreover, not only had he looted the Jerusalem Temple and insisted that the Jews worship Nebuchadnezzar as a God (Jdt 3:8), but his repeated characterizations in the text as "master" (Greek: *despota*),[70] suggest that he may have presented himself as a deity, as this term is used in the LXX with reference to God. Holofernes's association with Haman is reflected in the fourth-century CE Ethiopic *Didascalia*, which states that, "Esther, and Mordecai, and Judith were saved by fasting from the wicked Holofernes,"[71] apparently conflating Holofernes and Haman. Although this conflation is manifestly a genuine error of some sort, it demonstrates the close association between the two villains in late antiquity.[72] On the other hand, as with the depictions of Antiochus IV in the texts discussed above (but unlike depictions of Ahashwerosh in all ancient versions of *Esther*), Nebuchadnezzar is also portrayed as villainous, and one could make the case that Holofernes was merely executing the evil king's orders.

Like other Second Temple texts surveyed, the primary threat in the story is not to Jews but to Judaism, for there was in Hellenistic thought no hatred of Jews as such. They were free to choose between adherence to either a Hellenized or un-Hellenized version of their religious culture. It was through their decision to reject the king's request for submission that they fell foul of the story's villain(s). In fact, *Judith* makes it clear that the Jews were but one in a long list of nations targeted for rejecting Nebuchadnezzar's request (Jdt 2:5–13). Unlike Haman in *Esther*, who dislikes Jews *qua* Jews, Nebuchadnezzar and Holofernes dislike anyone who proves disloyal (regardless of their ethnicity).

Summary: Haman as a Second Temple Villain

The range of texts covered in the preceding survey demonstrates that there was much diversity of thought among Jews living in the Second Temple period as to the merits or demerits of Hellenization and of life in the Diaspora. And yet, the depiction of villains in these *Esther*-influenced texts does reveal quite a lot about the impact of Hellenism on Jews in this period.

First, with the exception of Menelaus—who is the only Jewish Haman encountered—all villains in these texts are *military* commanders; they are generals rather than viziers. This is no doubt a consequence of the Maccabean context in which Jews faced their enemies on a battlefield rather than in a royal court. Second, the villains are not anti-Jews as much as they are anti-Judaism. Third, the villains are all successful in their villainy, at least to begin with. Unlike Haman, the tragic villain who was punished "for a crime he did not commit," Menelaus, Holofernes, Nicanor, Bacchides, and Antiochus IV all deserved their comeuppance, thereby justifying (in Hellenistic terms) Jewish gloating over their demise. Fourth, the Second Temple "Hamans" almost always share their villainy with the ruler under whom they serve.[73] Antiochus IV—as himself, as the "king of the North," or as Nebuchadnezzar—is not Ahashwerosh. Whereas Ahashwerosh unknowingly enables Haman's plot, he is not himself a villain (even in Greek *Esthers*). In the Second Temple texts, by contrast, a villainous ruler equals or even overshadows his evil sidekick in his enmity toward the Jews. Interestingly, in ancient and late antique rabbinic sources, Haman often shares the status of villain with the king.[74] To that extent, these transformations of *Esther*—and of Haman within it—serve as a bridge not only between Purim and Hanukkah, but also between *Esther* and late antique interpretations of the story.

3 Maccabees and Haman

Before turning to Haman in late antiquity, there is one more text worth considering here. *3 Maccabees*, despite its title, is not about the Maccabean revolt and therefore belongs outside the group of Second Temple responses to *Esther*. And yet, it is very much in conversation with *Esther* (I will explain what this means presently), and it reflects many of the developmental stages through which Haman passed between MT *Esther* and late antiquity. As a bonus, it may even bridge an important gap between the biblical and Qur'ānic Hamans.

Composed in Greek, probably in Alexandria during the late first century BCE, *3 Maccabees* relates events that took place in the Egypt of Ptolemy IV (r. 222–205 BCE), following the latter's defeat of the Seleucids in 217 BCE. As part of a victory-lap of sorts, Ptolemy visited the cultic centers of his diverse subject population, but when he came to the Temple in Jerusalem, a supernatural force prevented him from entering the holy precinct, leading him to turn against the Jews in his kingdom. Initially, he intended to enslave them unless they abandoned their religion and adopted the pagan Dionysian rites that he himself followed. Subsequently, he decided to do away with the Ptolemaic Jews altogether. However, God intervened in the story repeatedly, and after a number of unsuccessful attempts at a massacre, the king decided to honor the Jews instead. In commemoration of their deliverance from genocide, the Jews instituted an annual festival.

That *3 Maccabees* is based to some extent on *Esther* has long been accepted by scholars.[75] Confusingly, having originated as a sort of Second Temple response to *Esther*, the book eventually repaid the debt, for Additions B and E to the Greek *Esther*s appear to have been influenced by *3 Maccabees*.[76] (This is the "conversation" between *3 Maccabees* and *Esther* mentioned above.) As with some of the other works considered here, the author of *3 Maccabees* was unhappy with elements of *Esther* and sought to correct them by rewriting a story that eliminated *Esther*'s perceived deficiencies. For our purposes, what is relevant is the story's portrayal of the Haman-ic villain. Here, as in other Second Temple works, the villain is represented by two characters—the ruler and his esteemed subordinate—and in *3 Maccabees* it is the ruler who is portrayed as the more villainous of the two.

Ptolemy planned to punish the Jews of Egypt by releasing 500 intoxicated elephants on Jews gathered in the hippodrome, and it was one "Hermon, the elephantarch," who was charged with executing the plan. As the king's subordinate and his agent, Hermon played the role in this story that Haman played in *Esther*. Indeed, when the king berates Hermon for failing to execute the order (by executing the Jews), we are told that his "face fell" (3 Macc 5:31–33; cf. Esth 7:8).[77] The author of *3 Maccabees* was thus encouraging his reader to associate the two characters. It may also be noted that the identification of Hermon as the ruler's elephant-handler channels the Haman-ic Nicanor, who, in 2 Macc 14:12, is the royal keeper of the elephants.[78]

In *3 Maccabees*, however, it is the king himself who is the story's villain: Like Haman in *Esther*, Ptolemy IV feels disrespected by the Jews (or their Temple) and hatches a genocidal, anti-Jewish plot, whose failure the Jews would celebrate in an annual festival. Thus, *3 Maccabees* presents the same balance of villainy encountered in other Second Temple works in which it is Antiochus IV (more than Nicanor/Holofernes or Bacchides) who is the story's villain-in-chief. Similarly, *3 Maccabees* reflects the Hellenistic model, whereby the Jews were targeted not for their ethnicity, but rather for their refusal to conform to the expected behavioral norms of the empire (in this case, the pagan Dionysian rites). In other words, in contrast to *Esther*, the Jews were given a chance to save themselves. The message of *3 Maccabees* is that it is best to resist such a self-serving temptation and instead to engage in God-serving prayer.

Thus, we might conclude that *3 Maccabees* is comparable to *1 Maccabees*, *Judith*, *Megillat Antiochus*, and *Daniel* 11, in portraying its Haman-ic villain as a gentile ruler, in contrast to *2 Maccabees*—where the villain, Menelaus, is a philhellenic Jew. Such an assessment, however, is complicated by the fact that *3 Maccabees* also vilifies Hellenizing Jews, in three ways: First, like the penitent Antiochus IV in 2 Macc 9, Ptolemy IV has a change of heart towards the end of the story and foe becomes friend. Second, following an assassination attempt against Ptolemy (before he turns friend), Dositheus, a Jew who has abandoned his religion, acts to save the ruler (1:3). The ruler then persecutes the Jews and attempts to annihilate them, as a direct result of this acculturated Jew's "heroism." Finally, when the Jews celebrate their salvation, they request the king's permission to exact revenge upon their co-religionists who had abandoned God's Law in order to appease the king: they massacre 300 of them (7:10–15). In other words, in *3 Maccabees* the Jews exact violent revenge on their enemies much as the Jews did in Esth 9. Thus, between Dositheus's dubious heroism and the massacre of paganized Jews, the story of *3 Maccabees* begins and ends with a critique of Jews who did not adhere to their religion.

There is one more element in *3 Maccabees* that relates to Haman, albeit in a rather unexpected way. As seen earlier (Chapter 5), in the Qur'ān Haman commands armies (Arabic: *junūd*) and serves under "Pharaoh," who overshadows him considerably. In *3 Maccabees*, Ptolemy IV, who was an actual Pharaoh of the Ptolemaic dynasty, overshadows Hermon, an underling ordered to execute the Pharaoh's orders, and one who, as elephantarch, holds a military position (rather than the sort of vizierate occupied by Haman in *Esther*). Furthermore, unlike other Second Temple authors who were influenced by *Esther*, who crafted entirely new works that were received by an audience that read them without reference to *Esther*, *3 Maccabees* continued to interact with *Esther* in shaping Additions B and E. Put another way, as the latest of the Second Temple texts surveyed here, *3 Maccabees* not only bridges the biblical and Qur'ānic Hamans temporally, but also bridges the two Hamans in its contents: It demonstrates that a reimagined version of *Esther* may relocate the narrative to a Pharaonic Egypt,[79] may downgrade its villain *vis á vis* the king, and—as is the case for most of the Second Temple Hamans discussed here—may exchange the villain's administrative garb for a military uniform.[80]

———

All of the texts considered here were to some degree canonic in one or more of the various eastern Christian churches. By contrast, although some of the Second Temple stories came to be very influential within Jewish circles, especially as etiologies for the Hanukkah festival, none of them was canonized in Judaism. Even the Greek *Esthers*, originally composed by and for Jews, were overshadowed by the MT version in the overwhelming majority of Jewish communities (and their contents largely forgotten). What this meant, of course, was that the array of remedies to the theological, historical, political, and other deficiencies in *Esther* that these Second Temple works provided, were rarely available to *Esther*'s many Jewish readers. The ancient and late antique rabbis stepped in to provide solutions of their own that had a formative impact on the development of the figure of Haman, due both to their sheer volume and to the communal authority that the rabbis came to hold in subsequent centuries.

3) Haman in Late Antiquity.

In many ways, the late antique period is the turning point in Haman's biography, perhaps because it is the turning point in the religious history of the Near East more generally. We are no longer conditioned to view the Middle Ages as a collapse of Greco-Roman antiquity's cultural brilliance, suddenly eclipsed before barbarism and backwardness. Instead, the period of 250–750 (give or take) in the Mediterranean and Near East has been reinterpreted and rehabilitated: These centuries are now recognized as marked by unparalleled cultural-religious dynamism and productivity. Christianity achieved "muscle" for the first time; Judaism produced some of its most important works, codifying the oral law that arguably would come to shape it even more than the Torah itself; and Islam emerged in the Arabian Peninsula, inarguably against the backdrop of this religious dynamism.[81]

The Abrahamic religions developed in contact and conversation with each other, a process through which the respective traditions were chiseled into the forms by which we recognize them today. Critical debates between (and within) religions produced communities that—despite sharing commonalities that still serve as the basis for water-cooler interfaith moments—came up with very different answers to shared questions. Perhaps most significant of all was the debate over scriptures: What are they, how were we to read them, and with what ramifications? As a scriptural character Haman was thus dropped defenseless into the fast-paced, multi-lane highway traffic of late antique religious controversies, where his story would be picked up and knocked about in different directions by the three monotheistic vehicles. In the previous chapters, we saw how Christian and Jewish interpretations of *Esther* and Haman's role within it shaped each other, both positively—through mutual influence, and negatively—though contradistinction.

No less significant than the debates themselves was the political backdrop against which they took place. It is not only that imperial rivalries shaped the intellectual activity occurring within them, but that the relationship between religion(s) and politics was redefined. The two polities under whose rule most of the Bible's audiences lived were the Byzantine and Sasanid Empires. Until the fourth century CE, Jews and Christians in the Mediterranean world were ruled by (Roman) rulers who were at best indifferent and at worst actively antagonistic to them. Debates about scriptures would have remained an intellectual curiosity of local proportions had Christianity not been transformed so thoroughly in the fourth century, with the Christianization of the (Eastern) Roman Empire. Nearly a century earlier, the Sasanid Empire had adopted Zoroastrianism as the imperial religion, and the political rivalry between the two great powers of late antiquity had a sharp religious edge to it.

The practical ramifications of this were numerous. Victories and defeats signaled theological no less than military superiority (just as earthquakes, plagues, and widescale destruction at the hands of plundering nomadic hordes were signs of God's displeasure, or of the impending Eschaton). It was supremely important to get religion *right*, and resources on both sides of the imperial divide were invested in the codification of orthodoxy and orthopraxy, the canonization of scriptures, and the standardization of the imperial religion's formal structures. In Byzantium, for instance, councils of experts were repeatedly convened to iron out unwanted wrinkles of diversity, thereby legitimizing those who were in line with a council's decisions and delegitimizing those who were not, in theory if not in practice, reducing the variety of Christianities into a single, carefully defined religion.

How does the late antique marriage of imperial and religious interests and identities bear upon Haman's formation? To answer this question we must consider such diverse perspectives as those of the Christian or Zoroastrian imperial ruling elites of the two empires and their Jewish, Christian, Samaritan, and Zoroastrian populations. (The latter two did not read *Esther* at all, the former read it very differently one from the other.)

We will begin with the Zoroastrian ruling elites and their Zoroastrian population. For them, *Esther* and the HB generally were not part of an imperial-religious package. That is not to say that the story and its villain were irrelevant to them. Some Sasanid rulers married women from communities that read *Esther*: Khusraw II (r. 590–628) had a Christian wife by the name of Shīrīn, and Yazdgird I (r. 399–420) married a Jewess known as Shūshān-dukht (lit. "the daughter of Susa"), whose father was the Jewish exilarch and whose son was the Sasanid ruler Bahram Gor (r. 420–438).[82] Moreover, the Jewish rabbinical academies at Sura, Nehardea, and Pumbedita operated under Sasanid rule, and the elaborate debates conducted therein often signaled cordial or even friendly relationships between rabbis and the Sasanid elite. Finally (for now), the Parthian storytelling heritage with its *Esther*-like novellas was part of the general cultural repository of Persian lands. Stories about Amalek-like Ṭūrānians led by a Haman-like Hōmān, to cite but two examples encountered above, were known widely. If a Sasanid-Zoroastrian encountered the *Esther* story, with its account of a Jewish victory over Haman and Jewish-Persian cooperation and mutual support, he would not likely have found much to dislike in it.

The Jewish and Christian populations in Sasanid lands most certainly knew and thought about *Esther*: Among Christians we have already encountered the Church Father Aphrahat with his typological reading of the story and his eschatological interpretation of its villain. As far as Haman's transformation is concerned, these are slim pickings and the really significant developments occur later, among the late antique rabbis. We will focus on their perspectives in some detail below,[83] but here it is important to distinguish between the perspectives of Babylonian and Palestinian rabbis.[84] The Babylonian rabbis were well aware of their privileged circumstances, at least as compared to those of their coreligionists to the west of the Euphrates,[85] and these circumstances had practical ramifications for the way they could interpret *Esther*: The relatively benign conditions enjoyed by Sasanid Jews allowed the rabbis to read the story from a position of comfort and confidence, to identify satire and humor in it, and to mock its villain. They knew from experience that Mordecai had, indeed, ensured the prosperity of future generations of Persia's Jews (Esth 10:3). For Jews living under Roman rule the political context was considerably less benign. In this region, Haman was not viewed as a tragic villain; in fact, as we will presently see, Haman's menace was deemed to have intensified and to have accumulated relevance.

Some of the most interesting developments in Haman's biography originate in Byzantine lands. For the Byzantine elite, *Esther* was not a perfect fit. It glorified the Persian Empire, it mocked earthly kings and vilified their closest advisors, its message resonated with protagonists living in a Diaspora, and it stressed ethnic or national bonds over religious ones. But that is not the end of it: As we will soon see, what came to be the greatest gap between Byzantine culture and

Esther's contents is the fact that the story culminated in a celebration of violent revenge, which included not only the widescale killing of one's enemies but the crucifixion of the story's villain. And should the similarities between Jesus and Haman have been lost on Christians, there were Jews who took the trouble to bring the offensive symbolism to their attention. To understand the intercommunal dynamics that led to such provocations, and generated profound re-imaginings of Haman's biography in late antiquity, we turn to rabbinic conceptions of the Byzantine context in which they lived.

Haman the Roman: Jewish Views of the Byzantine Empire[86]

If in late antiquity the salient equation was *political rule + religion = power*, then the trajectory of the Jews' fortunes in this period could hardly have been more different from that of the Christians, for just as Christianity gained an empire and all that comes with it, Judaism lost political power in spectacular fashion. The only thing the Jews and Christians had in common was that the former's fall and the latter's rise both originated with the Romans.

As noted, it was the (Eastern) Roman Caesar who adopted Christianity, reversing a three-century-long trend of Roman persecution that began with Pontius Pilate's execution of Jesus. Admittedly, the Kingdom of Armenia adopted Christianity as its religion of state two decades before Constantine converted, and the Eastern Romans only confirmed Christianity as the official imperial religion decades afterwards (in 380, under Theodosius I). But any list of historical Christian-influencers would surely place Constantine near the top. From the fourth century onwards, with few exceptions, the Roman Empire would be associated with Christianity, so much so that the early Muslims referred to the Byzantine Christians as *al-rūm*, "the Romans" (perhaps an echo of the Byzantines' own self-designation as *romaioi*). Any lingering Christian antipathy towards Rome could be downplayed, and biblical texts that cast aspersions on the Romans' role in history could be reinterpreted (often unsubtly) to portray them as divinely mandated saviors. Pivotal in this context are references in the book of *Daniel* (especially chapters 2 and 7) to a succession of four earthly kingdoms, of which the final would be exceedingly terrible (Dan 7:19, 23). Although until late antiquity most Jewish and Christian writers identified this fourth kingdom as Rome, the Christianization of the empire prompted a revision that viewed Rome as a fifth and eternal kingdom, founded by God himself (Dan 2:44; 7:27).[87]

By contrast, Jewish perceptions of the Roman Empire went from bad to worse, beginning in the second century BCE, when in both Seleucid Palestine and Ptolemaic Egypt Jews composed eschatological prophecies that sought to make sense of past empires and to predict the End Times and the fate that awaited the rulers of this world. While *Daniel*'s sequence of four kingdoms, composed in Judea in the 160s BCE, does not mention or even allude to the Romans, Dan 11:30 refers to the "ships of Kittim," almost certainly code for Antiochus IV's navy. Daniel was thus dealing with a leading Second Temple villain, but not a Roman one. Before long, however, the equation of the Romans and the "kittim" was made: A first-century BCE Qumran text refers to the Romans as "Kittim," and repeatedly criticizes their abhorrent behavior, which is interpreted as a prelude to the advent of the "Teacher of Righteousness" in the Final Age.[88]

In Alexandria, too, Jews were composing and circulating anti-Roman texts. The reference to "Kittim" in (the Judean) Dan 11:30 is rendered in the (Alexandrian) LXX as "Romans,"[89] but even earlier—some decades before Dan 11 was originally written—Alexandrian Jews were expressing virulently anti-Roman ideas in the earliest layers of the *Sibylline Oracles* (hereafter: *Sib.Or.*).[90] Although these Jews despised the Romans for interfering in internal Egyptian affairs in support of a rival to their ruler, that is to say for political reasons, the depth of anti-Roman sentiment apparent in their writings suggests a hatred of considerably more significance. The first oracle of *Sib.Or.* 3 (dating from the first half of the second century BCE) lists a sequence of eight kingdoms, which would be followed by a final, eschatological kingdom (vv. 97–161).[91] The second oracle also contains a list of kingdoms, but devotes much of its discussion to an unequivocal condemnation of Rome (vv. 162–195).[92]

While such negative focus on Rome may seem to us something of an overreaction, by the end of the first century CE, the Romans had proved themselves worthy of every denunciation imaginable: Their destruction of the Second Temple in 70 CE transformed them from a political enemy to an eschatological one, and virtually all Jewish eschatological texts that postdate 70 CE expect the Messiah to undo the Romans' act of destruction and rebuild Jerusalem and its Temple. One could become a "Christ" through involvement in the Temple's construction (recall the Persian Cyrus's epithet "God's Messiah" in Isa 45:1), and an "Antichrist" through involvement in the Temple's destruction.[93] Hence, in later layers of the *Sib.Or.* that date from the reign of Nero (r. 54–68) onwards, we find a thinly veiled equation of this emperor, whom Jews held responsible for the events that led to the Temple's destruction, with "Belial," a personification of cosmic evil mentioned already in the Qumran Scrolls as a sort of Satan or

Antichrist.[94] As time progressed, Nero's status as an eschatological adversary only worsened: The second oracle of *Sib.Or.* 5, dated to just before the Great Diaspora revolt of 115–118 CE, highlights Rome's destruction of the Temple and predicts Nero's eventual return as an Antichrist figure. His appearance will be followed by the emergence of a Savior who will descend from Heaven.[95] The *Sib. Or.* influenced numerous ancient Jewish and Christian writings, and Lactantius (d. 325), a Christian writing in Rome shortly before Constantine's conversion, enthusiastically adopted the anti-Roman prognostications of the *Sib.Or.* Before long, however, anti-Roman rhetoric came to something of a dead end in the Christian Roman Empire. But for the empire's Jews, things were just getting started.

The Jewish vilification of the Romans in the early Christian era and the following centuries was not simply a consequence of the faithful transmission of older traditions: Its features were constantly updated, altered, and supplemented—just as the Romans supplemented the list of their outrageous (from a Jewish perspective) actions. Nero the Antichrist was replaced by Titus (r. 79–81), both because he oversaw the destruction of the Temple as a military commander in the first Roman-Jewish war, and because Nero was strangely rehabilitated in rabbinic tradition.[96] One source had it that he eventually converted to Judaism and was the ancestor of the famous second century *tanna* Rabbi Meir.[97] As though the unforgivable crime of destroying the Temple was not enough, following the reign of Hadrian (117–138), who brutally suppressed the Bar Kokhba revolt (132–136), the Roman Empire came to be routinely referred to in rabbinic texts as "the evil empire," a phrase that required neither elucidation nor justification.[98] It was no longer simply that specific Roman rulers were evil on account of specific sins, but that the Roman Empire was itself the cosmic adversary whose rise and ultimate demise were part of a divine plan that would lead to the Messianic era. Accordingly, with the passage of time, the Antichrist figure of Nero (or Titus) became "Armilos" (Romulus), signifying that the Romans had been Evil from their very inception.

In late antiquity, the rabbis equated Rome with Edom/Esau, thereby granting even greater antiquity and depth to the dichotomy that separated the good (Jacob, the Jews) and the bad (Esau, the Romans).[99] That a large proportion of the world's Jewry lived in Byzantine lands, which included, importantly, the Holy Land, furthered the seriousness of the Rome-Edom conflation. By representing Greek, Roman, and Christian cultures, the Byzantines presented a three-headed challenge to the rabbis. They were purveyors of Greek,[100] destroyers of Jerusalem and its Temple, and missionizing apostates from Judaism who twisted its scriptures; in other words, an all-encompassing foe the likes of which the Jews had never before faced and whose eventual defeat would herald the Messianic age.[101]

We should not be surprised, then, to discover that the rabbis in late antiquity associated Haman with Roman Christianity. This act of reimagination was not simple, for one of the few biographical details about Haman that we learn from *Esther* is that he was an "Agagite," an epithet that implied he was an Amalekite.[102] The rabbis rose to the challenge in various ways: They mined *Esther* for allusions to the Esau story in *Genesis*,[103] supplemented Haman's biography with details that connected him to Esau or the Romans,[104] and, intriguingly, traced his genealogy back to Esau (rather than to Agag).[105]

The new biographical detail that Haman was a Roman also resonated for the Babylonian rabbis, despite the fact that they were not living under the yoke of the Christian Roman Empire.[106] This is for two reasons. First, living under Sasanid rulers who were rivals of the Romans for primacy in late antique international relations (and who were supportive of their Jewish subjects), the rabbis had good reason to vilify their masters' political rivals. Second, and more importantly, it is clear that the Babylonian rabbis were products of their Sasanid cultural context and integrated local traditions with their own works.[107] Thus, by identifying Haman as a Roman, the rabbis may have been echoing Sasanid traditions about their own Haman-ic character, namely Alexander the Great. A heroic figure in virtually all cultures that left writings about him (and these included post-Sasanid Persian texts), Alexander is vilified in Pahlavi works that reflect Sasanid-Zoroastrian perspectives,[108] which also identify him as a Roman.[109] Moreover, "Macedonians" was generally rendered as "Romans" in Pahlavi literature, and Macedonians take on an eschatological role in Sasanid sources.[110] In some texts, it is Alexander the Roman who has an eschatological role as the representative of *druj* (chaos), the antithesis of divine *aša* (order).[111] The Sasanid Alexander was thus an eschatological chaos-figure and a Roman one at that.

All this may suggest that when the Babylonian rabbis adopted the (Palestinian-rabbinic) idea that Haman was a Roman, it fit rather neatly into their cultural context, which shared similar notions about villains. In fact, it may well be that the idea travelled in the opposite direction, for there are other ways in which Sasanid traditions about Alexander appear to have informed rabbinic ones about Haman. The reason Alexander was hated in pre-Islamic Persian traditions is, first and foremost, that his forces conquered Iran and put an end to Achaemenid rule. Persian descriptions of this conquest naturally exaggerate the violence and trauma of the events, including such (undocumented) ideas that the Macedonians (often called "Romans") sacked Persepolis, plundered the royal treasures, and burned its library, which contained the sacred scriptures (the Avesta).[112] This could be seen as the Zoroastrian equivalent of the destruction of the Temple in Jewish tradition (combined with later traditions about Antiochus IV, who ordered the burning of Torah scrolls).[113] Interestingly, although Haman could not possibly have had anything to do with the mid-sixth-century BCE destruction of the Temple, later rabbinic midrashim place him at the scene of the events.[114] Similarly, although Haman in MT *Esther* (7:6) is described as "bad" (*ra'*), he is neither "evil" (*rasha'*), nor "cursed" (*arūr*).[115] Both of these adjectives were used for Alexander in Pahlavi sources,[116] and both came to be used for Haman in late antique rabbinic ones.[117] That the LXX identifies Haman as a Macedonian who plotted to transfer the Persian Empire to the Macedonians (Add E:10, 14) might also hint at a Haman-Alexander conflation. Regardless of the direction in which the ideas flowed between rabbinic communities, it is clear that Haman was reimagined as having been an Edomite/Roman, a label loaded with evil associations, including apocalyptic ones.[118]

Haman the Christ(ian)

If the rabbis could agree that Haman was a Roman, and if by the fourth century CE the Romans were Christians, then perhaps it is unsurprising that the rabbis also came to imagine Haman as a Christian. But Haman's purported Christianity is not simply a corollary of the Eastern Roman Empire's official adoption of the Christian religion. In fact, although Haman's Christian attributes evolved most fully in the Byzantine-Christian context, the association between Haman and Christianity did not originate there and was not limited to Byzantine lands.[119]

First, both Josephus and the LXX report that Haman was crucified (rather than hanged or impaled, as in the MT), which may well have influenced the NT's description of Jesus in terms that intentionally evoke Haman. Such a superficially scandalous comparison could drive home theological points—for instance, that Jesus in his accursed state bore a burden of sins of Haman-ic proportions. However, Jews who were aware of the parallels took them in a different direction, considering the two characters to have shared a sin (illegitimately demanding Jewish prostration) and an ignominious punishment (crucifixion).[120] Indeed, in late antiquity Jewish sources supplied details that strengthened both the idea that Haman was crucified and that prostrating to him was an act of idolatry.[121] But while versions of *Esther* could simply state that Haman was crucified,[122] exegetes had to prove that prostration to him was an act of idolatry. After all, the HB is replete with references to illustrious figures who bow down to others.[123] As

Saadiah Gaon put it, "Why did Mordecai refrain from prostrating himself before Haman? Was he better than the Patriarchs, some of whom prostrated themselves before others?"[124] Perhaps the most ancient answer to this question comes from Add C:4–7, in which Mordecai explains that he refused to bow to Haman, "so that I might not set human glory above divine glory, and I will not do obeisance to anyone but you, my Lord. . . ." Mordecai implies here what later midrashim would state unambiguously: To bow to Haman was to bow to another god, either because Haman wore an idol on his clothing,[125] or because he believed himself to be a god.[126] To be sure, the rabbis offered all sorts of other explanations for Mordecai's refusal to bow to Haman,[127] but the fact that Haman's story begins with his demand that he be worshipped and ends with his crucifixion encouraged parallels between him and Jesus.

The comparison between these two figures had real consequences, two of which merit our attention. First, midrashim circulated that described Haman in terms more reminiscent of Jesus than of the Persian vizier of the *Esther* story. According to one well-known tradition, Haman, whose father and ten sons in MT *Esther* have recognizably Persian names,[128] was a native of the Galilee in Palestine.[129] Perhaps related to this is the curious midrash according to which Bigthan and Teresh, the two eunuchs who plotted to assassinate king Ahashwerosh (Esth 2:21–23), were from Tarsus—a town that is not otherwise mentioned in the Talmud, but was (in)famous as being the hometown of Paul. Were the rabbis seeking to associate the Achaemenid eunuchs who betrayed their master and sought to kill the king with Paul, who likewise betrayed his Jewish roots and challenged "the King"?[130] This interpretation of the midrash about the eunuchs seems convincing when considered alongside parallels between Jesus and Haman.[131]

Second, Jewish Purim celebrations came to serve as devious ways of mocking Christ(ianity). Many literary works composed in Christian lands to celebrate Purim contained oblique references to Jesus or to Christianity. A Byzantine-era *piyyuṭ* refers to Haman as "the *shoṭeh* (fool) of Scythopolis": the rabbis used the term *shoṭeh* with reference to Jesus, and Scythopolis was a town in the Galilee.[132] More generally, Jews in late antiquity used "Amalek" as a code-word for Christendom.[133] The significance of this point may have been clouded by the discussion of Haman's Roman identity, for which reason it bears highlighting here: Howsoever the rabbis chose to (re)imagine *Esther*'s villain, among the few details about Haman that they manipulate and supplement were the facts that Haman was an Agagite, and that the story in other ways appears to be responding to the episode of Saul and Agag, the Amalekite king.[134] Unlike Haman's hometown, which is not referred to in *Esther* and which, therefore, may have been somewhere in the Galilee (despite the instinctive brow-furrowing that this idea may induce), Haman's ethnicity is mentioned in the text, and not as an incidental detail: His identity as an Amalekite imbues his story with an extraordinary measure of theological, national, and scriptural import. Rather than presenting Haman as either an Amalekite, or a Roman, or a Christian, the rabbis blurred the boundaries between the three categories, which enabled the three attributes to coexist in a single villain.

Although the rabbis continued to relate Haman's career to the Israelite-Amalekite rivalry, they also made it clear that the Amalekites were themselves Edomites (Amalek was the grandson of Esau in Gen 36:12).[135] Seeing as the Romans, too, were Edomites, there was nothing wrong with assigning multiple labels to this single villain, not least because in Jewish sources the eschatological roles of the Amalekites and the Romans dovetailed, with both featuring as the final rivals of the Israelites/Jews who would be defeated at the End of Times. We thus find Haman depicted as a Christian bishop in *Pirqe de Rabbi Eliezer*,[136] even though the chapter in which Haman features is devoted to "The Seed of Amalek."

The popularity of some of the *piyyuṭim* that relate Haman and Amalek to Christianity, and the midrashic equation of Haman and Amalek with Christians, endured well into the Middle Ages. According to an eleventh-century hymn, Haman and his ten sons were crucified,[137] and Kallir's liturgical poems on Amalekite Christendom continued to be read and studied in the eleventh and twelfth centuries, acquiring considerable prestige in synagogues.[138] In the early-fourteenth century, Kalonymos ben Kalonymos (d. after 1328) composed a parody of the *Esther* story, which depicts Haman as a wretched victim of the villainous Mordecai. This text playfully depicts Haman as a Torah scholar in a Bet Midrash who was forced to abandon Torah-study and Judaism when it was discovered that he was descended from Amalek. Such texts align Haman with the anti-Christian *Toledot Yeshu* genre,[139] which depicts Jesus as a Torah scholar who turned to heresy upon discovering that he was actually a bastard.[140] In fact, Haman was identified as a Christian even in Muslim lands: in Aleppo, Syria, the local Judeo-Arabic *Megillah* refers to him as *al-Naṣrānī*, "the Christian."[141] Moreover, many Jews (both those living in Christendom and those living in Muslim lands) believed that Haman was, specifically, an Armenian Christian.

Equating Haman with Christ(ians) in particular, and Amalek with Christendom generally, was surely offensive to Christian sensibilities, but the sting of such name-calling could be neutralized in two ways: First, it is unclear to what extent Christians were aware of the contents of the Hebrew *piyyuṭim* or midrashic elaborations on *Esther* that contained such comparisons. Their composition in Hebrew and Aramaic limited their readership considerably. Second, name-calling could do little real harm, especially when deployed by a downtrodden minority against a great imperial power. It is therefore particularly significant that Jews in late antiquity did not limit their anti-Christian interpretations of *Esther* to name-calling, as is demonstrated in the text of an imperial law, dated to 408 CE, which stipulates:

> [T]he governors in the provinces should prohibit the Jews from setting fire to [H]aman in memory of his past punishment during a certain ceremony of their festival, and from burning with sacrilegious intent a form cast in the shape of a holy cross in contempt of the Christian faith, lest they mingle the sign of our faith with their jests. They shall also restrain their rituals from ridiculing Christian law because if they do not abstain from matters which are forbidden then will promptly lose what had been thus far permitted to them.[142]

The fact that such a law was codified and circulated suggests not only that Jews practiced what they had been allusively preaching in their literary sources, but that such public displays of Jesus-as-Haman mockeries were known and widespread enough to draw official condemnation. Seven years later, in Inmestar, Syria, another public celebration took place in which—according to Socrates Scholasticus (d. 439)—some local Jews:

> indulged in many absurdities, and at length impelled by drunkenness they were guilty of scoffing at Christians and even Christ himself; and in derision of the cross and those who put their trust in the Crucified One, they seized a Christian boy, and having bound him to a cross, began to laugh and sneer at him. But in a little while, becoming so transported with fury, they scourged the child until he died under their hands.[143]

Although Purim is not directly named as the context of this anti-Christian celebration, if we bear in mind both the earlier Purim-edict and the many subsequent accounts of Purim celebrations in which local Jews would pay a Christian boy to represent Haman, it is likely that in this instance, too, Purim was the context.[144] Whatever the case may be, for centuries thereafter, Jewish converts to Christianity in the Byzantine Empire were required not only to renounce the observance of Jewish rituals, but also to vow to "curse those who keep the festival of the so-called Mordecai . . . nailing Haman to wood, and then mixing him with the emblem of the cross and burning them together."[145] Numerous records exist of Jews throughout the Middle Ages and into the early modern period mocking Christianity by likening Haman to Jesus.[146] Writing in the mid-seventeenth century, the Protestant commentator John Mayer (d. 1664) referred to Jews at Purim who, "make noises with voices and knockings . . . and then to take up a crosse, representing that whereupon Haman was hanged." For this reason, he advises:

> [L]et the Governours of Provinces forbid the Jews to carry about a cross and burning it in remembrance of Haman's punishment, to the contempt of Christ and Christians, so to do anymore, or to mingle any thing of ours with their rites, or else they shall not be permitted as hitherto they have been.[147]

As a Christian, Mayer was no doubt appalled by the Jews' equation of Haman with Jesus; but as a Protestant, he may well have agreed with their characterization of Haman as Roman.[148]

Haman's Reinvention in Late Antiquity

Thus far, we have come to appreciate how thoroughly the Roman-Christian challenge to Judaism shaped depictions of Haman. The intertwining of political and religious power and identity in late antiquity is reflected in Haman's transformations into both a Roman and a Christian. No less significantly, the details of Haman's biography—his origins, activities, death, and historical-theological significance—were also shaped (or created) in this period and against the backdrop of Christian challenges to Judaism. Thus, in the context of the reformulation of Judaism in this period, the sheer volume of biographical details that Haman acquired and the prestige with which these details were imbued, combined to make this period the most significant in Haman's (literary) formation. Therefore, not only did Roman-Christianity directly provide new identities for Haman, but the late antique context in which the rabbis operated indirectly provided the bulk of what came to be accepted as the authoritative details of his life, both for rabbinic tradition and for those (Christians and Muslims) who drew on it.

To understand the dynamics behind these developments, we must first unlearn a widely held notion about the historical development of the Abrahamic religions, namely that Judaism preceded Christianity, which preceded Islam. While it is true that the original manifestations of each religion emerged in that order, scholars have long appreciated that the forms in which these religions are recognizable to us emerged gradually, in conversation with (and contradistinction to) each other. Much of what we would now recognize as Jewish tradition post-dates (or at least overlaps chronologically with) the emergence of Christian traditions. Moreover, Christians who enjoyed imperial backing and patronage read and interpreted many of the same texts that the Jews did, and the Christian readings of these texts could be sophisticated and attractive in a host of other ways. For this reason, the rabbis were forced to respond with readings and interpretations of their own, including of *Esther*. When the rabbis judged (their) Haman to be Christian, they were probably unaware of how accurate this verdict was.

All this took place in the aftermath of a traumatic century. Following the Second Temple's destruction (70 CE) and, especially, the failure of Bar Kokhba's revolt (132–136), Jews came to accept that a third Temple would not be built any time soon. The question arose—how does one practice a Temple-based religion without a Temple? The rabbis sought to provide answers to this extremely critical question, and their answers are recorded in the Mishnah (early third century), whose contents were also the subject of rabbinical debates that are recorded in the Talmuds of Jerusalem (early fifth century) and Babylonia (early sixth century). In the meantime, Christianities were emerging,[149] developing, and competing with Judaism on every level: New Israel (Christianity) with the support of New Rome (Byzantium) were facing off in the Near East against the purveyors of New Judaism.

The need to reinterpret the HB in light of contemporary Christian challenges, led rabbis to (re-)read the Bible and to propose their own interpretations of its contents. Both in response to Christian readings of the Old Testament, and as a continuation of the very ancient Near Eastern inclination to read significance into every line, word, and even letter of a sacred text, the rabbis produced a striking body of exegetical elaborations on the HB.[150] *Esther*, of course, benefited from this intellectual attention, but it posed a unique set of problems to its readers. These were solved by the LXX and its additions on the one hand, and by the Second Temple's rewritten-*Esthers*, on the other hand. Because the rabbis used MT *Esther*, they could not benefit from the LXX's solutions; and because they were at best ambivalent towards the Hasmonean era and its literary products, they tended to ignore them. To *Esther*'s challenges the rabbis had to propose their own solutions, and this they did in a corpus of diverse midrashim. That fact that *Esther* was the subject of more Jewish extra-biblical elaborations than virtually any other biblical story (a remarkable fact considering the book's modest length) attests to the quantity and quality of the challenges that the book posed.

The well-known problems with *Esther* were compounded by the rabbis' twofold solution to life in a post-Temple world: The first solution was to see all that happens as part of God's plan for His nation (otherwise, Jews might interpret their misfortune as a sign that God had switched sides and joined the Roman-Christian camp). The second solution was to highlight and elevate the Law, its details and application, above all else, thereby replacing any roles that the Temple had previously played.[151] For all their general merits, these solutions were problematic: God does not make a single appearance in the *Esther* story, nor does Esther herself adhere to the Law (she married a gentile and ate food at the palace that was not kosher, among other apparent transgressions).[152]

The rabbis managed to solve both of these problems. To the problem of God's apparent absence from the text, they proposed (1) that every reference in *Esther* to "the king," without specifying Ahashwerosh was actually code for God;[153] and (2) that the various coincidences that pepper the story's plotline and tie its scenes together were carefully orchestrated by God himself.[154] As for Esther's apparent transgression of the Law, the rabbis relate traditions according to which she did, in fact, follow *halakha* while living in the palace.[155] And more generally, the elevation of the Law led the rabbis to impose a simple equation on their readings of *Esther*: Since the Jews had misbehaved (for instance, by partaking in Ahashwerosh's unkosher banquet in Esth 1:5–8),[156] God sent Haman to motivate them to repent,[157] which they did,[158] and for that reason they were saved. By relating the *Esther* story in this way, the rabbis conveyed the message that keeping the Law was of the utmost importance, while the failure to do so might bring about the annihilation of the Jews. It is therefore not surprising that, when imagining the content of Haman's detailed accusation against the Jews (Esth 3:8), the rabbis placed in Haman's mouth detailed descriptions of the sort of *halakhic* practices that characterized Judaism in their eyes (and vexed anti-Semites throughout history). One such Haman-ic description of Jewish law is recorded in *Targum Rishon* (3:8), as follows:

> There is a certain people scattered and distinct among the nations; some of them live throughout all the provinces of your kingdom; the decrees of their Law are different from those of every nation; our bread and our cooked dishes they do not eat, our wine they do not drink, our festivals they do not celebrate, and our customs they do not observe; they do not observe the decrees of the king's statutes, and the king has no profit from them; what benefit does he have from them if he lets them (live) on the face of the earth?

We may compare this description of *halakha* to a similar expansion on Esth 3:8, this time from the Babylonian side of the Euphrates, according to which Haman said:

> They do not eat our [food], nor do they marry from our [women], nor do they marry off [their women] to us. . . . They spend the entire year [unworking, by

claiming] "*shehi pehi*" [possibly an acronym for *shabbat hayom, pessach hayom* "it is Sabbath today, it is Passover today," hence we cannot work]. . . . They eat and drink and scorn the throne: Even if a fly falls into the cup of one of them, he will throw [the fly] out and drink [the contents], but if my master the king were to touch the glass of one of them, he would throw it to the ground, and would not drink it [due to the laws of wine-impurity through contact with a gentile].[159]

The more something is right about Judaism, the more Haman will dislike it. Accordingly, the focus here on Haman's objection to *halakha* tells us how important the Law was to the rabbis who placed these words in his mouth.[160] Moreover, Haman's biography was expanded to include midrashic descriptions of the various ways in which he sought to outlaw Jewish practices, including studying the Torah, observing the Sabbath and festivals, practicing circumcision, and wearing phylacteries (*tefillin*) during morning prayers.[161] These prohibitions generally echo the Hadrianic persecutions of the early second century CE,[162] and we have already seen that at least some of them were imposed by Antiochus IV already in the mid-second century BCE. What stands out here is the rabbis' willingness to pad Haman's résumé with the crimes of other historical villains.[163]

Another way in which the rabbis updated Haman's résumé was by depicting him as an arch-criminal. For Hellenized Jews, Haman's characterization in the MT as a failed villain was not sufficient: A just God would not have punished Haman for crimes he did not commit, and the LXX (and other Second Temple writings) duly attributed a litany of offences to him. Here as before, the rabbis produced their own catalogue of crimes independent of the Second Temple solutions, e.g. Haman killed the courtier Hatakh, who had temporarily served as a go-between for Mordecai and Esther (Esth 4).[164] Some midrashim explained that Hatakh was none other than Daniel;[165] thus, Haman was responsible not only for murder, but for the murder of a biblical hero. As suggested in Add A:16–17, Haman was behind the plot of the eunuchs to assassinate the king (Esth 2: 21–23),[166] and he attempted to kill Esther when she approached the king uninvited (Esth 5).[167] Additionally, Haman plotted to kill the king and take his crown.[168] As far as the rabbis were concerned, however, Haman's greatest crimes were the parts he played in the defiling, destroying, and plundering of the Temple, as well as sabotaging attempts to rebuild it.[169] The trauma of the Temple's destruction cast a long shadow over the rabbis' worldview, and accusing Haman of anti-Temple crimes was a sure-fire way of cementing his infamy.[170]

Perhaps the greatest exegetical challenge that Christians in late antiquity posed to the rabbis was their ability to tie together the various books of the Old Testament library into a unified narrative of theological significance, through typological readings. The rabbis responded to this challenge by engaging in limited typological readings of their own (finding prefigurations of Esther, Mordecai, and Haman in Pentateuchal texts, for example), and by identifying an overarching narrative in the HB that related what otherwise would appear to be the fragmented components of a biblical corpus to each other. As this grand narrative concerned the Israelite-Amalekite rivalry, of which Haman represented the final Amalekite antagonist,[171] the demise of this Roman-Edomite-Christian-Amalekite villain sent a message of eschatological proportions.[172] Moreover, the rabbis' various anti-Roman apocalyptic prognostications were nicely complemented by traditions about Haman the Edomite-Roman: With the aid of a Christian-like reading of history, Jews living under Roman rule could take encouragement from the dénouement of the *Esther* story, which served as a sort of parallel or precedent for their current predicament (a predicament that will also end well, perhaps even usher in the messianic era). All that Jews must do now to deserve this happy ending is what they in fact did: To place their trust in God, repent, and uphold the Law.

Haman the Divine Puppet

Haman's transformation in rabbinic late antiquity from tragic villain to arch-villain is something of a mixed-blessing for those of us seeking to chart the evolution of Haman's character in history. On the one hand, as the rabbis ascribed all sorts of evil traits and actions to him—thereby ignoring the nuanced, occasionally even empathetic depiction of him in MT *Esther*—they created a Haman who was more evil and villainous than ever.[173] As seen earlier, by the time the *'Āl ha-Nissīm* prayer was composed, Haman was not merely the enemy of the Jews, but the enemy of God Himself. The large and varied corpus of midrashim with which the rabbis inflated Haman's résumé would come to provide Jews, Christians, Muslims, and Samaritans with materials on which they could (and did) draw in their own writings, and will serve us well in later chapters, as we attempt to compose Haman's biography.

On the other hand, by stressing the extent of God's control over History, and by framing Haman (and the Romans) in eschatological terms, the rabbis absolved Haman of all the crimes that they had ascribed to him. If God orchestrates all that happens (including past events in Achaemenid Persia, and present events in the Roman Empire), then Haman is merely a tool of God, through which history is being manipulated. It was not just that God was behind events, for He had been from the very beginning of the biblical account, but that His striking absence from the text of MT *Esther* led the rabbis to read Him into the text heavy-handedly, attributing virtually every major and minor moment in the story to God's hidden hand, and thus shutting down any questions about His absence from the story.[174] Accordingly, the rabbis tell us that God incited Bigthan and Teresh to plot the king's assassination so that Mordecai could foil the plot and receive a royal reward;[175] that at the crucial moment when Esther was about to implicate the king himself in the plot against the Jews, God sent an angel who pushed her accusatory hand towards Haman instead;[176] and that when Haman sought Esther's forgiveness at a particularly dramatic moment in the story, God again sent an angel who pushed Haman, causing him to fall on Esther, leading the enraged king to misinterpret Haman's actions, thereby triggering the latter's execution.[177] God's micromanagement of the events in *Esther* is reflected in numerous other midrashim.[178]

With regard to Haman himself, the rabbis tell us that he was sent by God both to exact punishment for sins that the Jews had committed and to induce them to repent.[179] Employing a sort of "the bigger they are, the harder they fall" logic, God exalted Haman, so that his eventual demise would be all the more dramatic.[180] By the same token, we are told that Haman's exaltation was immediately preceded by Mordecai's uncovering of the eunuchs' plot, since God "prepares the remedy before the affliction."[181] Similarly, the rabbis tell us, when Haman offered the king money (Hebrew: *ha-kesef*) for the Jewish people, God was already plotting Haman's execution on the gallows (Hebrew: *ha-ʿeṣ*), as the numerical value of the letters that comprise each of the two words is equal.[182] In this case, too, there are numerous other examples of God's carefully planned management of Haman's behavior.[183]

Now, one might argue that God's hand—hidden or otherwise—is behind *all* the events in the HB, including the behavior of Pharaoh, Nebuchadnezzar, and other villains. Nebuchadnezzar, as seen, was a divine agent sent to punish the Israelites by destroying the First Temple and exiling the Judeans to Babylonia. This reasonable argument would stand were it not for the fact that Haman's role as a divine agent was not limited to his punishment (or more precisely: his threatened punishment) of the Jews, but overlapped with his role in the unfolding eschatological drama. Identified as the final manifestation of the Israelite-Amalekite rivalry (which was confusingly merged with traditions about Rome as the final empire and about Haman as a Roman), Haman was imbued with the characteristics of an eschatological chaos-figure. From an early reference to Haman as a Gogite (rather than Agagite), through the LXX's designation of Haman as *ho diabolos*, and the interpretation of particular Romans (and Romans generally) as Antichrist figures, Haman's career may be read on two levels, one political (Haman as the oppressor of Diaspora Jews), the other apocalyptic. And while throughout history Jews have chosen to draw parallels between the political Haman and other oppressors under whom they suffered, it was God who chose for Haman his apocalyptic role, and it is, therefore, God who directed his behavior. In other words, one important strand of rabbinic thought viewed Haman as no less than, but also no more than, a divine puppet.

Esther is the only biblical book that the Babylonian rabbis in late antiquity chose to parse systematically, verse-by-verse, in the varied and voluminous discussions that have come to comprise the Babylonian Talmud.[184] In more ways than one, then, Jewish thinking about villains, and about Haman in particular, came full circle. The rabbis of the late antique Persian Empire were pondering not only on the most famous story of Jews in the ancient Persian Empire, but also on the very relationship between the good and evil forces in the world, a relationship that ended up where it started, with God in total control. Having entrusted evil to Satan (through exposure, perhaps, to Iranian dualistic ideas and vocabulary), God was now reclaiming responsibility even for Haman's misbehavior (perhaps through exposure to Iranian eschatological ideas and vocabulary). What is clear from the foregoing is just how diverse ideas about Haman were—not only between periods and regions, but also within them. Within a single discussion, the rabbis could present Haman as an inherently evil arch-villain and as a powerless, divine puppet.[185] They could imagine him as a Persian, an Amalekite, or a Roman-Edomite, without settling decisively on a single option. Indeed, as anyone with even a passing knowledge of rabbinic literature knows, argumentation and diversity of opinion were fundamental to the rabbinic method.

And while the rabbis were debating virtually all aspects of their religion, varieties of Christianity were developing throughout the Near East and Mediterranean worlds, raising consequential questions about the most basic tenets of religion. Some of these questions—concerning, for instance, which version of *Esther* to include in the Bible, and how to read and interpret the text—would have direct impact on Christian views of Haman. To this intellectually dynamic environment we may add a very strong, yet often overlooked, element of the apocalypticism that was widespread throughout Western Asia in late antiquity, generated by the influx of hordes of Gog-and-Magog-like nomads to the region, by relatively frequent and destructive earthquakes, by pandemics, and by the intertwining of religion and empire (which imbued the centuries-long Byzantine-Sasanid rivalry with theological significance). In such heady times, it is little wonder that villains such as Haman came to be imagined and reimagined repeatedly and variously in the Near East on the eve of Islam. And in such heady times, it is little wonder that new religious movements arose that promised to make sense of momentous events and offered answers to the many questions that divided religions from one another (and internally). By far the most important of these was Islam. Its striking success had enormous impact on the world in general, and on perceptions of Haman in particular.

4) The Classical Islamic Period.

The consequences of Islam's rise, spread, and domination, both political and cultural may be assessed in two spheres: First are the affects that the new, Islamic polity had on Jewish and Christian readers of *Esther*, with fascinating implications for depictions of Haman. Second are the various traditions about Haman that developed among Muslim scholars, who reacted both to Haman's appearances in the Qur'ān and to his importance to Jews and Christians. We will consider these two spheres in turn.

4a) Holy Books and History Books: Jewish and Christian Hamans in Muslim Lands

The first centuries of Islamic rule brought rapid and immense changes to virtually all corners of the world in which *Esther* was read. And yet, the same period was also characterized by a measure of conservatism that consolidated the authority of ancient and late antique scholars. This is not to say that under Muslim rule earlier traditions were merely recycled, but rather that within the new Islamic context, the corpus of older materials was shaped into new forms and refracted through new cultural lenses.

As Muslims of various sorts ruled from the Iberian Peninsula to the Indus River and Transoxania (and, occasionally, beyond), over a period of thirteen centuries, it would be foolhardy to reduce Islam or Muslim rule to superficial generalizations. It would be just as foolhardy, however, to refrain from appreciating the impressions that this bewildering Islamic diversity left on Jewish and

Christian interpreters of *Esther*. Indeed, the rise of Islam transformed the biblical Haman in two ways, one scriptural, the other historical.

Scripture

Whereas the rabbis argued for rabbinic authority, the Qur'ān argued for Qur'ānic authority. It is not merely that Muslims had their own divinely inspired book, but rather that the Qur'ān purported to relate God's own speech. And while there were voices within late antique Judaism that held similar views about the HB, the Qur'ān took the idea a step further, arguing that the inimitability of the Qur'ān was the very proof of its divine providence (and, hence, of Islam's truth). Repeatedly, the Qur'ān tells us, the Prophet challenged disbelievers to produce verses of the same caliber as those revealed in the Qur'ān, and repeatedly the naysayers failed to do so.[186]

In the multicultural Abrahamic world of the first Islamic centuries, scripture became an interfaith flashpoint that compelled Jews, Christians, and Samaritans to respond to the Qur'ān's claim to divine authorship. Jews rose to this challenge in two ways that will concern us here. The first was an attempt to upgrade the Bible's status by downgrading that of the Oral Torah. There were Jewish scripturalists of a sort beginning in the Second Temple period with the Sadducees (who rejected notions such as physical resurrection due to their absence from the HB), but it was only with the emergence of Karaism[187] in the early Islamic period that Jews developed a systematic exegetical approach to the HB that rejected rabbinic authority. Rabbanite traditions could be seen to have devalued the HB's prestige, both because the rabbis' scripture had been supplemented by a voluminous corpus of materials that (inadvertently) diluted the unique importance of the HB, and because these extraneous materials were not of divine provenance—or at best they were mediated through fallible rabbis, whose protracted debates attested to the lack of a decisive authority for interpreting the HB.[188] Karaites generated an impressive library of resources that allowed ordinary Jews to read the HB, even in the original Hebrew, without recourse to what they considered irrelevant, illogical, and generally incorrect ideas peddled by self-serving rabbis who sought to hijack the Bible and recast Judaism in their own image.[189]

One must be familiar with an idea before rejecting it, and Karaite readings of *Esther* often display an awareness of Rabbanite midrashim,[190] in some cases arguing against them, in other cases, repackaging them and passing them off as their own.[191] Crucially for us, this Rabbanite influence appears to have particularly affected Karaite commentaries on *Esther*, many of which drew on Saadiah

Gaon's own commentary on the book,[192] even though the latter was an assertive rival of the Karaites who dedicated much effort towards refuting their ideas.[193]

The second way that Jews responded to the Qur'ān's (and—for the Rabbanites—Karaism's) challenge was by paying renewed attention to their own scriptural traditions, with the result that a genre of Jewish biblical exegesis independent of midrashic collections emerged. This took place between the seventh and twelfth centuries CE, that is to say, just when and where Islamic civilization was developing and flourishing.[194] That all of this activity took place against an Islamic backdrop was certainly not coincidental, even if we disregard the Qur'ān's challenge to Judeo-Christian scripture. The Muslim conquest of the entire Sasanid Empire as well as the Eastern Mediterranean and the North African provinces of the Byzantine Empire meant that the overwhelming majority of the world's Jews were now living under Muslim rule. The divided world of late antiquity that produced two Talmuds in two competing empires, was now united, and by the late eighth century, this enormous expanse, extending from the Atlantic to the Indus, was centered in Baghdad, the capital of the Abbasid Caliphate (750–1258). As an imperial capital and international commercial hub, Iraq was the center of a sprawling network of roads, way-stations, and communications systems (both imperial and private). These networks fortuitously benefited the Geonim (sing. Gaon) of the Talmudic academies in Iraq, who were able to circulate replies to legal questions ("*responsa*") throughout the Muslim world and beyond. In this way, Judaism acquired a measure of standardization and the authority of the Babylonian rabbis was enhanced (as was that of the Babylonian Talmud, which came to eclipse the Jerusalem Talmud in rabbinic culture). This does not mean that the Babylonian Geonim blindly accepted the traditions found in late antique sources,[195] but rather that these were the sources with which they were working—even if this work included manipulations of various sorts (from expansion to rejection), which benefitted from the sharpening of their exegetical tools in response to the scripture-wars waged against and within Judaism(s).[196] Indeed, even within rabbinic Judaism there was palpable tension between literal (Hebrew: *peshat*) and non-literal (figurative or midrashic; Hebrew: *derash*) readings of scripture, and this tension, too, was indebted to methods of Qur'ānic interpretation, which posited a distinction between explicit/exoteric (*ẓāhir*) and implicit/esoteric (*bāṭin*) exegetical methodologies.[197] The various theological problems with MT *Esther* meant that reading the story using only literal, exoteric methods created challenges, and the boundaries between various interpretational strategies for *Esther* were often hazier than they were for other biblical books.

Karaite exegetes added their own exegetical methodologies to the mix, often focusing on biblical philology, and/or relying on rationalism to interpret the HB, at the expense of instinctive adherence to earlier tradition.[198] Within the Karaite exegetical tradition there was plenty of diversity. To cite but one Haman-related example:[199] a group of Jerusalem-based Karaite ascetics known as the "Mourners of Zion" argued that God sent Haman to punish the Jews for not returning to the Holy Land, even after Cyrus made it possible to do so,[200] whereas the Karaite exegete Yefet ben ʿEli (d. 1009) argued that Haman was sent to punish the Jews for their decision to cancel First Temple fast days and lamentations after the Second Temple was constructed.[201]

One popular exegetical approach to *Esther* developed by Jews living in Islamic lands involved devoting attention to historical *realia* in the story by both sides of the Rabbanite-Karaite divide. In Judeo-Arabic commentaries on *Esther*, the circulation of imperial edicts is described with terminology from the Abbasid *barīd* postal system; royal chamberlains are rendered *ḥujjāb* (the term employed at the Abbasid court); and young women summoned to the king's beauty contest are referred to as *jawārī* (sing. *jāriyah*; the term for slave-girls at the Abbasid court); among other examples.[202] The instinct to compare (even conflate) Ahashwerosh's court with the Abbasid one is hardly surprising. In both the *Esther* story and Abbasid Iraq, a Semitic, monotheistic people were actors on an imperial Persian stage, where Persian words and ideas pervaded an otherwise Arabic or Hebrew narrative or culture. Similarly, we find Judeo-Arabic commentators—both Karaite and Rabbanite—explaining aspects of *Esther* (and Haman within it) by referring to contemporary culture. For example, Saadiah compares the expectation that courtiers would bow to Haman to Turkic peoples who worshiped their supreme leader (Turkic: *khāqān*), and to Shīʿa Muslims who worshiped ʿAlī.[203] Similarly, Yefet holds that Ahashwerosh ordered prostration before Haman because the latter possessed "Divine Light" (Arabic: *nūr*), a concept known from both Shīʿa and Ṣūfī vocabularies.[204] What Saadiah and Yefet have in common is their preference for *realia* over (historically less-convincing and scripturally unsubstantiated) midrashim, such as the notion that Haman wore an idol on his garments so that bowing to him constituted worship.

This historicized reading of *Esther* represents a major break from the sort of interpretative strategies encountered in late antiquity, when the story was often read apocalyptically, and its villain could be seen as an eschatological agent of Chaos. The shift away from *Esther* as a narrative relating events at the End of Times and back to *Esther* as a narrative relating events in ancient times is related to the efflorescence of history writing in Muslim lands between the eighth and fifteenth centuries. By reading *Esther* as a story of Jewish success in the Diaspora,[205] Islamic-era Jews (and Christians) rediscovered the earliest meaning and message of the book, this following centuries of circuitous meanderings through Hellenized and late antique intellectual pastures. Once again, the Haman character represents not a Satanic[206] Antichrist figure whose demise will usher in the messianic era, but rather a human, rival of the Jewish people whose elevated position imbued his genocidal plans with menacing potency, as in the original Achaemenid context. It is this historicized Haman who served as the prototypical evil vizier to whom Jews and Christians would compare their most threatening antagonists for centuries to come.

Historiography

The impression that may emerge from the foregoing is that Islam confronted Jews and Christians with challenges to which the latter two religious communities were compelled to respond. While not entirely inaccurate, this picture is incomplete at best, and misleading at worst. In fact, developments in Islamic lands created a civilizational context from which all its inhabitants benefited. This context was undoubtedly the product of Islam's rise and spread, but it was also open to, and in its earliest stages shaped by, non-Muslim inhabitants of the caliphate. Reading and writing in Arabic, and heavily indebted to Muslim colleagues and predecessors, these Jews and Christians were Muslim in every way, except in their religious identity and practices. To capture this unique cultural setting, Hodgson has proposed the term "Islamicate."[207]

Islamicate civilization was, to some extent, enabled by the introduction of paper-making techniques to Islamic lands in the eighth century, a technological breakthrough that created a highly literate society with an increasing appetite for written works on an ever-expanding variety of topics.[208] Rulers patronized libraries and research—most famously in the early-Abbasid *Bayt al-Ḥikma* (House of Wisdom), where the knowledge of pre-Islamic civilizations—chiefly Greek, Iranian, and Indian—was gathered, translated, and improved upon, laying the foundations for intellectual and scientific achievements far beyond the temporal and geographical limits of the medieval Islamicate world. One branch of learning that flourished in these circumstances was historiography, which, like many other branches of knowledge in medieval Islamic lands, developed into a veritable science.[209]

Jews and Christians took the contents of scripture to be historical,[210] for which reason all biblical narratives were included within this emerging genre. But

Esther stood out as a leading beneficiary of these developments, for two reasons. First, the book informs its audience that it is relating a story about ancient Persian political history, as evidenced by the "chronicles of the kings of Persia and Media" (Esth 10:2). Second, the Abbasid-era historiographical revolution was led by scholars who were largely of Persian ethnicity and cultural background, and who generally wrote in Arabic. This meant that the *Esther* story interested them not because it appears in the Qur'ān, but despite the fact that it does not. We will encounter an intriguing example of such de-scripturalization of *Esther* below, when considering al-Ṭabarī's summary of the story.

Evidence of the impact of Muslim historiography on Islamicate Jews and Christians abounds, discernible at both the elite and the popular strata of society. For example, *responsa* from Islamic lands give evidence of an interest in history-writing. In the *Epistle of Rabbi Sherirah Gaon* (987 CE), the leader of Babylonian Jewry provides a chronological history of the rabbinic sages and their writings in response to a Tunisian rabbi's query.[211] In both the Western (*maghrebi*) and Eastern (*mashreqi*) halves of the Muslim world, Jews sought to organize and rationalize, for the first time, the unwieldly body of historical data that they had accumulated.[212] This newfound methodical approach to historiography also applied to the contents of *Esther*, as it was the scriptural book for which the balance between theology, prophecy, law, and history was weighted most heavily towards the latter. One did not have to translate *Esther*'s contents into history, for—at least on the surface—that is predominantly what they were. It is in this intellectual ambience that the rabbanite Tanḥum ha-Yerushalmi and the author of the Aramaic *Targum Sheni* situated the *Esther* story, setting it in a global historical framework.[213] Such a broad contextualization of *Esther* is discernible also in other Jewish writings from the period.[214]

Christian historiography also integrated *Esther*'s contents in its narratives, with enduring ramifications for the development of Haman's character.[215] Christians in the Islamicate world could draw on the imperial historiographical traditions of previous and contemporaneous Christian empires, but they had the added "benefit" of living in Exile. A Diaspora story such as *Esther* might not have much relevance for Byzantine historians, but the high-ranking Christian administrators at the Abbasid or Fatimid courts may have seen things differently.[216] In other words, Islamicate Christians are likely to have related well to *Esther*'s contents and to have had their own Hamans.

Some of the most interesting Muslim summaries of *Esther*—such as those related by al-Ṭabarī and Ibn Khaldūn (d. 1406), which we will encounter shortly, drew on Christian sources. Already in the late eighth century, Theophilus of

Edessa (d. 785) included a summary of *Esther* in his *Chronicle*, and although this summary is no longer extant, it is noteworthy that Theophilus refers to the Arab-Muslim conquerors of the seventh century as Amalekites.[217] We know of Theophilus's summary from both Agapius (Maḥbūb) of Manbīj (d. *ca.* 945) and Bar Hebraeus (d. 1286), who used it in their own fascinating treatments of the story.[218] Agapius's treatment of *Esther* is found in his universal history *Kitāb al-ʿunwān* (*The Book of the Title*),[219] and appears to be based on MT *Esther*,[220] for three reasons. First, there is no reference to the Additions to *Esther* found in versions based on the LXX. Second, Haman's name is rendered with the initial "H" (rather than as "Aman," as in the LXX and its offshoots). And third, this Haman is clearly identified as an Amalekite (rather than a Bougean or Macedonian). Complicating matters is the fact that Agapius identifies Haman as the vizier (Arabic: *wazīr*) of Artaxerxes, the Persian king of LXX *Esther* rather than as the Xerxes of the MT.[221] Curiously, Agapius's summary ends with Haman's crucifixion (rather than hanging), thereby ignoring the final three chapters of *Esther*. That the events recounted by Agapius do not follow *Esther*'s chronology suggests that the narrative is based on an oral summary of MT *Esther*.

Bar Hebraeus's summary of *Esther* shares with Agapius all of the points made above, allowing us to trace them tentatively to Theophilus's original text. However, Agapius does break free of his source(s) on occasion, as when he refers to Bigthan and Teresh (the conspiring eunuchs of Esth 2:21–23), as "two Turkish eunuchs . . . one named Baʿthān, the other Ītnāḥ."[222] Whereas the former is transparently a slight mis-rendering of the Hebrew *b-g-th-n*, the latter bears no resemblance to Teresh. And why are the eunuchs described as Turkish? We must resist any instinct to relate their Turkish ethnicity to the Talmudic midrash that describes them as being from Tarsus (in Asia Minor), as Agapius was writing centuries before Central Asian "Turks" conquered Asia Minor in 1071. The solution to the mystery of both Teresh's name and the eunuchs' Turkish identity comes from the ninth-century Abbasid court, where Turkic eunuchs did indeed challenge the caliphs in all sorts of ways—including both attempted and successful regicides—and where one of the leading Turkic eunuchs was "Ītākh," a name whose consonantal structure in Arabic (*i-y-t-ḥ/kh*) is almost identical to that of Ītnāḥ (*i-y-t-n-ḥ/kh*), with only the addition or removal of dots making the difference. In other words, as in the case of Judeo-Arabic commentators on *Esther*, Agapius historicized the story by incorporating Abbasid *realia*. But what about the Abbasid historians themselves? What did they and later Muslim historians make of the *Esther* story and of Haman's role within it?

4b) Muslim receptions of Esther *and Haman.*

Haman's reception into the richly varied library of classical Islamic civilization brings with it good news, bad news, and then more good news. The first batch of good news concerns quantity and potential. Haman appears repeatedly in the Qur'ān, and Muslim authors who were acquainted with (and frequently drew on) Jewish and Christian materials on biblical topics (*Isrā'īliyyāt*) thus had two rich sources from which Haman-related traditions could reach their bookshelves. Qur'ānic and biblical Hamans obviously hailed from entirely different contexts, but Muslim authors seem not to have been troubled by this and pooled the Haman-traditions that reached them. This integration of traditions is apparent in the frequent references to Haman as Pharaoh's vizier (Arabic: *wazīr*), which bring him into line with the biblical Haman, despite the fact that in the Qur'ān itself, he is never identified as an administrator. Instead, he commands armies and is commissioned with building a sort of skyscraper, while playing second fiddle to the ruler, Pharaoh. In other words, the Qur'ānic Haman resembles Second Temple Haman-ic villains (who were military generals, often overshadowed by a ruler), whereas post-Qur'ānic Islamic tradition, through exposure to the biblical Haman, reimagined him as a vizier and a dominant voice of villainy.

An interesting example of the biblicalization of the Islamic Haman comes from al-Kisā'ī (fl. 1100 CE), who recounts the story of Pharaoh's rise to power in Egypt,[223] followed by what appears to be a garbled version of Esth 3:

> The first to bow before [Pharaoh] was Iblīs (i.e., "Diabolos"), who called him "lord." After him, Haman and all the viziers, sorcerers and soothsayers bowed down. Then he called for the elders of the children of Israel, who came and fell down prostrate before him. . . . Pharaoh called for the priests of Israel and said to them, "It has reached me that outwardly you obey me but that inwardly you disobey me. Bow down to me or I will punish you with all sorts of torture!"

When the Jews refused to bow, Pharaoh "executed them to the last" and said to Haman:

> "I think my destruction will not come but from the hand of the Israelites; but bring me Amram, the son of Muṣ'ab, who is their chief." So Amram came to him and was made grand vizier, with the result that Haman and the rest of the viziers were under him.

Al-Kisā'ī's account contains unmistakable echoes of *Esther*, where Haman insists that all bow before him and Mordecai refuses to do so. Due to the Jews' reluctance to bow before Pharaoh/Haman, the ruler decides to annihilate the entire nation. Whereas in the *Esther* story this plan fails and Mordecai is elevated to the vizierate, in al-Kisāʾī's telling the plan was successfully executed although Amram was spared and elevated to a Mordecai-like status. Amram here replaces Mordecai and Esther (or they are ignored), while Haman still features as Pharaoh's vizier, only to be overcome by a Jew (as in *Esther*). Al-Kisāʾī's passage presents a Muslim author's description of the Qurʾānic Pharaoh and Haman, with the details that are indebted howsoever loosely to the biblical story.

The bad news is that increased attention to historicity and *realia* opened the floodgates to a glut of spurious traditions about Haman that are the stuff of utterly ahistorical midrashim. Accordingly, many of these came to be viewed with suspicion within Muslim circles. Thus, while Islamic sources contain a selection of "midrashic" materials on Haman—filtered, of course, through the sieve of Islamicate civilization—these are rarely taken to be historically sound.

I promised yet more good news, and here it is: Despite the increasing tendency to downgrade *Isrāʾīliyyāt*, Muslim sources contain numerous materials that pertain to Haman, which *have* made the historiographical cut. Moreover, the emphasis placed on historiography in the Abbasid world—and particularly on Irano-centric traditions—meant that the *Esther* story came to be viewed not merely as an instalment in the biblical library (traditions about which may be rejected as *Isrāʾīliyyāt*), but as a crucial episode in the history of world empires that almost uniquely bridges the Abrahamic and Iranian historical traditions. That the overwhelming majority of Abbasid historians were Persians who wrote in Arabic appears to have increased *Esther*'s relevance to them, as noted.

There are four principal ways in which classical Muslim authors dealt with the *Esther* and Haman materials that reached them.[224]

A) Ignoring *Esther*

We begin with those Muslim authors who, despite being acquainted with *Esther* and its version of Haman, decided to ignore the book, even when writing on relevant topics. Leading scholars such as al-Yaʿqūbī (d. 897) and al-Masʿūdī (d. 956), who treat pre-Islamic Iranian and biblical history in their works, chose to ignore *Esther* altogether, and even Ḥamza al-Iṣfahānī (d. 961), who compiled an overview of Jewish history and a list of biblical books, ignores both *Esther* and the Purim festival. This omission is surprising both because he was a native of Isfahan—which then (as now) had a large Jewish population, so that he would likely have come across a Purim celebration; and because he names the Jewish informants who contributed to his knowledge of Judaism and the HB (including one "Pinḥas").[225] We cannot but conclude that al-Iṣfahānī's omission of *Esther*, Purim, and Haman was intentional.[226]

That al-Ya'qūbī, al-Mas'ūdī and al-Iṣfahānī ignored *Esther* may relate to two major inconsistencies between its contents and those of the Qur'ān. First, Haman's Achaemenid context in the HB is not consistent with his Pharaonic context in the Qur'ān. Second, the crucial moment in *Esther*, which triggers the story's plot, is Mordecai's refusal to bow to Haman. As mentioned, the Second Temple-era *Life of Adam and Eve* included a refusal-to-bow episode (in which Satan and Adam replace Mordecai and Haman, respectively), a version that circulated widely in late antique Christian circles and occurs (in multiple versions) in the Qur'ān itself.[227] It may well be that those knowledgeable, highly respected Muslim authors chose to ignore *Esther* because they regarded its contents as historically unconvincing. *Esther* placed the Egyptian Haman in Achaemenid Persia and reimagined the story of Satan's refusal to bow as though it related to (the mistakenly described) Haman. The science of Abbasid historiography simply could not tolerate such howlers.

B) Disguising Haman

Discrepancies between biblical and Qur'ānic data do not necessarily mean that Muslim authors had to reject the former out of hand. For just as the author of *Jubilees* rewrote the post-diluvian distribution of the world's real estate among Noah's sons (to bring it into line with Hellenistic sensibilities), so early Muslim authorities found ways to swallow difficult scriptural pills. Turning to another example from the post-diluvian biblical story, some Muslim sources Islamicized the description of Noah's drunkenness after disembarking from the Ark (Gen 9:20–21) by replacing the intoxicated Noah with a fatigued Noah who had fallen asleep.[228] Other examples of this Islamicization process abound.

We should not be surprised, therefore, to find that in the case of the two Haman-ic discrepancies between the Bible and the Qur'ān, some scholars amended the *Esther* story to neutralize offending details. Drawing on materials inherited from their Abbasid predecessors,[229] and on personal experience with the Jews of Egypt and Greater Syria, a handful of Mamluk-era (1250–1517) scholars included summaries of *Esther* in their works, conscientiously revised along Muslim lines. Among them were historians such as al-Waṭwāṭ (d. 1318),[230] al-Nuwayrī (d. 1332),[231] al-Qalqashandī (d. 1418), and al-Maqrīzī (d. 1442).

In his account of Purim, for instance, al-Nuwayrī places the events of the story during the reign of "Ardashīr . . . whom the Jews call 'Ahashwerosh,'" telling us that the latter,

> ... had a vizier *whom they called in their language "Haymūn."* In those days, the Jews had a rabbi (*ḥabr*) whom they called in their language "Mordecai." It came to Ardashīr's [knowledge] that he [Mordecai] had a niece of beautiful appearance, one of the best people of that period. So [Ardashīr] demanded from [Mordecai] that he marry [Esther], and [Mordecai] agreed to this. So [Ardashīr] married her. She gained his respect and Mordecai became close to the king. *For this reason, Haymūn wished to bring Mordecai down, out of jealousy, and thus sought to annihilate the Jewish community throughout Ardashīr's realms.*
>
> When news of this reached Mordecai, he informed his niece of what he had heard and urged her to undertake a scheme to extricate the [Jewish people]. So, she told the king about this situation, *[explaining] to him that the vizier planned this out of jealousy, due to Mordecai's closeness to [the king].* So [the king] ordered that Haymūn the vizier be killed, and that safety should be decreed for the Jews. Thus, they took this [day] to be a festival. For three days preceding it the Jews fast. This for them is a festival of happiness, frivolity, wantonness, and presenting gifts to each other. On [this day] they make a paper image of Haymūn, fill its stomach with bran, and cast it into a fire until it is consumed.[232]

Mamluk historians all agree that the *Esther* story took place in Achaemenid Persia, that it involved a plot against the Jews, and that the plot was unsuccessful, for which reason Jews instituted an annual festival. The basic outlines of MT *Esther* are thus retained. What changes, however, are the two details that clash with Muslim tradition: (1) the refusal-to-bow motif is entirely absent from this context, for the villain plotted against the Jews out of jealousy of Mordecai's position vis à vis the king;[233] and (2) the evil vizier is named Haymūn, which dissociates him from the Haman character who operated in Pharaonic Egypt. It would be easy to dismiss this change as incidental—perhaps al-Nuwayrī's Jewish informant(s) pronounced the villain's name "Haymūn."[234] And yet, the significance of al-Nuwayrī's re-naming of Haman is supported by two changes that al-Maqrīzī made to his account: First, al-Maqrīzī removed the clause "whom they called in their language 'Haymūn'," presumably because he knew that they did no such thing. Second, towards the end of his account, having referred to "Haymūn" throughout, Maqrīzī adds that "some of them on this day [of Purim] make an effigy of Haymūn the vizier, though they call him 'Haman.'"[235] Although he appears to have inherited al-Nuwayrī's summary of the Esther story and to have adopted it, consistently for the most part, his extensive acquaintance with Jews and their customs led him to introduce some improvements, two of which demonstrate that unlike Muslims (including al-Maqrīzī himself) who knew the vizier as "Haymūn," Jews knew him as "Haman." It is likely, therefore, that removing the refusal-to-bow motif and renaming Haman were conscious revisions made to bring the text into line with the Qur'ān's contents.

C) Al-Ṭabarī's solution: "Blotting out the remembrance of Haman from under the heavens."

Jewish tradition almost unanimously associates Haman with the Amalekites, and for this reason a variety of popular customs arose, from late antiquity onwards, that aimed to erase, efface, or drown out his name; this in accordance with God's command in Deut 25:19 to, "blot out the remembrance of Amalek from under the heavens." Children wrote Haman's name on the soles of their shoes and scuffed them on the ground until the name was erased; or they wrote Haman's name on stones or twigs and then rubbed or banged them on some other object until the name was gone. Perhaps best known and most enduringly popular was the custom of using noise-makers to obscure Haman's name every time it came up during the ceremonial readings of *Esther* on Purim.[236]

The Persian scholar al-Ṭabarī's chosen method of blotting out Amalek's memory was a more refined and orderly alternative to these popular customs: He simply wrote Haman out of the story. Concerning the events of Ahashwerosh's day, he writes:

> After that, Babylon and its environs were ruled on behalf of Bahman by one of his relatives. . . . Nicknamed "the sage" . . . Ahashwerosh had come to Bahman well recommended by Nebuchadnezzar, and it was at that time that Bahman appointed him to rule Babylon and its environs. [Ahashwerosh] stayed at Susa, gathered nobles around him and wined and dined them; he ruled the region from Babylon to India, and Ethiopia and the coast. . . . Ahashwerosh became entrenched in Babylon but spent much time at Susa, and he married a woman from among the Israelite captives. She was called Esther, the daughter of Abihail. She had been raised by an uncle of hers, Mordecai, who was her milch-brother, as Mordecai's mother milk-fed Esther. The reason he married her was that he had killed one of his wives, a noble, beautiful, bright woman, named Vashti. He had ordered Vashti to appear before the people in order that they might see her majesty and beauty, but she refused. Ahashwerosh slew her but then became anxious about it. It was suggested to him that he review the women of the world, which he did. He became attracted to Esther by a divine design for the sake of the Israelites. The Christians assert that she bore him a son on his way to Babylon, and that he named

him Cyrus. They also assert that the rule of Ahashwerosh lasted fourteen years, that Mordecai taught him the Torah, and that Cyrus embraced the faith of the Israelites and learned from the prophet Daniel and his companions, Hananiah, Mishael, and Azariah.[237]

There is a lot to unpack here, despite the efficient precis of the story. We will begin with the historical context in which al-Ṭabarī situates the events. For him, the ruler of "Babylon" was Ahashwerosh (rather than, say, Artaxerxes/Ardashīr), who was himself subject to king Bahman, known to us from the Parthian novels encountered earlier. Moreover, the reference to Mordecai and Esther as milch-siblings appears to echo the tale of *Vīs and Rāmīn*, who were nursed by the same woman (in Susa!), as seen earlier. In other words, al-Ṭabarī, a proud Persian, brought the *Esther* story into the framework of ancient Persian historiography. This may explain why he describes Ahashwerosh—who in Jewish midrashim, is at worst a villain and at best a buffoon—as "the sage," and Vashti as "a noble, beautiful, bright woman," despite the fact that she, too, received a bad press in late antique Jewish tradition. Al-Ṭabarī was both a leading Muslim scholar and a proud Persian, whose *History of Prophets and Kings* fuses the two sides of his identity. Hence, the Persian king and queen are here rehabilitated and presented as impressive Iranian royals rather than buffoons (Ahashwerosh) or leprous sinners (Vashti).

But perhaps Jewish midrashim are irrelevant here: After all, al-Ṭabarī cites "the Christians" as his source.[238] Moreover, he relates the events of *Esther* within his *History* (rather than his voluminous commentary on the Qur'ān), thereby contributing to the Abbasid historiographical context which, as noted, was indebted to early medieval Christian historiography of the sort composed by Theophilus, Eutychius, and Agapius, who were either al-Ṭabarī's predecessors or contemporaries.[239]

What interests us about al-Ṭabarī's *Esther* is what it excludes, namely reference to Haman and, by extension, to his genocidal plot, its failure, and the resulting Purim festival. By removing Haman, al-Ṭabarī obviates the need to solve the problem that the Qur'ān's refusal-to-bow episode is set in ancient Persia. Admittedly, it is possible that the "problem" never arose for him. Indeed, contemporaneous Christian-Arabic summaries of *Esther*, such as that of Agapius (perhaps reflecting Theophilus's earlier account) do not mention the refusal-to-bow motif either: In their view, Haman hated the Jews because he was an Amalekite, and there was centuries of bad blood between the Jews and his ancestors.[240] In Agapius's words:

> ... Then lived the minister (*wazir*) of king Artaxerxes, Haman the *Amalekite*. He remembered the old enmity and the wars that had formerly separated the

> Israelites and Amalekites; he kept the resentment of it. And he asked the king to kill and exterminate the Jewish people.[241]

Thus, if he was indeed using Christian-Arabic sources, al-Ṭabarī may not have had to smooth over the discrepancy between refusal-to-bow contexts at all.

But other Christian sources do include references to (Achaemenid) Haman and his plot, and—as we will presently see—there is evidence that Jewish midrashim contributed to his knowledge of *Esther*. Al-Ṭabarī, therefore, was forced to deal with the existence of a Pharaonic character in Ancient Iran, and he found an elegant way to do so: Not only did he remove Haman from the story, but he also seized the opportunity to aggrandize the ancient Persian king along the way. To understand the context to this point, we must go all the way back to AT *Esther* (Add A:16–17), where the king rewards Mordecai for foiling the plot of the eunuchs by "assigning" Haman to him. The idea that Haman was given to Mordecai arises thereafter in a handful of sources: In the Talmud, Haman is compared to a slave who sold himself for a loaf of bread,[242] a tantalizing statement that begs for elaboration. The famous French exegete, Rashi, explains that in the distant past Mordecai had been wealthy and Haman poor, for which reason Haman sold himself to Mordecai as a slave in exchange for loaves of bread.[243] While this laconic elaboration contributes something to the historical context, it does not fill all the gaps in the narrative. A full version of the story first emerges in the thirteenth century, in the German midrash *Yalqut Shim'oni*.[244] According to this source:

> It once happened that a city in India rebelled against Ahashwerosh. In great haste troops were dispatched thither under the command of Mordecai and Haman. It was estimated that the campaign would require three years, and all preparations were made accordingly. By the end of the first year, Haman had squandered the provisions laid in to supply the part of the army commanded by him, for the whole term of the campaign. Greatly embarrassed, he asked Mordecai to give him aid. Mordecai, however, refused him succor; they both had been granted the same amount of provisions for an equal number of men. Haman then offered to borrow from Mordecai and pay him interest. This, too, Mordecai refused to do. . . . When starvation stared them in the face, the troops commanded by Haman threatened him with death unless he gave them their rations. Haman again turned to Mordecai, and promised to pay him as much as ten percent interest. The Jewish general continued to refuse the offer. But he professed himself willing to help him out of his embarrassment on the condition that Haman sell himself

> to Mordecai as his slave. Driven into a corner, he acquiesced, and the contract was written on Mordecai's kneecap, because there was no paper to be found in the camp.[245]

The midrash records the full text of the contract, including the detail that Haman and Mordecai each received 60,000 soldiers in order to wage battle against the Indian rebel. How does this elaborate midrash relate to al-Ṭabarī's account of the *Esther* story, and with what ramifications? To answer this question we must go back to al-Ṭabarī's account of *Esther*, which was preceded by background information on Ahashwerosh's rise to power:

> Ahashwerosh had come to Bahman well recommended by Nebuchadnezzar, and it was at that time that Bahman appointed him to rule Babylon and its environs. He was appointed, so it is asserted, because a man who had administered the region of India (Sind and Hind) for Bahman, Karardashīr b. Dashkal, rebelled with 600,000 followers. Bahman therefore appointed Ahashwerosh over the region and ordered him to go to Karardashīr, which he did. He waged war on the rebel, slaying him and most of his supporters. Bahman continued adding to the administrative duties of Ahashwerosh, giving him various parts of the realm to rule over. The latter stayed at Susa, gathered nobles around him and wined and dined them; he ruled the region from Babylon to India, and Ethiopia and the coast. On a single day, he gave each of 120 military commanders[246] a banner and 1,000 choice soldiers,[247] each of whom equaled one hundred warriors.

Clearly, *Yalqut Shim'oni* and al-Ṭabarī are offering up two versions of the same story. In both Ahashwerosh is required to quash a rebellion in India, and both mention an army of 120,000 soldiers. But whereas al-Ṭabarī allocates the 120,000 soldiers to Ahashwerosh (who entrusted 120 military commanders with 1,000 soldiers), in the midrash Mordecai and Haman are given 60,000 soldiers each. Inasmuch as al-Ṭabarī died some four centuries before the midrash was written, it is reasonable to assume that he preserved the original story, which was then reworked by a Jewish author. Alternatively, if al-Ṭabarī's account was a link in a chain that began with AT *Esther*, continued in the BT and/or the *Targum Rishon*, was picked up by Rashi, and finally ended with the *Yalqut Shim'oni*, then it would be al-Ṭabarī who reworked the account. By now it should be clear why: For al-Ṭabarī, Haman can play no role in the *Esther* story. In reimagining the story of a rebellion in India quashed by Mordecai and Haman as a story of Ahashwerosh successfully suppressing a rebellion, al-Ṭabarī had to ignore an Achaemenid

Haman as required by his Islamic heritage, and magnify the achievements of the Persian king, as required by his Persian heritage.[248]

On the one hand, by including a terse version of *Esther* in his *History*, al-Ṭabarī, arguably the most important Muslim historian of the first three Islamic centuries, was lending the story a measure of Islamic legitimacy. On the other hand, by removing Haman and his anti-Jewish mischief from his summary of *Esther*, he was foregoing the tension, drama, and basic plot of the story, which, for him, was merely an episode in the chronicles of ancient Persian kings and queens (as Esth 10:2 promised it would be). The big loser, once again, was Haman, who was written out of the story. Fortunately for him, two outstanding scholars of classical Islamic civilization restored his place in the narrative, as we shall now see.

D) Accepting Haman: al-Bīrūnī and Ibn Khaldūn

Al-Bīrūnī (d. 1048; Central Asia) and Ibn Khaldūn (d. 1406; North Africa), two of the most highly regarded intellectuals of Islamic civilization, included summaries of the *Esther* story in their works, despite being aware of the challenges involved in receiving it *as is*. Al-Bīrūnī's summary of *Esther* is included in his overview of the Jewish calendar and holidays. After introducing Haman as Ahashwerosh's vizier,[249] al-Bīrūnī writes:

> *This Haman was an enemy of the Jews.* He asked the diviners and augurs which was the unluckiest time for the Jews. They said: "In Adar their master Moses died, and the unluckiest time of this month is the fourteenth and fifteenth." Now Haman wrote to all parts of the empire, ordering people on that day to seize upon the Jews and to kill them. *The Jews of the empire prostrated themselves before him, and appeared before him, crossing their hands upon their breasts, except one man, Mordecai, the brother of Esther, the king's wife. Haman hated her and planned her destruction on that day,* but the king's wife understood what he was intending. Now she received (in her palace) the king and his *wazīr*, entertaining them during three days. On the fourth day she asked the king's permission to lay before him her wishes. And then she asked him to spare her life and that of her brother. The king said: "And who dares to attempt anything against you both?" She pointed to Haman. Now the king rose from his seat in great wrath; Haman dashed towards the queen, prostrating himself before her, and then kissing her head, but she pushed him back. Now the king got the impression that he wanted to seduce her, so he turned towards him and said: "Have you in your impudence come so far as to raise your desire to her?" So the king ordered him to be killed, and Esther asked

> him to have him gibbeted on the same tree which he had prepared for her brother. Thus the king did, and wrote to all parts of the empire to kill the partisans of Haman. So they were killed on the same day on which he had intended to kill the Jews, that is, on the fourteenth. Therefore, there is great joy over the death of Haman on this day.[250]

Compared to the biblical account, al-Bīrūnī's summary is largely unexceptional, and the divergences from MT *Esther* are traceable to midrashic sources. Compared to Muslim versions of the story, however, this account is exceptional. Al-Bīrūnī retains the plot, tension, and significance of the *Esther* narrative, including a relatively full range of its characters, even in the face of contradictory data emanating from his Persian and Islamic heritages. What is particularly interesting is that he retains the refusal-to-bow motif, despite having established Haman's anti-Jewish inclinations.

More than three centuries later, and on the other side of the Islamic world, Ibn Khaldūn demonstrated a similar willingness to convey Judeo-Christian materials dispassionately, in this case basing himself largely on the works of the Arab-Christian historian Ibn al-ʿAmīd (d. 1273), who, as noted above, relied on Agapius of Manbīj (thereby likely taking us back to Theophilus).[251] Ibn Khaldūn does not summarize the *Esther* story in a single account. Rather, in two passages he displays familiarity with the story as it was known to Jews and Christians rather than as reworked in Islamic sources. In the first passage, which concerns the relationship between ancient Persian kings and the Jewish people, Ibn Khaldūn tells us that beginning in the reign of Cyrus, Persian kings would supply the Jews with all they needed for Temple service,

> . . . except for a short lapse during the reign of Ahashwerosh. *His vizier was Haman, who was an Amalekite.* Saul had sought to depose them by God's order *and for this reason Haman was opposed to [the Jews], and plotted to destroy them.* Mordecai, who was one of their leaders, had married off his milch-sister[252] to Ahashwerosh, and encouraged her to beseech the king to save her nation, and he accepted this, and returned things [to the way they had been].[253]

Ibn Khaldūn's assertion that Haman's antipathy towards the Jews related to the Israelite-Amalekite rivalry, rather than to Mordecai's refusal-to-bow (which Ibn Khaldūn—and Agapius—ignore), exposes his debt to Agapius.

In the second passage, included in his survey of ancient Persian history, Ibn Khaldūn weaves the events of *Esther* into the political history of the Achaemenid dynasty:

> Smerdis [= Bardiya] the Zoroastrian reigned for one or thirteen years. He was called "the Zoroastrian" because it was in his time that Zoroaster emerged with his religion.[254] After him reigned Ahashwerosh b. Darius for twenty years. His vizier was Haman the Amalekite. He is the one with whom the story of the Israelite girl (*al-jāriya min banī isrā'īl*) occurred. Then reigned Artaxerxes b. Ahashwerosh, known as Longimanus. His mother was a Jewess, the niece of Mordecai . . . and it is through her that the Jews were extricated from the plot of his vizier.[255]

Ibn Khaldūn's and al-Bīrūnī's passages demonstrate that there were corners within the vast expanse of Islamic religious and historical writing where versions of the *Esther* story recognizable to those familiar with the biblical *Esther* could be found. And yet, they were rare. Most Muslim authors adjusted or modified the *Esther* story in order to smooth over contradictions between the biblical *Esther*, on the one hand, and either the Qur'ānic Haman or the Persian mythological historical traditions, on the other.

Some Islamicate Christians took things in a different direction: The litterateur al-Jāḥiẓ (d. 868) relates that Christians challenged the accuracy of the Qur'ān by pointing out errors within it. One example he lists is the Qur'ān's claim that according to the Jews Ezra was the son of God (Q 9:30), which according to al-Jāḥiẓ's Christian source and to Jewish tradition itself, is incorrect. Another inaccuracy that al-Jāḥiẓ attributes to Christian polemicists concerns Haman's appearance in the Qur'ān alongside Pharaoh. He quotes them as saying:

> What proves your historical inaccuracies, and your information from those who are unreliable, is that your book says that "Pharaoh said to Haman, 'Build for me a Tower,'" whereas Haman lived in the time of the [ancient] Persians, and a long time after Pharaoh—as recognized by those who possess scriptures, and as well-known to scholars.[256]

This anti-Qur'ān argument may not have reached Christians in medieval Europe, but—as we will see below—they managed to discover it for themselves, and for centuries Christian polemicists have been using Haman's appearances in the Qur'ān as an intellectual stick to attack the Qur'ān and Islam. Unsurprisingly, Muslims used the very same Qur'ānic references to Haman to fend off the attack. Haman, it would seem, found a way to cause trouble many centuries after his anti-Jewish plots were thwarted. It is to Haman's deployment in interreligious rivalries and debates that we now turn.

7

Haman's Deployment: Four Contexts

IN ANTIQUITY, following some false starts and considerable disparagment, Haman gained legitimacy: *Esther* was canonized. In late antiquity, he underwent multiple transformations as scriptures were formed, read, and explained, until in the end Haman had accrued a résumé abundant in details and varied in interpretations. In fact, the richness of these traditions and the flexibility with which they were elucidated meant that when a "Haman" turned up in the Qur'ān, it was by no means clear whether or not this was the biblical character in yet another one of his guises. By the early Middle Ages, Haman and the myriad biographical details that he had accumulated were subjected to disciplined exegetical treatments by different schools of scriptural interpretation. Thus, by the time he had been absorbed and rationalized within the various Muslim contexts surveyed above, his development slowed down dramatically. Questions about him (and about *Esther*) had been answered, and most readers of Abrahamic scriptures had accepted that earlier scholars who studied Haman had authority that was superior to their own.[1]

This did not mean, however, that people began to pay less attention to Haman; in fact, he came to feature more frequently than ever before, albeit in different contexts and with different roles. In this chapter we examine how "Haman" became a byword for villainy among Jews, Christians, and Muslims. These religious communities had each settled on a corpus of authoritative opinions concerning him. But while this relatively stable repertoire of interpretations and exegetical elaborations could be recycled by later scholars, the late medieval and early modern periods (in virtually all lands where Haman was deemed of interest) witnessed the development of exegetical trends and strategies, some of which are of great significance to us: Protestant Christianity, for instance, challenged

Christian traditions to their very core and, as we will see below, Haman was to play interesting roles in the ensuing inner-Christian controversies.[2] In the Jewish world, the emergence and popularization of mystical trends such as Kabbalah mysticism engendered radically new ways of reading scripture (including *Esther*).[3] Whereas Protestants returned to exoteric literalism, Kabbalists produced esoteric readings of the sources, in which Haman was interpreted on multiple levels.[4]

To these developments may be added new roles and contexts for scripture's contents, enabled by the adoption of printing in Europe and the beginnings of globalization, both phenomena that enabled the production and circulation of Bibles more widely than ever before. The increasing popularity of public preachers led likewise to the proliferation of published sermons (in Christendom), and to the popularity of Purim-plays (in European Judaism, *Purimspiels*), Purim-parodies,[5] and commentaries on *Esther*, which manifest the many uses to which *Esther* and its villain were put. Thus, what we will encounter in what follows here are not additional "Hamans" but rather fascinating historical moments in which existing Hamans played leading roles. We will focus on four historical contexts of particular significance.

1) Haman in Inner-"Jewish" Rivalries.

As Haman was the prototypical enemy of Jews (and Judaism), to make polemical use of him one needed only to identify the Jews, on the one hand, and a figure who threatened them on the other. The second task was often simpler than the first. Already in *2 Maccabees*, the Haman-character was a Hellenized Jew, Menelaus. The debate there was not about who was threatening or not threatening the Jews, but rather who "the Jews" were. Such questions had arisen throughout Jewish history, of course. Let us examine two relevant controversies of this sort.

First, we return to the Rabbanite-Karaite rivalry. The exegetical tensions described above were not always reflected in inner-communal relations, as Rustow has forcefully argued,[6] and some Genizah documents portray Rabbanites and Karaites partaking in joint Purim celebrations (and in at least one instance they were joined by Muslims who enjoyed marking "Haman's" demise).[7] Similarly, Rabbanites and Karaites (as well as Muslims and Samaritans) were occasionally victimized by the same tyrannical functionary, whom they identified as "Haman."[8]

And yet, inner communal rivalries did occur and the "Haman" label would, on occasion, be used by one group of Jews to denigrate another. In 1030 Palestine, a rumor spread among Rabbanites that Karaites had burned effigies of three communal leaders on Purim (probably in response to a Rabbanite attempt the previous year to excommunicate Karaites).[9] In 1465, some Iberian Conversos who had arrived in Cairo faced the decision of whether to join a local Jewish Rabbanite or Karaite community. Their adoption of Karaite Judaism was celebrated in a triumphalist document modelled on *Esther*, in which the "evil" Rabbanite, Ibn al-Kashshāʿ, played the role of Haman.[10] From these examples we learn that Jews did not use "Haman" only with reference to those who identified as non-Jews, nor did they limit the term to viziers or other administrators considered to have acted unjustly towards them. Moreover, as both Rabbanites and Karaites read MT *Esther*, the label "Haman" in that particular arena will have been common to both sides of the dispute. For a radically different deployment of Haman among rival Israelites, we turn now to our second inner-Israelite context for Haman's troublemaking, namely Jewish-Samaritan rivalries.

In this case, the traffic was one-way, with Samaritans reimagining Haman to have been an evil Jewish vizier.[11] Jews did, of course, engage in centuries of bitter anti-Samaritan activities (mostly reflected in polemical writings),[12] and it may even be the case that the original historical context that is reflected in *Esther* relates in some way to a very early manifestation of the Jewish-Samaritan conflict: Dalley argued that the Purim festival originated in the Samaritan community of the seventh century (!) BCE,[13] while Zadok argued that the *Esther* story is a record of Samaritan-Jewish rivalry in the fifth century BCE.[14] Ezra 4:6 does in fact indicate that the Samaritans (whatever this term might mean in that context) sought to frustrate attempts to rebuild the Jewish Temple during the reign of Ahashwerosh, at whose court MT *Esther* is set.[15] Accordingly, early rabbinic exegetes explained that the scribe Shimshai, who is identified as one of the Samaritan petitioners against the Jews' plan to rebuild the Temple in Ezra 4, was Haman's son.[16] In the following chapter, we will consider Haman's origins. For now, it is sufficient to mention that in the fourteenth century CE, it was the Samaritan community that depicted Haman as a Jew.

The central text in this regard is the reworking of the *Esther* story by the Samaritan historian Abū al-Fatḥ ibn Abī al-Ḥasan (wr. 1356).[17] Written in Arabic and in the Muslim world, Abū al-Fatḥ's account reflects its Islamicate context. Thus, as with the classical Islamic acculturations of *Esther*, this version combines a historicization of the story with an attempt to rewrite it, introducing new characters while reimagining older ones, all with the goal of reconciling *Esther* with the native traditions of the Samaritans. Just as al-Ṭabarī removed Haman from the story and recast Ahashwerosh as an impressive Persian king (among other things), this Samaritan historian replaced the Jews with the Samaritans and Haman with a Jewish vizier. And just as Muslim writers included versions of

Esther in their works, despite the book's absence from their scriptures, Abū al-Fatḥ, too, brought a version into his *History*, even though Samaritans exclude *Esther* from their canon and Purim from their religious calendar.[18] Abū al-Fatḥ writes:[19]

> After Zoroaster the Magian[20] came king Ahashwerosh. And it was in his day that the Jews rebuilt Aelia, that is Jerusalem, by his command. *His vizier was a Jew, very skilled in sorcery, charms and natural magic. By these means he won over the heart of the king and provoked him to [attempt to] destroy the Samaritans.*[21] When the Samaritans became aware that the vizier sought their destruction, they looked into the matter. . . . When the edge had gone off his anger, and his violent emotion had subsided, he abandoned his planned action. So his vizier plotted with one of his servants to kill him. Yūṣadaq came to hear of this and told the consort (Arabic: *zawja*) of the king about it: Her name was Esther. When she learned about this she informed the king who had the truth of the matter looked into, and had the servant put to death. The vizier became very embittered by the death of the servant, and his hatred for them increased. So, he set about looking for [other] means of having them destroyed. Meanwhile, Yūṣadaq had won the hearts of the king's subjects. He attracted them to himself by his soft words and his kindness. He convinced them that he wished them well, by the purity of his intentions, by his greatness of soul and sublime zeal. He never set aside this gentle manner, even in his efforts to blot out all traces[22] of the intrigue that the king's vizier had nurtured in his heart, with the result that God granted his people a happy release from Ahashwerosh and his insolence.

Although it may come as no surprise that Abū al-Fatḥ adjusted *Esther*'s contents to conform to Samaritan historiographical notions, it was not inevitable that in this rewriting of the story the evil vizier would become a Jew. After all, Samaritans were not living under oppressive Jewish rulers (or Jewish rulers at all), so the only benefit in retelling the story in this way was to score points in a theological-historiographical rivalry with the Jews. In fact, even in Samaritan circles this recasting of Haman as a Jew does not appear to have gained popularity: An eighteenth-century Samaritan summary of *Esther*, whose author demonstrably knew Abū al-Fatḥ's work, chose to retell the story along MT lines, stating simply that "[The king] also had for his viceroy a man of the community of the Jews, whose name was Mordecai—Esther, the wife of the king at that time, being his niece. They did many favors to the community of the Jews who resided in the land of Canaan."[23] This author does not even mention Haman, let alone Judaize him.

Thus, unlike the Rabbanite-Karaite tensions, which saw "Haman" used as a codeword for some hated leader of the rival community, in the case of Jewish-Samaritan tensions, Abū al-Fatḥ was merely seeking to set the historical record straight.[24] And in neither of these inter-Jewish/Israelite rivalries was one side living under the political hegemony of the other, faced with a Haman-ic, tyrannical authority who represented the competing group. Rabbanites, Karaites, and Samaritans were *all* living in exile, and it was a Muslim or, more frequently, a Christian ruling authority who could wield the sort of capricious power that triggered Haman-ic associations. It is to such contexts that we now turn.

2) Haman in Jewish-Christian Rivalries.

Jews arguably fared better in most ways under Muslim rule than they did under Christian rule.[25] What this means for us, is that we are more likely to find Christian Hamans than Muslim ones, even though considerably more Jews lived in Islamdom than in Christendom (until relatively recently).

Islamic and Christian cultural contexts were perceptibly different, at least in the eyes of those Jews who were sufficiently well-placed to compare the two. In some cases, Jewish exegetes expressed their views on the contexts in which they lived through their interpretations of Ahashwerosh and Haman. Abraham Saba, for instance, analyzes the relative faults of these two characters as follows:

> Ahasuerus originated in Persia and Media, whose people were Ishmaelites, lacking in wisdom and science, counsel and speech and were a people unskilled in speaking. But Haman was a crafty villain from the family of Edom, possessors of wisdom and science. Edom was clever in every type of wisdom as it is written: "I will make the wise vanish from Edom" (Obad 8), like the wicked Esau, father of Edom, who was a skilled huntsman, clever in deception and unlike Jacob who was a simple person. Similarly, Haman was a slanderer who knew how to present his arguments properly and forcefully with boasting tongue and flattering lips to follow counsel. This also came to him from Esau, whose tongue was schooled in speaking clearly and smoothly in order to mislead his father and deceive him with his utterances. . . . Similarly, Haman would stalk Ahasuerus and seduce him with his carefully ordered speeches and smooth utterances which were softer than oil.[26]

As we will see below, Saba lived during a period of extreme Christian intolerance, but this did not prevent him from expressing his admiration for the persecutors' culture. As Jews used "Haman" to designate threatening political authorities, what matters to us Haman-hunters is that it is in Christian lands that the Haman label was deployed most frequently, impressive though Christian culture might have been.

2a) Muslim Exceptions to the Christian Rule

Jews faced Hamans in Muslim contexts, too. To the Genizah documents that identify oppressive Egyptian functionaries as Haman we may add the case of the Jews of Safavid Persia (1501–1737), who were forcibly converted to (Shīʿa) Islam during the reign of Shah Abbas II (r. 1642–66). While these forced conversions were part of a larger attempt to spread Shiism throughout Safavid lands, the poet Bābāʾī ibn Luṭf (d. 1662) still chose to refer to Muḥammad Beg, the Shah's Grand Vizier, as "Haman."[27] Compared to some of the other Hamans we will meet, the use of the label in this case was fairly accurate: after all, a Persian Grand Vizier did seek to eradicate Judaism in the Persian Empire. To whom else could the poet have compared Muḥammad Beg?[28]

Less accurate deployments of the Haman label are also found, albeit rarely, in Islamic contexts. In one case, in 1039, the famous Andalusian Jewish statesman and intellectual, Samuel ibn Naghrīla (Shmuel ha-Nagīd), composed a poem reporting the defeat of a competing Andalusian ruler in the context of the internal Muslim rivalries. Ibn Naghrīla, who served as vizier to the ruler of Granada, celebrated his side's victory in its war against the ruler of Almería, Zuhayr al-ʿĀmirī. In the poem, Ibn Naghrīla refers to Zuhayr as "Agag" (the title of Amalekite kings in the Bible), and to Ibn ʿAbbās—who sought Ibn Naghrīla's position as vizier—as "Haman."[29] Here again, the poet displays biblical literacy and consistency of thought: The Haman character is an evil vizier (rather than the king himself), and he is in the service of the Amalekites. And yet, Ibn ʿAbbās was hardly an anti-Jewish schemer: the entire episode concerns inner-Muslim rivalries, rather than a genocidal threat to the Jewish people.[30]

Another Muslim context in which the Haman label was deployed (albeit imperfectly) was the 1840 Damascus Affair, a well-known anti-Jewish blood libel. In this case, too, the arch-villain was referred to, inaccurately, as "Haman": The Haman-character was not a Muslim but a Christian (the French Count de Ratti Menton), and in any event, historians have concluded that the negative judgment of him is "a gross oversimplification."[31]

There was a qualitative difference in the Jewish experience of Hamans in Muslim lands as compared to the experience of their coreligionists in other regions, periods, and political contexts. Perhaps the best example of this difference is the

Cairo Purim established to celebrate the downfall of Aḥmad Pasha, who had rebelled against the Ottoman sultan Sulayman (r. 1520–66) in 1524.[32] In return for his support of the new sultan, Aḥmad Pasha had apparently expected to be appointed Grand Vizier. Instead, the sultan merely made him governor of Egypt, for which reason he rebelled, albeit unsuccessfully. Aḥmad Pasha was executed, and the local population—who had been extorted by Aḥmad Pasha to fund his rebellion—celebrated. The Jewish community produced a Judeo-Arabic version of the events modelled on *Esther*, which ends with the author comparing the rebel to "Haman the Amalekite."[33] Although one of Aḥmad Pasha's acts of rebellion was to mint coinage with his own name, and although the head of the local mint was a Jew by the name of Abraham Castro (who alerted the Ottoman authorities to the rebellious minting of this new local coinage), the episode was not about the Jews at all. They undoubtedly suffered (along with local Christians) during the rebellion: their property was confiscated and Aḥmad Pasha demanded an enormous sum of money from them (under the threat of violence). And yet, he was hardly an anti-Semitic vizier who plotted to exterminate the Jewish community. Half a millennium earlier, a greedy Egyptian tax-collector was called "Haman" in a document preserved in the Geniza, and according to Muslim traditions that date no later than the ninth century, the Qur'ānic Haman extorted the inhabitants of Pharaoh's Egypt. The villain of the Cairo Purim story may well have been compared to Haman, but what this meant in the medieval Egyptian context was not the genocidal, anti-Semitic Haman known to most other *Esther*-readers throughout history. A greater threat, with a greater connection to *Esther* and its villain, was to be found in centuries of forced conversions to Christianity in Iberia and the Inquisition(s) aimed at exposing insincere converts.

2b) Haman in Jewish-(New) Christian Rivalries

Although officially launched in 1478, the Spanish Inquisition followed centuries of similar initiatives, the broad context for which was the reconquest and re-Christianization of the Iberian Peninsula. This process began in the twelfth century and was concluded in the fifteenth century, with the mass expulsions of Jews and Muslims. (The Inquisition itself was abolished only in the early-nineteenth century.)

To understand Haman's relevance to these events, one must appreciate that *Esther* played a role of disproportionate significance among Conversos (pejoratively known as "Marranos"), who considered Esther to have been a crypto-Jew. Already Abraham Ibn Ezra (d. 1167) had associated Esther's concealing of her

Jewish identity (Esth 2:10) with the realities of Jewish life in Iberia at the end of the eleventh-century, during which Jews were exposed to both the Christian Reconquista and the arrival of the puritanical Muslim Almoravids (1040–1147) from North Africa.[34] As Lewis observes, the refusal of Jews to convert—either to Islam or to Christianity—was handled differently in culturally Christian lands, where martyrdom was the only option, than in culturally Muslim lands, where dissimulation, based on the Muslim ideas of *taqiyya* and *kitmān*—both roughly meaning "concealment"—was possible for those who wished to remain Jews.[35] Of course, the Inquisition was a Christian institution, but the fact that it took place in a region that had been shaped by Islamic traditions for over half a millennium meant that the dissimulation option was more readily accepted there. The Conversos, therefore, could draw on the precedent of the *Esther* story, and on the conduct of its heroine, to maintain both their Judaism and the optimistic hope that their story, too, would have a happy ending.[36]

Esther was also highly relevant to the Conversos because of the similarity between the peril faced by Jews in Haman's time and during the Inquisition: The Conversos were not exploited by an over-greedy tax-collector; the threat was more direct, aimed at the Jewish people and Judaism itself. And not only did the Jews in Haman's time emerge victorious, but the non-Jews Judaized (*mityahadim*, Esth 8:17), an ironic turn of events for those Jews who had been forced to Christianize.

For all these reasons, it is not surprising to find that Andalusian Jews referred to villains as "Haman." In his exegesis of the verse in which the non-Jews Judaize" Abraham Saba—who lived through the Inquisition—drew a parallel between Haman and the Christians of Iberia:

> Now this is what was supposed to happen to Israel out of fear of the wicked Haman, and there is no clearer proof of this than the attempt we have seen with our own eyes, by the Edomites [i.e., Christians] to do all kinds of things to the Jews to frighten and confuse them so that they would take pity on their children and convert. This was Haman's intention and the Lord, may He be blessed, overturned his plan so that the fear of Mordecai fell over the rebels and they declared themselves Jews.[37]

Similarly, in 1627, the Converso poet João Pinto Delgado rewrote *Esther* portraying Haman as an Inquisitor who sought to force the Jews to convert.[38] Delgado's poem alerts us to an interesting by-product of the crypto-Jewish experience, namely the exposure of Jews to Christian interpretations (and versions) of scripture. Already in the fourteenth and fifteenth centuries, Jews were forced to attend sermons in churches,[39] and crypto-Jews adopted Catholicism, whose Bible included the LXX version of *Esther*. Accordingly, Delgado's poem casually refers to Mordecai's dream,[40] and some aspects of Delgado's portrayal of Haman reflect Christian perceptions of the villain's character. For example, Delgado's Haman is greedy and lusts after wealth—unattractive traits, no doubt, but not the ones that had made Haman universally hated by Jews.[41] As we will see below, Haman's greed was commonly invoked polemically in inner-Christian rivalries, and Delgado is thus displaying the impact that Christian culture had on Conversos.

Alongside the obvious similarities between Haman and the Inquisitors,[42] we find Jews deploying Haman polemically against Jewish Conversos. In 1559, Benjamin ben Elnathan, an Italian Jewish moneylender, referred to the recent Converso Giovan Battista Buonamici (formerly, Aharon ben Menaḥem') as "the evil Haman." He writes:

> In the first days of his conversion, he made himself seem like a man who loved the people of Israel . . . but his heart was full of abominations, then he became an enemy of the Jews . . . and injured them with his speech. He was an evil man and an enemy like Haman who used his speech in a deceitful manner.[43]

The deployment of Haman with reference to Jewish traitors who adopted the dominant, non-Jewish culture brings to mind Second Temple texts in which philhellenic Jews (such as Menelaus) are portrayed as enemies of the Jews, at least as much as non-Jewish political rulers, and which serve as a bridge between those ancient contexts and modern ones in which Jews refer to co-religionist rivals as Haman.[44]

2c) Haman the Christian (again)

Benjamin ben Elnathan did not limit the Haman label to this treacherous (as he saw it) Converso. In his account of the Jews' suffering under Pope Paul IV, who, among other acts of anti-Semitism, confined Jews to ghettos and demanded they wear a yellow badge, he refers to the pope's nephew and counsellor, Cardinal Carlo Carafa, as "Haman." This Haman was accused of a series of violent acts against Jews, including rapes, murders, and thefts.[45] Thus, the same author applies the "Haman" label in two legitimate, yet very different ways: (1) The Converso made (false) accusations against the Jewish community (like Haman in Esth 3); and (2) the pope's counsellor was guilty of the sort of crimes that are attributed to Haman in late antique sources. The fact that the evil pope was called "the Amalekite" while his counsellor-vizier was equated with Haman, displays the author's careful and consistent application of the term in each case. This was not mere name-calling, but rather the deployment of a relevant label to people who fit descriptions of Haman.

Throughout history, the overwhelming majority of cases in which Jews labeled an antagonist "Haman" originated in Christian contexts. What is interesting here, though, is neither the frequency with which the label was used (lamentably, there was no lack of contenders for such vilification), nor the particularly Christian context (as stated, Muslim rulers were generally friendlier to their Jewish populations), but rather the fact that it was specifically Haman who was chosen to represent villainous characters. Haman was far and away the most popular choice, with Nimrod, Esau, Pharaoh, Nebuchadnezzar, and others much further down the list of evil-doers. Ancient and late antique Jews remembered the tyrannies of Titus and Nero, who could be represented as Antichrists, but medieval and early modern Jews apparently did not.

It is curious that the historical villain with whom Haman was compared was often the ruler himself rather than a high-ranking administrator; a comparison with Pharaoh or Nebuchadnezzar would have been at least as relevant, even for those Jews who had forgotten Titus and Nero.[46] As we have seen, in descriptions of Haman-ic villains in Second Temple sources, in the Qur'ān, and in early Islamic materials, these Hamans were in reality overshadowed by rulers such as Antiochus IV and Pharaoh (among others). This curious preference for the "Haman" label over other ancient tyrants persisted, however, into modern times: Saddam Hussein repeatedly compared himself to Nebuchadnezzar who, like him, ruled Iraq, and who, like him, sought to expel the Jews from their Holy Land,[47] but modern Jewish writers often consciously choose the Haman label for him.[48]

The list of Christian figures whom Jews labeled "Haman" is long, and scholars have collected as many examples as they could find,[49] dozens if not hundreds. From these a few general points are worth noticing. First, there is considerable variety in the use of the Haman label for describing particular hated officials. Thus, whereas some Jews used the label to describe the Russian Emperor Alexander III (r. 1881–1894), who oversaw the enactment of several anti-Jewish laws, other Jews referred to him as "Pharaoh," while reserving the Haman label for some of his leading functionaries (such as those who implemented the infamous May Laws of 1882).[50] Similarly, during the Crusades, some Western European Jews referred to their king as Haman, while others reserved the label for a particularly anti-Semitic functionary.[51]

Second, the label was wielded broadly to cover a wide range of villains accused of a wide range of anti-Jewish actions. It was not merely the very well-known anti-Jewish figures—such as the Cossack leader, Bohdan Khmelnytsky (d. 1657), who led a massacre of thousands of Jews in 1648–9,[52] or Adolf Hitler (and other Nazi leaders)—that were deemed to be the Hamans of their age,[53] but also minor figures whose memory History has barely bothered to preserve.

Third, the growing use of the label to describe Christian authorities was as much a result of technology as it was of the adverse historical circumstances in which Jews were living. The spread of printing and the resulting increase in rates of literacy in Europe, including biblical literacy, generated increased demand for exegetical works aimed at new readerships, and by the early modern period the Bible was a standard household item in Europe. The late-fifteenth century witnessed a proliferation of *Esther* commentaries, authored by both Jews and Christians, and the sixteenth century saw "a veritable explosion of commentaries on the Scrolls, including *Esther*," as one scholar put it.[54] Related to the mushrooming of *Esther* commentaries was the increasing popularity of public preachers, which combined with the foregoing trends to ensure that *Esther* and its villain would play greater roles among expanding populations and in more diverse contexts. In the sixteenth through the eighteenth centuries, public re-enactments of the *Esther* story (*Purimspiels*), which had long provided opportunities for venting anger and frustrations against oppressive ruling authorities through thinly veiled references to local functionaries,[55] included depictions of Haman wearing an ecclesiastical cross on his garments.[56]

While Jews undoubtedly deployed Haman to refer to Christian enemies from the earliest centuries of the Christian era, such deployments increased substantially with the passage of time, due to technological determinism and to the unhappy circumstances of Jewish life throughout Christendom. By the late Middle Ages, Christians were well aware of the phenomenon and, in some cases, even followed the Jews' example by using the Haman label against their own rivals.

3) Haman in Inner-Christian rivalries

While it is undoubtedly true—for reasons examined earlier—that *Esther* has played a more central role in Judaism(s) than it has in Christianity(ies), we must not forget that the book also is part of Christian scripture, which has two ramifications: First, Jewish comparisons of important Christians (from Jesus onwards) to Haman were effective not merely in a positive way for Jews (cathartically), but also in a negative way for Christians, who grasped the offensive implications of the label. Had Christians not cared about *Esther*, they would not have cared about being called "Haman." Second, Christians could legitimately deploy *Esther* and its villain with reference to their own Hamans. And although these Hamans tended to be other Christians, this was not always the case. To understand this latter point, we need to look at Christian responses to Jewish comparisons between Haman and Christ(ians).

3a) Christian responses to Jewish name-calling

Precisely because Haman was a biblical villain for Christians, too, the Jewish use of the Haman label for Christians (and Christ) stung. There are four ways in which specific Christians responded to the insult: (1) by outlawing it; (2) by turning it on its head; (3) by adopting it for oneself; and (4) by adopting it for use against other Christians. We will consider these in turn.

A) As early as 408, a Byzantine imperial law was promulgated that outlawed Purim celebrations on the grounds that it offended Christians to witness the public assaulting of an effigy of Haman, "in the shape of a holy cross in contempt of the Christian faith" (as discussed in Chapter 6). Some twelve centuries later, John Mayer forcefully argued that Jews should be forbidden from creating Christ-like effigies of Haman during their Purim celebrations, and we may legitimately assume that at other points in history Christians sought to ban public comparisons between Haman and Jesus. The demand to discontinue a deeply offensive practice of this sort is so intuitive that one would be surprised had it not been attempted everywhere the Haman-Christ comparison featured.

B) Given that "I am rubber, you are glue"-logic is transparent to even the youngest victims of schoolyard bullying, the decision on the part of some leading Christian scholars to argue that it is the *Jews* who are Haman may be an intuitive retort to the Jews who label Christ and Christians as "Haman." Turning the *Esther* story on its head is a legitimate exegetical strategy, which may promote a supercessionist theology. The fourth-century Persian sage Aphrahat deemed the repudiated queen Vashti to represent the repudiated Jews, who were to be replaced by Esther and the New Israel, respectively, while the ninth-century Rhabanus Maurus compared Vashti to the Synagogue and Esther with the Church.[57] Such maneuvers lean more towards theological argumentation than name-calling, and it is really only with Martin Luther and his follower John Brenz (d. 1570) that we get full-blooded, vitriolic interpretations of *Esther* that return the Haman label to the Jews, and that with interest.

In his *On the Jews and Their Lies* (written in 1543), Luther refers to the Jews and Haman in two passages. In the first, he writes:

> [T]hey also assign us our special share of slander. In the first place, they lament before God that we are holding them captive in exile, and they implore him ardently to deliver his holy people and dear children from our power and the imprisonment in which we hold them. They dub us Edom and Haman, with which names they would insult us grievously before God, and hurt us deeply.... They know very well that they are lying here. If it were possible, I would not be ashamed to claim Edom as my forefather... Moses himself commands them to regard Edom as their brother (Deut 23:71).[58]

Luther is familiar with the Jews' predilection for complaining about their treatment at the hands of Christians, whom they dub "Haman." To him, such accusations are slanderous and deeply offensive. By referring elsewhere to Haman as a "slanderer" (German: *Lästerer*)[59] Luther was implicitly equating the Jews with Haman. In the following chapter (Part XI, the most famous section of this work), Luther adds the following:

> And even if the Jews could give the government such sums of money from their own property, which is not possible, and thereby buy protection from us, and the privilege publicly and freely to slander, blaspheme, vilify, and curse our Lord Jesus Christ so shamefully in their synagogues, and in addition to wish us every misfortune, namely, that we might all be stabbed to death and perish with our Haman, emperor, princes, lords, wife, and children—this would really be selling Christ our Lord, the whole of Christendom together with the whole empire, and ourselves, with wife and children, cheaply and shamefully. What a great saint the traitor Judas would be in comparison with us!

In this passage, Luther implies that the Jews equate Haman with Jesus, and that allowing them to do so would make Christians worse than Judas. Just as Luther elsewhere expressed his opposition to *Esther*, here he opposes Purim, which should not be tolerated, no matter how much money the Jews offer for the privilege.

As for Brenz, he contributes two of his own opinions as to the relationship between the Jews and Haman. First, he disparages the Jews for celebrating Purim, saying that they "marvellously please themselves" when reading *Esther* and that, "should any magistrate handle them sharply and drive them out of his borders, they give him the name of [H]aman, and they hope that they may be allowed to take revenge on their enemies, that is, the Christians, among whom they live."[60] Clearly, Brenz, like Luther, was aware of the common Jewish practice of labeling their enemies "Haman." Second, Brenz boldly states that the Jews' pursuit of Christians, who are the "true Israelites," resembles Haman's pursuit of the Jews in *Esther*. For this reason, the Jews have become "the cousins and kindred of Haman the Amalekite."[61]

Just as Karaite and Rabbanite Jews labeled each other "Haman," and just as medieval Samaritans retold *Esther* with a Jew as the Haman-ic character, Brenz argued that the Jews had become the Hamans for persecuting the New Israel. The difference here, however, is that whereas Karaites, Rabbanites, or Samaritans labeled *individual* Jews "Haman," Brenz labeled every single Jew as a representative of "the kindred of Haman."

C) Perhaps even more surprising than Brenz's innovation was the decision on the part of some Jew-haters to embrace the Haman-ic label, presumably because in each case the oppressor identified more with Haman's hatred of Jews than he did with the historical-theological messages imparted in *Esther*. As a book that celebrates the triumph of Jews over their enemies, *Esther* has not endeared itself to anti-Semites, who express their rejection of it by ironically associating themselves with the story's villain. Two examples stand out. First is Vincenz Fettmilch, a baker and grocer, who led an uprising of local guilds in Frankfurt (1612–1616) that was economic in nature. Within the broader context of this uprising, he also targeted Jews (who were market competitors and hated for being usurers), and in 1614 an anti-Jewish pogrom led to the death of two Jews, the plundering of over a thousand more, and the expulsion of the Jews of Frankfurt. In 1616, the uprising was quashed, Fettmilch was publicly executed, and the Jews who had been expelled were allowed to return. The local Jewish community instituted "Purim Vincenz" (or, "Purim Fettmilch") to commemorate the events, thereby equating the villain of Frankfurt with the villain of *Esther*. In this case, however, Fettmilch beat the Jews to it, as he had earlier gloated to the city's Jews that he was their Haman![62] Second, and more controversial, is Hitler's (and other leading Nazis') self-identification with Haman, with Haman's genocidal plot, or with Haman's eventual demise (Julius Streicher shouted "Purimfest!" as he was led to the gallows).[63] Such examples of openly embracing the Haman label are rare, but they are important to us both for the high profiles of the self-identifying Hamans, and for their indication that non-Jews in Christian Europe (I do not wish to categorize Hitler as a Christian)[64] were aware of the Jewish deployment of the Haman slur.

D) The final stage in the Christian reaction to the Haman label was their adoption of the slur for their own polemical purposes. The outstanding example of this was the Protestant deployment of the *Esther* framework generally, and of the Haman label particularly, within the context of their rivalry with Roman Catholicism. In this case, the accidents of history again played an instrumental role in Haman's career. Protestants exploited increasingly efficient printing and the rise in European literacy rates to disseminate their interpretations of the Bible, and this included turning Haman into a tool wielded against political and religious rivals. Although the Protestants' adoption of *Esther* for polemical use was constrained by Martin Luther's open hostility to the book and by the fact that the Protestants did not subscribe to the Catholic equation of Esther with Mary (thereby depriving *Esther* of a Christological framework),[65] they nonetheless repeatedly deployed *Esther* in their battles against the Pope and the Catholic Church.[66]

Underpinning the early modern wars of religion in Europe and the anti-monarchic movements in subsequent centuries was the idea that old elites (religious, political, or, often, a combination of the two) might be challenged, especially when their conduct is morally deficient.[67] Because many seventeenth century Europeans saw the world through a biblical lens, grafting political rivalries onto *Esther* was an effective way of making (and scoring) points. What *Esther* had going for it was its subtly anti-monarchic tone, its overtly critical attitude towards ambitious courtly functionaries, and its pious heroes who were willing to stand up to the tyrannical authorities (at the risk of their own lives) in order to effect positive change to "the system." Such a narrative framework could ring relevant to virtually all the revolutionary parties and movements that arose between the sixteenth and nineteenth centuries in Europe, and later the Americas.[68] Scholars have produced detailed studies of the many characters labeled "Haman" throughout these centuries, but here we will focus on a single, significant example of the phenomenon.[69]

The Protestant-Catholic rivalry is interesting inter alia for the fact that each read a different version of *Esther*: Whereas Catholics knew some version of LXX *Esther*, Martin Luther translated the MT version into German (even though he had grown up with the LXX and its additions). Seeing as the LXX's Haman differs considerably from the MT's, the Haman insult used by one side would likely have been understood differently by the target of the insult on the other side.

Despite their use of MT *Esther*, and despite their championing of *sola scriptura* (scripture alone), there is evidence that Protestants were aware of both the Additions to *Esther* and Jewish midrashim on the story.[70] The latter point is particularly relevant for the Jewish equation of Haman with Rome in late antiquity.[71] The idea that Haman was a Roman dovetailed nicely with Protestant opposition to papal authority, and the French Protestant Pierre Merlin (d. 1603) had already equated the pope with Haman, while in a 1624 sermon the Calvinist priest Thomas Taylor referred to "Romish Amalek."[72]

In early-seventeenth-century England, the Protestant adoption of the *Esther* framework was, above all, related to the failed Gunpowder Plot. In 1605, English Catholics attempted to blow up the Houses of Parliament, assassinate the king, and restore the Catholic monarchy. The plot was unsuccessful and its leaders were publicly executed, a triumph whose celebration was widely related to Purim in writings and sermons delivered over the next two centuries. Already in 1609, Thomas Cooper wrote *The Churches deliuerance, contayning meditations vppon the Booke of Hester* (sic!), in which he equated the papists and Amalekites, while in 1626 George Hakewell published a pamphlet that made very much the same parallels between Haman's machinations and the Gunpower Plot. Such comparisons served as the basis for sermons as late as 1848.[73] And although there was no consensus on which particular conspirator in the Gunpowder Plot best represented Haman,[74] the relevance of the comparative framework was not questioned.

The polemical deployment of the Haman label within inner-Christian rivalries in the early modern period was thus varied and widespread. In the most general terms, these diverse contexts shared two attributes: First, the character labeled Haman was almost always a figure of high political status and/or immense wealth and influence. Second, the villainy attributed to these Hamans was usually related to their (illegitimate) access to the corridors of power and their abuse of their ill-achieved influence. Put another way, the Haman wielded politically by early modern Christians more closely resembled the disloyal, politically scheming Haman of the LXX than the genocidal Haman of the MT, even though many of the Christians who deployed Haman in such contexts were acquainted with a version of MT *Esther*.

The exceptionally broad remit of Haman's inter- and intra-faith troublemaking in the medieval and early modern periods is striking, especially when we consider the dozens of other biblical villains there were to choose from, both in the HB and the NT and in countless exegetical elaborations on both scriptures. Perhaps what made Haman so attractive a candidate for such polemical roles was the fact that he was a failed villain whose bite never came close to matching his bark.[75] Referring to one's enemy as "Haman" could be at once offensive to the recipient of the slur and strike a note of hope for the author who chose the term, thereby identifying with the party that would ultimately triumph.

Haman features in one interreligious polemical context in which the stakes were considerably higher than any encountered so far. For this, we return to the Middle Ages, where some Christian readers of the Qur'ān used Haman as a tool with which to destroy not merely God's chosen people, but God Himself—by attacking His book, the Qur'ān.

4) Haman in Christian-Muslim Rivalries

In the late eighth century, Theophilus referred to the Arab-Muslim conquerors as "Amalekites," and in his famous 1095 speech at Clermont, Pope Urban II equated the wars against the Muslims with wars against Amalek.[76] Otherwise, however, Christians do not appear to have come close to using "Haman" as an insult aimed at Muslims.[77]

Similarly, Muslim authors did not wield the Haman label against Christians: In fact, rather curiously, when Muslims used "Haman" polemically, it was with reference to other Muslims: To the examples adduced earlier,[78] we may add Shīʿa texts that compare the first two caliphs, Abū Bakr and ʿUmar (whom Shīʿa Muslims despised for depriving ʿAlī and Muḥammad's family, generally, of the right to rule) to Pharaoh and Haman, respectively. This comparison is in evidence both for Twelver and for Ismāʿīlī Shīʿa writers.[79] But on the whole, Haman was not the historical villain Muslims used to insult their rivals. It was not until the second half of the twentieth century that Muslims rediscovered Haman's value as a polemical weapon, a rediscovery that is largely owed to Christian deployments of (the Qur'ānic) Haman to disprove the Islamic belief in the Qur'ān's divine origins.

4a) Haman in Anti-Qur'ānic Polemics

In the ninth century, al-Jāḥiẓ was aware of Christian arguments against the Qur'ān's placement of Haman at Pharoah's Egyptian court, rather than at Ahashwerosh's Persian one. By whatever means—and perhaps independent of this—medieval Christian readers of the Qur'ān raised similar objections to the Qur'ān's accuracy by making similar arguments about Haman's depiction within it.[80] The earliest recorded example of this objection comes from the writings of Pedro de la Cavalleria (d. 1464), a (sincere) Jewish convert to Christianity, who wrote polemics against "Jews, Saracens, and [other] Infidels." These polemics included the following point about Haman's appearances in the Qur'ān:

> This madman makes Haman to be contemporary with Pharaoh, which how falsely and ignorantly it is said, all who understand the Holy Scriptures can declare; and he and his followers, like beasts, must be silent.[81]

De la Cavalleria's reference to Muḥammad as a madman is not surprising, both because of the polemical nature of his work, and because the Prophet's own Meccan opponents referred to him as such (e.g., Q 15:6). Less offensive in tone, but no less convinced of the erroneous historical context in which Haman features in the Qur'ān, was Father Ludovico Marraccio, confessor to Pope Innocent XI, who published his annotated translation of the Qur'ān (into Latin) in the late-seventeenth century. Marraccio states:

> Mahumet (sic!) has mixed up Sacred Stories. He took Haman as an adviser of Pharaoh whereas in reality he was adviser of Ahasuerus, King of Persia. He also thought that Pharaoh ordered construction for him of a lofty tower from the top of which he could see the God of Moses which if true would be inferior to him. There is no doubt that he borrowed the story of this tower from the story of the Tower of Babel. It is certain that in the Sacred Scriptures there is no such story of the Pharaoh. Be that as it may, [Mahumet] has related a most incredible story.[82]

Along similar lines, George Sale (d. 1736), the first translator of the Qur'ān into English, states concerning the Qur'ān's Haman:

> This name is given to Pharaoh's Chief Minister, from which it is generally inferred that Muḥammad has here made Haman, the favourite of Ahasueres, King of Persia, and who indisputably lived many ages after Moses, to be that Prophet's contemporary. But how-probable-so-ever this mistake may seem to us, it will be hard, if not impossible to convince a Muḥammadan of it.

Subsequently, Henri Lammens (d. 1937), a Christian clergyman and scholar of Islam, called the Pharaonic context in which Haman appears in the Qur'ān "the most glaring anachronism," while Eisenberg stated: "That Muḥammad placed Haman in this period betrays his confused knowledge of history."[83] With the passing of time, scholars have been more reserved (and less offensive) in their assessment of the relationship between the two Hamans: Vajda, for instance, describes the Qur'ānic Haman as "a person whom the Ḳur'ān associates with Pharaoh (*Fir'awn*) because of a still unexplained confusion with the minister of Ahashwerosh in the Biblical *Book of Esther*."[84] What these scholars hold in common are three ideas: That *Esther* and the Qur'ān refer to the same Haman; that *Esther*'s Haman is the original one, against whom the Qur'ān's Haman is to be compared; and that the Qur'ān's Haman is therefore out of place (both geographically and temporally).

Why should any of this matter? There are, after all, dozens of differences of many sorts between the Bible and the Qur'ān. What makes the Haman question so significant is the fact that, for over half a millennium, European (mostly Christian) scholars have highlighted the issue to prove that there is a historical inaccuracy in the Qur'ān. And while Christians and Jews do not like it when scholars challenge the historicity of their scriptures, such challenges are considerably more threatening for Muslims who regard the Qur'ān as the *proof* of Islam and of the legitimacy of its final Prophet. Thus, the identification of even one historical error in the Qur'ān—say, the placing of an Achaemenid functionary in Pharaonic Egypt—would undermine the very foundations of Islam.

It is hardly surprising, therefore, that Muslim scholars (and some quasi-scholars) have attempted to refute all three assumptions. (1) The idea that *Esther* and the Qur'ān deal with the same Haman was challenged by scholars writing in the early 1980s, who found Egyptian characters who resembled the Qur'ānic Haman, thereby allowing for a dissociation between the Qur'ānic and biblical Hamans.[85] (2) If the Qur'ān's Haman referred to an ancient Egyptian functionary, then *Esther*'s Haman was not the "original" villain by this name (if anything, he postdated the Qur'ān's Haman historically). (3) Therefore, the Qur'ān's Haman was not out of place in his Pharaonic context. By the time the *Encyclopaedia of the Qur'ān* published its entry on Haman in 2002, Johns simply stated that there is "no reason, other than the paradigmatic one of hostility to the Israelites, to make any direct connection between [the Qur'ānic Haman] and the eponymous minister of Ahashwerosh referred to in *Esther*. . . ."[86] Had that been the end of the story, it would have been judged a resounding validation for Islam: The danger to the very proof of the religion, the infallibility of its final Prophet, and the divine origins of its scripture, would have been averted. The story does not end there, however, and—with the help of a lapsed Christian doctor—Muslim internet warriors turned defense into offence in a fascinating twist on Haman's adventures in interfaith rabble-rousing.

4b) Haman in pro-Qur'ānic Polemics.

In 2012, a distressed, Arabic-speaking Muslim, who was exposed to Christian arguments about Haman's supposedly erroneous appearances in the Qur'ān, turned to a Muslim scholar in an online help forum for assistance. The scholar assuaged his respondent by pointing out, first, that the arguments were wrong; second, that Jews in the time of the Prophet heard the verses about Haman and—in the case of 'Abdallāh ibn Salām—eventually converted to Islam (rather than rejecting it on account of Haman's appearance alongside Pharaoh); and third, that Haman's appearance in the Qur'ān is proof of the Qur'ān's divine origins.[87]

To explain this third point, we turn to another (apparent) convert to Islam, Dr. Maurice Bucaille (1920–1998), a French physician to Middle Eastern rulers and an amateur (though well-published) Egyptologist. Bucaille discovered that a functionary in ancient Egypt by the name of "Ha-amen" was associated with building projects, a fact that came to light only after hieroglyphs were deciphered in 1822. It would be impossible, he reasoned, for a seventh-century Arabian to know about this functionary, and yet he appears in the Qur'ān as "Haman." For Bucaille this impossibility was proof that the Qur'ān is divine and is said to have contributed to his decision to convert to Islam.[88]

That the Qur'ānic Haman came to be the character who proved (for some) the existence of God, brings him into line with the biblical Haman in an important way, as both Hamans represent charmingly ironic reversals. Having built an incredibly tall gallows by which to hang Mordecai, *Esther*'s Haman was hung from the very same gallows. And having built an incredibly tall tower to the heavens by which to disprove the existence of God, the Qur'ānic Haman played a central role in contemporary Muslim efforts to demonstrate the divinity of the Qur'ān.[89]

Conclusions

In some ways, Haman's appearance in hundreds of historical contexts is simple to understand. As each of the scriptures read by Jews, Christians, and Muslims features an evil character by the name of "Haman," it is hardly surprising that scripturally literate people would make use of this paradigm of villainy to refer to their opponents. Readers who have slogged through the foregoing pages only to discover that "Haman was deemed to be a bad guy," may be forgiven for feeling short-changed by this anticlimactic conclusion.

However, as I have argued in this chapter, it is not the mere fact of Haman's frequent deployment that is interesting (although the preference for Haman over other villains is curious). Rather, what is striking is the variety of ways in which Haman has been deployed and, indeed, the variety of Hamans whom we have encountered, often in unexpected places. Jews called oppressive functionaries "Haman" because the Haman of MT *Esther* was such, but they could also use this label with reference to other Jews (Rabbanites, Hellenizers, or Conversos). Jews in Muslim lands referred to greedy tax-collectors as "Hamans," while the "Hamans" of Jews living in Christendom could be far more destructive in their intentions (which matched those of the MT's Haman) and actions (which far exceeded those of the MT's Haman). And, more often than not, Jews referred to antagonistic (usually Christian) functionaries as "Haman," some of whom repaid the debt by turning the slur back on the Jews, while others might even embrace it.

Christians, by contrast, balked at making full use of *Esther* in political contexts. This is both because of the book's uneasy reception from the earliest centuries of Christian history, and because the exilic power dynamic that had led Jews to denigrate their overlords as Hamans did not usually apply to Christians. And yet, the Protestant Reformation pitted an "oppressed" New Israel against the old, tyrannical elites represented (in their view) by the Catholic Church and the Pope. And despite the antagonism of Martin Luther and many of his followers toward *Esther*, the relevance of the story to the Protestant experience, and the ready-made batch of Jewish traditions equating Haman with Rome, encouraged Protestant preachers and authors to overcome the frosty reception with which *Esther* was received and to make extensive use of the Haman label.

We have also seen that the nature of Haman's villainy differed in each context: For early modern Christians, Haman was often a scheming courtier with illegitimate access to the corridors of power, which he exploited in unjust ways. This view of the villain most closely echoes the LXX's Haman (even if Protestants, in theory, did not read that version). By contrast, the Jews of Islamdom encountered Hamans who were over-greedy local functionaries (occasional exceptions notwithstanding), while the Jews of Christendom encountered anti-Semitic antagonists who most closely resembled the Haman of the MT. Muslims, for their part, rarely labeled their rivals "Haman" and when they did so it was not a Haman based on *Esther* but the Qur'ānic character who was overshadowed by the far more (in)famous Pharaoh whom Haman served. As Shīʿa Muslims often experienced a sort of exilic existence, living as minorities under the rule of Sunnīs, they, too, made occasional polemical use of Haman, always with reference to other Muslims. Despite Haman's relatively modest status in the Islamic hierarchy of villainy, modern Muslims have deployed Haman polemically (and counter-polemically) in contexts whose importance far outweighs previous uses of Haman—judging both by the sheer numbers of participants on either side of the debate, and by the significance of the issues at hand.

Not bad for a tragic villain who, in *Esther*, never harmed anyone.

PART III

Haman's Life

8

Haman's DNA

Introduction

That Haman features in scriptures ensured that he would enjoy centuries of exegetical and scholarly attention (as discussed in Part I). This attention, and specifically the fact that he could be remembered as anything from a pantomime villain to a role model for threatening tyrants (as seen in Part II), meant that for over two millennia Haman has been important. And while this importance has benefited us by motivating the production of many interesting historical and exegetical sources, it also poses challenges—specifically when we consider Haman's biography critically, as we will seek to do now, in Part III.

In the following chapters, we examine aspects of Haman's pre-scriptural background, his family, career, and death. Our interpretation of Haman's life throughout these chapters will be affected, more than anything else, by the contents of the present chapter, in which we consider whether Haman existed as a historical character. What complicates our inquiry into his pre-scriptural background is that its conclusions will have implications for billions of people: We have seen that the debate over Haman's portrayals in the Bible and the Qur'ān became no less than a debate over the veracity of these scriptures and their divine origins. With more immediate consequences for this book's readers, the question of Haman's historicity bears on all other details of his biography: Will we encounter a real person's family members or a cast of literary characters who served as supporting actors in a historical novel? Are traditions about Haman's career or demise imagined details about a fictional character, or memories—faint though they may be—of historical events?

Considering the importance of the topic, it is not surprising that there have been numerous approaches to it over the centuries. It is not merely that some have adopted an internal, "believers" perspective (according to which, all that the Bible or Qur'ān says about Haman is accurate and meaningful), while others have adopted an external, "critical" perspective (according to which, Haman is the make-believe product of ancient Israelites/Jews who sought to justify carnivalesque Purim celebrations). As we will see, there is an expected variety of answers to the question of Haman's pre-scriptural origins, as well as the unexpected possibility that the internal and external perspectives are far closer to one another than might be imagined.

Where, then, did Haman come from?

Scripture's answer(s)

The Hebrew and Greek Bibles tell us directly, and the Qur'ān indirectly, where Haman originated. MT *Esther* refers to him as an "Agagite," an epithet that, from a biblical perspective, relates Haman to the Amalekites. The latter appear earlier in the Bible as ancient tribes, inimical to the Israelites, who lived in the vicinity of Canaan, perhaps specifically in the Negev (Num 13:29). As descendants of Amalek, son of Eliphaz, son of Esau, son of Isaac (Gen 36:12), the Amalekites were Semites and distant relatives of the Israelites. Why Haman's father and ten (named) sons had Indo-Iranian names—a fact that would likely have been noticed, even if not in those terms, by *Esther*'s ancient Jewish-Persian audiences—is an interesting question, but one that did not pose difficulties for later generations of readers. After all, Mordecai and Esther also had foreign-sounding names (in the case of Esther, alongside her Hebrew name, Hadassah; Esth 2:7), and in any event, the biblical Table of Nations and modern philologists had different conceptions of the Semitic, Hamitic, and Japhetic ethnic families.[1] The MT's Haman has a clear backstory, which can be traced all the way to Adam, and which potentially endowed him with enormous significance for Jewish historiography from the very moment he was born into Amalekite royalty.

The Greek versions refer to Haman not as an Agagite but as a Bougean and specify that he was a Macedonian.[2] This latter reference may be an effort to connect Haman to Alexander the Macedonian, who put an end to Achaemenid rule (which, as Add E:14 explicitly states, was Haman's goal); to the generally unfavorable view that Jews in Ptolemaic Egypt had of Macedonians;[3] or to specific Macedonian rivals of the Jews, such as Flaccus (the Roman prefect of Egypt from 33 to 38 CE, during which time there were anti-Jewish riots in Alexandria).[4] Each of these interpretations of "Macedonian" has merit, and we may simply acknowledge that readers of *Esther* in Greek gave Haman a different backstory from the one offered in MT *Esther*.

As for "Bougean," we cannot be certain whether this epithet relates to Haman's origins at all (and most interpreters have in fact opted to read the term as an adjective, meaning "braggart").[5] However, Wechsler has astutely noted that the Greek form of the term suggests that it is actually a gentilic, implying that it indicates Haman's ethnicity rather than some aspect of his character. (The fact that "Bougean" appears in the Greek versions where "Agagite" appears in the Hebrew ones supports the theory that it is, in fact, a gentilic). Wechsler argues that this epithet connects Haman to the Beja tribe of south-eastern Egypt and areas of modern Sudan and Eritrea, infamous in Ptolemaic times (when *Esther* was rendered into Greek) for their warlike and inimical qualities.[6]

Regarding these non-Agagite options, we may add two points. First, as noted, some manuscripts of AT *Esther* contain the epithet "Gogite" in lieu of "Bougean." If this is read as a conscious decision to connect Haman to the people of Gog (and Magog), as opposed to a scribal misreading of *gwgy* instead of *bwgy*, for instance, it would imply that Haman was a northern barbarian of eschatological significance. Second, in addition to telling us what Haman *was* ethnically, the Greek versions also stress what he was *not*, namely a Persian.[7] Add E:10 in the LXX has Haman as "a foreigner to the blood of the Persians," whereas the AT calls him "a stranger to the *thinking* of the Persians" (which also indicates outsider status in Zoroastrianism, where the motto is "good thoughts, good words, good deeds").[8] Jewish and Christian readers of *Esther* are thus provided with ready-made answers to the question of Haman's pre-*Esther* background. And while these answers are clearly significant for readers and interpreters of each version of *Esther*, perhaps the most significant distinction to be drawn is between those readers of *Esther* who attached importance to Haman's ethnicity on the one hand, and those (such as Hellenized Jews and, later, Christians) on the other, who prioritized spiritual bonds over physical ones.

Muslims also replaced family and tribal affiliations with spiritual ones.[9] Furthermore, the Prophet himself belonged to the same Quraysh tribe that initially opposed him, and whose surviving members eventually embraced Islam, meaning that there remained no Amalekite foil to the Muslim *ummah*. Therefore, the Qur'ānic Haman was not described with reference to his ancestors, but rather to the company he kept, and this company—comprising Pharaoh and Korah—was Egyptian, or at least Egypt-based. Whether or not the Qur'ānic Haman *originated* in Egypt is not stated, leaving a biographical gap that centuries of exegetes, historians, and storytellers would attempt to fill.

Authoritative Interpretations of Haman's Origins

A: Muslim Traditions

Although the Qur'ānic references to Haman imply that he was active in, if not native to Egypt, and although Haman's Egyptian identity has played oversized roles in centuries of debate over the divine origins of the Qur'ān itself, most premodern Muslim authors held that Haman was a native of lands far to the east of Egypt—more often than not, specifically Iranian lands. For instance, the eleventh-century polymath al-Bīrūnī relates that Haman was a native of Tustar (or: Sushtar), a village just outside of Susa—that is to say, roughly where *Esther* places him.[10] Many other premodern Muslims, however, specified that he hailed from the easternmost regions of Iran and even beyond, suggesting such options as Balkh (Bactria), Sarakhs (northeastern Iran), the Khurasan region (modern Afghanistan) generally and within it the town of Būshanj specifically.[11] Two points of interest emerge from this data, the one obvious, the other subtle. The obvious point is that despite Haman's appearance in the Qur'ān in Pharaoh's Egypt, premodern Muslim authors, unlike their modern co-religionists, sought to place Haman (back) in Iran. The subtle point is that authors who related Haman to eastern Iran and Khurasan may have been tapping into cultural associations of this region that circulated in pre- and early-Islamic times. As noted, the *Shāhnāmeh*'s "Hōmān" was a bloodthirsty Ṭūrānian general, which places him geographically to the east of Iran's borders, in Central Asia, and culturally on the opposing side of the Iranian heroes of the Persian national epic. By tracing Haman's roots to the Ṭūrānian lands, these Muslim authors, (most of whom were themselves natives of what is today Iran) were associating him with the Persian equivalent of the Amalekites.

Perhaps even more interesting than these Ṭūrānian echoes, is the fact that eastern Iran, and specifically Khurasan, was the region from which eschatological hordes would emerge in the End of Times, as part of the apocalyptic events described repeatedly in the Qur'ān and in Prophetic traditions (ḥadīth). According to one "authenticated" (*ṣaḥīḥ*) tradition, the Prophet said: "The Antichrist (*dajjāl*) will emerge from a land in the East called Khurasan and he will be followed by peoples whose faces are like hammered shields."[12] By contrast, another such tradition predicts that the Antichrist will emerge from the Iranian town of Isfahan and be followed by seventy-thousand Jews wearing prayer-shawls.[13] A less trustworthy, though well-known tradition, quotes the Prophet as having stated that, "Black banners will come from Khurasan, and nothing shall turn them back until they are planted in Jerusalem."[14] The point here is not that anyone hailing from Isfahan, eastern Iran, or Khurasan was necessarily seen as a chaos-agent, but rather that the Far East in Islamic tradition played a role comparable to that of the Far North in ancient Jewish and Christian traditions. We have noted that when Haman is labeled a "Gogite" in versions of AT *Esther*, the term may relate to Second Temple depictions of Hamanic villains as northern barbarians, who are associated with the chaos-agents of Gog and Magog in Ezek 38–39. In its treatment of these eschatological events, however, the Qur'ān (18:90–100) turns the eschatological map ninety degrees clockwise, with Gog and Magog (Arabic: *ya'jūj wa ma'jūj*) prophesied to emerge from the *East*.

That (Qur'ānic) Haman's eastern provenance in these sources is indebted to Jewish traditions about (biblical) Haman is indicated by a detail that occurs in the Muslim sources on Haman's pre-Pharaonic background. Both those scholars who place Haman in Balkh and those who place him in Būshanj add the fact that he worked as a baker. We have noted that late antique Jewish midrashim associate Haman with the sale of bread, a datum that bears no apparent importance for descriptions of Haman and appears to be little more than wordplay on his name.[15] The traffic could flow in both directions, of course,[16] and in at least one case it would appear that a Muslim idea about Haman's origins made its way into Jewish sources. Both the early-Islamic-era *Targum Sheni* and a seventeenth-century Judeo-Arabic commentary on *Esther* from Morocco refer to Haman as having been an Indian. Although there is no identifiably Muslim tradition that places Haman in India, there are two reasons to see this idea as originating outside of Jewish tradition.[17] First, seeing as the opening verse of *Esther* describes India as the easternmost region of the Achaemenid Empire, an association between Haman with the Far East would conform with the Muslim ideas that we have just discussed.[18] Second, virtually all of the Jewish traditions concerning Haman's origins place him not to the east of Susa, but to the west, in lands associated with Christianity, as we will now see.

B: Jewish Traditions

In the foregoing chapters, we have encountered Jewish conceptions of Haman's pre-*Esther* origins. The dominance of MT *Esther* in Jewish circles from late antiquity onwards has privileged the Agagite epithet and its Amalekite associations over all others, which should in theory leave little scope for debate over Haman's background, the main question being which contemporary nation (if any) represented the Amalekites, and which inimical functionary represented Haman.[19] We have also seen that the late antique rabbinic equation of Amalek with Edom and, hence, with the Romans, produced the idea that Haman was a Roman or a Christian. Such ideas were shared by Jews in Byzantine and in Sasanid lands, albeit for different reasons. And just as "Agagite" required explicit interpretation as "Amalekite," and "Amalekite" required explicit interpretation as "Roman" or "Christian," these labels would themselves be interpreted, allowing us to zoom into Haman's origins with an even sharper focus. Hence, beyond the general Roman-Christian label, we hear that Haman was from the Galilee region of the Holy Land, particularly the towns of Bet Shean/Scythopolis, Kfar Qarnos/Qarnayim (Krenos), or Kfar Qarṣum.[20] These traditions may be based on a specific significance that these towns held at the time, or on wordplay that connects a town's name with Haman's villainy: Kfar Qarnos may signal "horns," with their demonic associations (the word for "horn" in both Hebrew and Aramaic is derived from the same *q-r-n* root; see Rev 13:11), while Kfar Qarṣum may signal Haman's role as an "accuser" (the Aramaic term for which is derived from the same *q-r-ṣ* root).[21] The Muslim conquest of the Holy Land, however, dissociated the region from its Edomite-Roman identity. In place of Haman's identity as a Roman Christian, it became commonplace to assume that Haman was an Armenian Christian.

Haman's Armenian identity has the benefit of keeping him both Christian and Amalekite. That Armenia and its people are associated with Christianity needs no elaboration,[22] and here it is worth dwelling briefly on the Jewish tendency to identify the Armenians with the Amalekites. It has long been assumed that the Armenian-Amalekite identification originated with the tenth century author of *Sefer Yosippon*, an assumption adopted by Horowitz, who connected its origins to the political strength of the Armenians in the tenth century.[23] There are, however, reasons to assume that the idea is considerably earlier than this, and was shared by Christians and perhaps some Muslims as well.

To begin with, in the late-eighth century, following a failed Armenian revolt against the Abbasid caliphs, Shapuh Amatuni and his son, along with some twelve thousand followers, fled Armenia for the Byzantine Empire. Notable for us is that Shapuh's son was named "Haman" (or "Hamam"), and the principality they founded in 790 was called "Hamam's Hamlet" (Armenian: *Hamamshen*).[24] This may not be where the story begins, however. Around the same time, in the first half of the ninth-century, a leading Byzantine general by the name of "Manuel the Armenian" was accused of seeking to overthrow the Byzantine Empire (even taking refuge in Abbasid lands for one year in 829). This Manuel was routinely dubbed "Manuel the Amalekite," a reference either to the fact that, like Haman in LXX *Esther* (Add E:14), this trusted figure conspired to hand over rule to a rival empire, or to the fact that Armenians were already associated with Amalek in

Byzantine sources. This latter point is supported by the fact that the Byzantine emperor Leo V (r. 813–820), who was ethnically an Armenian, was also dubbed an "Amalekite."[25] Leo has been compared specifically to the Neo-Assyrian king Sennacherib, assassinated in a conspiracy orchestrated by his son Arda-Mulissu (known in the Bible as "Adrammelekh"),[26] who was disgruntled for having been replaced by a younger brother (Esarhaddon) as crown-prince. Adrammelekh is said to have fled, with his co-conspirator, to Armenia (Urartu), and it has been argued that "Adrammelekh" was, through wordplay, replaced by "Amalek."[27]

Curiously, this may not be where the Armenian-Amalekite connection originated, either: Already in a Second Temple-era work attributed to Pseudo-Eupolemus, Abraham's battle against a force led by the Elamite king Chedorlaomer (Gen 14) describes the latter as an Armenian.[28] The point here is that the Armenians were being conflated with the Elamites, whose capital was at Susa, and who were correctly identified in ancient times as being relevant to the *Esther* story.[29] We will pursue Haman's Elamite connections shortly, but for now we may simply recognize that Haman's Armenian identity may not, in fact, be an elaboration on his more general, "Christian" label, but may relate to an independent exegetical tradition that predated *Sefer Yosippon* by over a millennium.

To summarize, although Jewish, Christian, and Muslim scriptures tell us something about Haman's background, the information provided is merely a springboard from which exegetes in each tradition plunged into greater detail. It is particularly curious that, whereas MT *Esther* portrays Haman in a Persian setting (with a father and sons who bear identifiably Persian names), the antique and especially late antique exegetes followed the Agagite breadcrumbs to the Amalekites, whom scripture placed somewhere in the Negev region, that is to say, far to the *west* of Iran and in the sphere of Egyptian cultural-political influence. Similarly, although the Qur'ān strongly implies that Haman was an Egyptian character, subsequent Muslim tradition traces his pre-Pharaonic beginnings to the east, thereby plugging him into a complex of traditions that intimate either Ṭūrānian enmity, an eschatological chaos-role, or some combination of both.

There is one stray tradition preserved by a ninth-century Muslim author, which appears to relate not to Jewish or Muslim traditions about Haman, but to ANE ones. The Egyptian scholar Ibn ʿAbd al-Ḥakam (d. 870) states that Haman was a "Nabatean," this being a term that—in the context of Abbasid writings—often related to the pagan ANE.[30] What, if anything, might Haman have to do with the prebiblical Near East? To answer this question, we turn away from internal perspectives on Haman's background, and towards the external, critical study of the Abrahamic religions.

Modern Scholarship on Haman's Origins

Scholars have devoted an enormous amount of attention to the question of *Esther*'s historical and literary contexts.[31] As is to be expected, these efforts have produced diverse results, with correspondingly diverse implications for our understanding of Haman's background. Before surveying these, and adding some options of our own, it is important to stress that "modern" and "scholarly" may be deceptive terms here: There are different types of scholarly approaches to scriptural questions, including internal ones that consciously privilege the experience of the believer over questions of historicity. And even scholars who adopt a non-partisan external approach may unconsciously be swayed by an array of presuppositions or biases. As we will see, the same pieces of "historical" evidence have been used to support arguments both for and against *Esther*'s historicity. *Caveat lector.*

A: Historicizing *Esther* (and Haman)

Many scholars accept that *Esther* reflects historical events from the period of Achaemenid rule.[32] It is not merely the "innocent until proven guilty" principle that is at work, but also the fact that *Esther* itself confidently sends its readers to extra-biblical Achaemenid sources for confirmation of the events it records (Esth 10:2). For these scholars, an evil vizier by the name of Haman the son of Hammedata was active in fifth century BCE Persia, and to understand his background we must understand his Agagite epithet.

It would be easy to reject this approach as naïve or theologically motivated, both because it overlaps with the traditional, internal perspective on *Esther*, and because many of its proponents belong(ed) to academic circles aligned with traditional approaches to scripture (such as seminaries, divinity schools, and so forth). Such a reaction is not entirely justified, however, as the historicizing approach is supported by various types of evidence that, at the very least, convincingly suggest that *Esther*'s author was familiar with Achaemenid Susa, and with its language and culture. The archaeology of the Persian palace at Susa, the etymologies of the numerous names listed in MT *Esther*, and aspects of Achaemenid court-culture described in the book are all in sync with our knowledge of fifth-century BCE Susa.[33]

Furthermore, the historicizing approach to *Esther* and Haman has not needed updating as our knowledge of the period (and scripture) has grown. In fact, new historical data has been used no less by those arguing for Haman's historicity as by those arguing against it.[34] It is not merely that scholars with contrasting biases have sought to twist the evidence to suit their point of view, but that the evidence is so fragmentary that it is difficult to know how far it can be taken. To cite but one Haman-related example: Stolper has shown, on the basis of an Aramaic seal from Susa dated 505 BCE, that a man by the name of HMDT' served there as a high-level administrator or judge.[35] Given the time, place, and occupation of this HMDT', it is possible that he had a son who served in the administration of Xerxes at Susa (vocations were generally passed down within families), and this son may have been named "Haman." For us Hamanologists, these are slim-pickings indeed,[36] but considering that some modern scholars categorically dismiss the question of Haman's historicity, the unexpected surfacing of a corroborative clue of this sort serves to remind us that the question remains ever-so-slightly open.

A related approach to MT *Esther* and Haman holds that the story does reflect historical events and characters, but that the narrative as we have it is overlaid with biblical language or should be read as allusive (so as not to implicate particular characters directly). Consequently, that which is historical has to be painstakingly retrieved. Haman existed, but the details of his *history* have been stylized in the course of becoming story. Lurking beneath the figure of Haman there is a historical enemy of the story's original protagonists. Some have placed these events in the reign of Xerxes, while others place them later, under Artaxerxes II (r. 405–358 BCE), or earlier, under Darius I (r. 522–486).[37] What they have in common is the assumption that Haman is a code for a historical villain (such as the Bagoas character encountered in Chapter 5), whose identity was intentionally obscured by *Esther*'s author, but can be recovered by *Esther*'s readers.[38]

One final historicizing approach to *Esther* and Haman has the merit of being compatible with the archeological evidence, while yet retaining a measure of agnosticism as to the historicity of the story. In this view *Esther* is a historical novella.[39] It was written by an author who was familiar with (if not native to) Achaemenid Susa, which would explain why the linguistic and archeological data appear to add up.[40] However, the author did not set out to relate historical events in biblical language, but rather to craft a work of literature, analogous to fifth-century writings about the Persian Empire by Herodotus, the Greek novellas of Ctesias, and Near Eastern court-tales such as the stories of *Aḥīqar* the Sage or *The Instructions of Ankhsheshonq*.[41] The existence of specifically *Jewish* court-tales set in the Achaemenid period, such as Dan 1–6 lends support to this hypothesis.

Such an approach carries both positive and negative implications for our study of Haman's background. On the positive side, the assumption is that whoever crafted MT *Esther*, and its villain, knew the world that he was describing and provided a verisimilar (if not historically accurate) portrait of an antagonistic

Achaemenid vizier, one that may benefit from our knowledge of ancient Persia, but also—in a circular way—contribute to our knowledge of that world. As Llewellyn-Jones put it: "[T]he book of Esther is a genuine Persian-period source. Therefore, it should be incorporated into the sources that historians employ in the study of Persia on a more routine basis than it currently enjoys. For a historian of ancient Persia to overlook Esther is a mistake."[42] On the negative side, we cannot tease out of *Esther*'s description of Haman anything really useful about his prebiblical origins, even if we draw on related historical novellas.

Somewhat ironically, the approach that attributes the smallest measure of historicity to *Esther* is the one that provides the most information on Haman's origins. The catch is that this information is not about the origins of Haman the person, but rather of Haman as an avatar of mythological characters.

B: Mythologizing *Esther* (and Haman)

Despite the efforts expended towards illuminating *Esther*'s context, two problems remain: First, to all but the most conservative, theologically committed reader of *Esther* it is clear that the narrative as it has reached us does not represent journalism from early-fifth-century BCE Persia. Even traditional sources have long been aware of the role that other biblical books played in shaping *Esther*'s contents. And as we have just noted, modern scholars assume that whatever kernel of historical truth lies at the heart of *Esther*, it has been swaddled in so many added layers that we may never be able to disentangle fact from fiction in the story. Second, despite the empire-wide implications of *Esther*'s plot and subplots, not a single source from the Achaemenid period describes an attempted genocide against the Jewish people, nor does any refer to a vizier by the name of Haman, a queen by the name of Esther, or any of the other minor or major characters or subplots in the story.

As our knowledge of the ANE increased, the problem of *Esther*'s absence from the sources grew in tandem: the more sources that made no reference to the story, the more acutely their absence was felt. But solutions to the problem began also to present themselves. The more we came to know about the cultural production of the Near East in the first millennium BCE, the more data we acquired concerning *Esther* as a product of that period and region. The debate about *Esther*'s—and hence, Haman's—origins was redirected in the nineteenth century by the scramble to relate the contents of newly discovered cuneiform documents to biblical texts. *Esther* featured prominently in these *Babel-und-Bibel* discussions because its two heroes bore names that uncannily resembled the names of leading ANE deities Marduk and Ištar.[43] For anyone even superficially acquainted with ANE civilization, it was hard to avoid the impression that its language and ideas underpin MT *Esther* and its characters. Various attempts were thus made to identify the ANE myth on which *Esther* was based, an enterprise that did not produce a scholarly consensus.[44] For the most conservative readers of *Esther*, the fact that Diaspora Jews then (as now) took local names alongside their Jewish ones meant that the discovery of Marduk and Ištar did not affect the historicity of *Esther*. For scholars willing to pursue *Esther*'s ANE connections further, the lack of a neat fit between *Esther* and a text from the ever-increasing library of cuneiform documents meant that the comparisons were either misguided or futile.

Not all scholars abandoned the comparative framework altogether,[45] but a certain stalemate set in.[46] Most chose to sidestep the question of the book's extrabiblical origins, preferring instead to examine *Esther* within its biblical-literary context.[47] We cannot afford the luxury of ignoring the epigraphical and archaeological materials, because in the case of Haman's DNA, they provide copious and crucial data, as we will now see.

The following exploration of Haman's origins in ANE mythology will allow us to break the scholarly deadlock concerning this topic in two ways. First, in the century or so since the first bevy of theories about *Esther*'s ANE background were proposed, and rejected, much progress has been made in our understanding of its ANE context, and particularly the (Neo-)Elamite civilization from which, I will argue, Haman emerged. Our pursuit of Haman's DNA will thus benefit greatly from this progress. Second, we will learn from two mistakes that have generally characterized studies of this topic. The first is the assumption that because *Esther* is commonly named for its heroine, the ANE myth on which *Esther* was based must be one that celebrates Ištar (rather than Marduk). The second is the assumption that because MT *Esther* is a single work, it must be based on a single ANE (Ištar-)myth, and the inability to identify a perfect match erodes the legitimacy of the enterprise altogether. This latter assumption is particularly odd, bearing in mind the multitude of biblical intertexts identified for *Esther* over the centuries. We will see that *Esther* may be contextualized within ANE literary genres *as well as* within biblical ones; that *Esther* alluded to ANE myths that were popular in the mid-first millennium BCE; that *Esther*'s contents reflect an anti-Elamite perspective; and that events in early-Achaemenid history raised issues of political relevance to the historical Babylonian-Elamite rivalry that is reflected in *Esther*. All this will allow us to conclude that Haman had Elamite genes and to identify particularly those aspects of his Elamite identity that contributed to his portrayal in *Esther*.

A: Literary Contexts

Underpinning the idea that Haman is related to prebiblical Near Eastern mythology is the assumption that *Esther* itself belongs to an ANE context, an assumption that requires more proof than the superficial similarities between the names Marduk/Mordecai and Ištar/Esther. In terms of its ANE genre, *Esther* fits neatly within existing categories, among them the (non-biblical) court-tales popular around the time of *Esther*'s writing,[48] and the reversal tales that were common for centuries before the Achaemenid period, some of which deal specifically with the fate of Marduk and his people.[49] That *Esther* is concerned with the theme of reversal has long been well-known, both because this theme is mentioned directly in the book (Esth 9:1, 22) and because it is manifested in the chiastic structure of the story.

Also pivotal to our ANE contextualization of *Esther* are the numerous Akkadianisms that occur in the text. It is not only that *Esther* contains more words of Akkadian origin than any other biblical book, but that the book's author seems to have expected his audience or readership to be familiar with the language and able to identify subtle bilingual (Akkadian-Hebrew) puns in the text.[50] Two examples of this will suffice for now, with the promise that we will return to some Haman-related puns later.[51]

The first comes from a reference to month-long joy during the month of Adar (Esth 9:22). Although we know that it was on the fourteenth and fifteenth of Adar that the Jews celebrated their extrication from Haman's schemes, in Esth 9:22, Adar is described as, "The *month* which was turned from sorrow to gladness." How did a one- or two-day festival become a month-long period of joy? The answer comes from Akkadian, where there are two nearly-identical lexemes—*Addaru*, the name of the twelfth month of the Babylonian calendar; and *adāru*, a verb meaning, "to be worried, disturbed, restless." *Esther*'s author was thus telling us that the month of Adar was no longer related to the verb *adāru*.[52] The fact that such a reversal was affected by Mordecai's actions might resonate particularly with an audience aware of some Babylonian traditions about the month of Addaru, according to which it is when "Marduk shattered his enemies," as we hear in a Neo-Babylonian text.[53]

The second bilingual pun concerns the reversal theme that we have just encountered. In this case, it is the Hebrew root *n-ph-l* ("to fall") that is punned with the cognate Akkadian verb *napālu* ("to turn upside down"). Commentators have pointed out that the Hebrew root *n-ph-l* is one of the most important verbal roots in the story, not just for its ubiquity, but also for the centrality of the scenes in which it occurs.[54] Akkadian *napālu* can be used in the physical sense of the word, as, for instance, in the sentence: "The wicked Elamite dismantled [the city's] temple" (*ṣēnu Elamu u-nappil emaḫsu*). It can also be used metaphorically to indicate chaotic reversal.[55] When the author repeatedly employs *n-ph-l* verbs in the text, an audience aware of the root's Akkadian meaning will not only hear about things falling and befalling, but will also catch numerous clever references to the theme of reversal.

Thus, just as *Esther*'s intended audience or readership was expected to pick up on allusions within the story to other scriptural texts, they were also expected to be *au fait* with ANE language and culture.[56] An acquaintance with some of the ANE myths that were widely known in the first millennium BCE may help illuminate various aspects of MT *Esther*, and of Haman within it.

B: ANE Myths and *Esther*

Just as we have been careful to distinguish between various types of Judaisms, Christianities, and Islams, and between different versions of *Esther*, we must recognize also that ANE civilizations were highly diverse. Accordingly, their mythologies can derive from a very wide range of sources, in various languages, which depict hundreds of gods and goddesses. To complicate matters, deities and their mythologies evolved over the centuries (often, millennia), and multiple versions of a myth may exist (with the names of a local deity replacing that of the myth's original hero, for instance), making the corpus of ANE mythology unwieldly even for experts. In our search for Haman's forebears, we thus limit our survey of ANE-*Esther* literary connections to those works known to have been in wide circulation (or widely known) in the Neo-Babylonian (1000–600)[57] and Neo-Elamite (1100–540) periods that immediately preceded the rise of the Achaemenid dynasty. The point will be to demonstrate that MT *Esther*'s author had some combination of these (and other) ANE myths in mind—alongside some early versions of the biblical tales of Joseph, Saul and Agag, Jacob and Esau, and so forth, which students of *Esther* now take for granted.

We begin with the very ancient Epic of Anzû. This is the story of an evil, demonic storm-bird (Anzû) who steals from Enlil, chief of the pantheon, the Tablet of Destinies—this being an item that grants its possessor rule over the universe and control over the fates. Eventually, the protagonist Ninurta reclaims the Tablet of Destinies for Enlil, and justice is restored. In this myth, as in *Esther*, the item that grants authority (in *Esther* it is the king's signet ring, which grants its bearer authority to issue immutable commands), is first obtained by the antagonist only for the protagonist to retrieve it, kill the villain, and restore order. Furthermore, in both stories the item is obtained from a figure of higher status (Enlil or Ahashwerosh, respectively), who is secondary to the action despite his superior rank. Whereas the Epic of Anzû celebrates Ninurta (rather than Marduk), scholars have shown that it had a formative influence on the most important Marduk myth, the *Enūma Eliš*.[58]

In the broadest terms, the *Enūma Eliš* relates the process through which Marduk was elevated to the head of the Babylonian pantheon. Along the way, he creates the universe out of the body of his defeated rival (for which reason the text has commonly been known as "the Babylonian Genesis"). As the formative impact of the *Enūma Eliš* on MT *Esther* has been adequately explored by scholars,[59] we will focus here only on the myth's villains, Tiamat and Qingu. Tiamat was the primordial goddess of the sea, who sought to have the race of younger gods (Annunaki) eradicated by eleven monsters she created for the job. She exalted her consort Qingu and gave him the Tablet of Destinies, which he used to ordain the destinies of the gods. Marduk was chosen to be the representative of the threatened gods, defeated Tiamat and Qingu in battle, and acquired the Tablet of Destinies. Tiamat, Qingu, and Tiamat's eleven monsters were captured, bound, and killed.[60] As in the case in the Epic of Anzû, the protagonist here fights to acquire the Tablet of Destinies from the story's villain, just as Mordecai secures the king's signet ring and its authority from Haman. That Qingu was "exalted" by Tiamat recalls Haman's exaltation by Ahashwerosh, and Tiamat's eleven monsters bring to mind Haman and his ten sons.

The *Enūma Eliš* was probably composed in the aftermath of Nebuchadnezzar I's (r. 1121–1100 BCE) recovery of Marduk's statue from its captivity in Elam,[61] and in a Babylonian text dated centuries later, Tiamat is openly equated with the Elamites.[62] Such instances of god-napping a rival's deity were not uncommon in the ANE: the gods' absence from their cultic-center was believed to be the cause of chaos in the abandoned city, and only with their return would order and justice be restored.[63] Marduk is named in more god-napping incidents than any other god, spawning texts such as the *Marduk Prophecy*[64] and the *Marduk Ordeal*,[65] which some scholars have also seen as having had a formative influence on *Esther*.[66] The point is that taking Marduk captive was not a mascot-snatching college fraternity prank, but rather an act with incredibly destructive—even genocidal—potential. The relief that accompanied the statue's return was commensurate with the level of threat averted, and the *Enūma Eliš* came to be the central text of the Marduk cult, generating commentaries and a complex of annual rituals in the New Year festival ("Akītu"),[67] and becoming a staple of the Babylonian school curriculum.[68] Moreover, as we will see, it left its mark on early

Achaemenid political propaganda. For now, it may be noted that *Esther*'s Haman shared attributes with Tiamat and Qingu, who, in the period preceding the rise of the Achaemenids, were equated with the Elamites and were occasionally merged into a single villainous character.[69]

The disastrous effects of Marduk's abandonment of Babylon are described in another highly popular ANE myth, the Erra Song (or "Erra and Išum").[70] This seventh-century BCE work relates how the villainous Erra sought to seize control of Babylon from Marduk and to exterminate the city's population. When Marduk agrees to leave Babylon, chaos ensues, and when Marduk returns to the city, order is restored (and the threat against the good people of Babylon is averted). The myth is transparently a celebration of Marduk, and the existence of dozens of copies of the text from the mid-first millennium BCE attests to its popularity and importance to the Marduk cult. More complex is the relationship between the text's contents and the overlapping worlds of Near Eastern politics, mythological rivalries between gods, and observations of the planets, whose movements were equated with interactions between the deities they represented, which in turn had real implications for a god's followers on earth.[71] Thus, as Erra was identified with Mars and Marduk with Jupiter, the Erra Song was interpreted as a description of the behavior of these planets,[72] and also as a narrative about Marduk's triumph over a villain's attempt to eradicate his people, with initial chaos caused by the Mars-deity giving way to the order restored by the Jupiter-deity.

Numerous other details in the text evoke aspects of *Esther*, one of which stands out for its relevance to Haman and takes us back to the bilingual puns in *Esther*. The reference to Haman as an "Agagite" in MT *Esther* has generally been taken to relate to the Amalekites in general, and in particular to Saul's rival in 1 Sam 15. The term "Agagite," however, may also evoke the Akkadian verb *agāgu*, "to be enraged," a verb that usually refers to the anger of gods.[73] It is surely significant that both Marduk and Ištar are described in some sources as coming up against an enemy who is described as raging or angry using this verb. In one text we are told that, "The Goddess Ištar has gone to rest, let not the turbulent one (*agāgu*) enter the Temple."[74] And in the *Enūma Eliš* (4:60), we hear that "Marduk went in the direction of Tiamat who was fuming with rage (*agāgu*)."

But that is not all: Scholars have shown that in the Erra Song, the opposing concepts of "violence" and "rest" are represented by the roots *a-g-g* (for the former) and *n-w-ḥ* (for the latter).[75] This is of interest to us in that the dénouement of the *Esther* story—where in Chapter 9 the many reversals from earlier in the story completed—we are told no fewer than four times that the Jews enjoyed *n-w-ḥ* (9:16, 17, 18, and 22). If *n-w-ḥ* provides the answer at the end of *Esther*, then *a-g-g* must provide the question in the early chapters of the story. This is apparently a case of multivalency, which allows us to read the story as *both* a corrective to the Saul-Agag episode *and* as an ANE myth about Marduk and Ištar fighting against a raging rival, until their eventual triumph brings about *n-w-ḥ*. Correspondingly, Haman's Agagite epithet would evoke both the age-old Jewish rivalry with the Amalekites and the infamous chaos-villain Erra, represented by Mars.

A final specimen of ANE mythology that sheds light on *Esther* and Haman is the Nergal and Ereškigal myth, a detailed version of which dates to the seventh century BCE. This text tells the story of Nergal's marriage to Ereškigal, the chief goddess of the Underworld. Although this text does not discuss Marduk, Ištar, Elamites, or reversals, it provides some important clues regarding Haman's formation.[76] The story begins with a banquet held by the gods, to which Ereškigal is invited but which she cannot attend as she is unable to traverse the boundaries between the Under- and Upper-realms. She thus sends Namtar, her vizier (Akkadian: *sukkallu*), to represent her at the gods' party. Namtar is received by the assembled gods with deference (in one version of the story, all of the gods stand up before him; in another version, all bow down to him), with one exception: Nergal, the god of pestilence, refused to bow (or rise) before Namtar. Nergal was thus banished to the Underworld and eventually married Ereškigal. The parallels with *Esther* are interesting if imperfect. On the one hand, as in *Esther*, central moments of both plots take place at banquets, in both the protagonist is the only one within a group who refuses to prostrate when expected to do so, and in both the object of prostration is not the most senior figure (Ahaswerosh or Ereškigal) but rather their representatives. Finally, and no less curiously, the name of the vizier Namtar means "Fate," a key theme associated with Haman in Esth 3:7. On the other hand, the protagonist of this myth is Nergal, an important Mesopotamian god (whose cult center was at Cutha in northern Iraq), who was equated with Erra and with the planet Mars.[77] As with Tiamat-Qingu, the Nergal-Namtar duo appears to share pivotal elements with the description of Haman in *Esther*, even if the narrative parallels are not exact. *Esther*'s author may have been making use of an ANE *topos* common at the time—Nergal (and Ereškigal) appears in early-Achaemenid texts[78] and even in the Hebrew Bible (2 Kgs 17:30)—or inverting the connection either for polemical aims or for comedic effect.[79]

Bearing in mind Marduk's long-standing centrality to Babylonian religio-cultural life, it is not surprising that copious materials praising him and relating tales of his rivalries with other deities have survived. The sheer volume of these increases the likelihood that some description of him will overlap with a detail in *Esther*, and it is therefore important—especially when following the breadcrumbs back to Haman's pre-*Esther* genetic makeup—to focus not on celebrations of Marduk (and Ištar) in the sources, but on denigrations of one of their great historical rivals, the Elamites.[80]

C: Elamites in Babylonian Perspective

Although the deities Marduk and Ištar appear to be the basis for the characters of Mordecai and Esther, there are actually more Elamite deities referenced in *Esther* than Babylonian ones.[81] Vashti (Mašti), Zeresh (Kiriša or Kiririša), and—most importantly for us—Haman (Humban),[82] each have been identified as Elamite theonyms.[83] Not all scholars have been convinced by this, however: Some have objected (until surprisingly recently) that there were no such leading Elamite deities,[84] while others have rejected the etymological connections between the characters either on philological grounds or because there are, in their view, better etymological theories to account for these names.[85] The first objection is no longer tenable in light of recent advances in our knowledge of Elamite civilization, particularly in the Neo-Elamite period that immediately preceded the rise of the Achaemenids.[86] The second, philological objection suffers from two misapprehensions: That *Esther*'s author held himself to modern standards of scientific philology, and that a word or name in *Esther* can only have one source. Biblical etymologies (especially concerning names) are demonstrably unscientific,[87] and bilingual puns pepper the text, allowing for playful multivalency. Vashti's name may well reflect both Old Persian wordplay[88] and the Elamite goddess Mašti, just as Haman's name may reflect both Old Persian wordplay[89] and the Elamite god Humban. Even the epithet "Agagite" might reflect Elamite multivalency: In addition to the Amalekite- and *agāgu*-connotations of the term, Zadok has pointed out that *agag* could be an Elamite name.[90]

An Elamite context for *Esther* is hardly surprising, both because the Elamites were, historically, the enemy *par excellence* of the Babylonians, and because the Elamite capital was Susa, where *Esther* is set.[91] It is therefore not surprising that such anti-Marduk rivals as Anzû, Tiamat, and Qingu came to be associated with the Elamites in the Neo-Babylonian period, even though the texts recording these myths do not mention the Elamites at all.[92] That specifically Mašti, Kiririša, and Humban feature in *Esther* is also no coincidence: Despite the existence of hundreds of Elamite gods and goddesses, only two of them—Mašti and Kiririša—were known as the "mothers of the gods" and continued to be invoked widely in the Neo-Elamite period. As for Humban, he was one of only two gods known as "the great god" (Elamite: *rišar nappipir/nappirra*) over the three millennia of Elamite history.[93] Crucially, in the Neo-Elamite and early-Achaemenid periods that are most relevant to us, Humban was by far the best represented deity in inscriptions and theophoric names.[94]

Reading into *Esther* a reflection of the Babylonian-Elamite rivalry—as seen from a pro-Babylonian perspective—illuminates several aspects of the text. For example, the insistence in Esther 3:7 that Addar is specifically the twelfth month, and that Haman cast his lots in Nissan, which is the first month, may be read as anti-Elamite point-scoring: In the Elamite calendar, Addar was the first month of the year,[95] and as the fates for the coming year were determined in the first month, describing Haman as casting his lots in Nissan (the first month according to the *Babylonians*) amounts to two corrections of the Elamite calendar. Similarly, as early as the middle-Elamite period there was an Elamite center known as "Bīt Hubban" (Humban's House),[96] and *Esther*'s references (8:1, 2, and 7) to the story's protagonists taking over "Haman's house" (Hebrew: *bayt haman*) may also indicate Babylonian anti-Elamite triumphalism. One might also read the reference to "the fear of Mordecai" (Esth 9:3), as a sort of pushback or even supersession of the phrase "the terror of Humban," which occurs in a late-sixth-century Elamite curse formula.[97]

Haman Is from Mars, Esther Is from Venus

Haman's Elamite origins may also relate to the (Babylonian) association of the Elamites with the planet Mars. In Babylonian planetary theology, Ištar was represented by Venus, Marduk by Jupiter, and Humban—and the Elamites generally—by Mars.[98] If we grant an association between Haman and Mars in *Esther*, and given what we know Babylonians in the first millennium BCE thought about Mars, it becomes possible to unlock some playful references to Haman in MT *Esther*, and this in four ways.

First, the most common name for Mars in Akkadian was *Ṣalbatanum*, a word of uncertain etymology, but which may have impishly been related to the "crucified" Haman in ancient interpretations of *Esther* (the most common verbs for "crucify" in Semitic languages come from the root *ṣ-l-b*, including in Imperial Aramaic from this period).[99] Recall that already the LXX has Haman as crucified rather than hung from gallows.[100] Second, another of the most widespread names for Mars in Akkadian was *Makrû*, the "red [planet]." This may relate to Esther's insistence to the king that she and her people, "had been sold" (*nimkarnu*; Esth 7:4) by Haman. The problem with the plain meaning of the verse is that the text indicates that the king had actually rejected the money that Haman had offered him for the Jews (Esth 3:11), and even if money had been exchanged, by complaining that the Jews were sold, Esther was actually implicating Ahashwerosh himself, rather than Haman.[101] Esther's claim that the Jews were "sold" (*m-k-r*) may be a pun on *Makrû*, meaning that the Jews had been Hamanated (or Marsified).[102]

Third, the Elamite god equated with Mars was not Humban, but Šimut,[103] whose name was rendered in Neo-Assyrian as Šumudu, and who appears in the Achaemenid era.[104] Haman's wish to *le-hašmīd* the Jews (Esth 3:6) may thus also refer to Hamanating them through his association with the Elamites' conception of Mars. Fourth, and finally, an allusion to Mars in Hamanic contexts may come from references to him as the *ṣorer* (enemy) of the Jews (Esth 9:24), as the Akkadian verb *ṣarāru* (Ntn) may refer to the repeated flashing of the planet Mars.[105]

The Haman-Mars connection may have left some traces in AT *Esther*, which—as noted in Chapter 2—is thought to be a rendering of a Hebrew *Vorlage* at least as early in date as MT *Esther*. In the AT (4:6 = MT/LXX 3:6), when Mordecai refuses to bow to Haman, we are told that Haman "was provoked and all his rage was stirred up, *he turned red* (Greek: *erethros*), driving him from his sight." The added detail of Haman's redness may evoke not only Mars (Hebrew: *ma'adīm*, "the one who reddens"), but "Edom" as well (also from Hebrew "red," which is overtly invoked as characterizing Esau in Gen 25:25 and 30). That late antique rabbis identified Haman as an Edomite might therefore indicate the endurance of some Mars-related traditions about this villain, alongside the historical Jacob-Esau rivalry. Readers who doubt that such ancient associations could have persisted into late antiquity should note that as late as the fourteenth century CE, the Spanish Rabbi Baḥya ben Asher (d. 1340) compared Mordecai to Jupiter and Haman to Mars.[106] In fact, as we will see at the end of this chapter, the entire mythological or anti-Elamite framework for *Esther* that is being constructed here, may have been known to ancient Jewish tradition, and to late antique rabbis. Our task for now, however, is to relate this framework to events in the Near East during the sixth and fifth centuries BCE, which will allow us to understand how our Elamite-Martian villain became the Haman of *Esther*.

D: Early Achaemenid History and the Babylonian-Elamite Rivalry

Thus far, we have discovered that the Jewish author of MT *Esther* had in his mind (if not on his bookshelf) earlier biblical texts, versions of various ANE myths, and a penchant for wordplay and even bilingual punning. To grasp how these ingredients were combined to produce Haman, we must understand the cultural-political context during the crucial transition period from the ANE to the Achaemenid era.

The empire of the Achaemenids, which stretched "from India to Kush" (Esth 1:1), was established on lands conquered from various polities, two of the most important of which (for our purposes if not for theirs) were the Neo-Babylonian and Neo-Elamite states. Culturally, linguistically, ethnically, and theologically, these two states were different from one another and from the Achaemenids, who inherited their lands and populations. The Achaemenids were known, however, for their tolerant attitude toward their diverse subject populations, and it is clear that the elite (specifically, the royal advisors and scribal class) consciously integrated elements of the civilizations that preceded them within their own ruling culture. This process was not always smooth, both because even within each civilization there was much diversity, and because acculturating the sixth-century Babylonian and Elamite political cultures and pantheons within the early-Achaemenid ruling culture (which was comprised of an early form of Zoroastrianism and Persian culture) was not an easy task, especially for kings who sought to legitimize their rule in terms familiar to their conquered populations. Public proclamations and propaganda were distributed in multiple languages (so as not to superimpose the ruler's culture from above); Achaemenid Jews saw Cyrus as God's Messiah;[107] Achaemenid Egyptians saw his successors as Pharaohs; and—as we shall see shortly—Achaemenid Babylonians saw Cyrus as a champion of Marduk. At the same time, however, their public proclamations make it clear that the Achaemenid rulers had their own religio-political traditions (which were occasionally at odds with those of their subjects), and that even when integrating local traditions into their own system, they occasionally had to insist on one local option over several competing ones.

In what follows, we will see how MT *Esther* gives expression to the ways in which three early-Achaemenid kings—Cyrus the Great (r. 559–530), Darius I (r. 522–486), and Xerxes I (r. 486–465)—dealt with tensions between their own and local traditions, and specifically, how they settled the competition between Babylonian/Marduk and Elamite/Humban traditions in favor of the former. Put simply: *Esther* is the story of how the Achaemenid king(s) decided to adopt Marduk as the divine legitimator of their rule, in lieu of Humban. To explain this, we will break the evidence down into four sections: 1) The status of Marduk in the Neo-Babylonian period; 2) Marduk's restoration under Cyrus; 3) Darius's consolidation of power following the Gaumata affair; and 4) Xerxes' transferral of Humban's *kitin* to Ahuramazda.

Marduk in the Neo-Babylonian Period

During the reign of the Neo-Babylonian dynasty, which immediately preceded the rise of the Achaemenid Empire, Marduk's prestige and centrality to Babylonian civilization was at its height. This is evidenced by two facts. First, of the six kings of this dynasty, five had theophoric regnal names that related either to Marduk or to his son Nabu. Considering that during the same period, virtually all Neo-Elamite rulers had theophoric names invoking Humban, one might be tempted to conclude that *Esther* reflects the actual political rivalry between rulers with names derived from Marduk and Humban.[108] However, we will see that there are far more convincing explanations for the Marduk-Humban rivalry reflected in *Esther* than this.

Second, rivals to the Neo-Babylonian ruling elite expressed their enmity by demoting Marduk's status or attacking him in some other way. The Assyrian ruler Sennacherib sacked Babylon in 689 and refused to pay Marduk respect, an offense that is said to have been avenged by the latter when Sennacherib was assassinated in 681. (Sennacherib's son, Essarhadon, reversed his father's anti-Mardukian policy, restoring Marduk's temple and returning the statue of Marduk to Babylon.) More significant to us is the challenge to Marduk from within the Babylonian ruling elite mounted by Nabonidus (r. 556–539). This ruler sought to promote the moon-god Sīn at the expense of Marduk-worship, an act deemed scandalous by the Babylonian elites who, in their highly partial accounts of the events, deemed Nabonidus to have gone mad. Chronologically bridging these two affronts to Marduk's status was the rule of Nebuchadnezar II (r. 604–562), who invested heavily in Marduk's cult, building the famous Ištar Gate in Babylon, which portrayed images of Marduk and Ištar, and through which the New Year processions (the Akītu) passed. It is in the New Year rituals that Marduk's supremacy was annually affirmed, as was the legitimacy of the king who patronized the Marduk-cult. That Marduk's enthronement ceremonies *passed through* Ištar's Gate may evoke the events described in *Esther*, especially Chapters 2 (vv. 21–23) and 4, where Mordecai's successes and his relationship with the king are enabled through Esther's mediation.[109] It is highly likely that the details of the annual Akītu rituals and their meaning were known to Jewish elites,[110] and the Bible contains various references (predictably, of the disparaging sort) to the Mardukian cult.[111] As stated, Marduk's centrality to Babylonian civilization was endangered by Nabonidus's attempt to replace him. To Marduk's rescue came not a subsequent Babylonian ruler, but rather the Achaemenid Cyrus, whose pro-Marduk policies seem to have left their mark on *Esther*.

Marduk's Restoration under Cyrus

To justify his conquest of Babylon, Cyrus claimed that Marduk had chosen him to conquer and rule the city. This claim is recorded in the famous Cyrus Cylinder, an Akkadian inscription deposited in Marduk's main temple in Babylon (the Esagila), and copies of which were distributed, apparently in a variety of languages, throughout the Achaemenid provinces.[112] This text is important to us for three reasons.

First, it reaffirms Marduk's primacy in Babylon, following the temporary demotion that he suffered under Nabonidus, the king whom Cyrus defeated. Second, it describes Marduk as having been furious (from Akkadian *agāgu*; ll. 9–10), details the unjust taxation imposed by Nabonidus on the Babylonians (l. 8), then tells of their removal by Cyrus (ll. 25–26; cf. Esth 2:18 and 10:1),[113] and ends with Cyrus establishing the connection between his just rule and Marduk's divine legitimation of it (ll. 34–36; cf. Esth 10).[114] Third, the Akkadian style employed in the text has been shown to draw on literary sources,[115] including the *Enūma Eliš* (which, as mentioned, left its mark in numerous ways on the contents of MT *Esther*).[116] On its own, the Cyrus Cylinder does not unlock *Esther*'s contents or context, but combined with comparably public and political proclamations authored in the name of Darius and Xerxes I, its role acquires significance.

Darius's Consolidation of Power Following the Gaumāta Affair

Cyrus the Great died in 530 and was succeeded by his son Cambyses II (r. 530–522), but for Hamanologists the really interesting events occurred upon Cambyses's death. While our knowledge of these is irretrievably skewed by the politicized accounts left by Darius I (r. 522–486),[117] it is clear that the latter's accession was contested by multiple challengers, whom he defeated (with the aid of named supporters). What concerns us here is Darius's version of the events: This was recorded in the Behistun Inscription, copies of which were circulated throughout the Achaemenid Empire in a variety of languages (including an Aramaic copy of c. 420 BCE that belonged to the Jewish community of Upper Egypt).[118] In the simplest of terms, this trilingual inscription (in Old Persian, Elamite, and Akkadian), tells how a Zoroastrian imposter by the name of "Gaumāta the Magus"[119] usurped the throne by impersonating the actual ruler (Bardiya or Smerdis, whom Cambyses had secretly killed). This was the first in a series of nine local rebellions against Darius's rule that took place in the first year of his reign (a tenth rebellion followed and was only quashed in his third year). Herodotus relates that, in celebration of the defeat of the Magus pretender, Darius's supporters went on an anti-Magi rampage, and an annual festival—"the killing of the magi" (Greek: *Magophonia*)—was instituted to commemorate the events.[120]

For a variety of reasons, some modern scholars have sought to relate parts of *Esther*'s story to the Behistun Inscription and to the Magophonia generally.[121] It is curious that Ibn Khaldūn (or his source) already had dated *Esther* to immediately following the reign of Smerdis or "Bardiya the Zoroastrian";[122] that is to say, to the early years of Darius I's reign. Similarly, Josephus immediately follows his succinct summary of the Magophonia episode with a discussion of events at Darius's court, a discussion that is unmistakably modelled on MT *Esther*.[123] As one of the arguments against *Esther*'s historicity is that there is no record of a mass-murder of the Jews in early-Achaemenid times, the fact that Magophonia accounts describe the mass-murder of a religious community in this period—commemorated by a triumphalist annual feast—may be relevant to *Esther*'s contents (disanalogies notwithstanding). In fact, the relationship between the Behistun Inscription and *Esther* runs deeper than has been hitherto recognized. The following seven points of overlap between the two texts, most of which have not been previously considered in the context of *Esther*'s origins, will contribute to our understanding of Haman's pre-*Esther* background.

A: According to the Behistun Inscription, Gaumāta rebelled on the fourteenth day of the twelfth month (Old Persian: Viyaxana). In the Akkadian version of the trilingual inscription, the month is specified as Addaru, placing the crucial moment of the rebellion on the date of Purim.[124]

B: In total, Darius was forced to fend off ten rebels (nine in his first year, one in his third year), all of whom are named. Compare Haman's ten sons, named in *Esther*'s recounting of the Jews' victory (Esth 9:6–9).

C: Among the named rebels who fought against Darius was one named "Vahyazdata," which is likely etymologically related to the name of Haman's son "Vayzata" (Esth 9:9).

D: Three of Darius's ten challengers rebelled in Elam, including—crucially—the final one, "Athamaita." This revolt is specifically related in the Behistun Inscription to the Elamites' loyalty to the wrong god (presumably Humban).[125]

E: One of the Elamite rebels, Martiya, called himself "Ummaniš," this being a theophoric name invoking Humban.

F: The first and final rebellions were quashed thanks to one "Gobryas" (in Latin; based on Greek *Gōbrýās*, or Akkadian *Gubaru*).[126] This character appears to be the basis for (aspects of)[127] *Esther*'s Mordecai:

- He had a daughter who married the king (Herodotus, *Histories*, 7.2.2; cf. Esth 2:5–6).
- When he is introduced in Xenophon's version of the events, he is described as being an elderly man (*Cyropaedia*, 4.6.1). Compare Esth 2:5, where Mordecai is introduced as having been improbably old.

- Upon defeating the final (Elamite) rebel, Gobryas was made governor of Elam and, according to the Persepolis Fortification Tablets, he received the largest amount of rations in the country, indicating that his status was second only that of the king.

G: Darius repeatedly credits Ahura-Mazda with his victories. In Babylonian versions of Achaemenid texts, however, Marduk ("Bel") replaces Ahura-Mazda.[128] Thus, like Cyrus before him, the Achaemenid king acknowledges Marduk's role in granting the king legitimacy and protection.

The Mordecai-Gubaru connection may, in fact, be yet another specimen of bilingual punning in MT *Esther*. For just as "Mordecai" invokes "Marduk," the name may also have alluded to the Old Persian word for "man" (*martiya*, with the "t" pronounced in a Semitic context as a "d," just as Šimut became Šumudu). The significance of this is that "man" in Hebrew is constructed on the same *g-b-r* root from which Gubaru derives. The penultimate verse of MT *Esther* associates Mordecai with this root by referring to his "might" (Hebrew: *gevurah*, again from the *g-b-r* root).[129]

If *Esther* is, at least in part, a reflection of the events recorded in the Behistun Inscription,[130] and Mordecai is based on Gubaru—who defeated both Gaumāta and the final, Elamite rebel—then Haman (and, perhaps, his ten sons) may correspond to the anti-Darius rebels, whose defeat is celebrated in the Magophonia festival and the texts of the Behistun Inscription. Intriguingly, Haman's origins in Gaumāta's *coup d'état* and the subsequent rebellions against Darius, may manifest in the LXX's depiction of Haman, in two ways. First, in Add E:10–14, Haman is accused of conspiring to overthrow the Persian Empire, in favor of the Macedonians. Tantalizing support for the LXX's association of Haman with disloyalty to the Persian king, and with the Macedonians specifically, comes from an ancient Sogdian version of the Magophonia events, which depicts Alexander the Great as the story's villain.[131] Second, Shapira has argued that Haman's "Bougean" epithet in the LXX was a misreading of an original epithet indicating "magus"; accordingly, he argues, Purim is based on the Magophonia.[132]

Thus far, we have seen that *Esther*'s author was evoking Cyrus's adoption of Marduk as the legitimizer and protector of his rule, as well as Darius's defeat of rebellions that began on the fourteenth of Adar and ended in Susa, in the third year of the king's reign. The final piece of evidence for an Achaemenid religio-political context for *Esther* comes from the reign of Xerxes I (r. 486–465), and it has to do with this king's decisions to replace Humban with Marduk.

Xerxes' Transferal of Humban's *kitin* to Ahuramazda

The recognition that "Ahashwerosh" and "Xerxes" are Hebrew and Greek renderings of the same Persian name (*Khshayarsha*) has led to numerous attempts to contextualize the events of MT *Esther* historically with reference to Xerxes I's reign.[133] The incompatibility of *Esther*'s contents with what we know of contemporary events convinced some that the story is entirely ahistorical and others that the story recounted historical events unrelated to the Jews of the empire at this time, but which were related in a biblicized version.[134] Here, we adopt the latter approach, with the important qualification that the key decision that Xerxes took, which is reflected in MT *Esther*, must be taken together with the evidence from the reigns of Cyrus and Darius I to provide a full historical context for the story.

In broad terms, it is argued here that Xerxes decided to downgrade Humban's status as the divine protector of the king, following his predecessors' decision to upgrade Marduk (or his Persian equivalent, Ahuramazda). Accordingly, MT *Esther* relates—among other things—a Judaized version of the Achaemenid replacement of Humban with Marduk as the deity under whose auspices the king ruled.[135] To understand this better, we must return to Humban's status in the Neo-Elamite and early-Achaemenid period, a topic for which our evidence has improved greatly in recent years. As noted, in this period Humban was far and away the most popular and powerful deity in the Elamite pantheon. There is considerable evidence, moreover, to suggest that well into the early Achaemenid period he continued to be popular—even among Iranians, who acculturated him within their own religious culture.[136]

Furthermore, in the late Neo-Elamite period, on the eve of the Achaemenid conquest of Iran-Iraq, Humban was closely associated with the Elamite concept of *kitin* (also: *kiten*), which generally refers to the protective aegis that a god bestows on a ruler. While some have traced this idea to earlier, Neo-Assyrian concepts, and other have connected it to later, Old Persian notions of charismatic rulership,[137] it is undeniable that the notion of *kitin* came to the fore in the Neo-Elamite period, with Humban as its chief purveyor.[138] As the early-Achaemenid rulers pragmatically portrayed themselves to local populations as champions of their cultures and theological systems (we have encountered Jewish, Egyptian, and Babylonian examples of this above), in the case of the Elamites, it would appear that Xerxes adopted the concept of *kitin*, but not its divine representative, Humban. In what is generally known as Xerxes' *Daivā* inscription, this ruler relates how early in his reign one of the countries under his rule rebelled and, with the help of Ahuramazda, he succeeded in putting down the revolt. He then added that he also destroyed a sanctuary (in another country) in which demons (Old Persian: *daivā*) were worshipped and established at this place a cult of Ahuramazda. Which country rebelled, and what *daivā*-sanctuary was destroyed, were not specified, and their identification has generated much scholarly debate. Based on a misreading of a passage in Herodotus, it was long thought that Xerxes was actually targeting Babylon and its Marduk-cult, an idea that has now been solidly refuted.[139]

Most important for us is the fact that in the Elamite version of this inscription, Xerxes refers to the *kitin* that *Ahuramzda* bestowed on him.[140] By invoking the term *kitin*, Xerxes was speaking the Elamites' own theological language, but by crediting Ahuramazda with what was in this period and region considered the preserve of Humban, Xerxes was unmistakably demoting the leading Elamite deity at the time.[141] Thus, just as Cyrus actively promoted Marduk (in the aftermath of Nabonidus's challenge to him), and just as Darius celebrated a Mordecai-like hero (Gubaru) and promoted Ahuramazda-Marduk, Xerxes was taking a side in the Babylonian-Elamite rivalry, specifically an anti-Humban one.[142]

To summarize, MT *Esther* draws on an eclectic combination of sources, three of which are official Achaemenid public pronouncements circulated throughout the empire's provinces in various languages (a process described in Esth 1:22).[143] These materials telescope within Ahashwerosh's reign events that in fact spanned the reigns of three Persian kings, and which describe how these rulers sought to make sense of the Babylonian-Elamite rivalry that they had inherited. Early Achaemenid kings promoted Marduk at the expense of Humban and celebrated their defeat of rebellious challengers to their reigns, which began on the fourteenth of Adar and ended with the defeat of the tenth Elamite rebel. As an impish connoisseur of bilingual wordplay, MT *Esther*'s author drew on both Old Persian and Akkadian etymologies as he winked his way through the story, alluding freely to public Achaemenid texts, but also to a selection of ANE texts that celebrated Marduk's triumphs (often against an Elamite enemy). Whether the author could reasonably expect his audience to pick up on the allusions to such a rich repertoire of political and mythological sources—to say nothing of the dozens of biblical intertexts identified by some two millennia of scholars—is impossible to determine.

What can be said with more certainly is that the biblical Haman was a composite character, whose background has eluded scholars both because it is so heterogeneous and also because those seeking his origins have labored under the misconception that there is a single origin that must be discovered and then privileged decisively over competing options. It is far more likely, that Haman had multiple forefathers, all of whom were consciously tapped in forming the story's villain. We can therefore accept that the name "Haman" is both a pun on the Old Persian for "same thoughts" (cf. Esth 8:3, 8:5, 9:24, and 9:25) and a reference to the chief Elamite deity of the time, Humban.[144]

Naturally, despite this deep-dive into ANE history and culture that we have taken with the aim of revealing Haman's prebiblical past, questions remain. Where, for instance, does Esther fit into all this? Is it enough to see her character as a reflection of Ištar's replacement of the Elamite goddess(es) Mašti (and Kiririša)? And why did a Jewish author choose to mythologize and then Judaize the political events of the first Achaemenid kings in this way?[145] Problematic though these issues may be, they are not our problems: Our pinpoint mission was to identify as much of Haman's DNA as the sources allow, and the foregoing represents the results of this effort.

Perhaps most surprisingly of all, it would appear that the gap between scripture's answer to the question of Haman's DNA and modern, scholarly approaches to it, is much narrower than might be imagined. For as we will now see, the author of MT *Esther* peppered the text with biblical intertexts relating to the Elamites to the point that even some ancient interpreters of the book displayed awareness of Haman's mythological and Elamite genes.

Bridging the Traditional and Modern Scholarly Options

We begin with MT *Esther* itself. Incredible though it may seem, the author of *Esther* appears to have woven an anti-Elamite polemic into the story, drawing for this purpose on earlier biblical intertexts—in addition to diverse references to ANE mythology, to Achaemenid political propaganda texts, and to the numerous biblical intertexts identified by centuries of scholars.

An important clue to the existence of an Elamite subtext comes not from what is written in *Esther* the book, but from what is not written. It has long been recognized that MT *Esther* seems deliberately to omit certain topics that it wishes to stress, two examples being God and the Passover festival. Both of these topics are strongly present between the lines of the text, yet absent from the lines themselves. The same can be said of Elam(ites), based on a comparison between the introduction of Susa in *Esther* with its introduction in the two biblical books that are closest in historical context to *Esther*, namely *Daniel* and *Ezra-Nehemiah* respectively.

In Dan 8:2 Susa is introduced as being "in the province of Elam . . ." Similarly, in *Ezra-Nehemiah* (Ezra 4:9) Susa's native population are introduced as the

Susanchites, who are the Elamites."[146] The lack of a comparable reference to Elam when Susa is introduced in Esth (1:2) represents the breaking of a literary mold, which may be an indication of Elam's centrality to the story.

Turning to pre-*Esther* biblical references to Elam, we find that in the Pentateuch, with the exception of a laconic reference to the eponymous ancestor of the Elamites in the Table of Nations (Gen 10:22), it is only in Gen 14 that this nation features. This chapter describes Abraham's defeat of the Elamite king Chedorlaomer and his allies, the account of which shares numerous features with MT *Esther*, including many parallels of plot and phraseology.[147] In the Prophets the Elamites feature a handful of times,[148] all of which appear to relate to MT *Esther*. Isa 21:2–3 refers to Elam apparently incidentally, yet the vocabulary employed strikingly prefigures the word choice in MT *Esther*. The relevant verses read:

> A grievous vision is declared unto me: "The treacherous dealer deals treacherously (*b-g-d*), and the spoiler spoils. Go up, O Elam! Besiege, O Media! All the sighing thereof have I made to cease." Therefore are my loins filled with convulsion (*ḥ-l-ḥ-l*); pangs have taken hold upon me, as the pangs of a woman in travail; I am bent so that I cannot hear; I am affrighted so that I cannot see.

These verses employ two verbal roots that are repeated in Esth 4:4, as follows:

> And Esther's maidens and her chamberlains came and told it her; and the queen was exceedingly pained (*ḥ-l-ḥ-l*); and she sent raiment (*b-g-d*) to clothe Mordecai; and to take his sackcloth from off him; but he accepted it not.

Not only are two verbs from Isaiah's reference to Elam repeated in this single verse, but the root *ḥ-l-ḥ-l* is relatively rare and its repetition in this Elamite verse and in *Esther* is intriguing.[149] It is difficult to read significance into *Esther*'s choice to employ these roots in this verse, other than as a playful nod to one of the Prophetic references to Elam.

More pivotal to our concerns is Ezek 32:1, 17, and 24–25. The first passage contains a prophecy about the demise of Egypt, who will eventually be destroyed and confined to Sheol, where she will meet the five (or seven) kingdoms that have already suffered this fate. One of these kingdoms is Elam.

> And it came to pass in the *twelfth year, in the twelfth month*, in the first day of the month, that the word of the Lord came unto me, saying . . . It came to pass also in the *twelfth year, in the fifteenth day of the month*, that the word of the Lord came unto me, saying . . . *There is Elam* and all her multitude round

> about her grave; all of them slain, fallen by the sword, who are gone down uncircumcised into the nether parts of the earth, who caused their terror in the land of the living; yet have they borne their shame with them that go down to the pit. They have set her a bed in the midst of the slain with all her multitude; her graves are round about them; all of them uncircumcised, slain by the sword; because their terror was caused in the land of the living, yet have they borne their shame with them that go down to the pit; they are put in the midst of them that are slain.

These verses regarding the demise of the Elamites are important for the date of the prophecy. Ezek 32 begins with "the word of the Lord" coming to the prophet on the first day of the twelfth month of the twelfth year (of Jehoiachin's captivity, viz. 587/6 BCE). The prophecy's particular reference to Elam's fate, however, was revealed later on in that month, specifically on the fifteenth (v. 17). In other words, Ezekiel received a prophecy recalling the destruction of the Elamites on the fifteenth day of the twelfth month of the twelfth year. According to *Esther*, the Jews defeated their enemies in the twelfth year (of Ahashwerosh's reign), during the "twelfth month, which is the month of Adar" (Esth 8:12). When in the twelfth month did this happen? Throughout the provinces of Ahashwerosh's empire this happened on the thirteenth of the month, but of Susa itself, the ancient Elamite capital, we are told (Esth 9:18):

> But the Jews that were in Susa assembled together on the thirteenth day thereof, and on the fourteenth thereof; and on the fifteenth day of the same they rested, and made it a day of feasting and gladness.

Until today, the fifteenth of the twelfth month is known as "The Purim of Susa." It seems beyond coincidence that the prophecy describing Elam's demise in *Ezekiel* was revealed on the fifteenth day of the twelfth month of the twelfth year, and that the celebration of Purim in the ancient Elamite capital of Susa was declared on the fifteenth of the twelfth month of the twelfth year.

Finally, Jer 49:34–39 contains a prophecy about Elam, self-dated to the beginning of the reign of Zedekiah (viz. 597 BCE), which ends with the following divine promise: "I will set My throne in Elam, and will destroy from thence king and princes, said the Lord. But it shall come to pass in the end of days, that I will bring back the captivity of Elam, said the Lord."[150] While there does not appear to be an allusion to this verse in MT *Esther*, some Talmudic rabbis made the connection, demonstrating an awareness of the Elamite backdrop to *Esther* and some of its characters. In the Talmud (b.Megillah 10b), we are told that Rabbah bar 'Ofran began his Purim sermon with Jer 49:38 ("And I will set my throne in Elam and will destroy from thence kings and princes"), explaining that, "By 'kings' is meant Vashti, and by 'princes' Haman and his ten sons."

Moreover, some rabbis suspected a mythological context for *Esther*. Esther herself is compared to Venus (*istahar*) in the Talmud (b.Megillah 13a), and in both the first and second targums to *Esther* (2:7), and these identifications continued to feature into the fourteenth century, as the Spanish Rabbi Baḥya ben Asher (d. 1340) compared Mordecai to Jupiter and Haman to Mars, while at the other end of the Islamicate world, the Judeo-Persian poet Shāhīn of Shīrāz composed his celebrated *ArdashīrNāma* (wr. 1333), in which Esther and Mordecai are compared to Venus and Jupiter respectively.[151]

Similarly, while some late antique rabbis held that Mordecai refused to bow to Haman as the latter had worn a symbol of idolatry on his clothing, others argued that Haman deemed himself to be a god.[152] This tallies with MT *Esther*'s employment of both the verbal roots *k-r-'* and *sh-ḥ-w* with reference to the prostration to Haman that Ahashwerosh commanded. This pair of verbs is only ever used in the HB with reference to prostration before God, whereas other, theologically acceptable episodes of bowing to humans use only one root or the other.[153] MT *Esther*'s author was telling his biblically literate readers that the king demanded recognition of his choice of divine *kitin*-bestower in Esth 3, only to replace Haman in this role with Mordecai (Marduk), in the final two verses of the book (Esth 10:2–3).

Two concluding points may be made in light of the foregoing. First, both the ANE evidence unearthed by modern scholars and the biblical intertexts deployed in MT *Esther* identify Haman as both an Elamite and as a deity, facts that did not escape some of *Esther*'s authoritative interpreters. Second, while it is conventional to observe that the divine actor does not appear (by name) in MT *Esther*, this is far from accurate. For while the *biblical* God goes unmentioned, various ANE gods are mentioned repeatedly.

All this assumes that the Judeo-Christian perspective on the historical evolution of scriptures is correct. Accordingly, the Elamite Humban produced MT *Esther*'s Haman, who was adopted (and reconceived) in the Greek versions of *Esther* and their offshoots, following which centuries of Jewish and Christian exegetes continued to reimagine their Hamans as refractions of the villains with whom they were forced to contend. In his final scriptural manifestation, Haman resurfaced in the Qur'ān.

However, as stated in Chapter 1, from a Muslim perspective it is the Qur'ān that predates the HB and *Esther* within it. Curiously, even from this perspective the Elamite Humban may prove illuminating: For just as the Qur'ānic Haman (unlike his biblical namesake) was known to have commanded armies and sought to build a tower to the Heavens, Humban literally meant "military commander" and in the Neo-Elamite period there appears to have been a ziggurat for him in Susa.[154] To this, as to the various theories concerning Haman's prebiblical DNA discussed in this chapter, perhaps the most fitting verdict is the common Arabic statement, *wa-allāhu a'lam*, "And God knows best."

9

Haman at Home and at Work

IN THE previous chapter we discussed the lead-up to Haman's birth and in the following we will discuss his death. In this chapter we will consider aspects of Haman's life—focusing on his family and career—as recalled by Jews, Christians, and Muslims. To the extent that this book promises to provide a biography of Haman, this is the chapter in which that promise will be fulfilled.

And yet, despite ending on an agnostic note, the previous chapter demonstrated that the three Hamans of the MT, LXX, and the Qur'ān, are not characters that a modern reader would necessarily recognize as historical. To be sure, it is likely that there were historical circumstances or even figures who underlie each Haman, but that is not the same as saying that a villain by the name of Haman existed in Achaemenid Persia, in Ptolemaic Egypt, or at Pharaoh's court. Moreover, even assuming that historical figures contributed to the scriptural Hamans, the latter will undoubtedly have undergone such thorough literary processing that each Haman has reached us as a tapestry woven of many threads. In what follows, therefore, we encounter a Haman created by the Jewish, Christian, and Muslim authors who encountered him in their scriptures. Accordingly, whereas in the preceding chapter we considered both internal and external approaches to Haman's origins, in this chapter there are no external data to consider.

Family

Any biography must surely include details of the subject's family context, but in the case of Haman this is particularly so for two reasons. First, the fact that Haman's epithet changed between the versions of *Esther* indicates that ancient readers of the book attributed significance to his group identity. It is perhaps within this context that we may understand the decision to include in both *Targum*

Rishon and *Targum Sheni* a complete genealogy for Haman, tracing his lineage back to Esau.[1] Along these lines, the two targums render the phrase "Haman's house," which Esther received from the king upon Haman's demise (Esth 8:1–2), as referring to his people or even to his children.[2]

Second, the importance of Haman's family to the plot of *Esther* is made apparent in the text itself, for his family is described in considerably more detail than that of any other character in the story: We know of his father (Hammedata), his wife (Zeresh), and of his ten sons (named in Esth 9:7–9), and we know that his sons were integral to his self-worth (Esth 5:11).[3] Zeresh, for her part, plays a pivotal role by recommending the means by which Haman is to punish Mordecai (Esth 5:14), which, famously become the means by which Haman himself is executed.

Moreover, the topic of Haman's family gained further significance in late antiquity. Not only was this when Haman's Amalekite or Bougean associations give way to Edomite and Christian ones (as seen), but this was the period in which the very concept of "family" within the Abrahamic religions would be contested. Judaism's ethnic character meant that patrilineal (eventually to be replaced by matrilineal) descent was what conferred Jewish status, as described repeatedly throughout *Genesis* (for all that "Jewish" was not yet a relevant label). If one's determining parent was Jewish then they too were Jewish. A Jew who ate pork on Yom Kippur, would be a sinning Jew, but a Jew nonetheless. There was (almost) no way in, and no way out. Family was thus absolutely essential throughout the HB, as well as for those who read and interpreted it from within the Jewish fold.

Jesus in the NT, however, introduced a momentous reinterpretation of the family concept. Familial bonds, like other aspects of the HB, were spiritualized, meaning that physical ties were replaced by spiritual ones. In Mark 3:31–35, we hear the following:

> Then Jesus' mother and brothers arrived. Standing outside, they sent someone in to call him. A crowd was sitting around him, and they told him, "Your mother and brothers are outside looking for you." "Who are my mother and my brothers?" he asked. Then he looked at those seated in a circle around him and said, "Here are my mother and my brothers! Whoever does God's will is my brother and sister and mother."[4]

For this reason we find the Greek word for "brothers and sisters" (*adelphoi*) used in the NT with reference to believers, for they belong to God's family.[5] Muslims, for whom "believers are brothers [to each other]" (Q 49:10), also replaced family and tribal affiliations with spiritual ones.[6] Accordingly, all of Noah's sons inherit the earth in the biblical flood story (Gen 10), whereas in the Qur'ān, Noah has a disbelieving son who does not survive the flood (Q 11:42–46). Bearing the foregoing in mind, it is perhaps unsurprising that we find the most attention paid to Haman's family members in Jewish tradition. It is to Haman's parents, father-in-law, wife, sons, daughter, and brother that we now turn.

Mother

Any modern psychological profile cannot but begin with the subject's mother, and although no version of *Esther* mentions Haman's mother, late antique rabbis generously supply one piece of information. In the Talmud (b.Baba Bathra 91a), we are told that two people in history had a mother by the name of Amthelai: Abraham and Haman. This is a rare name—in fact, it is not known from other sources, unless one relates it to the Islamic tradition that Abraham's mother's name was Amīla.[7] When discussing Haman's brother below, we will return to this curious detail. For the time being, we know only what Haman's mother's name was, and we may assume that she withheld affection from him.

Father

In the case of Haman's father, we are on firmer ground. *Esther* tells us that his name was Hammedata,[8] this being an authentic Achaemenid-era name that appears in official documents of the period (as discussed in Chapter 8). And although *Esther* itself does not contribute further details about him, late antique rabbis did, specifying that Hammedata had been a bath-attendant and a barber in the Galilean village of Kfar Qarnos.[9] We will return to the family profession in the following section, where some sense will be made of this detail.

Father-in-law

Unfortunately, we know nothing about Haman's mother-in-law, a figure one imagines had a negative influence on his character and mood. Of his father-in-law, however, we do hear something: According to two late antique Aramaic renderings of *Esther*, Haman's wife was "the daughter of Tattenai, the governor of the (province) across the river [Euphrates]."[10] As with Hammedata, there is contemporary documentary evidence for the existence of a "Tattenai," who served in precisely this administrative capacity.[11] Late antique Jews, however, probably knew of this character from the biblical book of *Ezra* (5:3, 6:6, and 13), where Tattenai opposes Jewish efforts to rebuild the Temple.[12] The association between Tattenai and Haman's family seems to be based on the numerous late antique midrashim that associate Haman himself with opposition to the reconstruction of the Temple. In any case, from Haman's perspective, he married well.

Wife

Unlike Hammedata or Tattenai, there is no external confirmation for the existence in the early-Achaemenid period of women by the name of Zeresh. Instead, as suggested in the previous chapter, it is likely that "Zeresh" relates to the theonym Kirirša, an Elamite "mother of the gods." As Haman's wife, Zeresh plays oversized roles in both *Esther* and the various exegetical elaborations on it.[13]

Zeresh's importance is indicated by the very fact that she is mentioned at all, which is not a given for three reasons. First, she is always referred to alongside "those who love [Haman]" (Hebrew:*'ohavav*; Esth 5:10, 14, and 6: 13) whereas she could have been included within this group. Her exclusion from "those who love [Haman]" may well have comic intent, implying a loveless marriage. Second, whereas Vashti is replaced by Esther and Haman by Mordecai, Zeresh does not have an obvious foil in *Esther*,[14] and her absence from the narrative would thus not weaken the reversal theme of the story. Third, from the various traditions concerning Haman's scores of sons (to which we turn shortly), it may be assumed that ancient exegetes believed Haman to have had numerous wives. That Zeresh, specifically, should be mentioned requires explanation.

We cannot determine whether Zeresh's appearance in *Esther* is a vestige of the anti-Elamite raw materials with which its author worked, or whether it is due to her father's stature generally (or to his anti-Jewish reputation particularly, as some have argued).[15] What we can determine, however, is that she was a divisive figure in antiquity and throughout the Middle Ages, with some traditions portraying her as villainous and others capturing her in a more (sym)pathetic light.

In support of Zeresh's villainy is the text of *Esther* itself, which not only places her in Haman's camp, but actually depicts her as the leading voice within it (Esth 5:10 and 6:13). Haman's complaint that Mordecai disrespects him is met not with spousal empathy, nor even with the sort of cautious advice that would have allowed Haman to bear the frustration calmly, but rather with the most uncompromising solution to the Mordecai problem, namely that a tall gallows should be constructed by which to hang him. Had Zeresh's advice been more moderate, so too would Haman's eventual suffering have been (when his plot was eventually turned on him). To make matters worse, Zeresh eventually admits that her advice was flawed (Esth 6:13). Considering the gravity of this realization and the danger to her husband that it implies, she makes the admission rather glibly, even using an alliteration (*naphol tippol le-phanav*) when breaking the bad news to him.[16]

Not only was Zeresh an unloving spouse, but according to some ancient interpreters she was responsible for Haman's downfall altogether, not merely for giving bad advice, but for having goaded Haman on with his evil plans. The fourth-century Church Father Aphrahat argued that Zeresh (acting on Satan's behalf) misguided Haman, thereby following in a long line of women, beginning with Eve herself, who brought about their husbands' downfall.[17] Some centuries later, the same idea surfaced in a midrashic commentary on *Proverbs*, which states that Haman and Korah had two things in common: their wealth, and the fact that they "fell" because they heeded their wives' advice.[18] The idea that male villains were manipulated by their wives also appears in the Elijah-cycle, where the evil Israelite king, Ahab, was "stirred up" by his wife Jezebel (1 Kgs 21:25).[19] From this single reference, the Talmudic scholar Rav ("Abbā Arīkhā," d. 247) is said to have stated generally that, "whoever follows his wife's advice will fall in Hell."[20]

That biblical women in late antiquity could receive bad press is also evidenced by the Qur'ān's contrasting the virtuous (Arabic: *ṣāliḥ*) Noah and Lot with their disloyal wives, who were committed to Hell (Q 66:10).[21] Whether or not this is relevant, by the time the medieval-era *Esther Rabba* was compiled, the Talmudic phrase "cursed be Haman," was upgraded to include Haman's sons and his wife, Zeresh.[22]

Traditions that view Zeresh as a sympathetic character, are relatively rare, but they are all the more interesting for it. An Aramaic *piyyuṭ* from late antique Palestine describes Zeresh's response to the execution and public hanging of Haman's (and her) sons, as described in Esth 9:5–10. In this *piyyuṭ* two aspects of Zeresh's response serve to refract her character through a sympathetic lens. First, Zeresh clearly blames Haman for the misfortunes which befell their family, and she directly curses him twice in the poem.[23] She is also described as wailing publicly and using language that invokes Jewish dirges recited on the ninth of Av (commemorating the destruction of the Temple). Just as Jews mourn the destruction of "God's House," so Zeresh mourned the destruction of her own house.[24]

Second, unlike Haman and his ten sons, who are punished for their behavior and publicly executed by others, the *piyyuṭ* has Zeresh taking her own life by hanging herself with a rope (*ḥ-b-l*).[25] This detail—in typical midrashic fashion—fills a narrative gap left by MT *Esther*, where we only hear of the fate of Haman and his sons. But this gap need not have been filled in this way: LXX Add E:18 *implies* that Zeresh was killed together with her sons when it states that Haman's "household" was executed, while OL *Esther* (7:9–10) states this directly.[26] Furthermore, the *Targum Rishon* (9:14), tells us that Zeresh actually fled with her surviving son, rather than dying with Haman and their ten (other) sons.[27] That Zeresh took her own life by hanging contrasts her with Umm Jamīl, Muḥammad's aunt and the wife of the Prophet's infamous opponent, Abū Lahab. The Qur'ān (111:5) tells us that Umm Jamīl has (or will have) a rope (*ḥ-b-l*) around her neck. Unlike Umm Jamīl, whose hanging by rope is the punishment due to this villainous woman,[28] Zeresh's hanging by rope is the self-inflicted result of her maternal anguish. Thus, at around the same time and in much the same place where the author of the *Targum Rishon* was describing Zeresh as "the evil one" (Aramaic: *reshīʿa*), the author of an Aramaic *piyyuṭ* was recasting her in a considerably more sympathetic light.

Sons

Like Zeresh, Haman's sons have pre-*Esther* DNA (in the form of Tiamat's eleven monsters, Darius's nine or ten challengers, and Zoroastrian *daivās*).[29] They play an important role in the text of *Esther* itself, where they serve as status-markers for Haman: their existence denotes his success, their demise his failure.[30] Also like Zeresh, the sons draw important exegetical attention, some of which reimagines them—either as a group or individually—in unexpected ways.

The implication in the Greek *Esther*s that Haman was a eunuch (and therefore could not father children) is not to be taken literally, both because these versions clearly state that he did have sons, and because the term "eunuch" in the HB could refer to a courtier generally.[31] Seeing as in most premodern societies one's sons followed in their father's professional footsteps, it is not surprising that ancient and medieval exegetes described Haman's sons as courtiers, too.[32] Motivated by an instinct to expand on even the smallest datum, the exegetes expanded not merely the quantity of our information about Haman's sons, but also the quantity of his sons. For just as it could be argued that Zeresh was but one of Haman's wives, it became commonplace in rabbinic tradition to assume that Haman's ten named sons in *Esther* were not the only sons he had; they were merely the ten sons who served with him at Ahashwerosh's court.[33] As is often the case with midrashim, the supplementary data provided strike a modern reader as somewhat doubtful. From the reference (Esth 5:11) to "the multitude of his sons," some rabbis argued that Haman actually had 202, 208, or 214 sons altogether, as the numerical sum of the Hebrew letters that make up the word "multitude" (*rov*) could equal one of these three numbers (the different numbers reflect different spellings of (*ve-*)*rov*).[34]

Not only do we hear of additional sons, but in some instances a character known from elsewhere in the HB is described as having been among Haman's progeny: Just as Tattenai (known from Ezra 5–6) was remembered as having been Zeresh's father, Shimshai the scribe who successfully petitioned the Persian king to halt the rebuilding the Jewish Temple in Ezra 4—was widely identified as Haman's son.[35] Some late antique traditions merely relate that Shimshai was the scribe who presented Ahashwerosh's diaries to him (Esth 6:1);[36] others tell us that he attempted to erase from the king's diaries a positive report about Mordecai, but did not identify him directly with Haman;[37] and still others explain that this Shimshai was Haman's son.[38] Segal has argued that the association between Haman and Shimshai derives from the similarity between the anti-Temple accusation in Ezra 4 and Haman's anti-Jewish accusation in *Esther* 3:8.[39] Bearing in mind that the anti-Temple accusation was associated in Ezra 4 with Shimshai and with "Rehum the chancellor," it is probably not surprising that some added Rehum to the list of Haman's additional sons.[40]

Perhaps more interesting than the names and numbers of Haman's sons is the question of their allegiance: Were they supportive of their father (and, therefore, also villainous), or innocent bystanders, caught up in Haman's evil schemes? Whereas in Zeresh's case the sympathetic reading of her character was very much a minority view, in the case of Haman's sons, the jury has traditionally been split.

That Haman's sons—or, at the very least, the ten sons named in Esth 9:7–9—were culpable collaborators in their father's anti-Jewish machinations is implied by the fact that they were executed and publicly hanged (9:10) in the context of the Jews' killing "their enemies" (9:5). The sons' specific culpability is indicated in the various traditions that identify them generally as royal scribes or provincial governors during Haman's viziership. (Other midrashim add details such as Haman's having acquired the wood for "Mordecai's" gallows from Noah's Ark, which came to rest in a province where Haman's son, Parshandata (*Esther* 9:6), had been governor.[41] Parshandata was thus able to supply Haman with a suitably large plank for the 50-cubit gallows.[42] That ancient (and modern) authors located Noah's Ark in Armenia[43] may relate to the common association between Haman and Armenia (discussed in Chapter 8).

There are, however, midrashic traditions which hold either that Haman's unnamed sons and their descendants were far from villainous, or even that the ten sons named and killed in *Esther* were themselves unwilling accomplices, who eventually turned on their father. This latter view is reflected in *Targum Sheni* (8:15), as follows:

> The ten sons of Haman (with) odorous hands walked in front of the righteous Mordecai and declared: "The one who gives reward to the Jews pays the wicked their compensation upon their heads; but this Haman, our stupid father who put his trust in his wealth and (in his) glory, Mordecai defeated him with fast and prayer."[44]

Having seen their father's rival emerge victorious, the ten sons came to blame Haman for their misfortune, just as a mourning Zeresh blamed her husband for the family's misfortune.

Regarding Haman's other descendants, we hear that they "studied Torah in Benei Beraq."[45] While this tradition may seem odd at first, it makes more sense when considered in both its immediate and broader contexts. As for its immediate context: the Talmudic text in which this tradition appears adds that other unsavory characters, such as Sisera and Sennacherib, had also studied Torah (the former in Jerusalem, the latter "in public") and Nebuchadnezzar's descendants had converted to Judaism.[46] Haman's Torah-learning grandchildren are thus not particularly exceptional for having followed a better path than their infamous ancestor.

The larger context is the debate over the inheritability of guilt. The pre-Hellenic HB takes it as a given that one's descendants can be punished (or rewarded) for one's own actions. God's covenants with Abraham and then Moses commit their descendants to rules and promise to reward them for following these rules, even though 99.9% of the beneficiaries of the contracts were not yet alive at the time of signing. God's punishment of Adam's and then Ham's descendants likewise affected hundreds of generations of people who were seemingly innocent of the sins that elicited the punishments.[47] In the post-Hellenic world of late antiquity, however, a just God was expected to reward and punish His people only for their own actions. The message imparted in these Talmudic passages is that one may choose a virtuous life (taken, in this context, to mean a life of Torah study) regardless of how unvirtuous one's ancestors were.

The extent to which villains themselves could repent was debated among Jews, Christians, and Muslims. Such figures as Nebuchadnezzar and Pharaoh were considered sincere penitents in some (usually Christian and Muslim) circles, but incorrigibly evil in other (usually Jewish) ones.[48] Already in the HB, following a period in which Nebuchadnezzar was transformed into an animal and dwelled in the wilderness, he openly repented and recognized the King of Heaven (Dan

4:31–34). This episode served as the basis for Christian renunciants in late antiquity, who sought to achieve spiritual heights by modelling themselves on Nebuchadnezzar's transformation. The rabbis, however, could not accept that the Temple's destroyer could ever be rehabilitated.[49] Similarly, whereas the Qur'ān (10:90–92) appears to indicate that Pharaoh became a believer in the moments preceding his death, and indeed some (predominantly Ṣūfī) scholars came to view Pharaoh's conversion as sincere and accepted, most Muslim authorities disagreed.[50]

Although it is true that some villains bred further generations of villains, and late antique traditions could invent villainous genealogies by which to emphasize just how evil a person was,[51] most agreed that individuals—including the offspring of villains—have freedom of choice and can, if they wish, reach the very heights of piety.[52] The Jewish traditions according to which Haman (and Sisera, Sennacherib, and Nebuchadnezzar) had pious descendants, originate in the same late antique Near East that produced the early biographies of Muḥammad, and these are replete with infamous characters who had pious sons: Abū Jahl (one son), Abū Lahab (two sons), and ʿAbdallah ibn Ubayy (nine sons), all had children who converted to Islam, despite having been archetypal opponents of the Prophet.[53] What these traditions demonstrate is not only that it was possible for the son of an exemplary villain to slip through his father's net and find his way to God, but that this was the norm. It might even be argued from the quantity and quality of these examples that it was a characteristic feature of villains to have sons who rejected their path. This may be why Haman's sons and descendants were rehabilitated in later sources, despite the clear statement in *Esther* that his sons were publicly punished and the strong implication in the text that they were enumerated among the "enemies" of the Jews.

Daughter

As there is no reference to Haman's daughter in any ancient version of *Esther*, it was left to the exegetes to invent her. In this case, they did not slot some existing biblical woman into Haman's household, but instead read her into the backstory. A puzzling phrase in Esth 6:12, describes Haman returning home after parading Mordecai "in mourning and with his head covered." One could easily imagine that he was in mourning either literally or metaphorically: literally, with his head physically covered, for having been forced to celebrate his archrival in public (as it would be a number of verses later, in Esth 7:8, where the same verb is used); metaphorically, as it is elsewhere in the HB, to imply shame.[54] Had the exegetes adopted those readings of the phrase, Haman would have remained daughterless.

Instead, it was imagined that when Haman was parading Mordecai, the following occurred:

> As they were walking opposite the house of the wicked Haman, Sh-k-ḥ-ṭ-n-t,[55] his daughter, looked down from the roof, and it appeared that the man walking on the road was Mordecai while the man riding on the horse was her father. So she took a pot of excrement and flung it on his head. He raised his head and said to her, "You, too, my daughter, you embarrass me?" Whereupon, immediately she fell from the roof and died from the balcony chamber.[56]

Other versions of the story, with minor differences, can be found in late antique and early medieval rabbinic sources,[57] all of which share the conclusion that Esth 6:12 referred to Haman "mourning" over his daughter, and "with his face covered" in excrement. The popularity of this midrash (and perhaps its very creation) may owe to the comic-ironic image that it creates, as the character who so craved public expressions of honor was so publicly dishonored. And yet, one may also notice two items of deeper significance within this midrash. First, that whereas Haman's sons were a source of pride to him (Esth 5:11), his daughter was a source of shame, with whatever gender-related implications this may have: Perhaps we are to conclude that daughters are a liability to "family honor" or, conversely, that Haman's daughter closely resembled her father, as a bumbling tragic villain whose evil plans were turned on their head (so to speak). Second, and also along gender-lines, we might relate this story to Zeresh's suicide in the late antique *piyyuṭ* discussed earlier, or to Jezebel's death by defenestration (2 Kgs 9:30–37).

Other midrashim discuss Haman's daughter, as a means used by her father in his pursuit of power rather than as a character in her own right. The *Targum Rishon* (5:1) relates that before she approached the king uninvited, Esther uttered a prayer that began as follows:

> Lord of the Universe, do not deliver me into the hand of this uncircumcised one, and do not accomplish the desire of the wicked Haman against me as it was accomplished against Vashti, whom he advised to the king to put to death because he wished [Ahashwerosh] to marry his daughter. Thus, when the maidens were assembled into the custody of Hegai, Haman's daughter was there too, and it was then determined from Heaven that each day she become defiled with excrement and with urine, so her mouth smelled exceedingly offensive, whereupon they hurried her out. . . .[58]

According to the tradition in this passage, Haman plotted to have his own daughter enthroned as queen of Persia, and this was his motive for conspiring against Vashti.[59] Conniving to raise a child to royalty is a plot element with a long legacy that perhaps had its origins in ancient Persian storytelling. *Samak-i 'Ayyār*, for example, relates that both the evil nurse of Mah-Parī and the evil vizier of the king of China plotted to have their sons marry a king's daughter. This is a theme whose antiquity is matched by its endurance, as it has resurfaced in modern times: Elizabeth Polak included it in her 1835 play *Esther the Royal Jewess or, The Death of Haman*,[60] and it has also been adopted by some modern scholars of *Esther*.[61]

That Haman sought to have his daughter marry Ahashwerosh, only for Mordecai to succeed in having his own (adopted) daughter enthroned, is consistent also with other examples of Mordecai's having achieved Haman's goals. And just as Esther's prayer indicates that God miraculously caused Haman's daughter to be unattractive to the king, another tradition (preserved by al-Ṭabarī) relates that Ahashwerosh, "became attracted to Esther by divine design."[62] What the foregoing traditions show is that Haman's daughter, like his sons, was imagined by exegetes to have been a victim of her father's schemes rather than an active contributor to them.

Brother

Did Hammedata (and Amthelai) have sons other than Haman? One might be forgiven for assuming so, or for expecting the exegetes and other *Esther*-readers to invent them.[63] And yet, no such materials exist in premodern Jewish and Christian sources. There is, however, a modern Persian resource that states matter-of-factly that Haman had a brother, and that this brother was none other than the prophet Abraham.[64] Such an assertion could be easily dismissed as a simple error based on a misreading of "Haran," the name of one of Abraham's brothers in the HB (Gen 11:26). Not only are these two names near-homophones, but in Semitic languages the letters "r" and "m" (which belong to the *l-m-n-r* group of liquid consonants) are interchangeable. Hence, "Haman" can become "Haran" and vice-versa. In fact, already in the first half of the twelfth century, a Persian text stated that (Haran's son) Lot was "the son of 'Haman.'"[65] Assuming "Haran" was misread as "Haman," and considering the numerous gaps—historical, geographical and others—between the careers of Abraham and Haman, we might reject the notion that they were brothers out of hand.

And yet, there are two reasons to give some consideration to this tradition. First it appears in 'Alī Akbar Deh Khodā's (d. 1955) monumental dictionary of the Persian language, *Lughat Nāma.*[66] This is the most complete and ambitious dictionary of Persian ever compiled. The work's cultural standing in Iran is such that the parliament in 1945 allocated a budget and staff to work solely on the project, and it is therefore worth consulting, if nothing else, for a snapshot of Iranian knowledge on a given subject. Deh Khodā's entry on "Haman" states: "Haman was the name of the brother of our Master Abraham, and he was consumed by fire at the time when the idols were burned." This entry is followed by one on Purim, known in Persian as "Hāmān-Sūz," and this entry, too, deserves our attention—for reasons that will become clear shortly. Deh Khodā writes:

> Hāmān Sūz is the fourteenth day of Adar, this being the month that is followed by Nissan. On this day, Jews make an effigy that they name "Haman" (the vizier of Ahashwerosh), hang it, throw it into a fire, and celebrate joyously.

Second, as we will now see, the gaps between Haman and Abraham in sources emanating from the culturally Persian world are far smaller than they are in Western, Judeo-Christian sources. Geographically, although Judeo-Christian sources place Abraham's homeland in modern Iraq, no less a figure than the (Persian) al-Ṭabarī relates the tradition that Abraham was actually a native of Susa.[67] Temporally, although Judeo-Christian tradition considers Abraham to have been a contemporary of Nimrod, builder of the Tower of Babel,[68] we have noted that in the Qur'ān and Islamic tradition it is Haman who is infamous for having been commissioned with the building of a tower that dared to aim for the heavens. All agree, therefore, that Abraham had a tower-building antagonist and in Islamic tradition he may have been Haman.[69] The temporal gap is thus also bridgeable.[70]

Perhaps even more significant is that both Haran and Haman were commonly associated in Persian lands with death by fire. We will encounter traditions about Haman's death in the following chapter; here it is sufficient to return to Deh Khodā's statement (which he attributes to al-Bīrūnī) that Purim was known in Iran as "Hāmān-Sūz," literally, "the burning of Haman." As for Haran, despite barely being mentioned in the HB itself, he plays a central role in postbiblical traditions concerning one of the most famous episodes of Abraham's life, namely Nimrod's testing of Abraham in a fiery furnace. An early version of this episode is found in the book of *Jubilees*, which relates that:

> Abram arose by night, and burned the house of the idols, and he burned all that was in the house and no man knew it. And they arose in the night and sought to save their gods from the midst of the fire. And Haran hastened to

save them, but the fire flamed over him, and he was burnt in the fire, and he died in Ur of the Chaldees before Terah, his father, and they buried him in Ur of the Chaldees.[71]

A similar description of Haran's death is found in the late antique *Genesis Rabba*,[72] where this story includes such added details as the fact that Abraham's antagonist, responsible for casting him into a furnace, was none other than Nimrod.[73] Admittedly, in virtually all midrashic elaborations on this event, whether from antiquity, late antiquity, or the early Middle Ages, Haran is a passive victim, rather than an instigator or ringleader. He dies in the fire for no other reason than that he hesitated when asked whether he would choose Terah's idolatry or Abraham's iconoclasm. However, the fourteenth century Judeo-Persian poet Shāhīn relates that Haran volunteered to cast Abraham into the furnace, and—through God's intervention—Abraham was saved from the fire, while Haran died in it.[74] This version of events brings Haran into line with Haman, who was an active antagonist and who was hanged on the very same gallows by which he sought to hang Mordecai. If Haman's biography underwent a "Haranization" (by absorbing the death-by-fire motif)[75] then here we have Haran undergoing a "Hamanization." Either way, the two biographies came to be intertwined in Persian sources, both Jewish and Muslim, perhaps because the geographical and temporal gaps between Abraham and Haman in these sources are smaller than they are in Western exegetical materials.

A reader of Deh Khodā's entry on Haman will thus be under the misapprehension that Haman had a particularly famous brother. Despite the apparent absurdity of the notion in the eyes of readers conditioned by Judeo-Christian traditions, they should perhaps consider that Haman's association with Abraham is no less historically defensible than our data on Haman's mother, daughter, or descendants in Benei Beraq. And at least the tradition about his brother has the benefit of being of local, Persian provenance.

Career

In premodern societies, and to a great extent in modern ones too, one's occupation says more about them than the mere facts of how they spend their time and earn their keep. This is all the more relevant in biblically literate societies, for the HB regularly imbues certain professions, careers, and lifestyles with a specific significance. For instance, in distinguishing between Jacob and Esau (Gen 25:27), the Bible characterizes them based on their lifestyles and skillset rather than on their appearance: Jacob is a tent-dweller, Esau is a man of the field, a hunter. This particular distinction acquires added relevance for our purposes when we consider that Haman was routinely related back to Esau and the Edomites in late antiquity (although we will see that he was not usually associated with hunter-like professions).

Another culturally loaded aspect of Haman's lifestyle was his wealth. Both Hebrew and Greek versions of *Esther* describe him as wealthy (Esth 5:11).[76] What, if anything, this signifies about Haman as a person differs according to the different meanings that wealth takes on in each Abrahamic community, and on this issue there is a noteworthy diversity of opinion. Jesus is memorably quoted as having said, "It is easier for a camel to go through the eye of a needle than for a rich man to enter the Kingdom of God" (Luke 18:25). Accordingly, for readers of the NT, Haman's wealth is unquestionably to be judged negatively.[77] By contrast, the Qur'ān's version of this statement reflects a different attitude to riches: "Surely those who receive our revelations with denial and arrogance, the gates of heaven will not be opened for them, nor will they enter Paradise until a camel passes through the eye of a needle" (Q 7:40).[78] Elsewhere in the Qur'ān it is strongly implied that some leading sinners were themselves wealthy, and that their wealth would be of no use to them on the Day of Judgment (Q 111:2 and 104:1–4, among others), but the conscious replacement of Jesus's "rich man" with arrogant deniers of revelation serves to downplay the negative associations of money.[79]

What the Qur'ān and the rabbis did seek to regulate was one's attitude to wealth: Overly relying on one's wealth (rather than on God), acquiring riches illegitimately, or attributing one's material success to one's own ingenuity (rather than acknowledging God's control over such things) may taint wealth. We therefore find that Korah (Arabic: Qārūn) was judged to have sinned by acquiring his treasures illegitimately (according to the rabbis), or for taking credit for them personally (according to the Qur'ān).[80] For his part, Haman is said to have relied too heavily on his wealth,[81] and to have acquired it by stealing treasures from the kings of Judah and from the Holy of Holies.[82] Korah and Haman, who were closely associated throughout history for their reliance on their wives and for their riches,[83] appear together in the Qur'ān (Q 28:6 and 8).

The association of Haman with Mammon, coupled with the fact that the Bible and Qur'ān directly refer to aspects of Haman's career, ensured that Jews, Christians, and Muslims throughout history would pay exegetical attention to this aspect of our villain's biography. We begin with the scriptures themselves.

Haman's Career in Versions of Esther

All versions of *Esther* describe Haman as having been a courtier of some description. In the MT, this courtier's fortunes fluctuate wildly: Already in the first verse in which he appears we are told that Haman was promoted by the king. From the statement that his seat was raised above those of "all the other princes (Hebrew: *sarīm*) who were with him," we may infer that he was originally one such prince. These princes, we are told in the following verse, were "servants of the king who were at the king's gate," a fairly general description that nonetheless reinforces the notion that he and his colleagues were court-functionaries of some sort. Later in the chapter, a sharp increase in Haman's authority is added to this ceremonial promotion, as the king gives Haman his signet ring and the empire-wide influence that comes with it (3:10–11). By the end of the chapter (3:15), Haman and the king have "sat down to drink," which adds "royal boon-companion" to Haman's résumé. The prestige, authority, and direct access to the king that Haman enjoyed, combine to create the impression that he was what might (anachronistically for the Achaemenid period) be called the king's "vizier," holding as he did the highest executive position in the imperial administration.[84]

Working with a Hebrew *Vorlage* that described Haman in such terms, the authors of the Greek versions of *Esther* also depicted Haman as ascending the administrative ranks of the Persian court, ultimately attaining the status of a second-in-command to the king (LXX 4:8, AT 4:4). There are, however, ways in which the Greek versions adjust and add to the MT's descriptions of Haman's roles. As noted, we learn that he was a eunuch at the Persian court (LXX 1:10, AT 2:8), worked for Mordecai (who was appointed senior chamberlain; Add A:16–17), and was a spy for the Macedonians (Add E:10–14).

The Qur'ān's Haman, by contrast, combined two functions, the one military (for commanding *junūd*, "armies"), the other more administrative in nature as Pharaoh's project-manager charged with building a rebellious skyscraper. The latter role deserves some attention for its Near Eastern associations, which may be lost on modern readers. Whereas in modern Western societies scientific knowledge is deemed to be an indicator of intelligence, in ancient and late antique Near Eastern societies architectural know-how was the yardstick by which intellect was measured. The Tower of Babel story, for instance, indicates that when all of humankind's resources and abilities are marshalled towards a single goal, they can produce a city and a tower that stretches up to the heavens. Neither a flying-machine, nor medical knowledge, nor quantum physics rival the ability to plan and execute an architectural mega-project. Perhaps the two most renowned wisemen of the ANE—Aḥiqar (the skyscraper architect) and Solomon (who built the Temple or *ṣarḥ*-palace, as per Q 27:44)—are famous for their building projects.[85]

In this wider context, the Qur'ān's depiction of Haman as Pharaoh's master-builder indicates that Haman was considered the wisest member of Pharaoh's retinue (Arabic: *malā'*). Wisdom and piety are two different things, however, and the Qur'ān contrasts Solomon's mega-project, which brings the Queen of Sheba to Islam, with Haman's, which represents a rejection of God.[86] Muslim exegetes and historians took things further and combined admiration for Haman's skills and achievements with unfavorable anecdotes about his unjust practices.[87]

From Rags to Riches: Haman's Pre-scriptural Career

Whether he was a middle-range courtier promoted by Ahashwerosh, or part of Pharaoh's inner-circle, Haman appears in Abrahamic scriptures mid-career, allowing premodern historians and exegetes to fill in the gaps in his résumé.

One question about Haman's early career that drew scholars' attention concerned the source of his wealth or influence at the imperial court. As is often the case with medieval midrashic expansions, the boundaries between Jewish, Christian, and Muslim traditions were far more porous than one might imagine: As we will see, the Qur'ānic Haman shared attributes with his biblical namesake, and vice versa.

Perhaps to enhance the dramatic effect of Haman's topsy-turvy life, most sources tell us that he began poor and powerless. What is probably the oldest tradition about Haman's pre-*Esther* career comes from the AT (Add A:16–17), which relates that he was "given" to Mordecai, a vague statement that produced a centuries-long tradition of Haman's having been Mordecai's slave. Some rabbis explicitly contrasted Mordecai, who came from a wealthy background, with Haman, who came from a poor one—a notion they based on the tradition that Haman was called, "the slave who was sold for a load of bread."[88] We have also encountered the tradition that Haman acquired his wealth by stealing the treasures of the kings of Judah and of the Temple, and that it was upon seeing his wealth and his ten accomplished sons who served as scribes, that the king decided to promote Haman to high office.[89]

Thus far, we have learned three things: Haman began poor; he achieved his wealth illegitimately; and his wealth impressed the ruler enough to earn him a political appointment (or promotion). All three of these feature in the works of

Muslim scholars from the tenth and eleventh centuries CE.[90] The earliest of them is al-Maqdisī (fl. 966), who writes:

> I have heard storytellers (*quṣṣās*) claim that Pharaoh was a native of Balkh, and Hāmān was [a native] of Sarakhs. [I have also heard] that they were the first to transport watermelon seeds to Egypt, where they planted them, became wealthy, and took control of the cemeteries there. [Thus,] they did not allow corpses to be buried unless a fee was paid. Thereafter, Pharaoh came to rule over Egypt and appointed Hāmān as his vizier (*istawzarahu*). And God knows best.[91]

About a century later, al-Kisāʾī (fl. 1100) and al-Bīrūnī (d. 1048) related similar accounts of Pharaoh's and Haman's rise from obscurity to influence through the practice of graveyard extortion, but with a significant difference: Rather than describing the two villains working together, these authors narrate the events as though they concern either Pharaoh (al-Kisāʾī) or Haman (al-Bīrūnī). According to al-Kisāʾī, having gambled away all the money that he had inherited from his previous employer (!), Pharaoh came up with a cunning business plan:

> The idea came to him to sit at the gate of the graveyard of Egypt to ask a pittance from those in funeral processions. He spread out a carpet, sat down, and charged everyone who came with the dead a voluntary amount, until at length he had amassed a large quantity of money. When the king's daughter died and was carried to the cemetery, Pharaoh prevented them from burying her. For this offense the king was determined to have him killed, but Pharaoh ransomed himself with the money that he had collected, so the king set him free and allowed him to resume his activity.[92]

Later, al-Kisāʾī explains that Pharaoh killed the real king of Egypt and put the royal crown on his head. "Thus all the kingdoms on earth became his, though he was no more than an Egyptian slave." Al-Bīrūnī, by contrast, recounts a version of the Maqdisī/Kisāʾī story that is interesting for identifying *Esther*'s Haman with the Pharaoh of Islamic tradition. He writes:

> Once a man called Hāmān, a man of no importance, travelled to Tustar in order to undertake some office. But on the way there he met with an obstacle which prevented him from reaching the end of his journey and this happened on the same day on which the offices (in Tustar) were bestowed. So he missed this opportunity and fell into utter distress. Now, he took his seat near the temples and demanded for every dead body (that was to be buried) three and

> one third dirhams. This went on until the daughter of king Ahashwerosh died. When people came with her body, he demanded something from the bearers, and on being refused he did not allow them to pass, until they yielded and were willing to pay him what he asked for . . . The king was astonished at the great sum of money which he mentioned, because he with all his supreme power had nothing like it. So he said: "A man who gathered so much money from the rule over the dead, is worthy to be made *wazīr* and councillor." So he entrusted him with all his affairs, and ordered his subjects to obey him.[93]

We have thus far encountered three accounts that include the three features found in earlier midrashim describing Haman: poverty, wealth obtained by dishonest means, and a political appointment resulting from the ruler's amazement at the villain's ingenuity. Among the three accounts, al-Kisāʾī's stands out for replacing Haman with Pharaoh. That both earlier and contemporary traditions tell this story about Haman, and that Pharaoh in al-Kisāʾī's narrative achieved political power "though he was no more than an Egyptian slave," strongly suggest that even his version of the story is based on Haman traditions. What is particularly interesting is that Haman in these Muslim sources is described as having attained the position of vizier, that is to say, he has come to resemble *Esther*'s Haman.

One aspect of these accounts that does not appear to be based on extant midrashic materials is the motif of graveyard extortion. The origin of this detail in Haman's pre-scriptural life exemplifies the complexity of advanced Hamanology, for in this case we must turn not to midrash but to Diodorus Siculus (first century BCE) and to Haman's epithet in the Greek versions of *Esther*, "Bougaios." In Chapter 5, we considered the possibility that this epithet might relate to the infamous Achaemenid courtier(s) named "Bagoas," as the latter shared many characteristics with the Hamans of the LXX and of the Qur'ān. Diodorus preserves the following anecdote about Bagoas:

> Artaxerxes, after taking over all Egypt and demolishing the walls of the most important cities, by plundering the shrines gathered a vast quantity of silver and gold, and he carried off the inscribed records from the ancient temples, which later on Bagoas returned to the Egyptian priests on the payment of huge sums by way of ransom.[94]

Both Bagoas and Haman/Pharoah thus obtained wealth by dishonest means. Admittedly it is a stretch to link Bagoas's holding "inscribed records" belonging to ancient priests for ransom with Haman/Pharaoh's use of Egyptian corpses as a means to wealth in Muslim sources. There is, however, a key to this ostensible incongruity, and it lies in the intricacies of Arabic orthography: The term used for the "corpses" in these texts is *nawāwīs* (نواويس), literally meaning "sarcophagi," whereas the word for "inscribed records" or "sacred writings" in classical Arabic is *nawāmīs* (نواميس). It is not simply that a single letter in the middle of the word distinguishes Bagoas's commodity of choice from Hāmān's or Pharaoh's, but that the "m" and "w" are orthographically very similar, and would be more so in handwriting. Accordingly, an Arabic text concerning Bagoas, which described him as having confiscated Egyptian *nawāmīs*, was read by a scribe as Egyptian *nawāwīs*, "sarcophagi." The story, with this new detail, was elaborated upon, reaching the forms in which it is quoted above.

Thus, a detail about Bagoas from a Sicilian historian, informed a Jewish midrash about Haman in Greek *Esther*, which was misread in an Arabic telling of the story. Within two centuries, a Turkish collection of *Isrā'īliyyāt* included its own, expanded version of Pharaoh's and Haman's rise from rags to riches. The author of this work, al-Rabghūzī (wr. 1310),[95] appears to have supplemented the tale with details taken from other late antique midrashim. In his words:

> A drought befell the land of Khorasan and the people were very hungry. When Pharaoh heard that there was abundant food and luxury in the land of Egypt, he set out from Khorasan for Egypt. He went from town to town. He entered Bushanj; he was hungry and came upon a bakery. Hāmān was the baker there. When Hāmān saw Pharaoh he asked him: "Where have you come from?" Pharaoh replied: "I've come from Balkh." "Where are you going?" Hāmān asked. "To Egypt," said Pharaoh. Hāmān was literate and had read in a written text that a king would arise at that time, and that he, Hāmān, would be the king's minister and would attend to all his affairs. It occurred to him: "This may be the man." Hāmān said: "Let us be friends." Pharaoh replied: "So be it." Then Hāmān said: "Just wait a little; I must make some necessary arrangements." Pharaoh bided his time while Hāmān sold his mansion and land, and all his possessions.

Whereas in the HB there was a famine in Pharaoh's Egypt, in this case the famine occurs elsewhere while Egypt enjoys abundance. But what interests us is the detail that in this tradition Haman was originally a baker, a detail found earlier in the work of Sibṭ ibn al-Jawzī (d. 1256).[96] That Haman was a baker may relate to the fact that Haman—like the Chief Baker in Gen 40:22—was executed by hanging (using the same Hebrew phrase as found in *Esther* 7:10), and to the complex of midrashim in which Haman sold himself to Mordecai for a loaf of bread. Alternatively, this detail relates to the traditions that describe Haman acquiring his wealth by plundering the treasures of the kings of Judah and the Temple, as these equate him with the evil Nebuzaradan, who is also described (in 2 Kgs 25 and Jer 52) as having plundered the Temple's treasures. Whereas Nebuzaradan is known in the biblical text as *rab ṭabbāḥīm* (literally, "chief of the cooks"—employing a Semitic root that can also denote "slaughter"),[97] in extra-biblical sources he was known (as "Nabû-zēr-iddina") by the title *rab nuḥatimmê*, which means "chief cook" in Akkadian, but is etymologically related to the Talmudic word for "baker," *naḥtom*.[98]

Whatever the case may be, al-Rabghūzī's acquaintance with Hebrew or Jewish sources is instructive, not least because a Hebraicized version of his account surfaces in the late midrashic work *Sefer ha-Yashar*.[99] The round-trip journeys of Haman lore between Jewish and Muslim sources is characteristic of the interplay between *Isrā'īliyyāt* and midrashic literature, and bears upon a significant ramification of the foregoing discussion: Although the Qur'ānic Haman is a military commander and wise master-builder, rather than a vizier; and although biblical Haman is a vizier rather than a military commander; during the Middle Ages Muslim sources would describe Haman as Pharaoh's vizier and Jewish sources would describe him commanding Ahashwerosh's armies to quash a rebellion in India.

From Riches to Rags: Haman's Demotion

Haman's progress from poverty and insignificance to wealth and influence would peak in those biblical and Qur'ānic references to him that also mention his demise. In the following chapter, we will consider Haman's death in detail. Here, we examine a final station on Haman's career path, one that exegetes fashioned out of the slimmest textual material, but which nonetheless greatly enhances Haman's professional portfolio. In Esth 6:11, we hear that Ahashwerosh commanded Haman to repay Mordecai for foiling the two eunuchs' regicidal plot, by publicly parading Mordecai. We have already seen how this scene ended for Haman's daughter who, in some midrashim jumped to her death having inadvertently humiliated her father. To Haman's disappointment and public humiliation in Esth 6:11, the rabbis thus added yet more humiliation plus the loss of his daughter.

The rabbis did not stop there, however, and in a selection of late antique traditions that expand on Haman's parading of Mordecai we are told that Haman had served in a variety of other capacities, specifically menial ones. In the Talmud (b.Megillah 16a) we discover that when Haman prepared Mordecai for the latter's ceremonial parade, Mordecai insisted on having a bath and a haircut out of respect for the royal garments that he was about to wear. Esther then cunningly ordered that all bathhouses and grooming facilities be shut, thus forcing Haman to undertake the grooming tasks himself. While trimming Mordecai's hair, Haman cut himself and sighed. Mordecai asked him, "Why are you sighing?" to which Haman replied, "The man whom the king once regarded above all his other ministers is now made a bathhouse attendant (Aramaic: *balnay*) and a barber (*sappar*)!" Mordecai then dismissed Haman's explanation by reminding him that he had previously served as a barber in Kfar Qarṣum for twenty-two years.[100]

A number of versions of this midrash exist, one of which replaces the phrase, "The man whom the king had once regarded above all his other ministers," with technical terms for functionaries in the Byzantine bureaucracy and suggests that it was Haman's *father* who had served as a "barber, a bath attendant, and a cosmetician" in Kfar Qarṣum (or "Qarnos") for twenty-two years.[101] Yet another midrash relates that Haman had previously served as a bath attendant, barber, equerry, and herald,[102] while a *piyyuṭ* from the eve of Islam refers to Haman as "a singer . . . and a blood-letter and barber, and a seeker of hairstyles."[103] These traditions may explain how Haman suddenly found the grooming utensils necessary for preparing Mordecai, and how he acquired the skills needed to undertake the tasks (although his injury in doing so suggests that his skills were a bit rusty). But in addition to answering questions these traditions raise some new ones: Exactly which jobs did Haman actually undertake? Was it Haman himself or his father who had served as a barber or bath attendant in the past? Do these traditions describe Haman's *ad hoc* actions in light of Esther's shutting down the relevant services in town, or do they indicate some aspects of Haman's work experience that belong on his résumé? The answers to these questions vary in the sources and portray Haman differently: Either we are being told that his rise from rags to riches began with low-level, menial work, or that his actions vis à vis Mordecai indicate yet another stage in the deterioration of his status, from riches to rags. According to other (admittedly rare) opinions, Haman did not himself undertake the grooming tasks, but rather commissioned his own, private barber and bath attendant, a tradition that indicates Haman's influence and authority rather than weakness.[104]

Fortunately, the Dura Europos panel provides pictorial evidence of Haman undertaking the actions described in Esth 6:11. Unfortunately, scholars disagree in their interpretation of Haman's attire in the panel, with some seeing him depicted as a Parthian stable boy, and others as a Roman competitor in a chariot race.[105] We might also question the readings of the various menial tasks associated with Haman in the late antique traditions. The term used for "barber," for instance, derives from a Semitic root (*s-p-r*) that in ancient and late antique contexts, more commonly indicates scribal work. That Haman's sons were thought to be scribes (using the same *s-p-r* root) supports the idea that Haman (and/or his father) might also have been scribes of some sort. Perhaps, then, a tradition about Haman the scribe was read as "Haman the haircutter," to which other humble vocations were then added.[106]

Not only could specific terms be misread, but the character of Haman's activities might be lost on readers detached from the social context of the story. This is evident in the interpretation of Haman's lot-casting as an offence—first as proof that he was an astrologer, and later as evidence that he was a gambler. As a practitioner of astrology,[107] Haman would not necessarily be engaging in a practice that was widely condemned, but neither was it officially authorized:[108] Abraham Shalom (wr. 1575), for instance, portrayed Haman as "an astrologer who denied God's providence and strove to undermine the Jewish faith."[109] Gambling, by contrast, was generally frowned upon, and Christian authors, particularly of the Victorian era, conflated Haman's lot-casting with gambling as yet another way of denigrating him,[110] while the reality was just the opposite. Lot-casting was deemed to be a legitimate practice, widely sanctioned in the most prestigious of ANE, Jewish, Christian, and Muslim texts throughout history.[111]

Conclusions

From an internal, Abrahamic perspective, numerous details of Haman's biography came to light in late antiquity and the Middle Ages. Sources from these periods informed us about Haman's parents, his wife and his father-in-law, his children and other descendants, and even his brother. They also testify to Haman's versatile vocational skillset, which included not only high administrative and military positions, but also menial tasks, street-swindling, espionage, racketeering, Temple-looting, baking, astrology, and haircutting. The extent to which these biographical details were deemed reliable by their purveyors and audiences is nigh impossible to determine.[112] The declining prestige of *Isrā'īliyyāt* in Muslim societies and the frivolity that often characterizes the contexts in which *Esther* lore was enjoyed in Jewish societies, certainly suggest that we are not dealing with traditions that can boast high historiographical pretensions.

Despite this, there is much to learn from the foregoing discussion of Haman's life at home and at work. These lessons concern not the minor details of

Haman's life, but instead shed light on larger issues: concepts of family, wealth, the inheritability of villainy, mega-project building, gender-relations, and of course the ways in which various religious communities in different regions and periods interpreted these concepts. Moreover, the decisions that exegetes, historians, scholars and liturgical poets took in elaborating on aspects of Haman's life are instructive—both for the questions they asked and for the answers they provided. And as seen repeatedly in this book, readers of scripture could pool their traditions to enrich their descriptions of Haman, with the unexpected results: the wider the range of Haman traditions an author consulted, the more uniform the portrayal of Haman became, until we see Qur'ānic and biblical Hamans merging in medieval Abrahamic sources. One detail about Haman's life that all could accept is that its ending was of enormous significance. Why this is so is the topic of our final chapter.

10

Haman's Death

Introduction

Haman's death is not interesting in itself (for everyone dies), and even in *Esther* (Esth 7:10), Haman's end was not the end of the story, for in the MT it continues for three more chapters. What is interesting, and will concern us here, are the ways in which Haman's death has been interpreted, reenacted, and celebrated, from the most ancient versions of *Esther* until the present day. It is not merely that as part of Purim celebrations Jews have routinely rejoiced in Haman's demise, but that Haman's death was imbued with meaning and significance, as we will discover in the following pages.

This chapter is divided into three sections. In the first, we examine descriptions of Haman's death in scriptures and their exegeses. In the second section, we consider the multiplicity of popular customs associated with Haman's death, some of which, such as burning or crucifying Haman in effigy, we have already encountered in passing. The most prominent of these traditions will be contextualized culturally, yielding analyses that enhance our understanding of practices that might otherwise appear random or merely cathartic. In the third section, we will contextualize Hamanicidal customs historically, tracing some of them to pre-*Esther* times, while also demonstrating the extraordinary influence that they had beyond the world of Purim celebrations, in Christian, Samaritan, and Muslim contexts.

Haman's Death in Scriptures

We begin with the Qur'ān, as it is in this scripture that we might expect a villain's death to hold the most significance, for two reasons: First, the Qur'ān contains a selection of what are commonly referred to as "punishment stories," which aim to dissuade us from ignoring the Prophet's message by recounting the fate of those who rejected prophetic warnings in the past. In this context, one would expect that, for his role as a Moses-rejecter, Haman's bitter fate would be described in some detail. Second, and related to this, is the fact that Haman is inextricably paired with Pharaoh in the Qur'ān, and Pharaoh's death is deemed to be particularly important. Q 10:90–92 relates that Pharaoh "and his armies" were drowned (cf. Exod 15:4), but that Pharaoh's body was to be preserved as a "sign" (or "wonder," Arabic: *āya*) for future generations. Indeed, the discovery in Egypt in 1881 of what is purportedly Pharaoh's well-preserved corpse has generated excitement in some Muslim circles.[1]

Unfortunately for us and for our serially disappointed villain, the Qur'ān does not mention Haman's death. The fact that Pharaoh drowned with "his armies" does not necessarily imply that Haman was drowned as well,[2] as the Qur'ān specifies that he and Pharaoh each had their own armies (Q 28:6, 8). For this reason, Muslim exegetes and historians have suggested that Haman died under the weight of his collapsing tower, which the angel Gabriel destroyed with his wing.[3] This latter option brings the Qur'ān's Haman into line with his biblical namesake, as it presents a sort of poetic justice, with Haman being defeated by the very same object through which he sought to challenge God.

As discussed earlier, the biblical accounts of Haman's death are highly significant, especially the references to his crucifixion in the LXX and other ancient and late antique sources.[4] The postulate that this detail influenced NT descriptions of Jesus's crucifixion would, if correct, make this the most influential event in Haman's biography. Before turning to the influence that biblical descriptions of Haman's death may have had in history, it is worth contextualizing these descriptions literarily, beginning with the instance of poetic justice cited above. *Esther*'s description of Haman's demise on the very gallows that he had prepared for Mordecai relates to two biblical intertexts. The first is the narrative in Dan 6:16–25, where Daniel miraculously survives being cast into a den of lions while his tormentors are devoured (together with their families; cf. Esth 9) in the very same den of lions. This passage is relevant to Haman's context as it concerns Jewish success in an eastern Diaspora court.[5] The second is the description in Esth 2:21–23 of Bigthan and Teresh's plot to kill the king, which results in the king killing them. Although not necessarily a case of poetic justice (for we do not know whether they had plotted specifically to hang the king from a tree), it is surely significant that the same terminology is employed to describe their execution (2:23) as is employed to describe Haman's (7:10).[6] If nothing else, this episode, like many details found in Chapters 1–2 either sets the scene or serves as a precedent for details that will be found in later chapters of the story. In this case, we learn that for merely plotting a crime one might be executed in Ahashwerosh's empire.

The foregoing points notwithstanding, there are three ways in which Haman's execution in *Esther* differs from these intertexts. First, Haman's gallows are described (5:14 and 7:9) as being fifty cubits high, which would make them the second tallest building project mentioned in the HB (the tallest being the golden idol set up by Nebuchadnezzar in Dan 3:1). Haman's execution was thus both monumentally public, and pleasantly ironic: Having initially been elevated by the king in a display of honor (Esth 3:1), Haman was now being elevated by the king in a display of shame. Second, and related to this, is the theme of reversals that is so central to *Esther* generally. It is not merely that Haman was executed by the means intended for Mordecai, but that his death represented a crucial stage in the reversal of his fate *vis à vis* his rival at court. Third, unlike Bigthan and Teresh's execution, which spelled the end of their story in *Esther*, Haman's death is followed in the MT by three more chapters related to his genocidal threat and its unmaking. It is, as far as the plain text(s) of *Esther* is concerned, less pivotal to the plot than it would come to be among *Esther*'s audiences, as we will now discover.

Haman's Death in Practice

As with virtually all scriptural verses, those in *Esther* that describe Haman's demise have generated exegetical attention. Various aspects of Haman's execution have been discussed and debated, most often regarding what appear to us to be superficial details of the event: the type of tree from which the gallows were constructed; the relationship between Haman's execution and those of his sons (and wife); and even the short dialogue that Haman had with Mordecai moments before the former was executed.[7] In previous chapters such midrashic details could compensate for the lack of historical corroboration or material evidence pertaining to Haman's life, but the case of his death is different. There are rich resources from diverse regions and periods of Jewish history that enable us to capture the ways in which it has been reimagined over time. These living commentaries on Esth 7:10, combine literary traditions on Haman's death with local customs in fascinating ways. Historians, anthropologists, and others have studied Purim rites generally, and Hamanicidal customs in particular, and it is not my intention here to survey the many thousands of such recorded traditions.[8] Rather, I will analyze in this section some of the most common methods of punishing Haman, with a particular focus on the cultural and historical contexts that shaped them.

Underpinning any discussion of these traditions are three general points. First, punishing Haman is a part of Purim celebrations, and these are (with a few, notable exceptions) carnivalesque occasions. The context of killing Haman is thus inherently frivolous, although the cathartic release that punishing Haman enabled might add a sharp edge to the festivities. Second, already in late antiquity these popular practices were couched in religious language and even classified as religious obligations. As seen regarding controversial Purim practices in Byzantine lands, where an effigy of Haman was crucified and burned, such customs were observed when and where rabbis and liturgical poets were active. The rabbinic emphasis on legalism and the widespread identification of Haman with Amalek had practical ramifications as responses to the commandment to "blot out the remembrance of Amalek from under the Heaven" (Deut 25:19) that was fulfilled during Purim celebrations. In the same period, the verse "the name of the wicked shall rot" (Prov 10:7) was connected to Haman specifically,[9] while a leading Talmudic sage stated that one is halakhically obligated to say, "cursed be Haman, cursed be his sons."[10]

Third, despite the regulated framework within which Hamanicidal practices were scaffolded, Jews on Purim did not necessarily apply Jewish law when punishing Haman; in fact, Purim celebrations have often been characterized by antinomianism, as they take place in an atmosphere that flaunts the letter of the Law rather than enshrining it.[11] In practice, Jews have tended not to act on Purim as though they were aiming for legal or literary consistency, but instead have unleashed on Haman whatever modes of punishment their cultural language might dictate. And although the following discussion treats the leading methods of punishing Haman in Jewish history individually, multiple forms of corporal and capital punishment were regularly visited upon Haman in a single ceremony.

Cursing Haman

We begin with the practice of cursing Haman, both because it was taken to be a religious obligation from late antiquity onwards, and because the significance of cursing Haman requires elucidation for modern readers. In Near Eastern contexts generally, and in biblical ones particularly, cursing someone was not only a verbal insult, but a practical way of invoking supernatural powers to punish the targeted figure.[12] It was believed that name-calling actually *could* break bones, no less than sticks and stones. This is reflected both in the popularity of magical objects meant to ward off such curses, and in the terminology used to describe the act of cursing: The Ethiopic root *r-g-m*, which in other Semitic languages often connotes "pelting" or "stoning," is used with reference to the accursed snake in Gen 3:13 (rendering the Hebrew: *arūr*, "cursed"), just as leading Muslim lexicographers interpreted Satan's epithet in the Qur'ān, *al-rajīm*, as meaning "accursed" (Arabic: *mal'ūn*).[13] Satan's accursed state is described in the Qur'ān itself (Q 15:35), using the same *l-'-n* root that some Judeo-Arabic commentators of *Esther* used for Haman, whom they referred to as *al-la'īn*, "the accursed."[14]

Moreover, deeming Haman to be accursed places him in the company of such infamous biblical characters as the snake in the Garden of Eden (Gen 3:14), Cain (Gen 4:11), and Canaan (Gen 9:25). In each of these cases, the damned figure is referred to as *arūr*, "accursed," this being the term used by the rabbis when on Purim they order that Haman be cursed. In late antiquity, Sasanid sources referred to Alexander the Great as "accursed" (Pahlavi: *gizistag*), precisely when and where the rabbis were adding Haman to the *arūr* list, while Muslim scholars (perhaps following Eastern Christian authors from late antiquity), labeled Satan in similar ways.

Bearing all this in mind, it is hardly surprising that descriptions of Haman-abuse often include the detail that Haman (and occasionally Zeresh, too) were publicly cursed during Purim celebrations.[15] We will also see below that villain-cursing came to be a central feature of Shī'a ceremonies that may have been influenced by Purim.

Effacing Haman

The various practices through which Haman was effaced or erased were also linked to the biblical commandment to "blot out the remembrance of Amalek from under the heavens" (Deut 25:19). Sanctioning informal practices by connecting them to a formal scriptural instruction imbued them with an unexpected measure of prestige,[16] which belies the eclectic and unregulated nature of some of the customs that claimed to fulfil the commandment. Haman's remembrance could be blotted out physically simply by writing his name down in some form—on the sole of a shoe, or on a rock, with the intention of erasing it shortly thereafter by scraping the sole on the ground, or by smashing the rock against another hard object. No less common, however, was the custom of blotting out Haman's name aurally, drowning it out by noise whenever it was uttered (either during the ceremonial Megillah-reading on Purim, or in the popular recitation of *piyyuṭim* following the Megillah-reading).

While the scriptural sanction for such practices probably enhanced their popularity, there is more to these customs than that, and here, too, some contextualization is in order. Just as cursing was deemed to be efficacious in ways that might not ring convincing to a modern reader, so the physical manifestations of religious texts were deemed sacred. Hence, most Near Eastern religions, from ancient to modern times, have swathed their religious writings in detailed regulations aimed at preserving the holy status of these texts. One must be in a state of ritual purity to handle a sacred text, and a Bible or Qur'ān reader might insist on placing the book on the top of a pile,[17] or even kiss a copy of the text that had fallen to the ground. Related to these rules is the well-known practice of burying holy texts that have fallen out of use, such as the Genizah idea, which is a feature of Islamic contexts as well as of the more famous Jewish ones. In fact, sacred writings could be taken to possess miraculous qualities (such as imperviousness to fire), by virtue of the physical words written in them.[18]

It is within this context that we may better understand the perceived significance of writing down Haman's name only to erase it soon thereafter.[19] Words were considered to have actual power, beyond the symbolic or metaphorical uses to which language may be put. Observers of Purim practices, particularly in Christendom (but elsewhere, too), have frequently noted the multitude of customs aimed at physically effacing Haman's name,[20] while the related custom of aural-effacement continues to be widespread wherever Purim is celebrated. The historical preference of Western Jewish communities to punish Haman by effacing and erasing him may relate to (or even originate in) the Roman legal concept of *Damnatio Memoriae*. This practice, which was reserved for an executed criminal, entailed erasing the criminal's name from documents and monuments and cancelling his ongoing charitable donations. It was so thorough a blotting out of a person's legacy that it was generally reserved for those who had committed such crimes against the state as treason, which tallies well with Haman's character in the LXX and its spin-offs. The Roman custom of effacing an illegitimate ruler's image from coins is similar in its intent.[21] What these precedents show is that Haman was not the first person in history to be "cancelled." And yet, given the spread of Haman-cancelling practices to other figures in Jewish history (and, as we will see below, beyond Jewish circles), Haman may arguably be considered as having generated an early form of "cancel culture."[22]

Crucifying Haman

Crucifixion is the only punishment inflicted on Haman (in some versions of *Esther*) or his effigy (in Purim celebrations), that has been discussed in some detail earlier in this book. We have seen that some very influential versions of *Esther* describe Haman as having been crucified; that such descriptions may have influenced the NT's accounts of Jesus's crucifixion; that even those Jews who knew *Esther* in its MT version were aware of traditions about Haman's crucifixion; that Jews in Christendom provocatively crucified effigies of Haman as part of their Purim celebrations; and that Christian observers of Jews throughout history were well aware of the barely concealed equation between Haman and Christ that Jews made. To these points, two further ones may be added here.

First, the act of crucifixion in the context of the ancient and late antique world could mean more than one thing, and our exposure to Christian iconography and jewelry has clouded our understanding of what this act meant in Haman's context. Haman's "hanging" may have been interpreted as crucifixion already in the Achaemenid period, based on the use of the Aramaic *zeqīf* in Ezra 6:11, where Darius threatens anyone who alters his decree, saying: "let a beam be pulled out from his house, and let him be lifted up and fastened thereon." The wording of this verse may be related to Haman's punishment in Esth 7:10,[23] for although *ṣ-l-b* is the most common root for crucifixion in Semitic languages, in Syriac the root employed is *z-q-f* (cf. Akkadian *zaqīpu*, "a cross for torture"). Moreover, in the Achaemenid period, hanging almost certainly indicated impalement rather than suspension from a gallows with a noose around one's neck (the latter practice probably does not predate late antiquity), and in some cases even impalement was referred to as "crucifixion."[24] Hence, the distinctions between crucifixion, impalement, and hanging (on a tree), in the pre-Christian Near East may have been far less pronounced than we might assume. Once the sort of crucifixion known from the NT became associated with Jesus, the haziness surrounding the term largely dissipated. Thus, when Jews are described as having crucified effigies of Haman in Christian contexts, we can be fairly confident that it is the sort of T-shaped suspension that was used.

Second, there is a difference between crucifying (or impaling) a criminal as a means of executing them, and doing so following their execution, as a means of publicly shaming them (or deterring onlookers from emulating them). In *Esther* itself both types of crucifixion are referenced. Haman (7:10), and Bigthan and Teresh before him (2:23), were executed through impalement,[25] whereas his ten sons were impaled publicly upon Esther's request (9:13–14), having already been executed (9:10).[26] That said, the fact that Haman was impaled on a wooden pole fifty cubits tall means that the method of execution doubled as a means of public-shaming. Whatever crucifixion meant, and whether it was a means of execution or display, it is interesting to note that Jews are recorded crucifying (*ṣ-l-b*) effigies of Haman even in Muslim lands—including in places such as Yemen that had not had a significant Christian presence for over a millennium.[27]

Burning Haman

Many Jewish communities celebrated Haman's downfall by burning an effigy of him on Purim. This custom may simply be interpreted as a cathartic means of torturing a villain to death, one that has immediate appeal and universal relevance (every culture has access to fire and dislikes being burned by it). There are, however, deeper layers of meaning to this practice that might be lost on modern readers.

First, unlike crucifying, impaling, or hanging an effigy of Haman, burning one eventually leads to the consumption of the effigy, which relates to the idea of effacing Haman. In Bukhara, for instance, children would make a snowman of Haman on Purim, around which they would light a fire that melted this Haman into nothingness.[28] Second, witnessing Haman's effigy consumed in flames might have evoked ancient ideas (originating in the Second Temple period, if not earlier) about evil persons suffering in hellfire. Burning Haman may therefore allude to his sorry fate in the Afterlife.[29]

Third, in some communities children would hold a mock trial of Haman on Purim at which they would condemn him to the four capital punishments applied in Jewish law (stoning, burning, decapitation, and strangulation). Following this, the children would burn an effigy of Haman.[30] Scholars of Jewish law might object that "burning" (Hebrew: *sereyfah*) in this context entails ingesting molten lead or the like, rather than being burned alive; that Haman's sins would have earned him death by stoning (whereas burning was generally applied in cases of illicit sexual relationships); and that Jewish law does not apply to gentiles in any case. At a popular level, however, such judicial minutiae and legalese are not of much concern.[31]

Fourth, and perhaps most significant of all, is the long-standing importance of fire ordeals in Near Eastern societies, and above all in Iranian cultures—which may explain why it is in these that Haman-burning customs appear to have featured most prominently. Simply put, it was widely accepted that guilt or innocence could be determined by subjecting a defendant to a trial-by-fire. While this practice was normally conducted in legal contexts,[32] the most famous examples of its application in Near Eastern history are theological episodes. Such religious heroes as Abraham, the three Jewish youths in Dan 3 (or, in some versions, Daniel himself), Zoroaster, the *ShāhNāma* hero Siyāvash, the Shīʿa Imām

Jaʿfar al-Ṣādiq, and others all survived fire ordeals through divine favor.[33] Burning Haman (in effigy) would thus have been a very public display of his guilt.

The cultural resonances of burning in Near Eastern contexts, and particularly in the Iranian sphere, may account for al-Bīrūnī's reference to "Haman-burning" (Persian: *hāmān-sūz*) as the name of Purim, and for the popularity of Haman-burning among Persian Jews throughout history.[34] Burning Haman is not limited to Iranian contexts, of course, and has been documented for Purim celebrations in other parts of the Muslim world,[35] as well as in Christian lands.[36] In fact, the well-known instances in which Byzantine Jews mocked Jesus on Purim concluded with the burning of a crucified effigy.[37] This was the case when, in 408, a Byzantine imperial law was passed banning Purim celebrations at which Jews burned an effigy of a crucified Haman, just as centuries later Jewish converts to Christianity in Byzantine lands would be forced to "curse those who keep the festival of the so-called Mordecai . . . nailing Haman to wood, and then mixing him with the emblem of the cross and burning them together."[38] That John Mayer, writing in seventeenth century England, railed against the practice of burning crucified effigies of Haman at Purim celebrations,[39] demonstrates the wide spread of the custom.

Corporal Punishment

Related to the various ways in which Haman was killed or erased (metaphorically and physically), are those customs that entailed punishing Haman (in effigy) before or after executing him. A good example of this—one that also serves to highlight the fluidity of the various categories adopted here—comes from a Jewish community in Kurdistan. Observers relate that once Haman's effigy had been publicly burned, a crowd would cast stones at its remains, thereby enacting "a stoning and a burial together."[40] Exposed as they were to both Jewish law and Muslim lore, this Jewish community may have been incorporating both halves of their identity by stoning Haman's burnt remains.

In Jewish law, execution by stoning was one of the four methods of capital punishment, and the widely held notion that Haman was promoting idolatry (either by presenting himself as a deity, or wearing an image of one on his clothes), would have earned him this type of execution. In Muslim lore, there was a practice of stoning the burial sites of hated figures, beginning with the legendary pre-Islamic Arabian traitor Abū Righāl, whose grave was stoned in pre- and early-Islamic times,[41] a custom that inspired numerous other instances of grave-stoning well into the Islamic period. Here we may also note the ritual stoning of Satan at the annual pilgrimage to Mecca (*Ḥajj*), which itself may be related to earlier rabbinic traditions about attacking Satan physically (or, at the very least, using language that implies physical attacks against him, such as "an arrow in the eye of Satan!").[42] Thus, although lapidation was a method of execution in Jewish law, there were also respectable precedents for casting things at villains outside of judicial contexts and without the intention of killing them.[43]

Stoning Haman at Purim was not only a custom in Kurdistan,[44] and one can imagine that it might have arisen spontaneously from the basic instinct to attack Haman with violence of whatever sort. For example, in some Russian communities, where the Near Eastern cultural resonances of stoning villains were not known, it was customary to attack Haman's effigy with sticks and metal rods.[45] Violence against an object representing Haman predated these practices by centuries: In Italy, between the thirteenth and eighteenth centuries, there was a Purim-custom of smashing a jar identified with Haman to symbolize the anticipated smashing of Christendom. As was the case with cursing or effacing Haman in other contexts, here, too, the practice was related to biblical verses that upgraded what might have seemed to be little more than an expression of anger to the status of a formal religious ritual.[46]

Eating Haman

Our final example of Hamanicide-in-context is the relatively widespread custom of eating Haman, or at least parts of him—a custom that may accrue greater significance when considered in its broader historical-cultural context. In the simplest of terms, eating a representation of the body, ears, or pockets of Haman (to name the best-known practices), may be seen as a symbolic gesture of triumphalism, celebrating either the complete subjugation of one's enemy, or—if the full process of eating is considered—the transformation of one's enemy into excrement. In either case, an ingested enemy ceases to be a threat.

Eating defeated rivals, or "exocannibalism,"[47] can also connote the absorption of the rivals' powers and positive attributes. And while this was not usually the intention behind consuming representations of Haman's body, it alerts us to the complexities inherent in the concept. In fact, the Eucharistic rite of eating sacramental bread and drinking sacramental wine—which are believed, through transubstantiation, to become the body and blood of Jesus—is an important Christian sacrament or an ordinance aimed at enabling communion between the one partaking in the eating and Jesus. Despite the very different contexts and interpretations of the Eucharistic and Purim practices, the intentionally provocative comparisons between Jesus and Haman encountered in previous chapters raises the possibility that, at times, Hamanivorism may have doubled as an oblique dig at Christian rituals.

While the Jewish children of Thessalonica are described as having eaten a life-size representation of Haman made of sugar,[48] and in Poland meat and pastry dishes representing Haman's body were consumed,[49] it is Haman's ears (Hebrew: *ozney haman*) or his pockets (Yiddish: *Hamantaschen*) that are most often consumed. For all that it is relatively well known in the West, the custom of eating Haman's pockets is the less interesting of the two, both because it does not involve Haman's body at all, and because the accidental invention of the term (if not of the concept itself) has long been known. The Yiddish word *Hamantaschen* is almost certainly a corruption of the word *Mohntaschen*, "poppyseed pockets," and although it has been argued that these poppyseed pockets were consciously meant to reflect either the seeds eaten by the Achaemenid Jews in Dan 1:12,[50] or the 10,000 talents of silver with which Haman offered to buy the Jews from Ahashwerosh (Esth 3:9), these are transparently popular aetiological explanations.

Eating Haman's ears, in contrast to his pockets, means eating part of Haman's body, and may derive from ancient Purim (or Purim-like) traditions. The reference to a pastry by the name of "Haman's ears" dates back at least to the sixteenth century,[51] which is around the same time as the phrases "Jew's ear" (in English) or "Judas's ear" (Latin: *auricula Judae*) are first attested.[52] While "Jew's ear" eventually came to refer to a type of mushroom, in medieval Europe it referred to a pastry eaten on Good Friday to commemorate Judas Iscariot's betrayal of Jesus on that day. Accordingly, for all that Haman and his death in LXX *Esther* may have influenced the NT's descriptions of Judas and of Jesus's crucifixion, in Christian Europe the tide of influence came to flow in the opposite direction.[53] Alternatively, eating Haman's ears has been connected to the Fettmilch uprising of 1612–1616, which was celebrated as a local Purim (as seen in Chapter 7). According to this theory, prior to his execution Fettmilch's ears were cropped and it is this Haman whose ears gave the pastry its name.[54]

The concept of dismembering Haman's body may also be kin to traditions about pre- and post-Hamanic figures who were cut up upon their defeat. The pre-Hamanic character is his ancestor Agag, who is said to have been cut to pieces by Saul (1 Sam 15:33), whereas the post-Hamanic character is Nicanor, descriptions of whom were shaped by *Esther* and whose head, arm, and tongue were cut off.[55] There is, however, no hint of exocannibalism in either of these cases.[56] An allusion to *Esther*-related pastry-pockets may underlie a biblical account of Judean women making cakes displaying the image of the Queen of Heaven, generally taken to be Ištar, with these cakes representing her reproductive organs

(Jer 44:15–25). Some have related this rite to ancient Purim practices (at which, it is argued, Esther-triangles were consumed festively).[57] Cumulatively, these accounts create the impression that long before the sixteenth century CE, Purim traditions relating to the consumption of Haman's body were in circulation.

Haman's Death in Context

Purim celebrations, and Hamanicidal ceremonies particularly, were typically public events. We have encountered moments in history when this created intercommunal tensions—such as the pushback from Christian authorities who were deeply offended by perceived comparisons between their most beloved figure and the Jews' most hated one. In other cases, however, broadcasting Haman's punishment yielded more positive results. There are, for instance, numerous accounts of non-Jews partaking in Purim festivities and then in some cases adopting aspects of Haman's punishment in their own communal celebrations. Sivan has noted that Purim in late antique Palestine was an integrative event that drew in non-Jewish observers;[58] in Fatimid Egypt Rabbanites, Karaites, and Muslims are portrayed as celebrating Haman's demise together;[59] and in Kurdistan, Jews and Muslims played Purim games in which balls representing Haman's head were smashed.[60]

One interesting testimony to Purim's public exposure comes from late-nineteenth century Ottoman Rhodes. As the story goes, the (Christian) governor had attempted to dissuade Jews from burning effigies of Haman on Purim, arguing that the local Christians themselves had recently discontinued the comparable custom of burning effigies of Jews as part of their Easter celebrations.[61] What we learn from this anecdote is not only that Jewish customs were widely known, but that non-Jews came to integrate similar behaviors in their own ritual calendar. And whereas Jews may have learned to eat Haman's ears on Purim from European Christians who ate Judas's ears on Easter, the very existence of an Ottoman-Christian ritual that was consciously compared to Purim indicates that Haman's annual punishment continued to shape not only Jewish communities that partook in these events, but also their neighbors who witnessed them. In the following section, I will attempt to demonstrate that punishing Haman on Purim informed a variety of non-Jewish rituals and ceremonies, which, in turn occasionally repaid the debt by enriching local Purim practices.

A: Pre-Purim contexts

The question of what makes a popular custom or ritual endure does not lend itself to simple answers. The necessary research most often produces tentative results whose value is outweighed by the immense efforts expended towards it.

In our case, for example, the fact that communities in the pre-*Esther* Near East ritually punished their enemies in symbolic ways is of such broad application that one wonders whether it is worth our attention here. Nonetheless, in the late-nineteenth and early-twentieth centuries, scholars endeavored to uncover the origins of various aspects of the Bible and biblical culture, including Purim. The most influential study to emerge was James Frazer's *Golden Bough*, in which he postulated that Purim was based on ANE New Year celebrations that included scapegoat rituals where a mock king was enthroned, temporarily, only to be executed publicly. Haman's elevation and subsequent public demise was, in his view, a Judaicized version of such earlier festivals as the Zagmuk, Akītu, or Sacaea holidays,[62] festivals that also contain elements of agricultural regeneration, temporary social reversals, the determination of fates for the coming year, and other themes familiar to us from *Esther* and Purim.[63]

Rather than attempting to analyze or contribute to the earlier work done on Purim's origins, we would simply note here the following three points. First, as we have come to discover in this chapter, and indeed throughout this book generally, there are as many Purims and Haman executions as there are Jewish communities, and attempts to reduce this rich diversity to some representative or typical institution, whose origins could then be traced to some similarly reduced ancestor, would be of questionable worth. But second, and despite this disclaimer, there are certain aspects of pre-*Esther* villain-punishing that either recur widely enough in Purim contexts, or are specific enough to suggest a relationship between pre-*Esther* practices and later Purim celebrations. These merit at least passing mention here. In pre-*Esther* New Year celebrations, for instance, a *hariu*-pot representing Marduk's defeated rival, Tiamat, was smashed, just as Italian Jews from the thirteenth to the nineteenth centuries would smash a pot representing Haman or Amalek. Similarly, a sheep representing Tiamat's viceroy, Qingu, would be burned in a bonfire—again, to celebrate Marduk's triumph, and again recalling Purim customs.[64] The relevance of the *Enuma Eliš* to *Esther* makes these New Year's rituals particularly relevant for us. Third, despite these details, and despite the variety of proposed precursors to Purim unearthed by scholars, there is no evidence of their enduring legacy in the Samaritan, Christian, and Muslim examples of villain-punishing to which we now turn. Conversely, we will see that the legacy of Purim and, particularly of Haman-punishing, is readily identifiable.

B: The Legacy of Haman's Death beyond Jewish Circles

A good place to start is the Magophonia festival, which we encountered earlier when investigating Haman's prebiblical origins. Although this festival is likely to have left its fingerprints on *Esther*, later incarnations of it seem to reflect Purim's reciprocal influence. The Achaemenid Magophonia celebrated the defeat of a Zoroastrian magus pretender who had challenged Darius's rule, and the ensuing massacre of magi throughout the Persian Empire. In the much later Sogdian version of the Magophonia, however, it is the Zoroastrians who are celebrated as the story's heroes, while the evil Alexander the Great (whose depiction in Sasanid Persia shared much with that of Haman in Sasanid-Jewish sources) was the villain.[65]

Another example of Purim's influence on non-Jewish communities comes from the Samaritan community in sixth-century Palestine. In this case, we hear of a violent rivalry between local Samaritan and Christian communities, which—from the Samaritan perspective—began when Christian children pelted their synagogue in 529, leading a group of Samaritans to murder a number of Christian children. In revenge, some Christians in Scythopolis (Bet Shean) publicly burned the leading Samaritan in the city, one Sylvanus. Sivan postulates that the burning of Sylvanus took place on Purim, indicating that Christians had been influenced by Purim practices.[66] The Samaritans of late antique Palestine are also said to have engaged in annual Purim-like rituals, when, on the festival of Sukkoth, they would burn effigies of Romans who had persecuted them in the distant past.[67] Unlike the Christians' burning of Sylvanus, which was a one-off event that involved burning an enemy in the flesh, the Samaritans commemorated the punishing of their tyrannical overlords annually, by burning them in effigy.

More historically significant are those Christian and Muslim festivals that appear either to be based on Hamanicidal rituals encountered at Purim, or to integrate elements from them.

Christian "Purims"

Writing in 1837, the Reverend J. W. Niblock remarked that the Jewish Purim, "is our Christmas and Easter."[68] While he was, of course, entitled to his opinion, there are in my view more accurate comparisons that can be made with Christian festivals. Here, we consider two of these—one predominantly celebrated in Catholic societies, the other in Protestant ones.

The (largely) Catholic Purim consists of a diverse complex of celebrations, attested throughout both Europe and Latin America, at which an effigy of Judas is ceremonially burned during the Eastern season.[69] As we have noted, it was during this season that a pastry called "Judas's ear" was eaten. Moreover, the noise-makers (Yiddish: *grogger*; Hebrew: *ra'ashan*) commonly employed to drown-out Haman's name during ceremonial Megillah-readings on Purim may also be traced to medieval anti-Judas customs.[70] What makes the possible relationship between Burning-Judas and Hamanicide ceremonies particularly interesting are the following three points. First, as implied in *Esther*, Haman was executed on the fifteenth of Nissan, that is to say, on Passover. Thus, the Easter timing of Burning-Judas ceremonies overlaps neatly with Haman's execution (for all that it does not overlap with Purim). Second, in Latin American communities especially, the Burning-Judas ceremonies (Spanish: *Quema del Judas*) were often an occasion for obliquely punishing unpopular political figures, just as Haman-punishing ceremonies have been throughout Jewish history. Third, it would appear that these celebrations reached Latin America from Spain shortly after the highpoint of the Spanish Inquisition. Considering the centrality of *Esther* to the Conversos, it may be that (former) Jews shaped anti-Judas festivities along the lines of anti-Haman celebrations in Latin America.

The Protestant Purim is Guy Fawkes Night, an annual commemoration of the failed Catholic conspiracy to overthrow Protestant rule in England by assassinating King James I and blowing up Parliament in 1605. Celebrated on the evening of November 5, virtually all descriptions of the festivities center on the public burning of the villain in effigy, for which reason the festival is commonly known as "Bonfire Night."[71] Its parallels with Haman-punishment are numerous and significant. Unlike most other comparable festivals, Guy Fawkes Night celebrates a failed conspiracy (as does Purim), and Guy Fawkes, like Haman, was a tragic villain. In fact, although burning him in effigy is meant to evoke Guy Fawkes' execution by hanging in 1605, he did not actually die by hanging: Shortly prior to his execution, Fawkes accidently fell and broke his neck. Thus, even in his bumbling, Guy Fawkes evoked Haman. Moreover, as seen in Chapter 7, the Gunpowder Plot was widely compared to Haman's machinations in *Esther*, and Guy Fawkes Night was routinely equated with Purim in sermons.[72] The variety of midrashim that equated Haman with Rome or the Romans made the comparison particularly apt.[73]

While for some English writers Guy Fawkes Night was perceived to be a new Purim, for others—particularly those travelling throughout Persian in the mid-nineteenth and early-twentieth centuries—the Shī'a festival of Omar Koshan (literally: "Killing Omar") was, "a Persian Guy Fawkes."[74] It is to these (Shī'a) Muslim Purims that we now turn.

Muslim "Purims"

Shīʿa cultures have produced a more developed repertoire of festivals and annual commemorations than Sunnī ones have. Two outstanding examples of this are the *Taʿziyah* (mourning) passion-plays, which bewail the massacre of a revered figure and his supporters; and the Omar Koshan festivities, which celebrate the murder of a reviled figure. While these are undoubtedly occasions of a very different nature (both in their ideological underpinnings and in their practical manifestations), there are points of overlap between them, as well as similarities between these two Shīʿa events and Purim.

Taʿziyah events mark the martyrdom, at Karbalāʾ, Iraq, of Ḥusayn, the third Imām of Shīʿa Islam and the Prophet Muḥammad's grandson, which took place on *ʿĀshūrāʾ*, (the tenth of the first month), in 680 CE. Detailed descriptions of the public mourning practiced on this day throughout the Shīʿa world date mostly from the sixteenth century onwards—probably because this was when Greater Iran (including Iraq) was conquered by Shīʿa rulers (the Safavid dynasty, r. 1501–1737),[75] who patronized Shīʿa culture and observed public commemoration of Shīʿa days of remembrance. That said, it is clear both that not long after the events in 680, a group of Ḥusayn's supporters began to deeply regret their inaction at the battle of Karbalāʾ, and that many aspects of the *Taʿziyah* as it is practiced in Persianate lands originated in pre-Islamic Iranian traditions (such as the commemoration of the death of Siyāvash, a leading hero in the *ShāhNāma*).[76] In other words, in Greater Iran, contact between Haman-punishing ceremonies and *Taʿziyah* events may predate the Safavid period by centuries.

The *Taʿziyah* is essentially a melancholy affair and, as such, it is not an obvious locus for overlap with carnivalesque Hamanicidal customs. Despite this, there are two ways in which the *Taʿziyah* may be relevant to us.[77] First, there are descriptions of Purim celebrations that bear more resemblance to *Taʿziyah* passion-plays than to Burning-Judas festivities: A Purim poem written in 1389 refers to, "those who make their way about the city reeling and staggering [cf. Ps 107:27] as they go, gashing themselves with knives and spears, according to their practice, until blood streams over them."[78] It would appear that in some historical contexts Purim celebrations resembled the public mourning rituals routinely witnessed at *Taʿziyah*s, at which, even today, mourners often engage in self-flagellation.[79]

Second, an important aspect of the recreation of the events at Karbalāʾ is the vilification of Ḥusayn's tormentor, accompanied by verbal and even physical abuse of the actor representing him (or of the villain in effigy). The precise identity of the tormentor was either the Umayyad caliph Yazid (r. 680–683), whom Ḥusayn challenged; or Shimr ibn Dhī al-Jawshan (d. 685), the soldier who actually killed Ḥusayn; or 'Umar ibn Sa'd (d. 686), the military commander who led the Umayyad forces against Ḥusayn. Observers of *Ta'ziyahs* in Iran relate that during the month of Muḥarram, when the *Ta'ziyah* occurs, people have the custom of cursing 'Umar,[80] while Piedro Della Valle (d. 1652) noted that on the eve of the *'Āshūrā'* there was a custom of burning effigies of 'Umar (alongside hated Sunnī figures).[81] Thus, just as the Burning-Judas festival focuses on punishing the antagonist of the martyred Jesus, the *Ta'ziyah* focuses on punishing the antagonist of the martyred Ḥusayn.

Closer to Purim generally, and to Haman-punishment particularly, is the Omar Koshan festival,[82] which commemorates the death of one of Shī'a Islam's most detested villains. Throughout history, from the Fatimid period (r. 969–1171) at the latest,[83] this Omar was generally understood to be the second caliph of Islam, 'Umar ibn al-Khaṭṭāb (r. 634–644), celebrated in Sunnī Islam as one of the greatest of the Prophet Muḥammad's companions and vilified in Shī'a Islam as a leading conspirator against 'Alī's right to lead the community of Muslims upon the Prophet's death. In Iran, 'Umar (Persian: *Omar*, hence "Omar Koshan") is doubly hated for being the caliph under whose rule Iran was conquered by Arabs, putting an end to 1200 years of Persian sovereignty. For these reasons, this 'Umar is among the most derided, ridiculed, and hated figures in popular Shī'a culture: his name is used as a swear-word, bathrooms are referred to as "'Umar's house" (Persian: *omar khāne*), and his death is celebrated in carnivalesque fashion during the Omar Koshan holiday. Curiously, despite its popular connection with the caliph 'Umar, the festival was almost certainly named after 'Umar ibn Sa'd, the Umayyad commander whose troops killed Ḥusayn.[84] The *Ta'ziyah* and Omar Koshan ceremonies are thus genetically related.

Some accounts of Omar Koshan mention that local Jews participated in the festivities, making this an integrative occasion that enabled contact between two villain-punishing traditions.[85] Accordingly, a variety of parallels may be drawn between Omar Koshan and Purim. To begin with, Omar Koshan has traditionally been held on the ninth day of the third month of the Muslim calendar (Rabī' al-Awwal),[86] when, according to Muslim tradition, Muḥammad was born. This brings the Shī'a festival into line with Purim, which takes place in Adar, the month of Moses's birth.[87] Moreover, during Omar Koshan celebrations, many communities stage plays recreating Omar's death, and one observer has specified that an Armenian Christian was hired to represent the evil Omar (recalling Haman's specifically Armenian identity).[88] Furthermore, it is a custom to consume

Omar-cakes that ooze blood-like syrup, while the ordinary cursing of Omar that peppers Shīʿa slang is intensified. Most importantly, effigies of Omar are made, abused in various ways, and ultimately burned publicly.[89] In fact, some practices witnessed at Omar Koshan appear specifically to echo Jewish ideas about Haman-punishment, as reflected in Purim-practices and midrashim on *Esther*. To cite but two examples: Writing in the mid-nineteenth century, Lady Mary Shiel noted that women would wait on rooftops with a pot of water, which they would pour on passers-by while shouting, "Omar, God curse him!,"[90] bringing to mind a midrash concerning Haman's daughter; and leathermakers would scratch his name into the soles of shoes so that walking in them would efface his name,[91] bringing to mind Jewish customs aimed at effacing Haman and Amalek.[92]

As Floor put it: "Omar is the most despised person, even more so than Judas to the Christians. No vilification is strong enough for him. Anything is allowed to dishonor him." And yet, the behaviors witnessed at Omar Koshan celebrations are not "anything." They are customs that tantalizingly overlap with Hamanicidal rituals associated with Purim.

Conclusions

From the centrality of Haman-punishing practiced at Purim, and the legacy that such rituals have had in comparable Christian and Muslim festivals, it would seem that Haman's death was the most significant event in his biography. The theological implications of his death—representing, as it does, the defeat of another manifestation of Amalek—are also significant, and it is no coincidence that images of Haman hanging from a tree with his ten sons hanging on either side of him, "was the most common illustration in the monumental illuminated Ashkenazi mahzorim produced in the thirteenth and fourteenth centuries."[93] The various means by which Haman was punished (along with Judas, Omar, Yazid, and others), can be appreciated at both superficial and more profound levels. Superficially, effacing, cursing, crucifying, beating, eating, and burning Haman were ways of cathartically alleviating the tensions and stresses inherent in the precarious Diaspora existence of Jewish communities throughout history. On a more profound level, these practices were pregnant with cultural and historical meanings that would likely be lost on modern readers. That Haman is executed every year, thousands of times, and in ceremonies in which men, women and children participate actively, makes his Sisyphean death particularly influential.[94] Typically of our tragic villain, the one thing Haman was most successful at was being ritually ridiculed, humiliated, and executed.

Conclusions

WHO, THEN, was Haman? In Part I of this book, we discovered that the answer to this question is complex. One's perception of Haman depended on the scripture through which one came to know him; on whether one read scripture literally, allegorically, or typologically; and which exegetical traditions shaped one's understanding of Haman's life and significance. In Part II, we analyzed the political, cultural, and religious contexts in which Hamans were formed and deployed polemically—in different regions and different periods of history. In Part III we sketched our biography of Haman on the basis of the accumulated Haman-lore produced by generations of Jews, Christians and Muslims.

We learned that Haman's family consisted of known parents, a famous father-in-law, numerous wives, somewhere between 10 and 214 sons (some of whom were well-known biblical characters), a daughter, descendants who engaged in Torah study, and a very famous brother. In terms of his religious affiliation, Haman was seen as a Christian (by Jews); a Jew (by other groups of Jews, and by Christians and Samaritans); a Catholic (by Protestants); and a Pharaonic Egyptian (by Muslims). Ethnically, Haman was variously identified as Persian (or, specifically *not* Persian), Macedonian, Roman, Egyptian, Amalekite, Armenian, Galilean, Elamite, or Indian. Vocationally, Haman was either a vizier, a military commander, a master-architect, a beautician, a gambler, an extortioner, a baker, a street-swindler, an astrologer, or some combination of these. Haman was executed by hanging, impalement, or crucifixion, while most annual celebrations of his demise have involved erasing, effacing, eating, beating, cursing, or burning him in effigy.

This bewildering diversity compels us to consider each Haman within the specific context that produced him.[1] And while historical and geographical circumstances are undoubtedly relevant to any such contextualization, cultural and religious contexts were the most pivotal variables in shaping perceptions of

Haman. In the broadest of strokes, we may summarize the ways in which Haman was situated within Jewish, Christian, and Muslim contexts respectively, as follows.

For Jews, Haman is primarily seen as a historical villain. He belongs not to the foggy, pre-Exodus period where we find Cain, Nephillim giants, Nimrod, and Pharaoh, and where God intervenes openly to orchestrate events, but to the more relatable, post-Exilic history, in which Jews lived under the rule (and, hence, at the mercy) of non-Jewish kings. Haman was also a familiar figure to Jewish readers of MT *Esther* as he was the ruler's representative, a position comparable to that of the various officials whom Jews encountered and occasionally despised.[2] Haman's inability in *Esther* to execute his genocidal plans was a source of relief for those Jews who felt threatened by their own Hamans, and the widespread identification of Haman with the Amalekites imbued him (and his defeat) with enormous significance.

For Christians, Haman's portrayals were shaped by several factors, including the version of *Esther* available to them, the interpretative strategies adopted in reading the book, and the political circumstances in which a Christian reader of *Esther* lived. To these may be added the fact that the OT came to be complemented by the NT, which introduced new archenemies and villains. Despite the theologically sophisticated identification of Haman with Jesus, the more readily apparent comparison was between Haman and Judas. Haman was influential for shaping Judas's character, but he was also downgraded in Christian cultures as he was replaced by Jesus's betrayer: Thus, some Christian communities celebrate a sort of Purim not as Burning-Haman but as Burning-Judas. Similarly, in other Christian communities, Haman's Roman identity (which originated in late antique Jewish circles) and his association, in Protestant eyes, with the Papal authorities in Rome, combined to produce a sort of Protestant Purim at which it is not Haman but rather Guy Fawkes who is burned.

For Muslims, Haman arguably played more significant roles in history than he did for Jews and Christians. He appeared in a scripture whose canonical status was never challenged; he featured on this scripture's most important historical stage; and he challenged not a particular nation but God Himself: The MT's Haman was an "enemy of the Jews" (3:10, 8:1), whereas the Muslim Haman was "the enemy of God."[3] Just as importantly, for over a millennium, the Qur'ānic Haman was used to challenge the very foundations of the religion, while in the twentieth and twenty-first centuries, the same Haman has been used—by those who see his appearance in the Qur'ān as miraculous—to strengthen these very same foundations.

On the other hand, Haman's appearance in the history of the Banū Isrā'īl—relevant though this period may be for its cautionary lessons and as the lead-up to the emergence of the "Seal of Prophets"—is not part of the final epoch that begins with the Prophet's rebooting of History: All prophets were considered impeccable, but it is only Muḥammad whose life is taken as a blueprint for subsequent generations of Muslims. Hence, just as Judas overshadowed earlier biblical villains for readers of the NT, a new cast of enemies comprised of such opponents of the Prophet as Abū Jahl and Abū Lahab, came to overshadow earlier villains.[4] And from among the ancient Israelite bogeymen it is Pharaoh, rather than Haman, who was taken to be the model villain. The Prophet is said to have stated that "Abū Jahl is the Pharaoh of this *ummah* (community),"[5] just as it is Pharaoh whose name has given the Arabic language the verb *tafarʿana*, "to be Pharaoh-like," which is used to describe those who are haughty or tyrannical.

As Shīʿa Muslims added their Imāms to the list of impeccable role models, they also added the most hated opponents of these Imāms to their list of villains. We therefore find ʿUmar paired with Haman in classical Shīʿa sources, and we find anti-Haman practices from Purim shaping Omarophobia in Iranian-Shīʿa culture. Thus, as with Judas and Guy Fawkes in varieties of Christianity, Haman's contributions to Omar Koshan celebrations in Shīʿa Islam demonstrate both his importance as an influential figure of evil and his vulnerability to replacement by more culturally relevant villains.

———

How evil was Haman? In the late eighteenth century, the eminent Lutheran Bible scholar Johann Michaelis (d. 1791) complained that Haman had been put to death without a trial, while in 1824, some Reform Jews sought to ban "striking the impious Haman at the festival of Purim."[6] Some two centuries later, the biblicist Phillip Davies (d. 2018) published a retelling of MT *Esther* from Haman's perspective, entitled "Haman the Victim," in which he argued that Haman has been misunderstood for millennia. My characterization of Haman throughout this book as a tragic villain is somewhat similar, based on the enormous gap between Haman's incompetence in MT *Esther* and his infamy throughout history.

Was Haman denied a fair trial? Was he perhaps guilty of nothing worse than impiety? And was he more victim than villain? In concluding this book, I would like to propose three answers to these questions.

The first answer, as we learned in Part I of this book, is that one's perception of Haman's crimes differs based on the scripture through which one accesses *Esther*. Michaelis, the Reform Jews of the early nineteenth century, and Davies, were all responding to the Haman of MT *Esther*, who was indeed an unsuccessful villain, and less culpable for it. Those acquainted with Haman from LXX *Esther* or from the Qur'ān, would tend to judge him less favorably (accusing him of being a hostile foreign actor or an enemy of God). It is notable that the rabbis in late antiquity (who read MT *Esther*) felt the need to inflate Haman's résumé with a litany of crimes that reflected the rabbis' own conception of evil (despite not reflecting the contents of *Esther*). That these rabbis emerged from late antiquity and the Middle Ages as the authoritative interpreters of Jewish tradition elevated their opinions to a level of prestige that, in practical terms, could override the literal meaning of *Esther*'s contents.

The second answer is that Haman, as a label of opprobrium that could be wielded in interfaith polemics, was guilty of causing immeasurable damage to relations between various groups of Jews, Christian, Muslims, and Samaritans over the past two millennia. We surveyed some choice examples of this interfaith mischief in Chapter 7.

The third answer, which appropriately reflects postmodern sensibilities, is that Haman was as evil as people believe him to have been, and the fact that he is annually "cancelled," attests to the depth of his culpability. A good measure of Haman's infamy is the fact that his name has been "retired." In 2016, the comedian Bill Burr remarked (drawing on the examples of Adolf Hitler, Attila the Hun, and Judas Iscariot) that one reaches the highest level of evil when their name is no longer deemed suitable as a human appellation.[7] The idea that villains' names need to be retired did not originate with Burr: The third century Talmudic rabbi Shmuel ben Naḥman remarked that parents choose names such as Abraham, Isaac, Jacob, Reuben, and Simon, but would never use Pharaoh, Sisera, or Sennacherib.[8] Along similar lines, the interior ministry in the modern State of Israel has included "Haman" in its list of names that may not be chosen for one's children.[9]

Since the middle of the twentieth century, psychologists have made use of the HTP personality test which asks the test taker to draw *h*ouses, *t*rees, or *p*eople, with the resulting drawings being interpreted as projective of the drawer's inner thoughts and attitudes. In some ways, individual or communal conceptions of

Haman formed over the past two millennia tell us more about those who expressed them than about Haman himself. This book, then, is a kind of extended HTP (Haman-Tree-Purim) test through which Abrahamic communities have shared with us their fears, worries, frustrations, and hopes by expressing their thoughts about Haman, each in their in own way.

Never has a character been hated so much for having done so little.

NOTES

Introduction

1. With few exceptions, Haman's depiction in art, music, and material culture will not be covered in this book.

2. I borrow this disclaimer from my previous monograph, *Veiling Esther*, 2. While researching the present book, I discovered new materials and new approaches to *Esther* and Haman in Islamic cultures that merited publication but might not interest most readers of a biography of Haman. I therefore chose to publish those findings separately (in *Veiling Esther*) and to refer to them succinctly in this book where relevant.

3. In Stone, *The Essential Max Müller*, 113. Müller was paraphrasing Goethe's famous statement, "He who does not know foreign languages, does not know his own [language]."

4. As Walfish (*Esther in Medieval Garb*, 201) noted: "In the exegesis of [the Book of Esther], perhaps more than in any other, the exegetes' personal experiences and attitudes figured prominently in their commentaries."

Part One: Haman in Scripture

1. Mordecai as the author: Esth 9:20; Great Assembly as the author: b.Baba Bathra 15a. Some earlier Christian authorities, such as Augustine (*City of God*, 18.36) and Isidore of Seville (*Etymologies*, 137 (VI.ii.29)) proposed that Ezra was the author of *Esther*.

2. b.Megillah 19a.

3. b.Megillah 9a (written languages) and 18a (publicly-recited languages).

Chapter One: Haman in the Hebrew Bible.

1. The following summary is based on Silverstein, *Veiling Esther*, 12–13.

2. That Ahashwerosh is the central character of the story may be reflected in the titles "The Book of Ahashwerosh"—given to *Esther* by the Karaite exegete Yefet b. 'Eli (d. c. 1009)—and "The Scroll of Ahashwerosh" given to *Esther* in an Indian manuscript from 1806 (Tabory, "Yefet in the House of Shem," 463, n 43, where the midrash on this scroll is entitled "midrash Ahashwerosh").

3. In fact, some scholars have argued that *Esther* originated in two or more independent stories, one of which focused on Esther, the other on Mordecai (see Silverstein, *Veiling Esther*, 203–205).

4. Clines (*Esther Scroll*, 16) asserts that Haman's decree against the Jews is "based on a lie and a bribe," both allegations that I find unconvincing, as the accusations against the Jews were far from inaccurate, and the money was rejected.

5. See also Mic 5:6, where "the remnant of Jacob shall be in the midst of many nations."

6. Later on in the story, Esther will also knowingly transgress the king's law by approaching him uninvited (Esth 4:16), although in the latter case it is not her Jewishness that accounts for the transgression. Thambyrajah ("Other laws") argues that the Jews did not, in fact, have a *dat* that conflicted with Persian law.

7. Admittedly, in this case there was no royal command that Mordecai was transgressing. And yet, here Mordecai disrespects Haman after the latter is described as "glad of heart" (Esth 5:9), recalling Esth 1:10, where Vashti disrespects the king after the latter is described as "glad of heart [with wine]." If Esth 5:9 is consciously echoing Esth 1:10, then Mordecai's disrespecting of Haman is as unjustifiable as Vashti's disrespecting of the king.

8. We will see that the rabbis added further details to the story that would have made it even more difficult for Haman to withstand the emotional and psychological pressures. Nevertheless, he maintained his composure.

9. To the list of Haman's misfortunes may be added the fact that precisely those things of which he was proudest—his wealth, his offspring, and his status (Esth 5:10)—were taken from him in turn, even after his death. (Haman's house is given to Esther in Esth 8:1; the signet ring that afforded him authority was transferred to Mordecai in 8:2; and his sons were killed in 9:7–9).

10. In b.Megillah 7a the opinion is attributed to Rabbi Eliezer (c. 45–117 CE). Not all rabbis agreed with him, and Rava (280–352) argued that *Esther*'s author was simply imputing thoughts to Haman. Subsequent commentators tended to agree with Rabbi Eliezer, with few exceptions (e.g., Tanḥum ha-Yerushalmi (d. 1291), in Wechsler, *Strangers in the Land*, 24, 38, and 272ff.).

11. Wills compares *Esther* to the Egyptian *Instructions of Ankhsheshonq* in this regard, writing that: ". . . it is Haman's foolishness that is being narrated, not Mordecai's wisdom" (*Jew in the Court*, 187).

12. The negative court-character in the Joseph story is Potiphar's wife, and although the episode in which she sought to tempt Joseph and then falsely accused him has left its marks on *Esther*, these are largely to be found in descriptions of Mordecai and Esther rather than Haman. In the *Daniel* 1–6 stories, the closest parallel to *Esther* may be *Daniel* 3, where Nebuchadnezzar commands Daniel's three companions to bow to a golden idol that he has erected. The Jews refuse to bow, triggering an existential threat against them, from which they emerge unscathed. Whereas in *Daniel* 3 unnamed Chaldean men bring an accusation against the three Jews for not bowing and seek the Jews' destruction (Dan 3:8), Haman is better compared to the golden idol set up by the king as the object of prostration. The relevance of the *Daniel* context to *Esther* is complicated by the fact that the relative dating of the two stories is uncertain.

13. Pseudo-Philo (writing at some point between 50 and 150 CE) already explains that in the gap between Saul's destruction of the Amalekites and Samuel's execution of Agag, the latter managed to impregnate the woman from whose descendants Haman, the final Agagite, would emerge (*Biblical Antiquities*, 58:4). This idea endured in rabbinic sources from late antiquity, e.g., in the second targum (*Targum Sheni*; hereafter: TgII) 4:11.

14. See McKane, "Note on *Esther* IX"; and Amit, "Saul Polemic," 653–56.

15. That Mordecai is introduced as "the son of Yair, the son of Shim'i, the son of Kish, a Benjaminite" (Esth 2:5) strengthens the association with 1 Sam 15, for Saul was the son of Kish (1 Sam 9:1–2; see also Acts 13:21) and Shim'i was also a relative of Saul (2 Sam 16:5–14).

16. The word "exalted" in Num 24:7 uses the same verbal root as that used in Esth 3:1 for the exaltation of Haman.

17. Other Pentateuchal intertexts include Deut 25:17–18, where the Amalekites "met [the Israelites] on their path," using the verb *qarah*. The rabbis (e.g. *Esther Rabba* 8:5) related this to Esth 4:7, where the same verb is used.

18. Clines, *Esther Scroll*, 68; and Meinhold, *Esther*, 101.

19. See Grossman, *Esther*, for a thorough study of biblical intertextual allusions in *Esther*.

20. Esau and Haman are also comparable through the references to their inner thoughts (Esau: Gen 27:41, Haman: Esth 6:6). See Koller, *Esther in Ancient Jewish Thought*, 172–175 and Grossman, "Dynamic Analogies," 399–403.

21. To the list of biblical intertexts for "hanging from a tree" we may add 2 Sam 21, where it is the descendants of Saul who were hanged (verses 6, 9, and 13 use a different Hebrew verb, *le-hoqi'a*, although verse 12 uses the verb *talah* that is common to Deut 21, Gen 40, and Esth 2 and 7). The fact that we are dealing with the house of Saul in this case is particularly significant to *Esther*. Note, similarly, that in Evagrius's fifth-century account of a debate between a Christian (Theophilis) and a Jewish antagonist (Simon), the latter uses the hanging of Absalom from a tree in 2 Sam 18:9 as proof that whoever dies in this manner is cursed (hence, Jesus, too, was cursed; see Chapman, *Perceptions of Crucifixion*, 238, and Berkovitz, "Jewish and Christian Exegetical Controversy," 235–238).

22. Wechsler, *Conviviality*, 332. Already in the Babylonian Talmud (b.Megillah 10b-11a) Haman is said to have been hinted at in various (pre-*Esther*) books of the Bible, such as Prov 28:15, 29:2, Ps 124:1–2, Jer 49:38, and others.

23. Rhabanus Maurus *ad* Esth 7:9. Nearly a century later, Saadiah Gaon also quoted this verse with reference to Haman (Wechsler, *Conviviality*, 305).

24. Talmon, "Wisdom," 445–446.

Chapter Two: Greek Versions of *Esther*

1. *Megillat Ta'anit*, s.v. eighth (sic!) of Tebet; and Massekhet Sofrim 1:7. The latter text includes the (presumably earlier) tradition that it was actually five sages who translated the Torah into Greek, rather than seventy.

2. b.Megillah 8b–9b.

3. Uniquely for *Esther*'s translation, the text's colophon details when it was rendered into Greek. Scholars are divided between those who understand from this colophon that the book was translated in 114 BCE and those who opt for 78–77 or 77–76 BCE. Here, I adopt 100 BCE for LXX *Esther*, both as it is a round-number compromise position and because the precise year has no perceptible bearing on our understanding of Haman in the LXX.

4. Note also that the king's insomnia in Esth 6:1, which is unexplained in the MT, is attributed to God in the LXX.

5. See de Troyer and Smith, "The Additions of the Greek Book(s) of Esther."

6. Such changes include different lists of Persian eunuchs and advisors (Esth 1:10 and 14) and of Haman's sons (9:7–9), as well as a different name for Esther's father (2:7).

7. Significant changes to the narrative that do not much impact Haman's depiction or role, include the fact that in the LXX Esther and Mordecai are described as having been married (Esth 2:7), and the fact that the Purim festival is rendered in the LXX as *Phrourai* (or *Phrourdai*), suggesting a Semitic root *p-r-r* (with a range of meanings that have to do with "destruction," but which might also point to an etymology in the Persian Fravardigan festival). The *pūrīm* of the MT, by contrast, is from the *p-w-r* root, and it probably refers to the Assyrian word for "lots," as per MT Esth 3:7, 9:24, and 9:26. Admittedly, the LXX also explains the name of the holiday *Phrourai* to mean "lots" (Esth 9:26), probably on the basis of the Hebrew it was translating. However, the fact that the name of the festival was remembered (despite this) as being from the root *p-r-r* may be an interesting clue to an alternative—or, for some scholars, the original—name for Purim (see e.g., Lewy, "The Feast of the 14th Day of Adar"; and Hintze, "Greek and Hebrew versions").

8. In the ANE, not all those labelled "eunuchs" were physically castrated. The Hebrew *sarīs*, is derived from the Akkadian *ša reši* ("the one of the king"), which often—but not

always—indicates a castrated functionary. See 1 Sam 8:15 for an example of *sarīs* with the general meaning of court-functionary. On the etymology of *ša reši*, see M. Frazer, "Heads and Beds."

9. The two eunuchs who plotted against the king in Esth 2:21–23 are described in the LXX with the language used in the MT for both the eunuchs and Haman ("hanged from a tree"). In the LXX, therefore, the parallelism between the executions of the eunuchs and of Haman is missing.

10. For an overview of the options, see Silverstein, *Veiling Esther*, 128; and Thambyrajah, "A Macedonian in the Persian Court," 745–47.

11. In the late nineteenth century, an attempt was made to equate Haman the dragon with the eschatological Beast of NT Rev 13:11–18, on the basis of a *gematria* that calculates the Aramaic for "the evil Haman" (*haman rish'a*) as being 666 (Cassell, *Esther*, xxiii; and Lees, "Intertextual Ripples," 132ff.). Mathematically, the calculation works, but only if one ignores the fact that the phrase "the evil Haman" is spelled in the targums with a "yod" between the "shin" and the "ayin" (the correct spelling would add up to 676). And in any event, arithmetic aside, how are we to interpret *Mordecai*'s depiction as a dragon alongside Haman?

12. The reference to Haman as "our second father" (in NETS "father" is capitalized) echoes the description of Joseph as "a father to Pharaoh, lord of all his house, and ruler of all of Egypt" (Gen 45:8).

13. Similarly, in both Greek versions (LXX 4:8 and AT 4:4) Haman is referred to as being second to the king.

14. In the second half of Addition C (Esther's prayer), Esther refers to *the king* as "uncircumcised" (C:26 = AT Esth 4:25).

15. That Josephus also uses the term *hubris* with reference to the builders of the Tower of Babel will prove relevant to our description of Haman in the Qur'ān in Chapter 5.

16. We learn little from Addition F about Haman, who is only in mentioned when Mordecai decodes the dream described in Addition A.

17. "Bougean": LXX A:17, 3:1, and 9:10; and AT 3:1, 7:25, and 7:44. "Macedonian": LXX 9:24 and Add E:10; and AT Add A:17.

18. Old Persian puns that connect Haman's name with "thoughts" may be reflected in the verses (Esth 8:3 and 5, and 9:24–25) that refer explicitly to Haman's "thoughts" (from the Hebrew root *ḥ-sh-b*).

19. Fox, "Three Esthers," with earlier scholarship.

20. Jerome recognized that the additions were not part of the HB and placed them at the end of *Esther*. Catholics—for whom the additions are deuterocanonical, that is to say "inspired," but not originally part of the story—also place them at the end of *Esther*, whereas Protestants (who see the Additions as apocryphal) place them at end of the Bible as a whole. Regardless of where they feature, the additions do not integrate well with LXX *Esther* in a number of ways.

21. For attempts to recreate the "original" story on which the AT is based, see Wills, *Jew in the Court*, 153ff. and the sources in 154 n 2. Such retroversions are necessarily speculative.

22. For example, the AT does not include the lists of eunuchs and advisors to the king (Esth 1:10 and 14).

23. What the king does not know is that Haman's plot targets the Jews. Similarly, in the AT (5:23), Zeresh and Haman's friends are aware from the outset that Mordecai is a Jew. In the MT and LXX, by contrast, Haman is advised to construct the gallows for Mordecai (5:14), and only later do Zeresh and Haman's friends warn him that if Mordecai is a Jew then Haman stands no chance against him (6:13).

24. For this and other reasons, those scholars who have argued for separate Mordecai and Esther plots that were woven together in MT *Esther* tend to see the Hebrew base-text (*Vorlage*)

of the AT as being close to the "Mordecai source." The term *Vorlage* (pl. *Vorlagen*) refers to the original work on which the text under discussion (often a translation) is based.

25. The LXX appears to have misread the initial "H" in "Hegai" as the definite article, and took the eunuch's name to be "[the] Gai," just as centuries later the Karaite Yefet ben 'Eli (d. 1009) would refer to Haman's father (Hammedata) as "the Madata" (in Wechsler, *Yefet ben 'Eli*, 140, 163, 212, and n 263 *ad* Esth 3:1 and 10; 8:5; 9:10 and 9:24).

26. Clines, *Esther Scroll*, 197–198 n 7. In a similar vein, Macchi ("Haman l'orgueilleux," 210–224), agrees that the AT does in fact represent the earliest *Vorlage* and that Haman's epithet was originally a word meaning "proud." He proposes that a Hebrew epithet close to גאה, meaning "proud," was rendered in Greek "Bougaios" (with the same meaning). A scribal error turned הגאה into האגגי. While this ingenious explanation can be neither proven nor categorically refuted, we will see in Chapter 8 that there are ways of understanding "Agagite," that do not require envisaging scribal errors.

27. Ezek 38–39. Note that in Qur'ānic Arabic (Q 18:94 and 21:96), "Gog and Magog" are rendered *ya'jūj wa ma'jūj*, both names being derived from the Semitic *'-g-g* root (from which "Agagite" is also derived).

28. See Lacocque, "Haman dans le livre d'Esther," and "Haman in the Book of Esther."

29. In the broadest of strokes, the term "midrash" refers to a genre of ancient rabbinic writings that served to interpret and supplement the information provided in biblical texts. These writings include both legal/halakhic and homiletical/aggadic narratives. The aggadic portions dealt with (and were based on) non-legal materials of many sorts, including myths and legends absorbed from local (non-Jewish) cultures. It is this latter groups of writings to which we refer when using the term "midrash" in this book.

30. See, in general Stone, *Literature of Adam and Eve*, and Minov, "Satan's Refusal to Worship Adam" (with richly detailed bibliographical references). For edited and translated versions of this text, presented side-by-side in parallel columns, see Anderson and Stone, *Synopsis of the Books of Adam and Eve.*

31. Translation adapted from that in: http://www2.iath.virginia.edu/anderson/retellings/Cave.html.

32. That a number of versions of this episode appear in the Qur'ān may have hindered the Muslim reception of the *Esther* narrative, as Muslims believe the refusal-to-bow motif to have been associated with Satan (Arabic: *Iblīs*) rather than Mordecai. Moreover, as we will see, the Qur'ān held Haman to have been an Egyptian at Pharaoh's court. Therefore, from the Muslim perspective, there were two weighty mistakes in *Esther.*

33. Note that the AT includes a description of Haman that does not occur in either the MT or the LXX, which adds yet another reversal to the Haman-Mordecai rivalry: In AT 6:5, we are told regarding the king's servants that, "fear of Haman lay in their bowels," anticipating Mordecai's description as the object of people's fear (LXX and MT 9:3).

34. Another difference between the AT and the LXX and MT versions enhances the impression that Haman is loyal to the king: Whereas in the MT and LXX Haman presumptuously casts lots to determine the day on which to destroy the Jewish people (3:7) before securing permission from the king to do so (3:8), in the AT, Haman only casts the lots (3:12) after the king agrees to the genocidal plan (3:11).

35. Earlier in the AT (5:14; equivalent to LXX and MT 5:4), Esther referred to Haman as the king's "friend," whereas the LXX and MT in this instance do not qualify "Haman" in any way.

36. In the first targum (*Targum Rishon*; hereafter: TgI) 1:1, Ahashwerosh is "the wicked," and in *Esther Rabba* 7:20 (*ad* Esth 3:1), we read that Ahashwerosh hated Israel even more than Haman did. A seventeenth century Judeo-Arabic commentary on Esther from the Maghreb states regarding Ahashwerosh "there never was and never will be another like him, evil from

beginning to end" (Rivlin, *Perush*, 8 *ad* Esth 1:1; on this source, see Wechsler, *Strangers in the Land*, 336f.). See also Feldman, "Hellenizations," 162.

37. See Tabory, "Yefet in the House of Shem." Much of his evidence comes from the tenth-century CE *Sefer Yosippon*, rather than from rabbis in pre-Islamic times.

38. To these may be added the similarity between Haman's jealousy in the refusal-to-bow episode, as reflected in the AT, and Satan's jealousy in a comparable episode in the *Life of Adam and Eve*. In b.Megilla 16a, the rabbis explain that Haman was jealous first of Vashti and then of Esther (see Silverstein, *Veiling Esther*, 170–71).

39. b.Megillah 12b and TgI 1:16, among many others. Note, however, that in the TgII 1:16 Memuchan is identified with Daniel, and in the Old Latin version of *Esther* the advisor in 1:16 is Mordecai (!).

40. Rashi (d. 1105) *ad* b.Megillah 16b and TgI 8:16, among others. Cf. discussions in Segal, *Babylonian Esther Midrash*; 3:146, Glickman, *Haman and the Jews*, 27ff.; Horowitz, *Reckless Rites*, 112 and 116 (re: Eleazar Kallir, writing in Byzantine Palestine, who, describes Haman's plot as intended "to cut down my cut [circumcised] ones.")

41. Antiochus IV (r. 175–164 BCE) and Hadrian (r. 117–138 CE) both prohibited circumcision as part of their anti-Jewish programs. For Antiochus's prohibition on circumcision, see 1 Macc 1:60–61 and 2 Macc 6:10; for Hadrian's, see Schäfer, *Judeophobia*, 103–105 (and, generally, 93–105 on gentile attitudes to Jewish circumcision).

42. One could argue that the AT was influenced by rabbinic midrashim that were circulating in the first century CE. However, the internal consistency between the AT and the details that it shares with rabbinic materials would imply that these details were organic to the text, rather than later interpolations. This cannot be said, however, for the Additions, which are plainly of non-AT provenance.

43. In Zoroastrianism (an early form of which was the imperial religion of the Achaemenid Empire), Falsehood (*druj-*) is the polar opposite of Truth (*arta-*), these being the two competing forces in the dualistic theology of the religion, where they embody Order and Chaos more generally. Referring to Haman as a "liar" in an Achaemenid context, therefore, is a far weightier accusation than it may sound to us. In Chapter 8 we return to this topic when discussing Darius's Behistun inscription and *Esther*.

44. In support of Haman's cosmic role we may note the messianic (perhaps even divine) language in which Mordecai is described in MT 10:3, as seen above. Similarly, Leach ("Kingship and Divinity," 297–298) offers a messianic interpretation of the Dura Europos Purim panel.

45. To clarify: Whereas the AT represents an earlier *Hebrew* version of Esther than that used by the LXX, in their current Greek forms the AT is later than the LXX.

46. For a critical edition of OL Esth, see Haelewyck, *Hester*; for an English translation, see Bellmann and Portier-Young, "Old Latin book of Esther." For a recent analysis of OL Esth's theological significance, see Bellmann, "Theological Character."

47. Accordingly, Esther's prayer in Addition C is much shorter in the OL than it is in the LXX and AT (Bellmann and Portier-Young, "Old Latin book of Esther," 268). The one way in which Esther's prayer is enhanced in the OL is the inclusion (C:16) of historical episodes in which God saved his people as part of Esther's plea that He do so once more.

48. Naturally, as the point of this "violent vengeance" may well have been to finish the job that Saul neglected to complete in 1 Sam 15 (eradicating the Amalekites), the absence of this aspect of the story from the OL is hardly surprising as the OL does not describe Haman as an Agagite nor Mordecai as the descendent of Saul and Kish. Thus, there is an internal consistency within the OL regarding this deviation from the other versions of *Esther*.

49. To the list of differences one may add the following: In the OL Esther prepares only one meal for the king and Haman (rather than two); Purim is rendered as "the guards" (OL 9:29), apparently translating the Greek *phrourai* (lit. "guards," but in the Greek versions

probably reflecting a Semitic words from the root p-r-r); Hatach in the OL remains the go-between throughout Esther and Mordecai's exchange in Esth 4; and the king gives Mordecai the 10,000 talents of silver that Haman had offered (OL 7:10); among numerous other divergences from the MT, LXX, and AT versions.

50. Furthermore, when the king promotes Haman in the OL, his seat is not made higher than those of the king's ministers (or the like), but rather, "he made his seat the first among all his friends." It is difficult to read significance into this change, except to note that, as we shall see below, Haman's friends are described.

51. "Thebari" appears to be a misreading of "the citadel" (Hebrew: *ha-bīrah*) as though it is part of Susa's name. That the OL misreads Hebrew and Greek words is evident both in the reference to Purim as "the guards" (see above, Ch 2, n 49), and in the reference in Add E:10 to Haman as, "Haman, Medadatum, a Macedonian." Haman's father appears here as Medadatum, presumably because the translator mistook the initial "Ha" of Hammedata for the definite article (for other examples of this, see above, Ch 2, n 25).

52. The reference to three hundred men may be based on MT 9:15, where the Jews of Susa killed this number of their enemies. Another option is that the number is based on 3 Macc 7:14–15, where the victorious Jews kill three hundred renegades who had adopted the Dionysian rites. In Chapter 6, we will see that *3 Maccabees* and *Esther* (especially the Greek version(s) thereof), were in conversation with one another.

53. Note that the OL (or its *Vorlage*) describes Mordecai's refusal to honor Haman in 5:9 as inconsistent with the behavior of others who were present (recalling 3:1ff., where only Mordecai refuses to honor Haman).

54. The AT (5:10) has: "So Haman went into his home and gathered together his friends, his sons, and Zosara his wife." He then takes pride in his invitation to a royal banquet. In the AT, Haman's sons exist, but no particular attention is paid to them, and they are not specifically mentioned as being a source of pride.

55. The closest one gets to the OL's assertions that Zeresh was also executed and that Haman, his wife, and sons were executed together, is the LXX (E:18), which states that, "[Haman] has been crucified at the gates of Susa with his whole household. . . ." (At the same place in the text, the AT excludes the words "with his whole household" (AT 7:28)). We return to Zeresh's demise in Chapter 9.

56. Thambyrajah ("A Macedonian in the Persian Court") argues that the epithet "Macedonian" for Haman originated in the Greek *Vorlage* of the OL.

57. Josephus, *Against Apion*, 1.37-41. Origen (wr. 245 CE) also considered *Esther* to have been the last of the twenty-two books of the HB. Rabbinic tradition considers *Chronicles* to be the last book of the HB (b.Baba Bathra 14b). Interestingly, the same passage states that the penultimate book was *Ezra* and the one before that was *Esther*. Bearing in mind that the HB in Judaism contains twenty-four books, we may deduce that here, too, *Esther* was the twenty-second book on the list. Moreover, in both the Aleppo Codex and the Tiberian Codex, the final three books are *Esther*, *Daniel*, and *Ezra*—this being a different order from that listed in the Talmud, but one that also places *Esther* as the third from the end of a list of twenty-four books.

58. Bellmann, "Theological Character," 4 n 2.

59. The classic treatments of this topic are those of Feldman (*Studies*, 513–538; and "Hellenizations"), to which may now be added Luria, *Josephus on the Book of Esther* and Chalupa, "The Book of Esther in Josephus."

60. On Josephus's sources for *Esther*, see Feldman, *Studies*, 525–526 n 22, and Lees, "Intertextual Ripples," 53f.

61. Josephus explains that the king was Cyrus the son of Xerxes, and that his regnal name was Artaxerxes.

62. Josephus preserves the names of "Bigthan" and "Teresh" (*contra* all Greek versions), and of "Memuchan" (*contra* the LXX "Mouchaios," AT "Bougaios," and OL "Mordecai").

63. The MT's "Harbona" in Esth 7:9 is "Sabuchadas" in Josephus (the LXX has "Bougathan," the AT has "Agathas," and the OL has "Buzatas").

64. Furthermore, as Feldman has shown, when paraphrasing Esther's prayer in Addition C, Josephus omits the reference to her abhorring the bed and food of gentiles, ("Hellenizations," 165). The desire to combat accusations that the Jews were misanthropic is found in such late antique rabbinic sources as TgI 9:6 and 16–18, where it is specified that those whom the Jews killed in Esth 9 were, in fact, Amalekites.

65. Maier, "Amalek in the Writings of Josephus." We will see (in Chapter 6) that the rabbis, too, equated Haman with Esau (and with Edom more generally).

66. Feldman, *Studies*, 537.

67. In Josephus's account, Haman amplifies his accusations against the Jews, referring to them as a "wicked nation," "unsociable," and "at enmity with thy people, and with all men, both in their manners and practices." These accusations of misanthropy are the low starting point from which the Jews rise up by the end of Josephus's account, when they are proven to be loyal to the king. Haman, by contrast, emerges as the one who sought to "transfer the government to others." Note that in Addition E (on which Josephus's text here is based) Haman is accused of working particularly for the Macedonians, a detail that might not sit well with Greek readers of his account. He therefore substitutes "others" for "Macedonians."

68. Feldman, *Studies*, 568.

69. It should be recalled, however, that Josephus was apparently familiar with Greek versions of the story that resembled the LXX, which do not share the MT's complete omission of God from the events. Still, the fact that *Esther* clearly could be told in this way (and Josephus likely also knew of the MT version) made it something of a model story for his purposes.

70. Feldman, *Studies*, 537. Josephus also used *Esther* to rewrite other biblical accounts, such as that of Rahab in Josh 2 (see Swart, "Rahab and Esther in Josephus").

71. Feldman, *Studies*, 528 and 537. For Josephus's use of *hubris* in referring to earlier biblical villains, see Levine, "Hubris."

72. On both Nimrod's role in the Tower of Babel episode and Josephus's relating of that episode to *hubris*, see Levine, "Hubris," 61.

73. Writing in the tenth century CE, Josippon, claiming to be Josephus himself, adds the detail that Saul killed 500,000 Amalekites in his war with Agag.

74. A good example of this is the suggestion (found in Josephus's account, and later in the Old Latin and Vulgate *ad* Esth 2:7) that Mordecai was Esther's *uncle* rather than her first cousin.

Chapter Three: Haman in Christian Scripture

1. Laniak, *Shame and Honor*, 2. In the words of Anderson, "It is significant that the Book of Esther is not once quoted in the New Testament" ("Book of Esther in the Christian Bible," 42).

2. On the Salome episode and Esther, see Aus, *Water into Wine*, 39–74.

3. Why the author of Mark chose to employ this quote from *Esther* is unclear. In Matthew's parallel account of the episode (14:7), Herod does not use the phrase. As Markan priority (viz. that Mark's was the first of the synoptic gospels) enjoys a near-consensus of NT scholarship, one can assume that the author of *Matthew* consciously chose to exclude the quote from *Esther* from his account.

4. These and similarly disdainful quotations may be found in Lees's "Intertextual Ripples," 16–17. See also the discussions in Lee, "Reflections," and Kalimi, *Book of Esther*, 251–288.

5. Bush, "The Book of Esther," 39.

6. Lees, "Intertextual Ripples," 180. The parallels are analyzed in ibid., 181ff. For a different approach to this topic, see Chapman, *Perceptions of Crucifixion*, 162–170.

7. This parallel was already noticed by Cassell, *Esther*, 241.

8. Damascelli ("Cross, Curse, and Redemption") argues that Purim is intentionally hinted at here. Lees ("Intertextual Ripples," 222–223) sees an earlier version of this framework in *Matthew* 5:3–12 at 10, where in the description of Jesus's Sermon of the Mount, we are told that one is blessed for being persecuted (using vocabulary found in descriptions of the Passion) for the sake of righteousness. In other words, by being crucified and reviled, Jesus was in fact being blessed.

9. LXX 7:4 and 8:1. See Ch 2, n 38 above for a Second Temple-era "refusal-to-bow" episode involving Satan, which shares numerous details with Haman's description in AT *Esther*.

10. Thornton, "Crucifixion of Haman," 422; Lees, "Intertextual Ripples," 202; and Chapman, *Perceptions of Crucifixion*, 236–241.

11. Lees, "Intertextual Ripples," 207ff.

12. As Lees ("Intertextual Ripples," 250) puts it: "The similarity between Jesus's crucifixion and Haman's led the author of Matthew to try to dissociate the two characters, nudging Judas towards Haman and Jesus towards Mordecai."

13. Lees ("Intertextual Ripples," 217) takes the parallel further, noting that Judas attempts (unsuccessfully) to return the money to the ruler, thereby linking him with Haman, in whose case the authority figure also refused the money.

14. b.Megillah 15b. Rabbi Levi b. Laḥm was a third-century CE *amora* from the Land of Israel. Other late antique Jewish texts similarly associated Psalm 22 with Esther (see Münz-Manor, "Carnivalesque Ambivalence," 838 and n 34).

15. Lees, "Intertextual Ripples," 244–246. The assumption that the NT was drawing on rabbinic traditions, rather than vice versa, suits Lees's argument, even though the alternative option is more consistent chronologically. In support of Lees, one might cite Jesus's well-known statement (Matt 19:24, Mark 10:24–27, Luke 18:24–27) that, "it is easier for a camel to go through the eye of a needle than for a rich man to enter the kingdom of God," which is generally thought to be based on a similar rabbinic turn of phrase, the oldest attestations of which are in the Babylonian Talmud (b.Berakhot 55b, and b.Baba Meṣi'a 38b; where an elephant rather than a camel is mentioned).

16. Writing in the eleventh century, the Benedictine theologian Rupert of Deutz called Haman's crucifixion, "the most beautiful image of the future triumph of the Redeemer" (in Carruthers, *Esther through the Centuries*, 30).

17. In Evagrius's fifth-century (fictionalized) debate between the Christian Theophilus and the Jew Simon, the Christian protagonist rejects the Jews' equating of Jesus with Haman (on the basis that they were both crucified and, hence, cursed), by asserting that Haman could not be a true exemplar of Jesus as the latter was without sin (in Chapman, *Perceptions of Crucifixion*, 240–241). It is impossible to determine whether this reflects Evagrius's opinion (demonstrating that even some Christian elites might not have grasped the sophisticated theology behind the Jesus-Haman equivalence), or a commoner's argument (as represented by Theophilus). Well into the twentieth century, Christian writers were aware of the similarity between Haman's and Jesus's crucifixions: In Sturge-Moore's 1931 poem *Judas*, he refers to "Haman's cross" when describing the crucifixion (in Carruthers, *Esther through the Centuries*, 232).

18. Other possible references to *Esther* in the NT include the notion that the "festival of the Jews" referred to in John 5:1 is Purim (Lees, "Intertextual Ripples," 154–161); that Matt 22:1–14 is modelled on parts of the *Esther* plot (ibid., 173); and that Gal 2:14 relates to Esth 8:17 (ibid., 292ff). To these sources may be added the arguments made in Fausett, "Typology of Christ in the Book of Esther."

19. Wechsler, "Shadow and Fulfilment."

20. Esther's fast is represented by the Hebrew *ṣōm* (Esth 4:16), whereas "humiliation" in biblical Hebrew is represented by the root *ʿn.h.* And yet the latter root came to be so closely related to fasting that the Fast of Esther on the thirteenth of Adar is known not as a *ṣōm*, but as a *taʿanīth* (from the same *ʿn.h.* root).

21. Lees, "Intertextual Ripples," 286.

22. The typological reading of OT stories is introduced by Paul (Rom 5:14), where he sees Adam as a type of Jesus. That he read *Esther* typologically, too, is certainly possible.

Chapter Four: Authoritative Exegesis of *Esther*

1. Literally, the word "scripture" refers to written texts, but as we will see, the Oral Torah, too, came to acquire the status of scripture (in its non-literal sense). "Revelation" might be more accurate here than "scripture," but for practical reasons I adopt scripture (to avoid such clunky phrases as "revelational exegesis" that would have to replace "scriptural exegesis," and so forth).

2. I prefer this translation to the more common, "both these and these are the words of the living God."

3. In the HB (Deut 6:7), God Himself commands us to: "teach [these words] diligently to your children, and you shall talk about them when sitting in your house, when you walk along the way, when you lie down [to sleep], and when you rise up." That this verse is part of the famous *shemaʿ* prayer has imbued the idea with exceptional weight and prestige.

4. The Christian doctrine of biblical inerrancy is both relatively recent and controversial.

5. In terms of its etymology, the word "*qur'ān*" itself may imply orality, and it is commonly translated as "recitation." Confusion may arise from the fact that the Arabic root *q-r-'* can imply both recitation and reading (as in other Semitic languages), and as the Qur'ān refers to itself as a "book" (Arabic: *kitāb*), it is likely that "Lectionary" (or the like) better captures the original meaning. On the other hand, according to Muslim tradition, the first revelation that Muḥammad received (Q 96:1) began with the word "*iqrā'*," generally understood to mean "Recite!" Whatever the case may be, there is no concept of a Written and an Oral Qur'ān in Islam along the lines described for Judaism.

6. Elaborating on Esth 8:9, which specifies that the *Esther* story circulated in various languages, the Mishna (m.Megillah 2:1) and the Babylonian Talmud (b.Megillah 18a) consider the precise details of reading *Esther* in other languages.

7. Scholars generally deem the traditional Jewish account of final canonization taking place at Jamnia/Yavneh in the first century CE to be legendary or, at the very least, a simplification of what was a protracted process. See Lewis, "Jamnia Revisited."

8. See Chapter 6 below.

9. As Koller (*Esther in Ancient Jewish Thought*, 135) put it: ". . . the Jews of Palestine were familiar with Esther, but many of them, at least, could not accept the book as sacred for many good reasons."

10. Sabar, "The Purim Panel at Dura."

11. Leiman, *Canonization of Hebrew Scripture.*

12. It should be noted that in the original, Mishnaic context, only *Song of Songs* and *Ecclesiastes* were challenged, and it was only in later Talmudic discussions that the rabbis raised the question of *Esther*'s status. See Baumgarten, "Sacred Scriptures Defile the Hands," and Lim, "The Defilement of the Hands."

13. Confusingly, Shmuel held that *Esther* did *not* defile the hands but *was* written with divine inspiration, a contradiction that was explained by asserting that what defiles the hands about scripture is the physical book itself, whereas *Esther* was scripture that could be recited orally.

14. In general, see Koller, *Esther in Ancient Jewish Thought*, 152–160. Koller (ibid., 160) adds the salient point that in the aftermath of the Bar Kokhba revolt in 135 CE, Holy Land Jews became Diaspora Jews too, and *Esther*'s Diaspora message would have resonated universally for Jews. Wechsler ("Esther [Book and Person]," 18) similarly argues for Jewish canonization "by the turn of the millennium."

15. The rabbis' aversion to the LXX may be reflected in a famous statement by Rabbi Akiba, according to which whoever reads "the external books" (viz. the apocrypha and pseudepigrapha; thus perhaps also the additions to *Esther*) "has no portion in the world to come" (m.Sanhedrin 10:1). A statement of this ferocity suggests that Jews were in fact reading "the external books," thereby precipitating such an extreme reaction.

16. On Josippon in Jewish culture, see Tabory, "Yefet in the House of Shem." Tabory attributes Josippon's knowledge of the Additions to Jerome's Vulgate.

17. y.Megilla 1:5. This statement was repeated centuries later by none other than Maimonides (*Hilkhot Megillah*, 2:18).

18. A no-less ringing endorsement for *Esther*'s importance comes from the Talmudic statement (attributed to Rabbi Abba bar Kahana), that Haman's removal of his signet ring to issue the anti-Jewish edict did more to encourage repentance among Jews than all forty-eight prophets and seven prophetesses of the HB, whose admonitions did not effect the same spiritual response (b.Megillah 14a). Similarly, in b.Shabbat 88a, we are told that God used Haman to draw a repentance from the Jews that was so sincere that it was as though they were accepting the Torah again.

19. On *Esther*'s canonization in Christianity, see Moore, *Esther*; idem, "Esther, Book of," 635–636; and Horowitz, "Esther (Book and Person) III.A Patristics and Western Christianity."

20. See examples in idem., 32–34. More often than not, objections to *Esther* came from Protestant Christians, who use the MT version of *Esther*, with its many potential deficiencies, whereas Catholics (whose Bibles tend to include the LXX Additions) have been less critical of the book's contents.

21. b.Megillah 18b. Rabbi Meir was a *tanna* of the fourth generation (i.e., 139–163 CE).

22. Lees, "Intertextual Ripples," 55–56. Note that in the *Apostolic Constitutions*, this statement is made regarding *Esther*, *1–3 Maccabees*, and *Sirach*, the latter two of which are deuterocanonical.

23. Haelewyck, "Le Canon de l'Ancien Testament," 149–150.

24. The Armenian reliance on the LXX is discussed in Cowe, "Scribe, Translator, Redactor," 272.

25. Aphrahat's use of the *Peshitta* (rather than the MT directly) is demonstrated in Owens, *The Genesis and Exodus Citations*, 247.

26. Wechsler, "The Purim-Passover Connection."

27. On Augustine's use of the OL, see Lees, "Intertextual Ripples," 52 n 105.

28. Carruthers, *Esther through the Centuries*, 8.

29. Lees, "Intertextual Ripples," 105–106: "One must remember that Christian critical writings have often been directed against the Hebrew text, and Origen is familiar with LXX Esther."

30. Ibid., 107.

31. Wechsler, "Esther (Book and Person)," 36; and Murray, *Symbols of Church and Kingdom*, 137.

32. Murray, *Symbols of Church and Kingdom*, 59 and 137.

33. For the eschatological significance of "the Wrath" see e.g., 1 Thess 1:10 and Rom 5:9, where "the Wrath" signifies apocalyptic tribulations.

34. Maurus used MT *Esther* (or a translation based on it), although he was also aware of Josephus's account of the story, which he recognized as being considerably different from the biblical version.

35. Perhaps Maurus understood Haman's name to be related in some way to Latin *malus.*

36. The reference to Haman as haughty recalls Josephus's use of *hubris* to characterize the villain. That Maurus opens his exegesis on *Esther* with references to Josephus's work increases the likelihood that he drew on Josephus's conception of Haman in this regard.

37. While it is not clear to what extent the rabbis were widely deemed to have been authoritative in their own time, I privilege the long tradition here, despite the uncertainties surrounding it.

38. That said, Prov 25:21–22 does state: "If your enemy is hungry, give him bread to eat; and if he is thirsty, give him water to drink. For you will heap coals of fire upon his head, and God will reward you." Moreover, these verses are deployed by the rabbis in explaining why Esther invited Haman to a banquet (b.Megillah 15b).

39. On the targums to *Esther*, see Damsma, "Targums to Esther," and Grossfeld, *Two Targums*, 1–25.

40. Torrey ("Older Book of Esther") proposed that *Esther* was originally composed in Aramaic, of which the Hebrew versions were translations. Despite their ingenuity, his arguments have not gained acceptance.

41. See Hayward, "Targum a misnomer for Midrash?" We have seen early examples of this in the Greek versions of *Esther*, which sought to solve textual problems by introducing extra-biblical details to the narrative. These additions were early Jewish midrashim.

42. See Segal, *Babylonian Esther Midrash.*

43. Note, however, that he relates the events as taking place during the reign of "Artaxerxes" (as in the LXX) rather than the reign of Xerxes (as in the MT). Moreover, he refers to Haman as having been crucified, again echoing the LXX rather than the MT.

44. Sulpicius Severus, *Sacred History*, ch. 12.

45. B.Ḥullin 139b. Rabbi Mattanah was a second generation *amora.*

46. Curiously, aside from the initial question about references to Moses before his birth, it is only *Esther* whose characters are thought to have been prefigured in the Torah (which may have been an attempt to buttress the book's canonical status).

Chapter Five: Haman in the Qur'ān

1. A convenient summary of the Qur'ān's view of its place in the scriptural timeline may be found in Q 5:44–48.

2. Q 28:6, 28:8, 28:38, 29:39, 40:24, and 40:36.

3. Q 29:39: "[We] also [destroyed] Korah, Pharaoh, and Haman. Indeed, Moses had come to them with clear proofs, but they behaved arrogantly (*istakbarū*) in the land. Yet they could not escape [us]." Q 40:23–24: "Indeed, we sent Moses with Our signs and compelling proof to Pharaoh, Haman, and Korah. But they responded: "Magician! Liar!"

4. The shift from Hebrew "Qoraḥ" to Arabic "Qārūn" is probably related to the pairing of this name with Aaron's, which in Arabic is "Hārūn." That Qārūn reflects the biblical Korah is clear from Q 28:78–82.

5. Q 28:4–8: "Indeed, Pharaoh elevated himself (*ʿalā*) in the land and divided its people into groups, one of which he persecuted, slaughtering their sons and keeping their women. He was truly one of the corruptors (*mufsidīn*). But it was Our Will to favor those who were oppressed in the land, making them models as well as successors; and to establish them in the land; and through them show Pharaoh, Haman, and their soldiers what they feared. . . . Surely Pharaoh, Haman, and their soldiers were sinful (*khāṭi'īn*)."

6. Q 28:38: "Pharaoh declared, 'O chiefs! I know of no other god for you but myself. So bake bricks out of clay for me, O Haman, and build a high tower so I may look at the God of Moses, although I am sure he is a liar.' And so he and his soldiers behaved arrogantly

(*istakbara*) in the land with no right, thinking they would never be returned to us." Q 40:36–37: "Pharaoh ordered, 'O Haman! Build me a high tower so I may reach the pathways leading up to the heavens and look for the God of Moses, although I am sure he is a liar.' And so Pharaoh's evil deeds (*su' 'amalihi*) were made so appealing to him that he was hindered from the Way. But the plotting (*kayd*) of Pharaoh was only in vain."

7. Despite the similarities between the two rebellious towers, we will see below that the Qur'ān's *ṣarḥ* has closer Abrahamic relatives than the Tower of Babel. Abū al-Fidā' (*al-Bidāya wa l-nihāya*, 2:91), for instance, equates Haman's tower with the building projects forcibly undertaken by the Israelites in Pharaoh's Egypt, as described in *Exodus*.

8. We return to the debate surrounding the Qur'ānic Haman in Chapter 7.

9. For a critique of this characterization of Qur'ānic typology, see Tannous, "Negotiating the Nativity."

10. It is interesting that this advice to turn to Jews and Christians comes immediately after the Qur'ān relates (a potted version of) the story of Pharaoh and the Israelites (Q 10:90–93).

11. See Silverstein, *Veiling Esther*, 23–24 (with further sources). To the evidence supplied there may be added that Origen compares Esther with Joseph (*Comm.Rom.* 9.2.4-5; see Lees, "Intertextual Ripples," 109), and that God barely features in the biblical Joseph story, where events seem to be coincidental rather than Providential (see Koller, *Esther in Ancient Jewish Thought*, 101).

12. Thus, Fox detects in *Esther* "clear echoes of the Joseph story—in phraseology, motifs, and formal structural-features" (*Redaction of the Books of Esther*, 98–99); while Paton simply states that "the author [of *Esther*] knows the story of Joseph" (*Commentary*, 95).

13. See e.g., Esth 9:4: (". . . the man Mordecai became increasingly great . . .") and Exod 11:3 (". . . the man Moses was very great in the land . . ."). These are the only two places in the Bible where the pattern "the man X" occurs. Moreover, Gerleman (*Esther*, 11–23) and Loader (*Esther*, 148–151) have argued that *Esther* is modelled on the Exodus story. See also TgII 2:7 and 20, where Mordecai is compared to Moses, drawing on verses such as Num 12:3 (compared with Esth 2:5) and Deut 4:5 (compared with Esth 9:30).

14. al-Maqdisī, *al-Bad' wa l-ta'rīkh*, 3:81. Note also that some scholars (e.g., Wills, *Jew in the Court*, 182) have related the "plot of the eunuchs" in Esth 2:21–23 to the Egyptian *Instructions of Ankhsheshonq*, which dates from the Achaemenid period (if not earlier).

15. An Aramaic *piyyuṭ* (liturgical poem) from Palestine, dated from about the eve of Islam, describes Haman and Pharaoh engaging in one-upmanship over which of them was the more wretched (in Yahalom and Sokoloff, *Jewish Palestinian Aramaic Poetry*, *piyyuṭ* no. 33; and see the discussion in Münz-Manor, "Carnivalesque Ambivalence," 833ff., and Lieber, *Jewish Aramaic Poetry*, 114–125). Despite this description of Haman and Pharaoh interacting, it is clear that the two characters were not thought to have overlapped historically, for the same *piyyuṭ* also describes Haman debating with Goliath, Nimrod, Sennacherib, Nebuchadnezzar, and Jesus.

16. Silverstein, *Veiling Esther*, 24 nn. 27–30.

17. Ibid., 24–27.

18. Ibid., 25 nn. 32–34.

19. Although the fifty-cubit gallows that Haman builds for Mordecai, and upon which he is hanged, is the second-tallest building mentioned in the Bible, it is specifically referred to as a "tree" (*'eṣ*) in *Esther*.

20. Nicanor's story is related in the Jerusalem Talmud (y.Ta'anit 2:12), and "Nicanor's Day" is discussed in b.Ta'anit 18b and in the first-century Megillat Ta'anit s.v. "thirteenth of Adar." Nicanor is said to have quoted Judg 8:9, where Gideon promises to smash the tower (*migdal*) of Penuel, which he then does (Judg 8:17). Note that in this verse, not only does Gideon smash

the tower but he also massacres the inhabitants of the city, just as in the Tower of Babel episode (Gen 11:4–5) the plotters build both a tower and a city. Nicanor thus (scandalously) compares the Temple to Penuel's *migdal*. A similar dynamic is found in the Qur'ān's use of *ṣarḥ*, where Pharaoh commissions Haman to build a *ṣarḥ* (through which he displays his *disbelief* in God), whereas the only other *ṣarḥ* mentioned in the Qur'ān is the one that Solomon built (Q 27:44), and through which the Queen of Sheba displayed her *belief* in God. That the positive *ṣarḥ* is attributed to Solomon, brings it in line with the Temple. The rabbis' Nicanor and the Qur'ān's Haman are thus comparable in their opposition to a Solomonic edifice. We return to the relationship between the characters of Nicanor and Haman in Chapter 6.

21. Levine, "Hubris."

22. In Silverstein, *Veiling Esther*, 22.

23. See Silverstein, "The Qur'ānic Pharaoh." For exegetical discussions of Pharaoh's *ṣarḥ* that appear to draw on midrashim about the Tower of Babel, see Schwarzbaum, *Mi-maqor yisra'el*, 188ff.

24. On the nephew's name, see Bledsoe, *The Wisdom of the Aramaic Book of Ahiqar*, 34 n 42.

25. One disanalogy between the Aḥiqar story and that of Haman in the Qur'ān is that Nadab did not ultimately build the tower, whereas much of the exegetical tradition holds that Haman did in fact build the *ṣarḥ* for Pharaoh. That said, some Muslim scholars did hold that Haman failed to carry out Pharaoh's order to build the *ṣarḥ* (e.g., Ibn 'Abd al-Ḥakam, *Futūḥ Miṣr*, 41).

26. "[H]aman" appears in the Codices Vaticanus and Alexandrinus of LXX *Tobit* 14:10, whereas "Nadab" appears in Codex Sinaiticus.

27. See Silverstein, *Veiling Esther*, 31–33. For further parallels between Haman and Nadab in the Aḥiqar story, see Bledsoe, *The Wisdom of the Aramaic Book of Ahiqar*, 195, 235, and 310–11. A systematic comparison between the Aḥiqar tale and MT *Esther* was first undertaken by Talmon, "Wisdom," esp. 438ff.

28. To our evidence we may tentatively add the tradition recorded in *Pirqe de Rabbi Eli'ezer* (Palestine, c. 800 CE), which links Haman with Korah as the two most famous wealthy men, Haman among "the gentiles," and Korah among the Israelites (*Pirqe de Rabbi Eliezer*, 50:5; trans. 398–399). As noted, twice Korah is listed alongside Haman and Pharaoh in the Qur'ān.

29. Note also that in a sixth-century *piyyuṭ*, Haman is described as denying the existence of God (Yahalom and Sokoloff, *Jewish Palestinian Aramaic Poetry*, 206, no. 33 l. 22, and Lieber, *Jewish Aramaic Poetry*, 117).

30. This is a recurring theme in the Qur'ān where, for example, we are told: ". . . But they scheme and Allah schemes; and Allah is the best schemer" (Q 8:30). The verb for "to scheme" in this and comparable verses is *m-k-r*, which will prove relevant to our discussion of Haman's origins in Chapter 8.

31. Whereas the Qur'ān implies this strongly, in later Muslim traditions it is stated explicitly, for instance in Ibn Taghribirdī's *al-Nujūm al-zāhira*, 1:56, where Haman is referred to as "Haman, the enemy of God."

32. Admittedly, the dating of the *'Āl ha-Nissīm* is problematic, for whereas the second-century CE Tosefta (t.Berachot 3:14) refers to "a summary of the event" being inserted into prayers precisely where *'Āl ha-Nissīm* should be, the earliest extant version of the prayer's text dates from the ninth century, some two centuries into the Islamic period (see Silverstein, *Veiling Esther*, 36–37).

33. A detailed presentation of the evidence may be found in Silverstein, *Veiling Esther*, 127–135.

34. Other Persian characters by this or related names are known and frequently conflated in ancient sources (see ibid., 131–132).

35. Note that Aelian (d. 235; *Var.Hist.* 6:8) considered Bagoas himself to have been an Egyptian (in Stanley, *Claudius Aelianus,* Book VI, 133–143).

36. See below, Chapter 9.

37. Note that some early Islamic sources and late antique rabbis (b.Mo'ed Qatan 18a) suggested that the Pharaoh who ruled at the time of Moses was originally a Persian, as we will see in Chapter 9. Conversely, Zlotnick-Sivan ("Moses the Persian?") argues that the biblical Moses was modelled after the Achaemenid Cyrus.

38. More often than not, Haman is mentioned as part of the fixed phrase "Pharaoh and Haman" used to refer to tyrants or other unjust rulers (e.g., al-Ṭabarī, *Ta'rīkh,* 2:717, where the rebel Muṣ'ab ibn al-Zubayr refers to the Umayyad dynasty as "Pharaoh and Haman"; and ibid., 3:209, where the rebel Muḥammad ibn 'Abdallāh "the Mahdī" rebelled against the caliph al-Manṣūr in Medina and used "Pharaoh and Haman" when referring to the unjust regime). Note, however, that centuries later we find the order reversed, with Tīmūr's son counselling his father not to covet earthly power, saying: "[D]ismiss worldly affairs and give constant care to the life to come; [even] if you possessed the kingdom of Shaddād and there came to you the power of Amalek and 'Ād, and victory and fortune so aided you that you attained the position of Haman and Pharaoh and a quarter of the earth paid tribute to you. . . ." (in Sanders, *Tamerlane,* 101–102).

39. The ḥadīth, which is categorized as trustworthy, may be found here: https://sunnah.com/mishkat:578. 'Ubayy ibn Khalaf was an enemy of Muḥammad at Mecca.

40. In al-Ṭabarī, *Ta'rīkh,* 1:476 (translation adapted from Brinner, *History,* 60). Al-Ya'qūbī (*Ta'rīkh,* 1:33) recounts a similar anecdote, in which Pharaoh is on the verge of accepting Moses's God, only for Haman to dissuade him from doing so by summoning local magicians to demonstrate that Moses's miracles were not of divine origin.

41. Yāqūt, *Mu'jam al-buldān,* 3:210 s.v. "sardūs." Cf. Ibn 'Abd al-Ḥakam, *Futūḥ Miṣr,* 26.

42. A good example of this comes from a relatively late historical source (Ibn Manẓūr's late-thirteenth-century epitome of Ibn 'Asākir's twelfth-century work), which relates that when Hārūn al-Rashīd's famous vizier al-Faḍl ibn al-Rabī' (d. 823/4) complained that a functionary referred to him as "Haman," the caliph retorted that the insult was even worse for him, as it made him Pharaoh! (Ibn Manẓūr, *Mukhtaṣar ta'rīkh dimashq,* 5:234). The clear implication is that it is worse to be called "Pharaoh" than "Haman."

43. This tradition is attributed to Bishr ibn Mu'ādh al-'Aqadī (d. 859), who derives it ultimately from Qatādah ibn Nu'mān (d. 644). See al-Ṭabarī, *Ta'rīkh,* 1:469 (trans. Brinner, *History,* 3:54).

44. The technical term for Haman's baked bricks in Islamic tradition, *ājurr,* is used by the Jewish traveler Benjamin of Tudela (d. 1173) in his description of the remains of the Tower of Babel (Benjamin of Tudela, *Itinerary,* 43, where the word is spelled *agūr*).

45. Al-Ṭabarī (*Ta'rīkh,* 1:479–80) relates this on the authority of al-Suddī.

46. In ibid., 1:527–28 (trans. Brinner, *History,* 3:110), quoting Q 29:40.

47. Exceptionally, in his Friday sermon, the Palestinian preacher Kamāl Khaṭīb referred to the stories of "Haman, Nimrod, Khusraw, Heraclius, and Pharaoh, who were tyrants (*ṭawāghīt*) whose unhappy ending should serve as a lesson to us." Here, Khaṭīb both dissociates Pharaoh from Haman and suggests that Haman's death was a significant lesson for future generations. The sermon, delivered July 22, 2022, may be found at: https://m.youtube.com/watch?v=trIaewkdkOA. Khaṭīb's deployment of Haman in this way may reflect the Jewish-Israeli context in which he lives and of which he displays considerable knowledge.

48. Ibn Manẓūr (*Mukhtaṣar ta'rīkh dimashq,* 28:16) preserves an interesting account of a desert Arab in the Hijaz, according to whom people were to be judged in pairs, such as (the infamous Umayyad governor) al-Ḥajjāj ibn Yūsuf, who had Yazīd ibn Abī Muslim (d. 721); Pharaoh, who had Haman; and (the Umayyad caliph) 'Umar ibn 'Abd al-'Azīz, who had Rajā'

ibn Ḥaywah (d. 730). A similar tradition may be found in a tenth-century Ismāʿīlī work *Kitāb al-shajarah* ("Book of the Tree"), according to which every prophet has been paired with a Devil (*iblīs*) and a Satan (*shayṭān*), and in the case of Moses, the Devil was Pharaoh and the Satan was Haman (in De Smet, "The Demon in Potentiality," 616).

49. See Kister, "Ḥaddithū ʿan banī isrāʾīla wa-lā ḥaraja."

Chapter Six: Haman's Historical Development: Four stages

1. The rabbis held that Nebuzaradan converted to Judaism after killing two million Jews (b.Gittin 57b), and that Nero converted to Judaism in lieu of his original plan to attack Jerusalem (b.Gittin 56a), but did not take Nebuchadnezzar's repentance seriously. We return to the question of villain-rehabilitation in Chapter 9.

2. Naturally, exegetes have found various ways to interpret the term "Messiah" in this context, vexed no doubt by the fact that here the term refers to a non-Jewish king. On the possibility that early Achaemenid kings saw themselves as eschatological redeemers (*saošyants*), see Silverman, "Achaemenid 'Theology' of Kingship," 186.

3. Admittedly, this summary of the Jewish experience in Achaemenid lands is something of an oversimplification. For a more nuanced view of biblical attitudes to the Achaemenids, see Sweeny, "Contrasting Portrayals."

4. Koller, *Esther in Ancient Jewish Thought*, passim, esp. 55–106.

5. A striking example of the non-Jewish vocabulary adopted during Exile is the retention of Babylonian month names, even though some of them are named after pagan gods.

6. Although the synagogue is usually dated to 245 CE, thereby post-dating the Parthian period, the art depicted in it—and specifically the *Esther* panel—has been shown to reflect Parthian culture (see e.g., Curtis, "The Iranian Revival in the Parthian Period," 18).

7. For a detailed presentation of the arguments, see Silverstein, *Veiling Esther*, 92–126.

8. One exception to the predilection for Greek sources in this context is de Goeje's attempt to compare *Esther* and the frame story of the *1001 Nights*, which was met with fierce resistance and even ridicule.

9. The pioneer in this regard was Bickerman (*Four Strange Books of the Bible, passim* esp. 177–96) who made frequent reference to storytelling from a number of cultures in his influential discussion of *Esther*. More systematic treatments of this topic, focusing on the Greek storytelling context may be found in Berlin, "Esther and Ancient Storytelling," Wills, *The Jewish Novel*, 93–131, and Day, *Three Faces of a Queen*, 214–232.

10. See Silverstein, *Veiling Esther*, 92–98. Although the Parthian novels all survive in versions no earlier than the eleventh century CE, numerous studies have established the antiquity—and particularly the Parthian provenance—of each work. That virtually no biblical or midrashic influence on these works is discernable indicates that there was no conversation between the two cultural corpuses.

11. Ibid., 93.

12. For a detailed discussion of the *ShāhNāma-Esther* connection, see ibid., 104–106.

13. On the preservation of Achaemenid history in the *ShāhNāma*, see Jamzadeh, "Shahnama Passage," and Davidson, "Traces."

14. There are numerous, confusing traditions about Ḥomāy's name, including Khumānī, Khumāna, and Shahrazād.

15. Shapira, "Judeo-Persian translations," 232.

16. Al-Ṭabarī, *Taʾrīkh*, 1:652–4. Al-Ṭabarī notes that Esther and Mordecai were nursed by the same woman (Mordecai's mother), a detail not found in versions of *Esther*, but which does overlap with the originally Parthian story *Vīs and Rāmīn*, where the two eponymous heroes were nursed by the same woman in Susa. We return to *Vīs and Rāmīn* below. There is a

rabbinic tradition according to which Mordecai nursed Esther miraculously (*Genesis Rabba* 30:8), but this is not quite the same.

17. Confusingly, Dārāb the son of Bahmān and Ḥomāy had a son named Dārāb, and it is the latter whom Alexander defeats.

18. A shorter version of this intrigue at Dārāb's court may be found in al-Ṭabarī, *Ta'rīkh*, 1:692–3.

19. In describing events from the very end of the Achaemenid period, the *DārābNāma*, necessarily postdates MT *Esther*. And yet, the existence of several ancient Persian versions of the "plot of the eunuchs" would suggest that it is that literary context (rather than *Esther*'s imagined influence) to which the *DārābNāma* may be related (see Shayegan, *Aspects of History and Epic*).

20. Note that in al-Ṭabarī's version of the story (*Ta'rīkh*, 1:697–8), the two courtiers are chamberlains (Arabic: *ḥujjāb*), which brings the account into line with the MT's subplot on the same theme (2:21–23).

21. For sources, see Silverstein, *Veiling Esther*, 116 and n 76.

22. E.g., Paton, *Commentary*, 136.

23. Whereas the *Samak-i 'Ayyār* uses the Persian phrase *khāṣṣ va-'ām*, which is patently post-Islamic, this phrase may be an updated version of the older, pre-Islamic Persian *kahtar o mehtar*, "smaller and bigger," which also signifies "everyone."

24. The nurse who raises Vīs is comparable to Mordecai, who is referred to as an *omen* (Esth 2:7, 20), a term derived from a verb meaning "to nurse" (e.g., Ruth 4:16). Moses is also described as an *omen*, meaning "nurse," in a childbirth metaphor (Num 11:12).

25. Whereas most modern commentators take this detail to be a sign of the narrator's exaggeration (comparable to the 120-day banquet described in *Judith* 1:16), the description in *Vīs and Rāmīn* demonstrates that six-month long banquets were a feature of the ancient Persian storytelling repertoire.

26. Silverstein, *Veiling Esther*, 121.

27. Admittedly, the Parthian novels emanate in their current forms from the eastern lands of the Abbasid caliphate where, in the tenth century, Bal'amī translated al-Ṭabarī's *Ta'rīkh* into Persian, around the time that the *ShāhNāma* was being compiled. And yet, as we will see below, al-Ṭabarī's summary of the *Esther* story does not mention Haman, nor does it refer to the "plot of the eunuchs," to the details of celebrations referred to here, or even to a plot against the Jews.

28. Davis, *Panthea's Children*.

29. Wechsler, "Two Para-biblical Novellae."

30. In *Samak-i 'Ayyār*, a week-long wedding feast marked Marzbān Shāh's marriage to an Iraqi princess (Golnār), just as early midrashim from Sasanid Iran (b.Megillah 10b) note that Vashti herself was a Babylonian princess, the granddaughter of Nebuchadnezzar (II) (b.Megillah 10b).

31. b.Megillah 13a. A similar idea is attributed to one Rabbah bar Lima (b.Megillah 13b).

32. On the love-triangle in *Esther*, see Walfish, "Kosher Adultery?"

33. Late antique midrashim also share traditions about Haman with the Parthian novels. For instance, in *Samak-i 'Ayyār*, the evil nurse and evil vizier plot to have their daughters marry the king, just as midrashim relate that Haman plotted to have his daughter marry Ahashwerosh. Similarly, in *Samak-i 'Ayyār*, the (benign) vizier Haman is an astrologer, a detail related about the biblical Haman in midrashic literature (we return to both of these details in Chapter 9).

34. As we will see, in practice the demand that Jews Hellenize was often accompanied by an expectation that they forego the Law.

35. The rabbis made an exception, even to the ruling against Greek wisdom, for those who worked closely with the governing authorities, for whom knowledge of Greek thought was necessary (b.Baba Qama 82b-83a).

36. Every traditionally educated Jewish child is taught that the Hanukkah story is about a Jewish victory over "the Greeks," whereas in fact un-Hellenized Jews were victorious over Hellenized ones.

37. Goldberg, *Curse of Ham*; and Haynes, *Noah's Curse.*

38. Presumably, Noah's naked body was exposed, although the text is not clear, and from the severity of the punishment, many exegetes concluded that more than mere exposure took place.

39. Jub 8:10–10:34, especially 10:28–34.

40. It is worth noting that many Ethiopian Christians and Jews regard *Jubilees* as canonical.

41. Moreover, when Haman is accused of a crime and punished for it (Esth 7), it is for a crime that he did not commit: the king misinterpreted Haman's begging Esther for forgiveness as an attempt to seduce her.

42. An alternative interpretation of "Bougean" is proposed by Wechsler ("The Appellation βογγαιος"), for whom the context is not broadly Hellenistic but specifically Ptolemaic: He argues that "Bougaios" refers to members of the Beja tribe of modern Sudan, Eritrea, and southeastern Egypt, who were infamous in Ptolemaic times for their violence. The epithet "Bougean" may thus refer to the Beja, while also evoking the Greek for "braggart."

43. The work was composed at some point in the second century BCE in a Semitic language. In Antiquity it was translated into Greek, Latin, Armenian, Coptic, and—eventually—Arabic (the story occurs more than once in the Qur'ān).

44. For cosmic meaning in Additions A and F, see De Troyer and Smith, "Cosmic Events."

45. In the court tales of Dan 1–6, which—in their present form—date from the mid-second-century BCE, Jews are challenged by a tyrant who seeks to punish them for their refusal to behave in the required way.

46. Hellenization took more than one form among Jews in this period. Some eagerly adopted Greek culture, which they believed would improve Judaism and the lives of Jews, others were less consciously complicit purveyors of Hellenism, and still others were openly antagonistic to Jewish philhellenism. It is the latter group whose adherents authored some of the rewritten *Esthers* that we discuss here. Nonetheless, all educated Jews in this period were forced to interact with Hellenism in some way and were, by necessity, shaped by it.

47. Schäfer, *Judeophobia*, 208–209.

48. On the assumption that LXX *Esther* (without its Additions) was composed around 100 BCE, it is likely that *2 Maccabees* was the earliest attempt to "correct" MT *Esther.*

49. In Bush, "The Book of Esther," 39.

50. Lacocque (*Esther Regina*, 35) goes so far as to date MT *Esther* to Antiochus IV's reign on account of the story's reference to state-organized genocide. We shall see in Chapter 8, however, that one may find just such examples of state-organized genocide in the early-Achaemenid period.

51. In 2 Macc 8:34ff., Nicanor is "thrice accursed." He suffers from overweening pride, and he is said to have invited a thousand slave-dealers to buy Jewish captives (cf. Haman's attempt to buy the Jews from Ahashwerosh in Esth 3:9). Moreover, Nicanor was eventually humiliated and had to escape "like a fugitive slave," hinting at the sort of reversal/poetic justice found in *Esther.*

52. Nicanor's interaction with the Jews is described in 2 Macc 14–15, where he is generally antagonistic to them (on the instructions of Antiochus IV). That said, in 14:24 we hear that Nicanor, "always kept Judas in his company, for he felt affection for the man." By contrast, in 1 Macc 7:26–32, there is nothing like a positive relationship between the two.

53. For midrashic accounts of Haman's having looted the treasures of the kings of Judah, see the sources in Glickman, *Haman and the Jews*, 42 n 3.

54. One presumes that the author of *2 Maccabees* used an early (pre-additions) Greek *Esther*, but we cannot know this with certainty.

55. When relating the account of Menelaus's demise, 2 Macc 13:8 adds to the fact that he was hanged from a 50-cubit tower the statement that, "because he had committed many sins against the altar whose fire and ashes were holy, he met his death in ashes." This brings Menelaus into line with Haman, who died by the same gallows on which he had intended to hang Mordecai.

56. On Nicanor in later Jewish sources, see Noam, *Shifting Images of the Hasmoneans*, 32–58.

57. A rabbinic summary of the events is recorded in Megillat Ta'anit (s.v. "Adar, Thirteen: Day of Niqanor"), which relates that Nicanor was a general of the Greek kings, who would blaspheme Jerusalem and the Holy Temple on a daily basis, proclaiming his intention to destroy the Temple. The events are also related in Josephus's *Antiquities* (XII.10.4-5), and in the Jerusalem and Babylonian Talmuds (y.Ta'anit 2:11 [12a], and b.Ta'anit 18b).

58. This Aramaic text relates much the same events covered in *1* and *2 Maccabees*, while also reflecting the events as they are recorded (in disguise) in the book of *Judith*. Kaddari ("In what form of Aramaic was the Scroll of Antiochus written?" 144–5), argues on the basis of the MA's language that the text dates from the second to fifth centuries CE, with an earlier date within that range more probable than a later one.

59. Aramaic *ḥayyāvā* is employed, this being a term that routinely translates *rāshā'* ("evil") in Aramaic biblical translations (e.g., Onqelos *ad* Gen 18:25 and Targum *ad* Job 27:7). *Haman ha-rāshā'* ("the evil Haman") had been a commonplace phrase in Jewish sources since antiquity, for all that it is absent from MT *Esther* itself.

60. In both cases, the contents of the villain's inner thoughts turned out to be misguidedly optimistic.

61. The Aramaic text, with Hebrew, Yiddish, and English translations may be found here: https://opensiddur.org/readings-and-sourcetexts/festival-and-fast-day-readings/jewish/hanukkah-readings/megillat-antiokhus/. Saadiah Gaon, who may have translated the book into Arabic, refers to it by the (Arabic) title *kitāb banī ḥashmona'ī*.

62. MA details the various ways in which the enemies of the Jews were killed: ". . . some of them they burned in fire, some they pierced with the sword, and some they hung (Aramaic: *ṣelabū*, lit. "crucified") upon trees. And Bagris who led his people astray, was burned by the House of Israel in fire" (MA 59). In other words, although crucifixion on a tree was one of the options, Bacchides was burned. This may be an example of MA correcting *Esther*, or a reflection of the fact that already in this period Haman's effigy was burned at Purim celebrations in the Holy Land. In Chapter 10 we will encounter examples of Haman-burning rituals from the early fifth century CE.

63. I will not discuss here the "Animal Apocalypse" in 1 Enoch 85–90 (mid-second century BCE), comparable to Dan 7–12 for its eschatologization of the reign of Antiochus IV.

64. By contrast, in the Qur'ān (18:90–94) and Islamic thought generally, Gog and Magog will arrive from the East.

65. Koller, *Esther in Ancient Jewish Thought*, 136–138.

66. Mordecai is specifically identified as the Jew in Esth 2:5, 3:4, 5:13, 6:10, 8:7, 9:29, 31, 10:3. Bearing in mind the Hasmonean background of the text, "Judith" may also be the female equivalent of "Judah [the Maccabee]."

67. Judith's beheading of Holofernes may be compared with Bīzhān's beheading of the Ṭūrānian general Hōmān in the *ShāhNāma*, but more directly echoes descriptions of Nicanor's mutilation in *1* and *2 Maccabees* (see Wilk, "The Abuse of Nicanor's Corpse," 56).

68. Mackey ("'Nadin' [Nadab] of Tobit is the 'Holofernes' of Judith") argues that Holofernes in *Judith* is in fact the Nadin/Nadan of the Ahīqar story, specifically as the latter

narrative occurs in *Tobit* 14:10. If so, then the associations with Haman are strengthened, seeing as the LXX to Tob 14:10 has "Aman" in lieu of Nadab (see above, Ch 5, n 26).

69. Jdt 2:4, 4:1, 5:1, 6:1, 10:13, and 13:15.

70. Jdt 5:20, 24, 7:9, 11, and 11:10.

71. Lees, "Intertextual Ripples," 100ff.

72. Note that *Judith* is canonical in Catholic, Eastern Orthodox, and Ethiopian churches (as are *1* and *2 Maccabees*).

73. On Second Temple attitudes to tyrannical kings in general, see Rajak, "The Angry Tyrant."

74. See below, Ch 6, n 185.

75. See Koller, *Esther in Ancient Jewish Thought*, 139–141, and Lees, "Intertextual Ripples," 73–75 (with sources).

76. Hacham, "3 Maccabees and Esther" and, earlier, Alexander, "3 Maccabees, Hanukkah, and Purim." To the evidence offered by Hacham and Alexander, we might add the fact that OL 5:9 refers to Haman as having 300 friends, a possible allusion to 3 Macc 7:14–15, where the victorious Jews kill 300 renegades (see above, Ch 2, n 52). Recall that OL *Esther* is probably based on a Greek *Vorlage* composed roughly when *3 Maccabees* was written.

77. Strictly speaking, and contra Hacham ("3 Maccabees and Esther," 768), Haman's face in Est 7:8 did not "fall" but "was covered." It is with reference to Cain (Gen 4:5) that the phrase "his face fell" may be found.

78. To these points may be added the possibility that Hermon was chosen to represent a northern enemy: In LXX Amos 4:3, Harmon (which is often equated with the northern Mt. Ḥermon) is rendered "Ermon," which is how "Hermon" is spelled in *3 Maccabees.*

79. Another example of the recasting of an *Esther*-related narrative in a Pharaonic context, which also dates from the Second Temple period, is the *Genesis Apocryphon*, found among the Qumran Scrolls, in which *Esther* clearly shaped a retelling of Gen 12:10–20. In that passage, Abram and Sarai interact with Pharaoh and the latter's servants, demonstrating the transferal of *Esther*-language to an Egyptian setting. As Gen 12:10–20 does not include a Haman-ic villain, I have not considered it here. On this text's relation to *Esther*, see Koller, *Esther in Ancient Jewish Thought*, 142–46 and the sources provided in nn. 24–27 thereto.

80. Beck (*Evolution of the Qur'ān*, 1–78), argues plausibly that *3 Maccabees* was known to the Qur'ān's author, which, if correct, may enhance the relevance of this rewritten *Esther* for our understanding of the Qur'ānic Haman.

81. Brown, *World of Late Antiquity*. The precise temporal boundaries of late antiquity are debated, with such ranges as 150–750 and 300–800 CE (among others) featuring in scholarly literature. Common to the proposed options is the understanding that late antique civilization developed gradually.

82. See e.g., Gross, "The Curious Case of the Jewish Sasanian Queen Šīšīn-duxt," and the earlier scholarship cited there. Gross is skeptical as to the existence of this Jewish queen, but even a fictitious account of Sasanid kings marrying (or being the son of) a Jewess tells us much about the relations between the Jews and their Sasanid rulers.

83. The midrashic corpus on Haman, in particular, and on *Esther*, generally, is enormous. In this chapter we relate only those traditions that bear directly on the historical development of rabbinic interpretations and depictions of Haman.

84. Admittedly, the neat dichotomy between rabbis on either side of the Euphrates belies the diversity of opinion within each community and the complexity of the subject as a whole. To these may be added the difficulty in ascribing traditions to particular rabbis and, related to this, securely identifying the chronological and geographical coordinates of midrashim. I thus resort to imprecise generalizations.

85. The extent to which the Jews of the Roman Empire were persecuted and hindered in their practice is reflected in the notion of a "Babylonia of Pure Lineage," a concept promoted by the Sasanid rabbis to argue that their traditions were more faithfully preserved than those of the Holy Land.

86. For a survey of the rabbinic sources (*midrash*, *piyyuṭ*, and *targum*) that we use here, see Shinan, "The Late Midrashic, Paytanic, and Targumic Literature," and Novick, *Piyyuṭ and Midrash*. As a general rule, it is safer to date the general corpus that preserves rabbinic quotations than it is to date those rabbis to whom the quotations are ascribed, as such ascription is notoriously unreliable. To complicate matters, the form in which a source has reached us is almost centuries later than the period in which the source was originally composed. My assumption in drawing on the late antique rabbinic materials is that they reflect the ideas found in the sources, even if they do not represent an accurate record of the individual statements attributed to specific authorities.

87. The classical treatment of the subject is Swain, "The Theory of the Four Monarchies." See also, Silverstein, "Q 30:2–5," esp. 32 n 44 (with sources), and Herman, "Persia, Rome, and the Four Kingdoms Motif."

88. *Pesher Habakkuk* (1QpHab, especially column 9). Josephus, too, relates the *Daniel* vision to Antiochus IV, following which he adds, "In the very same manner, Daniel also wrote concerning the Roman government . . ." (*Antiquities*, XI.7).

89. 1 Macc 1:1 also tells us that "Alexander the Great the Macedonian" had come from "the land of Kittim."

90. A more detailed treatment of this topic, may be found in Silverstein, "Q 30: 2–5," 28–32.

91. See also the NT prediction of the destruction of "Babylon the Great" (clearly a cipher for Rome) by an eighth empire (Rev 17:1–18).

92. The fourth oracle of *Sib.Or.* 3 predicts that an Egyptian ruler will defeat the Romans, which evidences the pro-Ptolemaic patriotism of the oracle's Alexandrian author (vv. 652–656).

93. Note the Talmudic statement (b.Yoma 10a) that the Persians were the Temple's builders and the Romans its destroyers.

94. In the Early-Christian-era *Ascension of Isaiah*, Belial is closely associated (perhaps even equated) with Satan (*Ascension of Isaiah*, 1:8–9, 2:2–4, 3:11–13, 4:14–18, etc.)

95. *Sib.Or.* 5 vv. 111–178 and 179–285.

96. In some Christian circles, by contrast, Nero continued to occupy a special place as the first Roman ruler to persecute Christians (cf. Eusebius, *Ecclesiastical History*, II.25.4; and Sulpicius Severus, *Sacred History*, II.28). The identification of Nero with the Antichrist persisted among some Christian authors (long after the Jews transferred the role to others), perhaps because the *Syb.Or.* was adopted and supplemented by Christian communities (while late antique Jews marginalized the work). Other Christians, by contrast, disputed the Nero-Antichrist theory (cf. Augustine, *City of God*, XX.19.3).

97. b.Gittin 56a. The tradition about Nero's conversion to Judaism aligns him with such penitent tyrants as Nebuchadnezzar (Dan 4) and Pharoah (Q 10:90–92; see n 771). That the Antichrist should convert is, however, odd.

98. Himmelfarb, *Jewish Messiahs*, 27ff.

99. On the identification of Esau with Rome, see Sivertsev, *Judaism and Imperial Ideology*, 9ff., and Feldman, "Some Observations," 47. It is surely also relevant that biblical texts (Obad 1:11–14, Ps 137:7) tell us that Edom partook in the destruction of the first Temple.

100. In theory, pre-Christian Hellenism and Christianity were incompatible. In practice, the Byzantines inherited and were thoroughly shaped by ancient Greek culture (see Kaldellis,

Hellenism in Byzantium). It is against this backdrop that Rabbi Shim'on ben Laqish (d. 275) equated Greece with Haman (in Herman, "Persia, Rome and the Four Kingdoms Motif," 192).

101. Note that TgII 1:1 lists the ten universal kings/kingdoms who were destined to rule, a list that includes the Romans, followed by "the Greeks" (read: Byzantines), after whom the Messiah would rule.

102. Had the rabbis used the LXX, where "Agagite" is replaced with "Bougean" or "Macedonian," there would be no problem. But they did not, and repeatedly connected the *Esther* story and the Agag episode in 1 Sam 15 (e.g., b.Megillah 11a, b.Yoma 22b, b.Shabbat 56b, etc.)

103. The Bible uses the verb *va-yivvez* with reference both to Haman's actions (Esth 3:6) and Esau's (Gen 25:34), just as it reports the inner thoughts of both (Gen 27:41 and Esth 6:6). Moreover, the phrase, "he cried out a bitter cry" is used only twice in the HB, once concerning Esau (Gen 27:34), the other time in Esth 4:1. Curiously, in the latter context it is Mordecai rather than Haman who "cries a bitter cry," but the unique parallelism remains nonetheless (as noted in *Genesis Rabba* 67:4).

104. Thus, for instance, TgI 3:6, 4:9, and 5:1 suggest that Haman targeted the Jews to repay them for Jacob's stealing Isaac's blessing from Esau. Similarly, a number of midrashim relate that on a military campaign to which both Haman and Mordecai were sent by the ruler, Haman exhausted his provisions and was forced to sell himself to Mordecai for food, just as Esau sold his birth right to Jacob for food (see Silverstein, *Veiling Esther*, 53f., with sources).

105. See Grossfeld, *Two Targums*, 211 "Table X: Haman's Genealogy," and ibid., 140 where TgII 3:1 traces Haman back to Esau. Note, also, that the oracle against Edom in Jer 49: 7–22, includes the phrase, "[God's] thoughts that he thought" (v. 20), which occurs elsewhere in the HB only with reference to Haman (Esth 8:3).

106. If Levit-Tawil ("The Purim Panel," 104–107 and "Queen Esther at Dura," 296) is correct, then Haman is depicted in the Purim panel of the Dura Europos synagogue as a "a Roman competitor in a chariot race."

107. The Talmudo-Iranica scholarly enterprise demonstrates this point aptly. With particular regard to rabbinic traditions on *Esther* and Haman, we have already seen striking similarities between the Parthian novels and the rabbinic sources (see above, Ch 6, n 30).

108. See e.g., do Nascimento, "From Blessed to Accursed," Gignoux, "La démonisation d'Alexandre le Grand," and, most recently, Agostini, "The Perception of the Romans," esp. 8–9 and 13 n 86.

109. See e.g., *Ardā Wirāz Nāmag* 1:7, where Alexander is referred to as "Aleksandar ī Hrōmāyīg" ("Alexander the Roman"), and *Zand ī Wahman Yašt* 7:32, where Alexander is both "the Roman," and is associated with *Xešm* ("demonic wrath").

110. See Agostini, "The Perception of the Romans," and do Nascimento, "From Blessed to Accursed," 31–35 (with sources).

111. do Nascimento, "From Blessed to Accursed," 35.

112. For the Near Eastern pedigree of descriptions of villains as sacrilegious rulers who rob temples, destroy holy writings, and interfere in the conduct of rituals, see Weitzman, "Plotting Antiochus's Persecution," esp. 234. We have already seen that Second Temple sources describe both Antiochus IV and Menelaus as plunderers of the Temple's riches.

113. 1 Macc 1:56. See also m.Ta'anit 4:6, where "Apostomus" is said to have burned the Torah scrolls. This otherwise unknown character is thought to have been Antiochus IV (perhaps through a misreading of the Greek epithet *epiphanes*). For a similar case of transferring this package of felonies to other villains with undecipherable names, see al-Ṭabarī, *Ta'rīkh*, 1:678, where the Ṭūrānian king "Kharzasf" (sic! Probably "Arjasb"; see Tafażżolī, "Arjāsp") "burned the archives, slew Luhrasp and the priests, destroyed the fire-worshipping sanctuaries, seized the wealth and treasures, and captured two daughters of Bishtasp, one called Khumānī, the other Badhafrah." That Khumānī was an Esther-type Jewish queen in ancient Persia increases

the likelihood that we are dealing here with a composite villain whose description reflects some admixture of descriptions of Alexander (Persian), Haman (rabbinic), and Antiochus IV (Jewish). Note that later al-Ṭabari (*Ta'rīkh*, 1:718) relates that Khumānī was defeated by none other than Alexander.

114. E.g., *Esther Rabba* 7:5 (and Glickman, *Haman and the Jews*, 42 and n 2).

115. A number of villainous characters in the HB are described by the term *arūr*, such as the snake in the Garden of Eden (Gen 3:14), Cain (Gen 4:11), and Ham's son, Canaan (Gen 9:25; who is labelled "evil" on account of his father's misbehavior.

116. In the *Dēnkard* (5:3) Alexander features in a list of evil characters (*wadgarīh*), and in the *Ardā Wirāz Nāmag* (1:4) he is referred to as "the accursed (*gizistag*) Alexander, the Roman."

117. *Rasha'* (evil): b.Megillah 11a (where Haman is identified with the "evil ruler" of Prov 28:15), *Exodus Rabba* 33, and *'Al ha-Nīssīm*. *Arūr* ("cursed"): b.Megillah 7b. It should be noted that the Haman-ic character Bacchides in MA (vv. 29, 32, 36, 43, 48, 59) is also referred to as "wicked" (*ḥayyava*, the usual Aramaic rendering of Hebrew *rasha'*), and it is impossible to determine where Haman first acquired the "evil" label. As always, it may simply be that the adjective was applied to Haman independently of other villains. Similarly, the application of *arūr* to Haman may be related to his association with Esau, as in Gen 27:29, where Isaac blesses Jacob, saying that those who curse Jacob will themselves be cursed (*arūr*). The designation of Haman as *arūr* also appears in a Byzantine-era *piyyuṭ* (Yahalom and Sokoloff, *Jewish Palestinian Aramaic Poetry*, 196–197, and Lieber, *Jewish Aramaic Poetry*, 110) while other *piyyuṭim* use *rasha'* for Haman (Münz-Manor, "Other Voices," 71f.).

118. To the evidence that Haman was identified with the Romans, we may add that the ancient Iranian Jewish Queen Ḥomay sent armies against "the Romans," thereby equating the Romans with Ḥomay/Esther's enemy (Ḥamza al-Iṣfahānī, *Ta'rīkh*, 37–38).

119. In fact, the same Sasanid (Pahlavi-Zoroastrian) context in which Alexander is called a "Roman" also occasionally referred to him as "the Christian" (*kilīsāyīg*; in Agostini, "The Perception of the Romans," 9 and n 93, where it is suggested that Alexander acquired the Christian label in the sixth century CE).

120. To the Jesus-Haman parallels may be added the idea that both were reportedly executed on Passover (Münz-Manor, "Carnivalesque Ambivalence," 834 and n 18).

121. On Mordecai's refusal to bow to Haman, with fuller references to sources, see Silverstein, *Veiling Esther*, 146–182.

122. On Haman's crucifixion: *Genesis Rabba* 30:8, and *piyyuṭim* from Byzantine Palestine (Münz-Manor, "Carnivalesque Ambivalence"). See also Thornton, "Crucifixion of Haman."

123. Talmudic rabbis make it clear that Mordecai could have bowed to Haman as a gesture of respect (b.Sanhedrin 61b). That the Babylonian rabbis accepted local legal systems (Aramaic: *dīnā de-malkhūtā dīnā*, "the law of the land is the law") as legitimate in civil contexts, implied that bowing to Haman had religious implications. Thus, the Babylonian and Palestinian rabbis reached the same conclusion (that bowing to Haman was idolatry) via different routes, with only the Palestinian rabbis comparing Haman to Jesus.

124. Wechsler, *Conviviality*, 216. Note that Mordecai's ancestor, Jacob, bowed before Haman's ancestor, Esau (Gen 33:3). See also Tanḥum ha-Yerushalmi's catalog of pre-*Esther* biblical figures who bowed to others (Wechsler, *Strangers in the Land*, 237).

125. TgI 3:2; TgII 6:1; *Esther Rabba* 7:6; *Pirqe de Rabbi Eliezer* 50:5 (trans. 399).

126. b.Megillah 10b and 19a. The idea that Haman viewed himself as a god is supported by the use of the two verbal roots *k-r-'* and *sh-ḥ-w* in *Esther* 3: whereas earlier Jews/Israelites bowed to humans, in the Bible, these two verbal roots are combined only when referring to prostration before God (e.g., Ps 95:6, 2 Chron 7:3 and 29:29). Some Talmudic rabbis held that one may commit idolatry under duress (b.Avoda Zara 54a).

127. Tanḥum ha-Yerushalmi is a rare Jewish exegete who suggested that bowing to Haman was *not* meant as an act of worship (Wechsler, *Strangers in the Land*, 26–27, 39, and 233–237).

128. Most rabbinic sources did not consider Haman to have been a Galilean, and even the corpus of *piyyuṭim* on which we draw here for the idea that Haman was born in Palestine includes the (contradictory) idea that Haman was a "son of Hamadan," i.e., a Persian. The *piyyuṭ*'s reference to him as "the son of Hamadan" may relate (consciously or erroneously) not to his birthplace but to his father's name, Hammedata. That the tomb of Esther and Mordecai is in Hamadan rather than in Susa may also be relevant in this context. Note that al-Samʿānī (d. 1166) states on the authority of al-Ḥasan al-Baṣrī (d. 728), that Haman was a native of Hamadan (*Tafsīr*, 5:20).

129. The idea that Haman was from the Galilee is found both in the Talmud and in Byzantine *piyyuṭim* (see b.Megillah 16a, where it is stated that Haman was from Kfar Qarnos (Krenos) near Scythopolis/Bet Shean; and see the elaborate discussion of the relevant *piyyuṭ* in Sivan, *Palestine in Late Antiquity*, 143–186, and Lieber, *Jewish Aramaic Poetry*, 120).

130. b.Megillah 13b and TgI 2:21. Note that Rhabanus Maurus (ad Esth 2:21–23) compares the Pharisees who (in his view) sought to kill Jesus with Bigthan and Teresh.

131. To these parallels we may add the reference to Ahashwerosh in a Byzantine-era *piyyuṭ* as "Caesar" (Aramaic: *qeysar*, rather than "king"). See Yahalom and Sokoloff, *Jewish Palestinian Aramaic Poetry*, 218–219, Münz-Manor, "Carnivalesque Ambivalence," 836, and Lieber, *Jewish Aramaic Poetry*, 124.

132. For the *piyyuṭ*, see Lieber, *Jewish Aramaic Poetry*, 118, and Sivan, *Palestine in Late Antiquity*, 152. On Jesus in the Talmud as a *shoṭeh*, see b.Shabbat 104b. On anti-Christian tropes in Byzantine-era *piyyuṭim*, see Van Bekkum, "Anti-Christian Polemics." For the scholarly debate as to whether these anti-Christian poems were parodies, see Münz-Manor, "Carnivalesque Ambivalence," 831, n 10.

133. On Amalek as a cipher for Christendom, see Horowitz, *Reckless Rites*, 116–118 (with sources).

134. The Andalusian exegete Abraham Ibn Ezra (d. 1167) is a rare exegete who dissociates Mordecai from the Saul of 1 Sam 15, arguing that if *Esther*'s author wished to indicate that Mordecai was a descendant of Saul, then he would have said so, rather than mentioning the less illustrious Kish (Esth 2:5) who was Saul's father (in Ibn Ezra's second commentary on *Esther*, *ad* 2:5 s.v. "son of Kish"). In his earlier, first commentary on *Esther*, Ibn Ezra merely questioned why Mordecai was not explicitly described as Saul's descendant, but he stops short there of denying the connection altogether (Mishaly and Zipor, *Abraham Ibn Ezra's Two Commentaries*, 70 *ad* 2:5 s.v. "son of Kish," and 129–130).

135. Josephus identifies the Amalekites with the Edomites (*Antiquities*, II.1-6). A similar, slightly later tradition may be found in b.Baba Bathra 21a-b, while subsequent rabbis added that Esau directly ordered his grandson Amalek to antagonize the Jews (Glickman, *Haman and the Jews*, 21).

136. Horowitz, *Reckless Rites*, 157, where Horowitz skillfully parses the nuances of Haman's description as a bishop.

137. Ibid., 87.

138. Ibid., 116–118. Similarly, the conflation of Esau with Amalek and the eschatological significance of Esau's (read: Christendom's) demise, acquired the status of received wisdom for centuries thereafter (ibid., 126ff.).

139. On anti-Christian parallels between Haman and Jesus in the *Toledot Yeshu* genre, see Gribetz, "Hanged and Crucified."

140. Cohen, "Cursed be Haman?" 481. Note also the Genizah document (T-S AS 152.103), which contains a Judeo-Arabic paraphrase of *Esther*, refers specifically to Haman, and includes

at the document's center a drawing of a man "chained to a yoke or possibly a cross. . . ." (https://geniza.princeton.edu/en/documents/22036/).

141. Aleppo Megillah Esth 3:1. See also Harel, "'Likhvod Ha-Umah,'" on the late-nineteenth-century Jewish initiative in Ottoman lands to cancel Purim celebrations that were offensive to Christians.

142. In Sivan, *Palestine in Late Antiquity*, 144. See also Thornton, "Crucifixion of Haman," 423, and Horowitz, *Reckless Rites*, 17 and 158.

143. Socrates Scholasticus, *Ecclesiastical History*, 349–50.

144. James Frazer was convinced that the Inmestar incident was indeed a Purim celebration, but he also argued that Jesus himself was crucified as part of a Purim ritual! See Horowitz, *Reckless Rites*, 223–224. Roth ("The Feast of Purim," 227) also argues that the Inmestar incident took place on Purim, but that it reflected exceptional rather than recurring behavior.

145. Thornton, "Crucifixion of Haman," 424, and Horowitz, *Reckless Rites*, 158. In late antiquity, burning effigies of Haman could also relate to the description in *Megillat Antiochus* of Bacchides's punishment, as seen.

146. See Horowitz, *Reckless Rites*, Chapters 6 and 8 for detailed descriptions of both literary comparisons between Haman and Jesus, and of Purim celebrations that mocked Jesus and Christianity. Although Horowitz also enumerates dozens of examples of Christian authorities whom Jews compared to Haman, these generally appear to reflect the deployment of "Haman" as a label for an enemy of the Jewish community rather than intentional equation of Haman with Jesus or Christianity.

147. Carruthers, *Esther through the Centuries*, 272. Similarly, about one century later, Polish bishops discouraged local Christians from allowing their sons to serve in the paid role of Haman in Purim celebrations (Teter, *Jews and Heretics*, 90).

148. In Carruthers, *Esther through the Centuries*, 135. We return to Haman's deployment in the Protestant-Catholic rivalry below.

149. Almost inevitably, this breakneck summary of religious developments in late antiquity is couched in generalizations, which do not do the subject justice, but nor do they challenge the basic inter-religious dynamics described.

150. Hence, for instance, some rabbis suggested that Haman had no fewer than 202 (or 208, or 214) sons, based on the numerical value of the letters in the word (*ve-*)*rov* in the phrase (*ve-*) *rov banav*, "the multitude of his sons" (Esth 5:11). We will encounter dozens of other such midrashim in later chapters of this book. For impressive studies of the midrashic sources on *Esther* see Börner-Klein and Hollender, *Midraschim zu Ester*, and Segal, *Babylonian Esther Midrash*.

151. Similarly, the rabbis, as creators, interpreters, and purveyors of the Law, became the sole religious authorities of Judaism, displacing the roles played previously by Temple elites (such as the Sadducees).

152. By contrast, when Daniel, Esther's predecessor (by the rabbis' reckoning), was taken to a Diaspora court, we are told that he managed to keep kosher by adopting a vegan diet (Dan 1). Unsurprisingly, one rabbi suggested that Esther acted in the same way, citing Daniel's precedent directly (b.Megillah 13a).

153. E.g., *Esther Rabba* 3:10.

154. Virtually every midrashic treatment of *Esther* in late antiquity assumes that the events related in the story were the fulfilment of a conscious, divine plan.

155. E.g., TgI 2:20, where we discover that Esther ate kosher food. Elsewhere it is asserted that Ahashwerosh's marital relations with Esther were non-consensual (b.Megillah 15a and b.Sanhedrin 74b). More generally, rabbis (e.g., b.Megillah 13a) interpreted Esth 2:20, "and Esther did the commandment of Mordecai," to mean that she fulfilled the minutiae of *halakhic* detail that Mordecai had taught her.

156. The Jews sinned by partaking in the banquet: TgI 1:5, 7; *Esther Rabba* 7:13; and more generally, where we are told that God sent Haman to punish the Jews for sinning and to encourage them to repent (b.Shabbat 88a). Other sins for which God sent Haman to punish the Jews include: The brothers' sin of having sold Joseph, Jacob's sin of having cheated Esau out of their father's blessing, and the Jews' prostration before Nebuchadnezzar's idol (Dan 3), among other offences.

157. b.Megillah 14a, where the removal of the king's signet ring (to endorse Haman's plot) was more effective in motivating the Jews' repentance than all previous prophets and prophetesses had been.

158. The rabbis enumerated the various good deeds that undid Haman's plot, including, for instance, "studying the laws of the *omer*" (b.Megillah 16a and *Esther Rabba* 10:4).

159. b.Megillah 13b. On this passage, and the phrase *shehi pehi* in particular, see Segal, *Babylonian Esther Midrash*, 2:114–133 at 128 n 136.

160. See Berman, "Aggadah and Anti-Semitism," for a survey of rabbinic expansions on *Esther* 3:8 that demonstrate the diversity of the rabbis' experience of anti-Semitism.

161. TgI 8: 16; and similar ideas in b.Megillah 16b, and Rashi's commentary thereto.

162. Segal, *Babylonian Esther Midrash*, 3:146. Elsewhere (ibid., 2:114ff.), Segal points out that the Talmud's version of Haman's slander in Esth 3:8 resembles Shimshai's slander against the Jews in Ezra 4:7–16. That the rabbis related Shimshai to Haman (either equating them, or suggesting that the former was the latter's son is therefore not surprising; see below, Chapter 9).

163. Along similar lines, Berman ("Agadah and Anti-Semitism," 189–90) has argued that the earliest exegetical expansions on Haman's anti-Jewish accusation in *Esther* 3:8 echo the classical anti-Semitic accusations of Roman authors such as Cicero (first century BCE) and Juvenal (first century CE).

164. TgI 4:12; TgII 4:11.

165. Hatakh is Daniel: TgI 4:9. Note, however, that other sources (e.g., TgII 1:14) identify Daniel with the eunuch Memuchan (Esth 1:16). According to TgI 1:16, Memuchan was Haman not Daniel. The implication of the latter opinion is that Haman was the eunuch who advised the king to dispose of Vashti (Esth 1:19), which would be a necessary first step in his plot to enthrone his own daughter as queen (on the latter point, see the sources in Glickman, *Haman and the Jews*, 38–39 nn. 60–61).

166. Laniak, *Shame and Honor*, 116 n 37 (who cites Josephus, the Greek versions, and the Targums); and Clines, *The Esther Scroll*, 196–197 n 2 (citing Josippon on Haman as a relative of the two eunuchs).

167. TgII 5:2, where Haman is characterized by an Aramaic rendering of the Greek *speculator*. Grossfeld (*Two Targums*, 161) translates this term as "executioner," although "spy" might be more accurate. That the Byzantine *agentes in rebus* were both spies and—when needed—agents for special missions (including executions) might explain the confusion (see Silverstein, *Postal Systems*, 32).

168. TgI 7:5–6 (where Esther also claims that Haman attempted to assassinate the king in his sleep). Further sources for Haman's ambition to replace the king may be found in Wechsler, *Strangers in the Land*, 266 n 34. For an eighteenth-century British author who compared James II to Haman for attempting to take the throne illegitimately, see Carruthers, *Esther through the Centuries*, 45.

169. Haman defiling, looting, or contributing to the destruction of the Temple: TgI 3:1; Haman sabotaging attempts to rebuild the Temple: *Esther Rabba* 7:2; and TgI 3:1. Abraham Saba (d. 1508) makes a similar point in his commentary on *Esther* (in Walfish, *Esther in Medieval Garb*, 91–92). According to Ezra 4, the rebuilding of the Temple was halted during the reign of Artaxerxes (rather than Xerxes); thus, some rabbis identified Ahashwerosh with

Artaxerxes (as the LXX does), thereby rationalizing Haman's activity (Koller, *Esther in Ancient Jewish Thought*, 176–77). Similarly, some rabbis understood "Shimshai the Scribe," who plays a leading role in foiling attempts to rebuild the Temple (Ezra 4:8ff.), as having been one of Haman's sons (see Ch 6, n 162 above).

170. A Byzantine-era *piyyuṭ* reflects Haman's increasingly villainous status by attributing to his wife, Zeresh, various complaints against him (Yahalom and Sokoloff, *Jewish Palestinian Aramaic Poetry*, 196–197, Münz-Manor, "Carnivalesque Ambivalence," 837, and Lieber, *Jewish Aramaic Poetry*, 110).

171. Numerous rabbinic sources relate the *Esther* story to 1 Sam 15, including b.Megillah 11a, b.Yoma 22b, b.Shabbat 56b, TgII 4:13, and so forth. Naturally, for those (predominantly Christian) readers of *Esther* who accessed the text via the LXX (or a version based on it), the Amalekite associations of Haman were largely lost.

172. Both the Jerusalem and the Babylonian Talmuds (y.Megilla 3:4; b.Sanhedrin 20b) mention the importance of publicly reading the Torah portion that mentions the eradication of the Amalekites (Exod 17:14) on the Sabbath preceding Purim.

173. Hence, for instance, we are told that Haman is one of the historic villains who "set his eyes on that which does not belong to him," referring in his case to his attempt to exterminate the Jews despite not having divine sanction for his plot (b.Sotah 9a-b).

174. Relating the *Esther* story to Deut 31:17, where God says that He will "conceal [his] face" (*haster astīr et panay*—the verbs here share a root with Esther's name), the rabbis justify the need to mine *Esther* for hidden references to God, as He had promised to be concealed in the story (b.Ḥullin 139b).

175. *Esther Rabba*, 6:13.

176. b.Megillah 16a.

177. b.Megillah 16a, *Esther Rabba*, 10:9.

178. An instructive example of God's micromanagement of the events is the idea that God caused Haman's daughter, whom Haman sought to enthrone as queen following Vashti's banishment, to become unattractive, thereby foiling the plan (TgI 5:1). What is interesting here is that the midrash about God's intervention seeks to explain another midrash (concerning Haman's plot to enthrone his own daughter, which does not feature in *Esther*).

179. b.Shabbat 88a. Other sources explain that God caused Haman to misbehave so that He could then legitimately punish Haman for his sins (Glickman, *Haman and the Jews*, 78).

180. *Esther Rabba* 7:1, where Haman is compared to a lamb fattened up before its slaughter.

181. b.Megillah 13a. On God "preparing the remedy before the affliction," see Segal, *Babylonian Esther Midrash*, 2: 105–110.

182. Glickman, *Haman and the Jews*, 85.

183. See, generally, Glickman, *Haman and the Jews*, 65–78.

184. b.Megillah 10a-19a. The most thorough studies of this running commentary are those of Segal, *Babylonian Esther Midrash*, and Börner-Klein and Hollender, *Midraschim zu Ester*, 1:103ff.

185. There was a third interpretation of Haman's career, namely, that he was a culpable villain, but one who acted together with the equally-evil Ahashwerosh. Although MT *Esther* presents the king as an ineffectual buffoon (a characterization supported by TgII 6:1, where he is labeled "the stupid"), late antique rabbinic sources refer to him as "the wicked" (TgI 1:1; see Grossfeld, *Two Targums*, 34 n 45). The Babylonian rabbis agreed with both judgements and considered Ahashwerosh both a buffoon and a villain (b.Megillah 11a). Interestingly, perhaps through exposure to Muslim ideas about Haman as a villain overshadowed by the ruler (Pharaoh, in the Muslim case), Saadiah suggests that Ahashwerosh was no less evil than Haman (Wechsler, "Ten Newly Identified Fragments," 271).

186. Q 2:23, 10:38, 11:13, 17:88, and others.

187. Although "Karaism" is in general use, a more accurate transliteration would be "Qaraism," which retains the *q-r-'* root that gives us both Hebrew *miqrā* (scripture) and Arabic Qur'ān. Those who continued the traditions of the rabbinic academies that were rejected by the Karaites, are generally known as "Rabbanites."

188. Even leading Gaonic authorities such as Saadiah Gaon were influenced by Islamic traditions (Friedenreich, "The Use of Islamic Sources"), and some scholars have even seen in Saadiah's commentary on *Esther* the influence of such (un-Islamic) litterateurs as Ibn al-Muqaffa' (d. 756; Nir, "The development of the literary character," 318).

189. In general, see e.g., Polliack, "The Emergence of Karaite Bible Exegesis."

190. Tirosh-Becker, "The Use of Rabbinic Sources in Karaite Writings."

191. Wechsler, "The Reception of Saadia Gaon's Commentary on Esther," and idem, "Sa'adia Gaon on Esther's Invitation of Haman," 334f., on Karaite scholars who used Saadiah's Esther commentary; and ibid., 336–337 on the Byzantine Karaites who consciously incorporated ideas from Saadiah's commentary on *Esther* into their own works.

192. In some cases, a Karaite scholar might openly express admiration for Saadiah's commentary on *Esther* (see e.g., Wechsler, *Conviviality*, 304 n 131, where the Karaite Salmon b. Yeruḥam, acknowledges that in Saadiah's commentary on *Esther*, "there is indeed benefit for those who are educated").

193. A convenient summary of the Karaite and Rabbanite Judeo-Arabic scholarship on *Esther* may be found in Wechsler, "Medieval Judaism: Judeo-Arabic Commentary," 24–27.

194. Nir, "The development of the literary character."

195. Late antique Palestinian traditions continued to wield influence on later generations of Jews since the pre-Islamic *piyyuṭim* composed in the Holy Land were highly popular in prayer services well into the late medieval period, including those held on Purim, both in Islamic lands and Christendom. On the medieval Jewish commentators' selective use of earlier, rabbinic materials on *Esther*, see Walfish, *Esther in Medieval Garb*, 12, which focuses mainly on exegetes living in Christendom.

196. An illustrative example may be found in Saadiah's reworking of Talmudic materials on Esther's invitation of Haman to the king's banquet (b.Megillah 15b; see Wechsler "Sa'adia Gaon on Esther's Invitation of Haman," 326ff.).

197. On this exegetical tension in Judaism, and the Islamic models on which it is based, see Cohen, *Rule of Peshat*.

198. Unsurprisingly, Karaite exegetes were influenced by their Muslim environment and drew heavily on Islamic exegetical vocabulary and techniques (see e.g., Zwanowska, "Islamic exegetical terms").

199. There are other examples of diversity within the Karaite tradition concerning Haman. For example, Yefet ben 'Eli routinely quotes the earlier Karaite exegete Salmon, often adopting the latter's ideas—such as the fact that Haman was crucified (Arabic: *ṣ-l-b*), and that he was "accursed" (Arabic: *al-la'īn*)—but occasionally straying from them, as in the case of Haman's father's name, which, according to Salmon (and Saadiah) was "Hammedata," but which Yefet misreads as "the Madata" (see above, Ch 2, n 25).

200. Erder, "Mourners of Zion," 218.

201. For the purpose of comparison, we may note that Saadiah held that God sent Haman to punish the Jews for marrying gentiles (Wechsler, *Conviviality*, 257–258).

202. Both the Rabbanite Saadiah and the Karaite Salmon use Abbasid terminology to describe Ahashwerosh's court. Saadiah even calls Ahashwerosh's palace the *Jawsaq*, the name of the Samarran palace built by the caliph al-Mu'taṣim (r. 833–42).

203. In fairness to mainstream Shī'a tradition, it should be noted that only extreme fringe groups within the Shī'a spectrum (such as the 'Alī-ilāhīs) can be said to worship 'Alī.

204. Saadiah: Wechsler, *Conviviality*, 218–219. Yefet: Wechsler, *Yefet Ben 'Eli*, 225.

205. For Saadiah Gaon's list of seven rules (Arabic: *tadābīr*, "organizational principles") for success in the Diaspora, derived from his reading of *Esther*, see Wechsler, "Saadia's Seven Guidelines."

206. A good example of the shift back to historicizing readings of *Esther* may be found in the tenth-century Karaite exegetical idea that Haman was an adversary (Hebrew: *satan*), sent by God to provoke the Jews to repent, a usage of "*satan*" that is manifestly temporal rather than eschatological. See Yefet ben 'Eli's commentary on *Esther*, where he attributes this interpretation of *satan* to Salmon ben Yeruḥam (Wechsler, *Yefet Ben 'Eli*, 240 n 386).

207. Hodgson, *Venture of Islam*, 1:58.

208. Paper is more widely available and cheaper than the writing materials previously used in the Near East (such as parchment and papyrus), which were restricted to elites, who had limited interests—largely imperial, religious, and mercantile. The impact of papermaking on Islamicate civilization is described in Bloom, *Paper before Print*.

209. See Robinson, *Islamic Historiography*, and Khalidi, *Arabic Historical Thought*.

210. Even Christian exegetes who read the OT allegorically assumed that the (far less important) base-story that is related in the Bible reflects historical events.

211. The historiographical relationship between the contents of Sherirah's *Epistle* and other Jewish chronologies (such as the *Seder Tannaim ve-Amoraim*, which shares some contents with Sherirah's *Epistle*) is examined in Brody, "Sources for the Chronology of the Talmudic Period." What these sources have in common is the Islamicate context in which they were composed.

212. An obvious exception to this generalization is *Seder Olam Rabba*, composed in the second century CE, which relates Jewish history from Creation to Alexander the Great's career (see Milikowsky, *Seder Olam*). Other exceptions, such as Josephus's *Antiquities*, strike me as less organic to Jewish culture, reflecting the interests of the author's non-Jewish context and audience.

213. Tanḥum's commentary on the opening verse of *Esther* includes a detailed treatment of Ahashwerosh's reign from a "global history" perspective (Wechsler, *Strangers in the Land*, 175–180). TgII, which draws on numerous pre-Islamic sources but clearly reached its current form in early Islamic centuries, also displays a concern with the historical context of the events described in *Esther* that far exceeds the TgI's (and other late antique Jewish sources') concern with historiography.

214. The late-ninth-century yarn-spinner "Eldad the Danite," who claimed to be an emissary from the lost tribe of Danite Jews who live beyond the Sambatyon River in Ethiopia, knew to present these supposedly pristine Jews as unaware of *Esther*, as the Danites continued the traditions of pre-Exilic Judaism and were uninvolved in events in the Diaspora. See Perry, *Eldad's Travels*.

215. In his modern classic *Zakhor*, Yerushalmi argues that Jewish historiography never really existed as an independent genre. By contrast, Christian and Muslim historians in the medieval Near East and Mediterranean belonged to an identifiable historiographical enterprise.

216. Christian functionaries had governed Sasanid Ctesiphon in late antiquity, while Sasanid Christian authors—such as Aphrahat, encountered earlier—referred to *Esther* in their writings. And yet, the systematic treatment of *Esther* in Islamicate Christian historiography is likely to have been a unique product of (and contributor to) Muslim historiographical traditions. On the symbiotic interplay between Christian and Muslim historiographies, see Hoyland, "Eutychius of Alexandria Vindicated."

217. Hoyland, *Theophilus of Edessa's Chronicle*, 90.

218. If, as some have argued, Agapius was the source for the thirteenth-century Christian-Arabic historian Ibn al-'Amīd (also known as Jirjis al-Makīn, d. 1273), then we may trace the

influence of Theophilus's lost *Esther* summary via Agapius to Ibn Khaldūn, who is known to have drawn on Ibn al-ʿAmīd's work. On Agapius and Ibn al-ʿAmīd, see Seleznyov, "al-Makīn Ibn al-ʿAmīd on Moses of Crete." On Ibn Khaldūn's debt to Ibn al-ʿAmīd, see Silverstein, *Veiling Esther*, 56.

219. *Kitāb al-ʿunwān* was only the second world history composed in Arabic by a Christian, the first having been written by Eutychius (d. 940). The Arabic text of Agapius's *Esther* summary may be found in Agapius, *Kitāb al-ʿunvān* (sic!), 217–226.

220. Alternatively, Agapius's summary of *Esther* may be based on a the Peshitta, which rendered the MT into Syriac.

221. The shift from Xerxes ("Ahashwerosh") to "Artaxerxes" is found among both Jewish and Christian authors in pre-Islamic times. As noted in Chapter 2, according to Josephus, the events of *Esther* took place during the reign of Artaxerxes, which he understood to be the regnal name of Cyrus. Like Agapius, Josephus described Haman's execution as crucifixion. Unlike Agapius, Josephus appears to have been familiar with (some version of) the Additions to *Esther*. A better parallel may be found in Sulpicius Severus's summary of *Esther*, which appears to be based on the MT, in which, however, Haman is crucified and the ruling king is Artaxerxes.

222. Agapius, *Kitāb al-ʿunvān* (sic!), 221.

223. Al-Kisāʾī, *Qiṣaṣ al-anbiyāʾ*, 1:200 (translation adapted from Thackston, *Tales of the Prophets*, 212–213).

224. The following is based on Silverstein, *Veiling Esther*, 41–58, where further references may be found.

225. On Ḥamza al-Iṣfahānī's treatment of Israelite history, see Adang, "Chronology of the Israelites."

226. Abū al-Fidāʾ (d. 1331) and his continuator Ibn al-Wardī (d. 1348) similarly ignore Purim and its story, despite including descriptions of Jewish holidays in their works (cf. Frenkel, "Al-Maqrizi on the Jewish Fesitvals," 328 nn. 12–13).

227. Silverstein, *Veiling Esther*, 172–175.

228. Al-Kisāʾī, *Qiṣaṣ al-Anbiyāʾ* (trans. Thackston), 105.

229. Mazuz ("al-Waṭwāṭ's description of Jewish Festivals," 447–448) suggests that al-Waṭwāṭ took his information from such sources as al-Maqdisī's *al-Badʾ wa l-taʾrīkh*, and al-Bīrūnī's *al-Āthār al-bāqiya*.

230. al-Waṭwāṭ's description of Purim may be found in his *Mabāhij al-fikar*, 1:218.

231. It is almost certain that al-Nuwayrī based his account on al-Waṭwāṭ, and it would appear that al-Nuwayrī's version of the Purim story was used by the influential al-Maqrīzī (among others). See Mazuz, "al-Waṭwāṭ's description of Jewish Festivals," 450.

232. Al-Nuwayrī, *Nihāyat al-Arab*, 1:196–197 (emphasis mine).

233. It is worth noting that Haman is motivated by jealousy already in the AT (3:5): "Now when Haman heard, he was provoked to jealousy against Mardochaios, and rage burned within him. So he was seeking to destroy Mardochaios and all his people on one day." I do not think it is reasonable, however, to suggest that the Mamluk authors had access to AT *Esther*.

234. Some two centuries before these Mamluk authors lived, Nāṣir-i Khusrō (d. 1088) composed a verse of poetry, in which Hām*ān* is rhymed with Hār*ūn* (quoted in Deh Khodā, *Lughat-Nāma*, s.v. "Hāmān"). Note that in modern colloquial Persian, too, a final *ān* is commonly pronounced *ūn*.

235. Al-Maqrīzī, *al-Mawāʿiẓ wa l-iʿtibār*, 4:377.

236. We discuss these and other Purim customs in Chapter 10.

237. Al-Ṭabarī, *Taʾrīkh*, 1: 652–654 (translation adapted from Perlmann, *The History of al-Tabari*, 4: 50–51). Al-Ṭabarī's summary of *Esther* is analyzed in Silverstein, *Veiling Esther*, 47–49.

238. Note that in Sulpicius Severus's late antique summary of *Esther*, Vashti is also unequivocally lauded.

239. The historiographical interaction between Christian and Muslim historians in the early Abbasid centuries, with particular reference to *Esther* traditions, is demonstrated by al-Mas'ūdī's statement that the ancient Persian city of Iṣṭakhr was built by Queen Homāy (*Murūj*, §1403), who—as seen—appears to be at least partly based on Esther. Over a century before al-Mas'ūdī, the Christian Theodore bar Koni (writing in the late eighth century), mentioned that the Persian town of Iṣṭakhr ("Saṭhar") was named after Esther (in Wechsler, "Esther (Book and Person)," 8:36).

240. Similarly, an anonymous thirteenth- or fourteenth-century Judeo-Persian summary of the *Esther* story, aimed at non-Jewish Iranians, mentions that Haman "hung on his chest a sign, on the face of which was engraved the likeness of one of the ancient idols." Despite the relevance of this detail to Mordecai's refusal to bow, the author ignores the refusal-to-bow motif altogether, explaining simply that "Haman . . . conceived a hatred of Mordecai and his people in his heart." See Silverstein, *Veiling Esther*, 58–63.

241. Agapius, *Kitāb al-'unvān* (sic!), 218. Subsequently (ibid., 221), however, Esther explains to the king that Haman seeks to destroy the Jews because, "It is he who is jealous of you because of me and who does not want you to have a wife like me, it is your minister Haman who is here." Haman's jealousy as the motive behind his genocidal plot is mentioned as early as AT 3:5, and recurs later, in the Mamluk summaries of *Esther* (see above, Ch 6, n 233).

242. b.Megilla 15a (and see the similar account in TgI 3:2). The Aramaic word for "bread" is *nahma*, which may be a pun on Haman's name, of which it is an anagram in Hebrew/Aramaic (as it is in English).

243. Rashi composed the earliest complete Hebrew commentary on *Esther* (Walfish, *Esther in Medieval Garb*, 2).

244. *Yalqut Shim'oni*, §1056. Grossfeld (*Two Targums*, 141–142), who provides the full text of this midrash together with the bill of sale, is of the opinion that these are later interpolations.

245. This translation is taken from Ginzberg, *Legends of the Jews*, 4:397–399. In the "Purim Panel" of the Dura Europos synagogue, the contract is written on a horse's abdomen, rather than on Mordecai's kneecap or boot (as in most versions of the midrash). See Steinhaulf, "Frescoes of the Dura Europos Synagogue," 52.

246. This is probably a reference to the 127 provinces that Ahashwerosh ruled (Esth 1:1). While this number does not tally with the ancient Persian division of the realm into 20 or so satraps, it does echo the 120 Achaemenid satraps appointed by Darius, mentioned in Dan 6:1.

247. Muslim sources from this period often use the number 120,000 topologically in e.g., Abū Zayd al-Sirāfī's account of the Guangzhou massacre: "120,000" Muslims in southern China are said to have been killed in the riots of 878/9 (al-Mas'ūdī, *Murūj al-dhahab*, 1:303); and in al-Rāzī's description of Baghdad during the reign of Hārūn al-Rashīd, there were 120,000 houses in the city (in Antrim, *Routes and Realms*, 168 n 64).

248. Perhaps following al-Ṭabarī's lead, the influential Judeo-Persian poet Shāhīn of Shīrāz (wr. 1333) rewrote *Esther* in his "Ardashīr-Nāma" ("Book of Artaxerxes"), which integrates elements from the *ShāhNāma* and combines Jewish triumph with Persian heroism. See Moreen, "Iranization," eadem, *Queen Esther's Garden*, 90–105, and Asmussen, "Judeo-Persica."

249. We return to this passage in Chapter 8, when considering Haman's pre-*Esther* origins.

250. Al-Bīrūnī, *al-Āthār al-bāqiya*, 280–281 (translation adapted from Sachau, *Chronology of Ancient Nations*, 273–274; emphasis mine).

251. We might also consider the possible influence of the tenth-century Jewish *Sefer Yosippon*, which had been translated into Arabic by the eleventh century (Dönitz, "*Sefer Yosippon*," 386), and whose account of *Esther* presents a similar historical context to the one offered by

Ibn Khaldūn. According to *Sefer Yosippon*, Cyrus and the other ancient Persian kings supported the Jews and their Temple until the reign of Ahashwerosh, when Haman the Amalekite arose and stirred up trouble (*Sefer Yosippon*, 1:48–49 = viii:40-ix:10).

252. As noted, al-Ṭabarī describes Mordecai as Esther's "milch-brother."

253. Ibn Khaldūn, *Muqaddima*, 2:136 (emphasis mine).

254. In Chapter 8, we return to the relevance of Smerdis/Bardiya's to the *Esther* story.

255. Ibn Khaldūn, *Muqaddima*, 2:196.

256. Al-Jāḥiẓ, *al-Radd 'alā al-naṣārā*, 54–55, and *Rasā'il*, 3:304 (I owe this reference to Nathan Gibson). Some three centuries later, al-Sam'ānī (*Tafsīr*, 5:14) describes the same objections to the Qur'ān's historical accuracy, which he solves by suggesting that "Haman" may have been the name of two separate people.

Chapter Seven: Haman's Deployment: Four Contexts

1. As Walfish puts it, "[B]y the end of [the twelfth] century, northern France was producing fewer exegetes and these were largely derivative of earlier ones. The thirteenth century saw the return to more traditional commentary incorporating a great deal of midrashic material" (*Esther in Medieval Garb*, 4).

2. On medieval and early modern Christian interpretations of *Esther*, see Carruthers, *Esther through the Centuries.*

3. On medieval Jewish interpretations of *Esther*, see Walfish, *Esther in Medieval Garb.*

4. Hence, the Kabbalist exegete Abraham Saba (fl. mid-fifteenth to early-sixteenth centuries) viewed Esther as the manifestation of the "*shekhīna*" (Divine Spirit), and Haman as representing the demonic forces of the Universe (Aramaic: *siṭrā akhrā*, "the other side"; in Walfish, *Esther in Medieval Garb*, 38). Similarly, Abraham Saba's Karaite contemporary, Judah Gibbor, compared Haman to the Evil Inclination (Hebrew: *yeṣer ha-ra'*; in Walfish, *Esther in Medieval Garb*, 50–51).

5. See e.g., Cohen, "Cursed be Haman?" (with sources). Cohen deals with perhaps the earliest such Purim-parody, an early-fourteenth century mock-tractate of the Talmud.

6. Rustow, *Heresy and the Politics of Community.*

7. Goitein, *Mediterranean Society, Volume II*, 299, and Rustow, *Heresy and the Politics of Community*, 307. The joint Purim celebration took place in 1039. Other Genizah texts refer to local Jew haters as "Haman" (e.g., T-S 32.8 recto ll. 41–43 available here: https://geniza.princeton.edu/en/documents/1812/). See also Goitein, *Mediterranean Society, Volume III*, 171.

8. A twelfth-century Judeo-Arabic document refers to such an administrator, who exploited local Jews, Muslims and Samaritans by extracting illegitimate requisitions, and earned the label "the wicked (*rasha'*) Haman" (T-S G1.1 1v ll.3-4 available here: https://geniza.princeton.edu/en/documents/3923/). This document is discussed in Goitein, *Mediterranean Society, Volume II*, 393. As noted in Chapter 5, Muslim literary traditions about the Qur'ānic Haman relate that the latter engaged in illegitimate taxation practices in the Egyptian countryside.

9. Rustow, *Heresy and the Politics of Community*, 224–226.

10. Rustow, "Karaites Real and Imagined," 54–56.

11. It is important to note that the version of *Esther* on which the Samaritan account was based was probably the LXX, rather than the MT used by the Jews whom they were insulting (Silverstein, *Veiling Esther*, 73–77).

12. See, e.g., Ophir and Rosen-Zvi, *Goy*, 185–192 (with sources).

13. Dalley, *Esther's Revenge at Susa*, 219ff.

14. Zadok, "Historical Background."

15. Note that the tenth-century Karaite commentator Yefet ben 'Alī connected the *Esther* story with this rivalry (in Wechsler, "Early Karaite," 119 n 90; and idem, *Yefet Ben 'Eli*, 167).

16. See Segal, "Esther and the Essenes," 139–45. On Shimshai as Haman's son, see above, Ch 6, n 162.

17. Crown, *Companion to Samaritan Studies*, 8, s.v. 'Abū 'l-Fatḥ ibn Abī al-Ḥasan.'

18. The Samaritans observe only those festivals that have Pentateuchal sanction (thus omitting Purim and Hanukka).

19. Translation adapted from Stenhouse, *Kitāb al-Ta'rīkh*, 98–101. For an analysis of Abū al-Fatḥ's rewritten *Esther*, see Silverstein, *Veiling Esther*, 64ff.

20. Compare Ibn Khaldūn's statement that "Smerdis [= Bardiya] the Zoroastrian reigned for one or thirteen years. He was called 'the Zoroastrian' because it was in his time that Zoroaster emerged with his religion. After him reigned Ahashwerosh b. Darius for twenty years" (*Muqadimma*, 2:196). Presumably, Ibn Khaldūn and Abū al-Fatḥ based their respective statements on a common source.

21. Emphasis mine. The equivalent section in Esth 3:8 includes Haman's accusations against the Jews. By contrast, in this text the author avoids even suggesting that there might be an objective reason to dislike the Samaritan community: If the king agreed to persecute them, it can only be because he had fallen under the influence of a Jewish magician.

22. Cf. Exod 17:14 ("I will blot out the memory of Amalek") and Deut 25:19 ("you shall blot out the memory of Amalek"). The implication is that the Jewish vizier, like Haman, was related to Amalek.

23. Bowman, *Samaritan Documents*, 103. The text is the *Chronicle Adler*, likely a composite work to which later authors added subsequent materials.

24. A modern Iranian example of this dynamic may be found in the writings of Nāṣir Pūrpīrār (d. 2015), a revisionist historian of ancient Iran, who read into *Esther* the story of a Jewish genocide perpetrated against the Iranian protagonists (see e.g., https://web.archive.org/web/20070811122505/http:/www.naria.blogfa.com/86013.aspx). Pūrpīrār argued that Jews and their allies have fabricated Iranian history since that genocide to cover up their shame and guilt.

25. See Cohen, *Under Crescent and Cross*.

26. Walfish, *Esther in Medieval Garb*, 136. In earlier periods it was in Islamic lands that a more worldly, "scientific" approach to scripture was cultivated, drawing on poetry, philosophy, astronomy, and other sciences. This intellectual milieu is well-represented in the work of Ibn Ezra (ibid., 4).

27. Moreen, *Iranian Jewry's Hour of Peril and Heroism*, 76 (Haman), and 31 (the influence of *Esther* on Bābā'ī's writings).

28. Similarly, when serving as the President of Israel, Shimon Peres referred to Iranian President Mahmoud Aḥmadinejad, who repeatedly vowed to "wipe Israel off the map," as "Haman" (https://www.timesofisrael.com/ahmadinejad-is-like-a-modern-day-haman-says-peres/). Aḥmadinejad could be seen as a Persian villain, who served as "the second in command" (to the Supreme Leader—in this case, Ayatollah Khamenei), and who threatened to exterminate the Jewish state.

29. Horowitz, *Reckless Rites*, 302–303.

30. Curiously, in the same year that Ibn Naghrīla composed his poem, Rabbanites, Karaites, and Muslims celebrated Purim together (as seen above).

31. Frankel, "Ritual Murder," 7.

32. Hary, *Multiglossia*, 115–129.

33. Both versions of the text, which have been studied by Hary (*Multiglossia*), may be found in English translation here: https://www.hsje.org/Holidays/Purim/purim_misrayim.htm. Another Muslim "Haman" in Ottoman lands from this period was a Muslim judge in Salonika, Muslih al-Dīn, whom the famous Solomon ha-Levi al-Qabeṣ (d. 1584) labelled "Haman" for having imprisoned a number of Jews in 1573 (in Sapperstein, *Jewish Preaching*, 80).

34. Lazarus-Yafeh, "Queen Esther—One of the Marranos?" That Ibn Ezra's only surviving son is said to have converted to Islam may have encouraged him to imagine that not all those who outwardly repudiated Judaism were sincere apostates from the religion.

35. Lewis, *Jews of Islam*, 83–85. On "dissimulation" in Abrahamic traditions, see Wechsler, "Dissimulation."

36. Roth, "Religion of the Marranos," Meyerson, *Jewish Renaissance*, 217–221, and Gilitz, *Secrecy and Deceit*, 377–79, where in 1491 a Converso mentioned that his grandmother would observe "a fast that they call the day of Saint Haman" (!). Gilitz (ibid., 355–56) suggests that the reference to "Saint Haman" indicates that the crypto-Jews had a garbled understanding of their culture, which strikes me as unconvincing. The reference to Haman as a Saint may have been employed ironically, or to reflect the topsy-turvy nature of the crypto-Jews' experience.

37. Walfish, *Esther in Medieval Garb*, 140, and Kalimi, *Book of Esther*, 206–207.

38. Carruthers (*Esther through the Centuries*, 146) writes: "In Delgado's poem, the accuser Haman declares that 'a demonstration of force will better compel,' echoing medieval inquisitional policies."

39. Walfish, *Esther in Medieval Garb*, 54–55.

40. Delgado, *The Poem of Queen Esther*, 43. Delgado displays knowledge of late antique rabbinic traditions on *Esther*, such as the idea that Bigthan and Teresh were from Tarsus (ibid., 33), as well as non-rabbinic ideas, such as the positive interpretation of Vashti's refusal, which occurs in Sulpicius Severus's late antique (Christian) commentary and in al-Ṭabarī's summary of *Esther* (ibid., 19).

41. Delgado, *The Poem of Queen Esther*, 57; and see Carruthers, *Esther through the Centuries*, 219.

42. Even some exceptional Christians deployed "Haman" with reference to Inquisitors. For example, Cardinal Juan de Torquemada (uncle of the infamous chief Inquisitor, Tomás de Torquemada), compared those who persecuted Conversos to Haman (Izbicki, "Torquemada's defense of the 'Conversos,'" 200). Similarly, the Spanish playwright Lope de Vega (d. 1635) compares inquisitors who look down upon the Conversos with Haman (in Cairns, *Esther in Early Modern Iberia*, 67).

43. Mampieri, *Living under the Evil Pope*, 242.

44. A well-documented example is the reference to Jewish communists as "Hamans" (in Horowitz, *Reckless Rites*, 141ff.). To this we may add the use of Haman by Israeli public figures against their (Jewish) political rivals. To cite but a few examples: In his pre-Purim sermon (March 2000), the Sephardi chief Rabbi Ovadiah Yossef compared the education minister Yossi Sarid, to Haman; on March 2, 2018 (which was Purim in Jerusalem), ultra-orthodox Jews hung Haman-like effigies of ultra-orthodox Jewish soldiers; in early 2022, ultra-orthodox politicians labeled Israeli ministers Yair Lapid and Avigdor Liberman "Haman" and "Liberhaman," respectively; and in the same year the singer Ahinoam Nini referred to Benjamin Netanyahu as "Haman" (see Iddo David Cohen in *Haaretz*, February 16, 2022, available here: https://www.haaretz.co.il/opinions/2022-02-16/ty-article-opinion/0000017f-e329-d38f-a57f-e77bd7a60000).

45. Mampieri, *Living under the Evil Pope*, 294–295 n 30 (and, more generally, 56–59).

46. Another disanalogy between the biblical Haman and the Jews' Christian antagonists is that the former—despite his genocidal intentions—ultimately created no damage, whereas the Hamans with whom the Jews of Christian lands dealt were often successful in persecuting local Jews.

47. P. Magid, "Inside the Abandoned Babylon that Saddam Hussein Built," *AtlasObscura* December 2, 2019 (https://www.atlasobscura.com/articles/babylon-iraq-saddam-hussein).

48. Carruthers, *Esther through the Centuries*, 150, quoting Rabbi Shimon Apisdorf.

49. Two important collections of such references include Horowitz, *Reckless Rites, passim* and especially 81–106, and Kalimi, *Book of Esther*, 198–231. Scholars have also compiled lists of Special (or "Second") Purims instituted throughout history to commemorate salvation from some (usually Christian) antagonist, such as those found in Yerushalmi, *Zakhor*, 46–48, and Goodman, *Purim Anthology*, 14–37.

50. Horowitz, *Reckless Rites*, 83.

51. Ibid., 262 (on the possible comparison between Haman and King Phillip II (r. 1180–1223), who ordered the forced conversion of Jews and/or their expulsion from France), and ibid., 149 (on Ephraim of Bonn's [d. 1200 or 1221] comparison of Haman with the anti-Jewish monk "Radulph the Cistercian," who incited mobs to massacre Jews).

52. On Khmelnytsky as "Haman," see Glaser, "Introduction," 4.

53. On the Nazis as "Haman," see Kalimi, *Book of Esther*, 221–226. Note that even early on in Hitler's career, he was compared to Haman, as seen in the 1933 Ladino *La vida de Adolf Hitler: el Haman moderno* (ed. Refael). Gilbert (*The Holocaust*, 297–299), describes the Nazis' conscious committing of anti-Jewish atrocities on Purim.

54. Walfish, *Esther in Medieval Garb*, 5.

55. One may analyze the "updated" contents of medieval commentaries on Esth 3:8 (Haman's accusation against the Jews) for references to the historical circumstances in which a particular exegete was writing (examples of which may be found in Walfish, *Esther in Medieval Garb*, 147ff., and Berman, "Aggadah and Anti-Semitism.")

56. Horowitz, *Reckless Rites*, 86.

57. The notion that Vashti represented the rejected synagogue resurfaced in various historical contexts (see, for instance, the American theologian John Edwards' early-eighteenth-century comments on the matter, in Carruthers, *Esther through the Centuries*, 29).

58. *The Jews and their Lies*, Part X (Martin H. Bertram's translation may be found here: https://sourcebooks.fordham.edu/basis/_1543-Luther-JewsandLies-full.asp). See also Kalimi, *Book of Esther*, 208.

59. Ibid., 286.

60. Horowitz, *Reckless Rites*, 87–88; Kalimi, *Book of Esther*, 291; translation adapted from Carruthers, *Esther through the Centuries*, 257.

61. Horowitz, *Reckless Rites*, 88. As Carruthers (*Esther through the Centuries*, 271) put it: "In an astounding rhetorical move, Brentius likens the Jews to Haman, and Christians to the chosen people."

62. Horowitz, *Reckless Rites*, 89 and 310; Kalimi, *Book of Esther*, 219.

63. Carruthers, "Esther and Hitler," and Beal, *Book of Hiding*, 6.

64. Fettmilch, by contrast, was unmistakably Christian, and his uprising—though predominantly economic—probably reflected his Calvinist rivalry with the Lutheran authorities.

65. Cohen (*The Martyrs*) argues that the Conversos' attachment to Esther was a reaction to Catholic exaltation of Mary, which—if correct—demonstrates how well-known the Esther-Mary equation was.

66. And at any event, even Martin Luther had positive views of *Esther*'s heroes (as prototypes of Jesus who risked their lives to save their people), even though he despised the book's broader, "Judaizing" message (Kalimi, *Book of Esther*, 247).

67. There were rare instances in which Jews who joined anti-monarchical movements also used *Esther* as their comparative framework and "Haman" as the term of opprobrium for the villain. For example, in 1848 Leopold Zunz (d. 1886) joined an (unsuccessful) rebellion against Kaiser Friedrich Wilhelm IV, whom he dubbed "Haman," in the hope of securing civil rights for German Jews (Kalimi, *Book of Esther*, 209–210).

68. In his 1831 sermon "Haman's Gallows," delivered in Troy, New York, the Unitarian minister C. F. Le Fevre compared Haman to "the priesthood," who, like Haman, are "highly favored," "rich," "promoted above the rulers of the people," and "excused from [. . .] taxation" (in Carruthers, *Esther through the Centuries*, 137). Similarly, during the American Revolution, Lord North was compared to Haman and George III to Ahashwerosh (in Bailyn, *Ideological Origins*, 126–127).

69. Horowitz (*Reckless Rites*), Carruthers (*Esther through the Centuries*), and Kalimi (*Book of Esther*), include dozens of examples of direct relevance to the topic.

70. In rarer cases, one detects overlap between Christian ideas about Haman and Muslim ones, such as the idea that Haman was Satan or the Devil, a notion that appears in Ibn Manẓūr, *Mukhtaṣar ta'rīkh dimashq*, 25:330.

71. In 1904, Theodore Herzl described his meeting with the Pope in terms that depicted Herzl as a Mordecai figure (who refused to kiss the Pope's hand, thereby losing favor with him). The implication of Herzl's description is that Pope was the Haman figure (see Horowitz, *Reckless Rites*, 79).

72. Ibid., 72 (Merlin) and 311 (Taylor). The Pope continued to be compared to Haman throughout the seventeenth century: thus, in 1647 John Mayer equated Haman's rise and tyranny with the Pope (see Carruthers, *Esther through the Centuries*, 135).

73. Carruthers, *Esther through the Centuries*, 256 and 311–312.

74. For Henry Case (wr. 1679), the Haman-like character of the Gunpowder Plot was Sir Everard Digby (ibid., 250). It is Guy Fawkes, however, who came to be most closely associated with Haman, as the ritual torturing of his effigy became a central feature of Guy Fawkes Night, which is commemorated annually on the fifth of November (see Chapter 10 below).

75. Jewish, Christian, and Islamicate sources compare Haman to a dog: The seventeenth-century (?) Judeo-Persian author Mullah Gershom refers to him as "the vile dog" (in Moreen, *Queen Esther's Garden*, 215–218 at 216); in 1890 Reverend William Matson referred to Haman as the "dog of Amalek" (in Carruthers, *Esther through the Centuries*, 42); in the Babylonian Talmud Esther refers to Haman as a dog (b.Megillah 16a); and in a sixth century *piyyuṭ* Haman's behavior is compared to that of a dog (in Lieber, *Jewish Aramaic Poetry*, 116, *piyyuṭ* 33, l. 13).

76. Krey, *First Crusade*, 33–36.

77. It may be that Muslim authors rarely used "Haman" polemically because the term did not have the sting for Muslims that it did when used by and against Christians and Jews, but this is mere conjecture.

78. See above, Ch 5, n 48.

79. Twelvers: Kohlberg, *In Praise of the Few*, 73, and 163–164. Ismā'īlīs: De Smet, "The Demon in Potentiality," 607–609, and 616. The anonymous tenth-century author of *Kitāb al-shajarah* ("Book of the Tree") refers to Q 25:31, "We have made an enemy from among the wicked for every prophet," and enumerates the Islamic-era equivalents of Qur'ānic enemies of several prophets, to which he adds a typically Ismā'īlī esoteric spin. The result is that Haman was deemed to be equivalent to 'Umar, a point to which we return in Chapter 10.

80. The following is based on Silverstein, *Veiling Esther*, 19–21.

81. The quotation appears in an apologetic article published online ("Biblical Haman» Qur'ānic Hāmān: A Case of Straightforward Literary Transition?" https://www.islamic-awareness.org/quran/contrad/external/haman), in which the author refutes Christian arguments against the Qur'ān's accuracy that focus on the "error" of Haman's depiction in Muslim scripture.

82. For this and the following anti-Qur'ānic quotations, see Syed, "Historicity of Haman," 51–52 (with sources).

83. Eisenberg, s.v. "Haman" in *EI1*, 2:244–245.

84. Vajda, s.v. "Haman" in *EI2*, 3:110.

85. E.g., Syed, "Historicity of Haman," especially 53–54; and Badawi, "Le problème de Haman," 29–33, where Haman is identified with Amon; and see Johns, "Haman," for the theory that "Haman" is "an Arabized echo of the Egyptian Hā-Amen, the title of a high priest second only in rank to Pharaoh."

86. Johns, "Haman." Note that Johns was writing in a post-Saidian academic environment, which encouraged respectful engagement with Islam and Muslims. The softened tone in which the debate is couched is also in evidence in Tottoli's entry on Haman in the third edition of the *Encyclopaedia of Islam*, where he writes that "Western scholars have tried to explain the origin of the name and consequently the possible influence of previous narratives on the Qur'ānic passages."

87. http://shubuhat3arabic.blogspot.com/2012/03/6.html.

88. Bucaille was also impressed by the Qur'ān's reference to Pharaoh's preserved body as a sign for future generations (Q 10:92). He related this verse to the discovery of what was deemed to be Pharaoh's relatively well-preserved corpse, which he was invited to examine (https://www.arabnews.com/news/443500). There remains some controversy over whether Bucaille formally converted to Islam or merely expressed his belief in the miraculous nature of the Qur'ān.

89. Such "influencers" as the Palestinian shaykh Bassām Jarrār (https://www.youtube.com/watch?v=ertXVN3fkww) and the Pakistani-American Nouman Ali Khan (https://www.youtube.com/watch?v=azBmsssf0ts) have incorporated the Bucaille-Haman idea into their sermons. A quick search on relevant websites reveals that dozens of clerics have used Haman's appearance in the Qur'ān to demonstrate the divine nature of the Muslim scripture.

Chapter Eight: Haman's DNA

1. Note, for instance, that the Mesopotamian (hence, Semitic) Nimrod is Hamitic (Gen 10:8), while such un-Semitic peoples as the Elamites, whom we will encounter throughout this chapter, were Semitic (Gen 10:22).

2. "Bougean" occurs in LXX A:17, 3:1, and 9:10; and in AT 3:1, 7:25, and 7:44. "Macedonian" occurs in LXX 9:24 and Add E:10; and in AT Add A:17.

3. Hacham, "3 Maccabees and Esther," 781.

4. Domazakis, "Date of Composition."

5. The possibility that "Bougean" is derived from a Persian word, such as *baga-* (relating to god), or *mwgy* (relating to "magus"), will be explored below, where we also return to the possibility that "Bougean" was reflecting the ancient Persian Bagoas.

6. Wechsler, "The Appellation βογγαιος." See above, Ch 6, n 42.

7. A version of Addition E is found in TgII 4:1, where the king says of Haman: "A certain man came to us (who is) not from our place and not from our country. Now he came to join us that we may prevail over our enemies. We investigated him; his name is Haman, son of King Agag, son of great Amalek, son of Reul, son of Eliphaz, Esau's first-born, a son of nobles, owner of property and rich land."

8. The three-pronged theology is mentioned in Zoroastrian liturgy in Avestan (*Yasna* 48:5).

9. We return to the spiritualization of family bonds in Christianity and Islam in Chapter 9.

10. Al-Bīrūnī, *al-Āthār al-bāqiya*, 280 (trans. Sachau, *Chronology of Ancient Nations*, 273).

11. Balkh: Wahb ibn Munabbih, in Sibṭ ibn al-Jawzī, *Mir'at al-zamān*, 2:30; Sarakhs: al-Maqdisī, *al-Bad' wa al-ta'rīkh*, 3: 81–82; Khurasan: Mujāhid, in Sibṭ ibn al-Jawzī, *Mir'at al-zamān*, 2:30; Būshanj: Muqātil ibn Sulaymān, in Sibṭ ibn al-Jawzī, *Mir'at al-zamān*, 2:30; and al-Rabghūzī, *The Stories of the Prophets*, 2:253.

12. The ḥadīth is preserved in Aḥmad ibn Ḥanbal's *Musnad* and may be found at: https://sunnah.com/ahmad:12 and at https://sunnah.com/ahmad:33.

13. The ḥadīth is preserved in Muslim's *Ṣaḥīḥ* and may be found at: https://sunnah.com/muslim:2944.

14. The ḥadīth, which has been categorized as "weak" (*ḍaʿīf*), may be found at: https://sunnah.com/tirmidhi:2269. Despite its shaky status in Muslim tradition, this ḥadīth has played important political roles from the Abbasid Revolution (747–750 CE; see Sharon, *Black Banners from the East*) to the rise of twenty-first century Jihadi groups (Raine, "Why Jihadis are Drawn to Khorasan").

15. See above, Ch 6, n 242.

16. See e.g., Lowin, *Making of a Forefather.*

17. TgII 8:12 (Grossfeld, *Two Targums*, 185). On the seventeenth century source, see Rivlin, *Perush*, 40ff.

18. A particularly *Indian* provenance for Haman might also conform to (Iranian?) Muslim ideas about hated figures who claim to be Iranian: Some of Ayatollah Khomeini's opponents famously claimed that he was actually an "Indian," which—regardless of the facticity of the claim—indicates that "Indian" can be used as an insult.

19. For the various Jewish answers to this question proposed over the centuries, see Horowitz, *Reckless Rites*, 107–146.

20. See above, Ch 6, n 129, and also y.Demay 2.1:3 (Kfar Qarnos).

21. Jews in late antiquity may have been familiar with the use of the *q-r-ṣ* root to refer to an (evil) accuser from Dan 3:8: In that context, too, Jews were threatened in a refusal-to-bow episode.

22. Note also that Armenia was the first polity to adopt Christianity as its state religion (in 301 CE).

23. Horowitz, *Reckless Rites*, 122–125, with sources. Horowitz traces the Jewish identification of Haman with the Armenians well into the nineteenth century.

24. Toumanoff, "Amatuni," and eadem, *Studies in Christian Caucasian History*, 198.

25. Codoñer, *The Emperor Theophilos*, 83. In the words of Ignatius the Deacon, "Leo displayed to the New Israel actions even more terrible than those of the Amalekitai" (ibid., 84).

26. 2 Kgs 19:37, Isa 37:38.

27. Codoñer, *The Emperor Theophilos*, 83–87. Sennacherib was deemed to be a villain in Jewish tradition (for his attack on Jerusalem, recorded in 2 Kgs 18–19 and Isa 36–37), and is referred to by the rabbis as "Sennacherib, the evil one" (*ha-rashaʿ*; b.Sanhedrin 95b). Interestingly, for his sack of Babylon in 689 and godnapping of Marduk's statue, Sennacherib was deemed evil by Babylonian supporters of Marduk, too. In fact, Dalley (*Esther's Revenge, passim* esp. 114–115) relates these events to the original historical kernel on which *Esther* is based.

28. Wacholder, "Pseudo-Eupolemus," 104f., and Charlesworth, *Old Testament Pseudepigrapha*, 880 and note to 886.

29. b.Megillah 10b, where Rabbah bar ʿOfran is said to have introduced his sermon on *Esther* with the verse, "And I will set My throne in Elam and will destroy from there king and princes" (Jer 49:38).

30. Hence, in his work *al-Filāḥa al-Nabaṭiyya* ("Nabataean Agriculture"), Ibn Waḥshiyyah's (wr. 904) deals with ANE traditions rather than what modern scholars deem to be Nabataean ones. See Hämeen-Anttila, *Last Pagans of Iraq*.

31. For the sake of neatness, the discussion here will refer to MT *Esther* as the earliest biblical version of the story, despite the fact that it probably represents the final edition/redaction of earlier *Vorlagen* (as seen in Chapters 1–2).

32. E.g., Gertoux, *Queen Esther*; Yamauchi, *Persia and the Bible*, 226–239; Shea, "Esther and History," among numerous others.

33. Shaked, *Iranian Functions*; Millard, *The Persian Names in Esther*; Sarbanani, *Revisiting the Book of Esther*; Gehman, *Notes on the Persian Words*; Russell, *Zoroastrian Elements*; and others.

34. See, for instance, the exchange between Clines and Yamauchi concerning the discovery of an Achaemenid functionary by the name of "Marduka" active around the time of Xerxes' reign (Clines, "In Quest of the Historical Mordecai," and Yamauchi, "Mordecai of the Persepolis Tablets").

35. Stolper, "Paper Chase."

36. From the last quarter of the fifth century BCE, we have evidence from a Jewish Aramaic letter from Egypt of two Achaemenid officials by the names of Marduk and Haumadāta: Taylor, "Bodleian Letters," 34 (Aramaic) and 35 (English), ll. 1–2; and Tuplin, "Bodleian Letters," 163–164 for commentary. The reconstruction of Haumadāta is tentative, and neither does the geographical context (Egypt-Syria) nor the historical one (the reign of Darius II) tally with the contents of MT *Esther*. Moreover, Haumadāta would—if anything—represent Haman's father. Nonetheless, it is clear that the piecemeal evidence that we have may still yield data that confirms the verisimilitude of *Esther* (if not its historicity).

37. Xerxes: Zadok ("Historical Background") and Littman ("Religious Policy"); Artaxerxes II: Hoschander (*Book of Esther*) and Lewy ("The Feast of the 14th day of Adar"); Darius: Shapira ("Judeo-Persian translations," 231); Wills (*Jew in the Court*, 154 and 164), and others. We return to this latter option below.

38. Dalley (*Esther's Revenge at Susa*), for instance, argues that MT *Esther* reflects historical events of the seventh century BCE, specifically the Assyrian sack of Susa in 647.

39. See, most recently, Llewellyn-Jones, *Ancient Persia and the Book of Esther*.

40. Gindin's commentary on *Esther* focuses in great detail on the philological and historical background of MT *Esther* (Gindin, *Book of Esther Unmasked*).

41. Wills, *Jew in the Court*, 182 and 191; Laniak, *Shame and Honor*, 5 n 7; Bickerman, *Four Strange Books*, 177–196; Talmon, "Wisdom"; Berlin, "Esther and Ancient Storytelling"; and others. In Chapter 6, we added Parthian-era novellas to the mix.

42. The once-popular view that MT *Esther* was written in the mid-second century BCE (see Russell, "Zoroastrian Elements," 32–33; Haupt, *Purim*, 5 and 28–30; and Lacocque, *Esther Regina*, 35) has fallen out of favor in the light of advances within relevant fields of scholarship, which point to a late-Achaemenid provenance for MT *Esther*.

43. Roaf ("Aššur in Esther") has suggested that behind Ahashwerosh lurks the Assyrian Aššur, which—if correct—means that the names of all six of the leading characters in *Esther* can be associated with those of Near Eastern deities.

44. Paton, *Commentary*, 87–94, provides a succinct summary of the various theories proposed by the turn of the twentieth century, concluding with the verdict: "The [*Esther*] story . . . has many points of similarity to Babylonian mythology, but no close counterpart to it has yet been discovered in Babylonian literature." The earliest studies on this topic are those of Jensen, "Elamitische Eigennamen," 70; Zimmern, "Ursprünge des Purimfestes"; and Schrader, *Keilinschriften*, 514ff.

45. The most detailed treatment of the subject is Dalley's richly documented, if controversial, monograph on the subject, *Esther's Revenge at Susa*.

46. In the words of Laniak, "The evidence, although highly suggestive, was consistently inconclusive" (*Shame and Honor*, 3).

47. As no one would question the threading of biblical intertexts throughout MT *Esther*, contextualizing the book in this way is, of course, a legitimate scholarly pursuit. What it yields for us, however, is very limited: Mordecai's refusal to bow to Haman is frequently compared to Joseph's rejection of Potiphar's wife's advances (Gen 39:7–20), and accordingly, Haman in the MT is evoking Potiphar's unnamed (and otherwise inconsequential) wife. As we will see

in this chapter, an ANE contextualization of *Esther* and Haman provides much more substantial parallels.

48. Llewellyn-Jones, *Ancient Persia and the Book of Esther*, 5.

49. Reversals and Marduk: Kruger, "World Turned on Its Head" *passim*, esp. 70–71 and n 49. ANE reversals and *Esther*: Winitzer, "Reversal of Fortune Theme," who proposes other Near Eastern literary contexts for *Esther*.

50. Alternatively, the author imbedded such bilingual puns for his own amusement. The widespread use of puns and wordplay in virtually all Near Eastern cultures makes it more likely that the punning was not an inside joke of sorts (see Noegel, *Puns and Pundits*).

51. I discuss these and various other bilingual puns in *Esther* in "Did Esther Lose Her *huile d'olive*?"

52. Owing to this Akkadian pun, the Talmudic sages (b.Ta'anit, 29a) declared that "when Adar commences, joy increases," a statement that had surprisingly practical implications, such as the advice that one is encouraged to sue a gentile in this month. See also Haupt, "Cuneiform Name of the Second Adar."

53. Reiner, "Inscription," 101–102, based on a Neo-Babylonian (626–539 BCE) commentary on the names of the months of the Elamite calendar.

54. E.g., Levenson, *Esther*, 10. The root is used in: 3:7 (Haman's lots), 6:10 (Haman parading Mordecai), 6:13 (Zeresh predicting Haman's demise), 7:8 (Haman pleading for his life), 8:3 (Esther pleading for her nation), 8:17, 9:2, and 9:3 (fear of the Jews/Mordecai befalling the nations).

55. *CAD* N1, 11:275, s.v. *napālu*.

56. Alternatively, it is possible that allusions to ANE civilization in *Esther* were inserted at an early stage in the text's development and were no longer intelligible (or even noticed) by the time *Esther* reached its MT form.

57. The Neo-Babylonian period is defined by the use of that dialect of Akkadian. The Neo-Babylonian dynasty, by contrast, lasted from 626–539.

58. Wisnom, "Blood on the Wind," and Seri, "Borrowings." Anzû was equated with Mars (Reynolds, "Unpropitious titles of Mars," 355), a fact whose relevance to Haman will be explored below.

59. Silverstein, "Book of Esther and *Enūma Elish*" (with sources).

60. Note, moreover, that Marduk sliced up Tiamat's body, just as Saul cut up Agag in 1 Sam 15:33.

61. Lambert, *Babylonian Creation Myths*, 439–444.

62. Reynolds, "Stellar Representations," 369.

63. The Babylonian elites who produced the myths discussed here put an interesting spin on the instances of Marduk's captivity: Rather than interpreting them as (temporary) triumphs of their political rivals, which must be reversed through victory over these rivals, godnappings were presented as being motivated by Marduk himself, who *chose* to abandon his city. The locals' behavior was thus responsible for the chaos, but would also be responsible for its correction and for the restoration of order. In other words, Marduk's Elamite enemies were seen as divine puppets, as Haman would be in some late antique rabbinical traditions.

64. Johnson, "Time and Again."

65. See Freymer-Kensky, "The Tribulations of Marduk," for a nuanced analysis of this text's contents and its near-exclusive focus on the captivity theme.

66. Dalley, *Esther's Revenge*, esp. 114–115.

67. On this see now Kutsko, *Between Heaven and Earth*, 105ff.

68. Gaspa, "State Theology," 142 n 62.

69. Reynolds, "Stellar Representations," 371 l. 5 and 377. Other texts from Nebuchadnezzar I's reign overtly celebrate Mardukian triumph over the Elamites (see e.g., Lambert, "Enmeduranki," among others).

70. See now Taylor, "Erra Song" (with a new edition and translation of the text in Appendix A, 336–387).

71. It is not for nothing that the rabbis referred to pagans as "planet-worshippers" (Hebrew: *'ovedey kokhavim*).

72. Brown, *Mesopotamian Planetary Astronomy-Astrology*, 256–257.

73. For the association of Near Eastern and Mediterranean tyrants with anger, see Rajak, "The Angry Tyrant."

74. VanderBurgh, "Babylonian Legends," 31.

75. Machinist and Sasson, "Rest and Violence."

76. The following is based on Silverstein, *Veiling Esther*, 155–156 (with sources).

77. Taylor, "Erra Song," 102ff.; Wiggermann, "Nergal," 217 and 222–223; and Reiner, *Astral Magic in Babylonia*, 4, 6–7, and 22. To complicate matters, one of the six Neo-Babylonian rulers was named Neriglissar (r. 560–556 BCE), a theophoric name meaning "Nergal, protect the king," indicating that Nergal was held in high esteem in what was perhaps the most Mardukophile dynasty of Babylonian history. Mordecai's refusal to bow in *Esther* may thus parallel the story's hero with Nergal rather than its villain.

78. Beaulieu, *Patheon of Uruk*, 295 and 297.

79. That Namtar is Ereškigal's vizier in *Ištar's Descent to the Underworld* may provide an important clue here, for in that myth Namtar imprisons and attacks Ištar, thereby better aligning the heroes and villains with MT *Esther*'s cast.

80. Very little is known concerning the relations between the Neo-Babylonian Empire and Elam. However, as noted regarding the composition of the *Enūma Eliš*, some of the most important moments in the Babylonian national memory were shaped by rivalry with the Elamites.

81. I recognize both that there were various "Ištar"s (including those of Akkad, Arbela, Uruk, and others) and that Dalley (*Esther's Revenge*) has seen Ištar of Nineveh (rather than Ištar of Babylon) as being the crucial goddess in contextualizing *Esther*. I nonetheless use "Ištar" inelegantly here both for the sake of convenience and because *ištaru* in Akkadian means "goddess" generally.

82. Note that Humban's name could be rendered "Huban," "'Umman," and "Hubban," among other spellings, depending upon the language, region, and period in which the name featured. I adopt "Humban" here throughout for the sake of uniformity, inaccurate though it may be in some contexts.

83. Jensen ("Elamitische Eigennamen") proposed these Elamite etymologies already in 1892.

84. For Humban skepticism, see e.g., Littman, "Religious Policy," 147 n 9 (quoting Gaster, *Purim and Hanukkah*, 8–10). For Mašti skepticism, see Llewellyn-Jones, *Ancient Persia and the Book of Esther*, 90 (quoting Gindin, *Book of Esther Unmasked*, 64). The shift between the Old Persian and Elamite languages allows for a shift between "v" and "m" (see e.g., Shea, "Esther and History," 248 n 39, and Stolper, "Iranian Loanword").

85. See van Koppen and van de Toorn's entries on "Humban," "Vashti," and "Kiririsha," in Brill's *Dictionary of Deities and Demons in the Bible Online*.

86. Additionally, it has been pointed out that an entrenched anti-Elamite perspective has tainted our view of the pre-Achaemenid Near East, as argued by Henkelman ("Humban and Auramazdā," 294ff.).

87. To cite but two examples: Noah's etymology from *n-ḥ-m* (*Genesis* 5:29) and Samuel's etymology from *š-'-l* in 1 Sam 1:20, would be deemed philologically unacceptable by modern scholarly standards. Similarly, the French-Jewish exegete, David Kimḥi (d. 1235) notes *ad* Gen 5:29 that when it comes to name-origins, biblical Hebrew does not necessarily apply grammatical rules accurately.

88. Accordingly, *Vahešti*, meaning "the best," plays on Esth 1:19, where the king seeks to appoint a queen, "better than her," while the morphology of *vahešti* itself may be hinted at in Esth 1:8 (*ve-haštiyah*, which immediately precedes Vashti's introduction).

89. Accordingly, Haman's name derives from *vohu-manah* ("of good thoughts") or *hama-manah* ("same thoughts"), which plays on Esth 8:3, 8:5, 9:24, and 9:25, in all of which there are references to Haman's "thoughts."

90. Zadok, *Elamite Onomasticon.*

91. While this statement concerning Babylonian views of the Elamites is an oversimplification (the Assyrians challenged and rivalled the Babylonians throughout history, too), we will see that the Elamite rivalry almost certainly underpins *Esther.*

92. Reynolds, "Unpropitious Titles," 355; Jastrow, "Signs and Name;" and see Walker, "Myth of Girra and Elamatum," 147, where the "star of Elam" came to be equated with both Mars and Anzû. In general, the very fragmentary *Girra and Elamatum* relates how "Girra," who is equated with "Gibil," the latter being one of Marduk's epithets—defeated an Elamite woman.

93. Henkelman, "Humban and Auramazdā," 316 and n 71.

94. Ibid. 316, and idem, *The Other Gods Who Are*, 331 (Kirirša being venerated in Susa at the very end of the Neo-Elamite period); 353 and 358 (Humban as the most popular god). An early-sixth-century BCE Elamite text refers to "the curse of Napiriša, *Kiririša* and the benevolent lord that created water and earth. The salvation of *Mašti* will be removed from him!" (in Quintana, "Elamite Religion and Ritual," 735, where "Humban" is tantalizingly (though inaccurately) read in lieu of "Napiriša," as the latter's name merely means "the great god," by which Humban was also known (Elamite: *rišar nappira*) in the Neo-Elamite period). Kiririša was specifically known to have had, "a certain taste for death" and to have been associated with tree-burials (Henkelman, *The Other Gods Who Are*, 330 and n 70), which may be reflected in Zeresh's advice that Haman build a "tall tree" from which to hang Mordecai in Esth 5:14.

95. Reiner, "Inscription," 97 and 99.

96. Henkelman, *The Other Gods Who Are*, 360 n 839. Temples dedicated to Humban endured into the late Neo-Elamite period (ibid, 362).

97. Ibid., 362–363.

98. Reynolds, "Unpropitious Titles," 351, where Mars as "the Enemy Star" (*Nakrû*) refers specifically to Elam, and 352, where Mars is "the Elam star."

99. The root *ṣ-l-b* with the meaning of "to crucify" appears in the Aramaic version of the Behistun Inscription (column 3, line 35, in Cowley, *Aramaic Papyri*, 253, and 263 *ad* l. 35 for comment), to which we return below.

100. Haman's "hanging" may have been interpreted as crucifixion already in the Achaemenid period, based on the use of the Aramaic *zeqīf* in Ezra 6:11, where Darius threatens anyone who alters his decree, saying: ". . . let a beam be pulled out from his house, and let him be lifted up and fastened thereon. . . ." The wording of this verse may be related to Haman's punishment in Esth 7:10 (see Ron, "Tattenai and Haman," 257). Whereas *ṣ-l-b* is by far the most common verbal root for crucifixion in Semitic languages (including most forms of Aramaic), in Syriac the root normally employed is *z-q-f*.

101. Esther's implicating the king, rather than Haman, in the Jews' predicament is presumably what motivated the author of *Pirqe de Rabbi Eliezer* to rewrite the story, with Esther telling the king: "My lord, O king! I ask nothing of you except my life and my people. Because one man has come and has *bought* us to destroy, to slay, and to cause to perish" (50:10; trans. 406).

102. Note that Levenson, *Esther*, 10, reads into the verb *le-hummam* (Esth 9:24) a play on Haman's name, which he argues would mean "to Hamanate" (the Jews).

103. Reynolds, "Unpropitious Titles," 354.

104. Šimut appears in the Persepolis Fortifications Tablets (PF 0338).

105. See Black, *Concise Dictionary of Akkadian*, 334 s.v. "ṣarāru[m]."

106. In Walfish, *Esther in Medieval Garb*, 58–59. It is also interesting to note that in the Talmud (b.Megillah 10b), Haman is compared to "thorns" for having considered himself a

god (following from the reference in Isa 7:19, where the Talmudic rabbis interpret the same phrase as referring to an idolatrous context), while in the early-tenth century CE, Ibn Waḥshiyya associates thorny plants with Mars, explaining that "an enmity between Mars and Jupiter" led to the creation of thorns (in Hämeen-Anttila, *Last Pagans of Iraq*, 155–156).

107. In addition to being God's Messiah, Cyrus is described in the Bible as God's agent (Ezra 1:1–4) and shepherd (Isa 44:28).

108. See Mitchell, "Biblical Archaeology," 70–71 n 94, who suggests that Haman reflects a Neo-Elamite ruler with a Humban theophoric name.

109. See Frankfort, *Kingship and the Gods*, 313ff., for vivid, text-based descriptions of Marduk's enthronement in the Akītu ceremonies—some of which appear to be echoed in *Esther*.

110. Gane and Gane, "Cosmic conflict."

111. E.g., Isa 46:1–2, Jer 50:2, and 51:44. Most famously, the refusal-to-bow episode in Dan 3 describes Nebuchadnezzar (II)'s setting up an idol of his god (whom we may assume to have been Marduk).

112. In general, see Finkel, "Cyrus Cylinder." A translation of the text may be found in Cogan, "Achaemenid Inscriptions," and an online transliteration of the Akkadian text and an earlier translation of it into English may be found here: https://www.cais-soas.com/CAIS/History/hakhamaneshian/Cyrus-the-great/cyrus_cylinder_complete.htm.

113. The analogy is imperfect since in both cases in *Esther* the same Ahashwerosh removes and then reimposes taxation on the population, whereas in the Cyrus Cylinder, the removal of taxation is a sign of Cyrus's justice and is contrasted with Nabonidus's imposition of corvées.

114. In fact, the ideological portions of the text end with Cyrus's prayers in these lines, whereas there is a (fragmentary) continuation of the text that deals with technical descriptions of building activities. To these points we may add the reference in the Cyrus Cylinder to enemies of civilization by the name of the "Umman-manda," a cryptic phrase that Adali (*Scourge of God*) relates to the Elamites.

115. Schaudig, "Magnanimous Heart of Cyrus," 72–77, and Tadmor, "Erudite Savagery," 46 (for other Babylonian literary references in the text).

116. In the interests of completeness, it is worth pointing out another possible connection between Cyrus's career and *Esther*, namely the possible relationship between Purim and the Sacaea festival. The latter, like Purim, is a festival of reversals, which Strabo related to the goddess Anahita (the Iranian manifestation of Ištar) and to two other Persian gods named "Omanes" and "Anadatos." The similarity between the latter two names and the names "Haman" and "Hammedatha" has led some to relate the Sacaea to Purim and to *Esther* generally (Langdon, "Babylonian and Persian Sacaea," 72; Paton, *Esther*, 88; and Dalley, *Esther's Revenge*, 170 n 14). However, de Jong (*Traditions of the Magi*, 150–155; and more generally, ibid., 379–384) has rejected this theory forcefully.

117. For a careful study of the interplay between the competing accounts, as well as the impact that oral (re)tellings of the events had on historiography and literature, see Shayegan, *Aspects of History and Epic*, esp. 27–34 (on the historicity of the events), and 73–108 (on the interplay between the inscriptions and orality).

118. Granerød, "Favour of Ahuramazda," 470ff; Benson, "Violence in the Behistun Monument," 22; and Tavernier, "Achaemenid Royal Inscription," 161.

119. "Magus" in this context has Zoroastrian-Iranian connotations (as Talmudic *amgūshī* and Qur'ānic *mājūs*) rather than the Eastern wise-men associations of the magi in the NT (Matt 2:1–2).

120. Herodotus, *Histories*, 3.79. The classic treatment is Henning, "Murder of the Magi." See also Dandanmaev, "Magophonia," and de Jong, *Traditions of the Magi*, 377–379.

121. Koller (*Esther in Ancient Jewish Thought*, 44), postulates that *Esther*'s author was arguing *against* the ideas reflected in the Behistun Inscription, whereas many other scholars see a

genetic relationship between the two texts or between the Purim and Magophonia festivals. On this, see Gunkel, *Esther*, 115; Shapira, "Judeo-Persian Translations," 231; and Ruiz-Ortiz, *Dynamics of Violence*, 204 and n 58; among others). Sarbanani ("Revisiting the Book of Esther," 23, and 25–29) and Llewellyn-Jones (*Ancient Persia and the Book of Esther*, 23, 42, 61, 70, 160, and 199) see the Behistun Inscription and *Esther* as representing accurately the early-Achaemenid context in which *Esther* is set.

122. See above 136.

123. Josephus, *Antiquities*, XI.3.1 (Magophonia) and XI.3.2, 7 and 9 ("Tale of the Three Guardsmen," modelled on *Esther*). Josephus transparently drew his own version of these events from the Second Temple text 1 Esd 3:3–4:4.

124. Tantalizingly, the rebellion was quashed on the tenth of the seventh month (Old Persian: Gamayadi; Akkadian: Tašrītu), which in the Jewish calendar is the date of Yom Kippur.

125. This point is made in Granerød, "Favour of Ahuramazda," 465. And see Henkelman, *Other Gods Who Are*, 362–363, for the curse formula, "may the terror of Humban and the Protective Gods be placed on upon him!" which Henkelman dates to the "reign" of Athamaita.

126. There appear to have been more than one Gubaru/Gobryas character who played significant roles in the early-Achaemenid period, and—as was the case with the various Bagoas functionaries—their careers may have been conflated into that of a single character. Schwenzner ("Gobryas") has argued that some of the "different" Gubarus are in fact a single person.

127. The other character from this episode who appears to have informed *Esther*'s Mordecai is Otanes (Akkadian: Utānu), who discovered Gaumāta's plot with the help of his daughter (Herodotus, *Histories*, 3.68.2 and 3.70; cf. Esth 2:21–23), who married the same daughter to the king, who suggested that ruling offices be determined by drawing lots (Herodotus, *Histories*, 3.80; cf. the lots theme in *Esther*), and who proposed that he and his people live in the Persian Empire under their own rules while remaining loyal to the Persian system (ibid., 3.83; cf. Esth 3:8, where Haman describes the Jews as having different laws from the other nations). See Haupt, *Purim*, 8.

128. See Granerød, "Favour of Ahuramazda," 467–468, and Nilsen, "Creation in Collision?" 4 n 19, for Marduk replacing Ahuramazda in the Behistun Inscription; Gaspa, "State Theology," 142, for Marduk's influence on "the cosmic traits of A[h]uramazda"; and Soudavar, *Aura of Kings*, 92, for an instance of comparison between Ahura-Mazda and Marduk in this period. In general, as the chief gods of their respective pantheons, as the Creator gods in their respective religions, and as gods represented celestially by Jupiter, Ahuramazda and Marduk were identified with each other.

129. Note that the repeated references to "men" (from *martiya*) in the Old Persian version of the Behistun Inscription are rendered in the Aramaic version with the same *g-b-r* root. Note, also, the reference to "the man Mordecai" (Esth 9:4), a formulation that unnecessarily refers to Mordecai as a man (Hebrew: *'īsh*), although this may simply be an echo of Exod 11:3 (regarding Moses).

130. To the list of similarities between the texts we may add both texts' apparent obsession with enumerating their dead enemies, as well as the calendar motif, whose significance has been argued (separately) for each text (see Freigburg, "A New Clue in the Dating," and Kosmin, "New Hypothesis" [Behistun]). Freigburg argues that the calendric evidence points to an origin for *Esther* in the years immediately following Darius I's reign.

131. Henning, "Murder of the Magi." This version recounts the events from a Persian/Zoroastrian perspective, with Alexander named as the persecutor of the Magi. The relationship between Haman and Alexander in pre-Islamic Iran (as discussed above), and the recasting of the villain of the story as genocidal (rather than as a "hostile foreign actor"), are particularly noteworthy.

132. Shapira, "Judeo-Persian translations," 229–232. In his view, a presumed *mwgy* (magus) became *bwgy* (Bougean).

133. See above, Ch 8, n 37.

134. Littman, "Religious Policy," is perhaps the most influential study of this sort.

135. Note that the near-complete equating of "theological" and "national" concerns in ANE rivalries (with Babylon's social and political fates being affected by the presence or absence of Marduk's statue, for instance) transfers smoothly to an ancient Jewish context in which religion, ethnicity, and territory overlapped.

136. See Granerød, "Favor of Ahuramazda," 464, and Henkelman, *Other Gods Who Are*, 371ff., where documentary evidence from Achaemenid Persepolis bears out Humban's acculturation and popularity. Henkelman (ibid., 372) demonstrates that officiants in Humban's cult had overwhelmingly Iranian (rather than Elamite) names.

137. Assyrian origins of *kitin*: Gaspa, "State theology," 138ff. Old Persian *khvarnah* and *kitin*: Root, "Defining the divine," 52–54 (drawing on Garrison, "By the Favor"), but see Soudavar, *Mithraic Societies*, 177, for the counter-argument. Whereas the Sumerian *melam* and the later, Akkadian *melammu*, also represent a sort of "kingly aura" (and it is this concept that Llewellyn-Jones, *Ancient Persia and the Book of Esther*, 65–68, relates to *khvarnah* and to Ahashwerosh's "honor" (Hebrew: *kavod*) in *Esther* 1:4), the Elamite *kitin* is clearly a more relevant context to MT *Esther* and Xerxes' reign for reasons that will become clear below.

138. The fact that *kitin* is thought to overlap with the Old Persian concept of *Arta*, which invokes divinely instituted Order but literally means "Truth," dovetails nicely with the depiction in Darius's Behistun Inscription of all those who rebelled against him as liars. On *kitin* and *Arta*, see Silverman, "Achaemenid 'Theology' of Kingship," 178. Xerxes' continuation of his predecessor's ideological policies may be seen in his importation of a life-size statue of Darius I from Egypt to Susa (Stronach, "Cyrus and the Kingship of Anshan," 59–60).

139. Herodotus, *Histories*, 1.183. For the refutation of Xerxes' targeting the Babylonians' Marduk statue and temple, see Kuhrt and Sherwin-White, "Xerxes' destruction."

140. On this, see Henkelman, *Other Gods Who Are*, 367–370, and Henkelman, "Humban and Auramazdā," 317–319 and n 75.

141. In the words of Henkelman (*Other Gods Who Are*, 9): "Whereas *kitin* is connected in particular with Humban, the supreme male god and protector of kings in the Neo-Elamite period, it is associated with Auramazdā, the new royal god, in [the *daivā* inscription]."

142. To the similarities between the *Daivā* Inscription and MT *Esther* we may add that the former ends with Xerxes imploring Ahuramazda to, "protect me from harm, and my house, and this land. . . ." (cf. Esth 10), and slightly earlier, implores its readers to, "worship Ahuramazda at the proper time and in the proper manner" (cf. Esth 9:27 on establishing Purim, "according to the writing thereof, and according to the timing thereof").

143. Mitchell, "Biblical Archaeology," 70, sees Esth 3:12 (the dissemination of anti-Jewish edicts throughout the Achaemenid realms) as reflecting the dissemination of public texts such as the Behistun Inscription.

144. By the same token, Mordecai was both a pun on the Old Persian *Mart/diya* ("man"), a playful cognate on Akkadian Gubaru (from the *g-b-r* root meaning "man"), and a reference to the chief Babylonian deity, Marduk.

145. One might surmise that the author is here evidencing the fact that the empire's Jews were loyally siding with the pro-Marduk and anti-Humban public policy of the early Achaemenid rulers (for, as Henkelman, *Other Gods Who Are*, 363, puts it, ". . . royal ideology demanded that . . . 'rebellion' against the king be presented as a rebellion against the king's god").

146. See also Jub 8:21 and 9:2, where the Elam mentioned in the Table of Nations is said to have had a daughter called "Susa."

147. The parallels were first noticed by Gunkel (*Genesis*, 282–284), and are most fully explored in Silverstein, *Veiling Esther*, 81–83.

148. In addition to the passages discussed here, Elam is only referred to either as a place from which Israelites will be ingathered (e.g., Isa 11:11), or as a divine instrument in Isa 22:6 ("And Elam bore the quiver, with troops of men, even horsemen; and Kir uncovered the shield"), or in Jer 25:25, where "all the kings of Elam" are mentioned in a long list of nations who will be subdued.

149. *ḥ-l-ḥ-l* is derived from *ḥ-y-l* and in the hitpa'el form it should be rendered *titḥolel*, as it is in Job 15:20 and Jer 23:19. The employment of this unusual form strengthens the association between the Isa 21 and Esth 4 references.

150. On this passage, see generally Peels, "God's Throne in Elam."

151. In Moreen, *Queen Esther's Garden*, 91 ll. 15 and 24. See Leach ("Kingship and Divinity," 292) for the argument that Esther in the Dura Europos Purim panel is depicted as Anahita/Ištar.

152. b.Megillah 10b and 19a.

153. E.g., Ps 95:6 and 2 Chr 7:3 and 29:29. See above, Ch 6, n 126.

154. Haman's armies in the Qur'ān: Q 28:6 and 8. Haman's tower to the Heavens: Q 28:38 and 40:36–37. Humban's ziggurat in Neo-Elamite Susa (Henkelman, *Other Gods Who Are*, 361). It must also be recalled that in the *ShāhNāma*, Hōmān is a Ṭūrānian commander of armies, reflecting perhaps a faint memory of Humban.

Chapter Nine: Haman at Home and at Work

1. TgI 5:1 and TgII 3:1.

2. That the Targum Rishon employed the Aramaic (originally Indo-Iranian) root *g-n-z* here, with the meaning of "treasury," may be relevant as the emerging word could resemble the Greek *genos*, "people" (see Grossfeld, *Two Targums*, 79). It is perhaps on the basis of such traditions that Yefet ben 'Eli explains the king's awarding "Haman's house" to Esther as meaning Haman's "dependents and his children" (in Wechsler, *Yefet ben 'Eli*, 274 *ad* Esth 8:1–2).

3. See Laniak, *Shame and Honor*, 128.

4. Cf. Matt 12:46–50; and Luke 8:19–21.

5. Cf. 1 Cor 1:10, 11, and 26; 2:1; 3:1; 4:6; 6:8; 7:24; and so forth. This is not dissimilar to Hellenistic ideas discussed earlier, according to which one may accept or reject Hellenism regardless of one's ethnicity. It is thus unsurprising that the Hellenized Josephus mentions Haman's sons only once (*Antiquities* XI.6.13), and even then he does not list their names.

6. Similarly, when Abraham asks God whether his descendants will benefit from the Covenant, God replies that it will not extend to those descendants who are sinners (*ẓālimūn*; Q 2:124).

7. Lowin, *Making of a Forefather*, 53 n 38. Arabic orthography allows for confusion between 'Amīla' (اميلى) and 'Amthelai' (امتلي), assuming a misreading of diacritical marks.

8. Note, however, that some readers mistook the initial "Ha" of Hammedata's name for the definite article and thought his name was "the Medata" (see Ch 2, n 25).

9. *Leviticus Rabba* 28:6.

10. *Targum Jonathan ad* Esth 5:10 and TgI 5:10 (in Grossfeld, *Two Targums*, 66 and notes 30–31 thereto). It is odd that the later, and more expansive, *Targum Sheni* does not include this detail, suggesting that its author did not hold it to be accurate.

11. Olmstead, "Tattenai."

12. Medieval exegetes debated whether Tattenai was an adversary of the Jews (see Ron, "Tattenai and Haman," esp. 255–256).

13. In some Jewish communities, a mock-*ketubah* ("marriage contract") for Haman's marriage to Zeresh was produced, with comedic contents (Lewinsky, *Smiting Haman in the Diaspora*, 35–36).

14. Zlotnik (*Dinah's Daughters*, 77) suggests that *Esther* relates the success of Mordecai and Esther as contrasted to the failure of Haman and Zeresh. This reading suits the LXX and exegetical readings of *Esther*, which have Esther as Mordecai's wife rather than his adopted daughter (as she is in the MT). I would add that Zeresh in Esth 5:10 mirrors Esther in Esth 4:4: In both cases, the main male character informs his wife of events, to which the wife responds with a bad idea (Esther offers Mordecai clothes, while Zeresh proposes that Haman create a gallows for Mordecai, an idea that, in 6:13, Zeresh concedes was misguided).

15. Grossfeld, *Two Targums*, 66 and nn. 30–31.

16. For these and other reasons, Zlotnick has argued that the text portrays Haman's and Zeresh's relationship as lacking in intimacy (*Dinah's Daughters*, 82–84). Zlotnick notes that the only intimacy that Haman shares with a woman is with Esther herself (Esth 7:8, where Haman and Esther are alone in a room, and Haman falls onto Esther's bed).

17. In Lees, "Intertextual Ripples," 115.

18. *Midrash Mishle*, 11. This work is thought to date from the eighth to eleventh centuries. That the late-eighth century *Pirqe de Rabbi Eliezer* (50:5; trans. 398) compares Haman and Korah for their wealth, without implicating their wives in their "fall," suggests that the latter idea post-dates this source.

19. Grossman ("Dynamic Analogies," 403–404), and Lees ("Intertextual Ripples," 144) have argued that the Jezebel episode is one of the biblical intertexts in *Esther*.

20. b.Baba Meṣi'a 59a. By contrast, in his *Instructions for Proper Conduct at Court*, the French rabbinic authority, Gersonides (d. 1344), uses the case of Haman consulting Zeresh to demonstrate that one may seek advice wherever it is to be found (in Walfish, *Esther in Medieval Garb*, 170).

21. The following verse (Q 66:11) takes things in the opposite direction, praising Pharaoh's wife for having been a believer despite her husband's villainy. It is worth clarifying here that the Qur'ān attributes to Pharaoh's wife the actions of Pharaoh's daughter in the biblical account, rendering this counter-example problematic.

22. "Cursed be Haman": b.Megillah 7b. "Cursed be Haman, cursed be his sons, and cursed be Zeresh": *Esther Rabba* 10:9 (where the phrase is attributed to the same Rav, who condemned to Hell those who heed their wives' advice).

23. Yahalom and Sokoloff, *Jewish Palestinian Aramaic Poetry*, 196–197, *piyyuṭ* no. 32, l. 4 (Hebrew) and l. 24 (Aramaic). On Zeresh's depiction in this *piyyuṭ*, see Lieber, "Stages of Grief," 118–121, and Münz-Manor, "Carnivalesque Ambivalence," 837–840.

24. Lieber, "Stages of Grief," 120. Thus, whereas the text of *Esther* portrays Zeresh as an unloving wife and implies (through her silence in Esth 9:5–10) that she "never displays maternal affection" (Zlotnick, *Dinah's Daughters*, 81), this *piyyuṭ* describes Zeresh as a mourning mother, motivated by her grief to take her own life.

25. Yahalom and Sokoloff, *Jewish Palestinian Aramaic Poetry*, 200–201.

26. Stal ("End of Zeresh," 79–80) reasons his way to the same conclusion, by drawing on the comparable context of Dan 6:25, where "wives" are specified as having also been cast into the lions' den.

27. Stal (ibid., 74 and 76–77) suggests that Zeresh survived because, as the daughter of Tattenai, she was not an Amalekite and thus did not merit death. Stal (ibid., 78), offers yet another suggestion as to Zeresh's fate, on the authority of the Moroccan Rabbi David Ṣabbāḥ (d. 1858), namely that Zeresh became a slave-woman to Esther (as *Esth* 8:2 says that Esther received Haman's "house" in 8:2, which Ṣabbāḥ interprets to mean, "wife"). See above, Ch 9, n 2.

28. The meaning and significance of the rope around Umm Jamīl's neck has puzzled exegetes for centuries. Al-Qurṭubī (d. 1273; *ad* Q 111:5) cites two relatively early opinions that interpret the verse to refer to Umm Jamīl's strangulation.

29. On the various etymological theories that relate Haman's sons' names in MT *Esther* to Zoroastrian *daivās*, see Yamauchi, *Persia and the Bible*, 237–238. The early-sixteenth century Karaite exegete Judah Gibbor also related the ten sons to the non-physical realm, arguing that Haman represented the evil inclination (*yeṣer ha-ra'*) and his ten sons were the five internal and five external forces that support it (in Walfish, *Esther in Medieval Garb*, 50–51).

30. As noted, both the OL and Josephus barely mention Haman's sons, presumably due to their attempt to downplay intercommunal tension between Jews and non-Jews.

31. See above, Ch 2, n 8.

32. In *Pirqe de Rabbi Eliezer*, 50:11 (trans. 408), for instance, we are told that ten of Haman's sons were royal scribes. That sons are expected to inherit their father's vocation is the starting point of another ANE court novella, the Aḥiqar tale, in which Aḥiqar is dismayed by his lack of a son to succeed him at court.

33. Hence, in b.Megillah 15b we are told that in addition to the ten sons who were hanged, Haman had ten sons who had previously died, as well as ten (or seventy!) other sons who, following the events recorded in *Esther*, became beggars seeking bread, a fact that brings them into line with Haman's own career as a beggar (to which we return below). Similarly, *Pirqe de Rabbi Eliezer*, 50:11 (trans. 408) tells us that in addition to the ten sons of Haman who served as royal scribes, thirty more sons served as governors in the empire's provinces (perhaps following in their grandfather Tattenai's footsteps).

34. b.Megillah 15b. On the number of Haman's sons in rabbinic literature, see Glickman, *Haman and the Jews*, 111 n 51. *Pirqe de Rabbi Eliezer*, 50:11 (trans. 408) holds that Haman had 40 sons, based on the fact that Haman's ten sons are mentioned on four different occasions in *Esther*.

35. Shimshai's activity in this regard is described in Ezra 4:8ff.

36. TgII 6:1.

37. b.Megillah 15b-16a. In TgI 6:1, Shimshai does not attempt to erase the writing but rather to turn the page so as to prevent the king from reading the account of Mordecai's heroism.

38. Stal ("On the identity of Shimshai the Scribe") analyzes various late antique and early medieval traditions on Shimshai as Haman's son. On Shimshai as Haman himself, see Glickman, *Haman and the Jews*, 44 n 6.

39. Segal, *Babylonian Esther Midrash*, 2:114ff.

40. In Stal, "On the identity of Shimshai the Scribe," 12 (quoting an early-medieval commentary on a late antique *piyyuṭ*).

41. The Hebrew uses the Greek term *hegemon* for "governor."

42. This midrash may be found in *Yalqut Shim'oni* §256, among other sources.

43. The midrash in *Yalqut Shim'oni* tells us that the son was governor of Qarduniya (modern Corduene). *Targum Jonathan* (*ad* Gen 8:4) mentions that it is in Qarduniya that Noah's Ark was to be found. Josephus (*Antiquities*, I.3.5) mentions more generally that Noah's Ark came to rest in Armenia.

44. Grossfeld, *Two Targums*, 187. This tradition is also found in a seventeenth-century Judeo-Arabic commentary on *Esther* (in Rivlin, *Perush*, 61).

45. b.Gittin 57b and b.Sanhedrin 96b.

46. In this passage, Nebuchadnezzar is referred to as "that wicked one" (b.Sanhedrin 96b), indicating that he was so reviled that his name could not be pronounced, and implying that he was more evil than even Haman (whose name could be uttered). And yet, in Esth 2:6, Nebuchadnezzar is described merely as "the king of Babylon," while it is Haman whose name is qualified by negative adjectives throughout the text.

47. The physical inheritability of Original Sin came to be a central doctrine of Christianity (see Rom 5:12–21, and the related Ps 51:5), in spite of the spiritualization of family bonds referred to earlier.

48. Curiously, although most Jewish authorities rejected the notion that Nebuchadnezzar and Pharaoh could repent, we have seen above (Ch 6, n 97) that no less a villain than Nero—deemed by some to be the Antichrist—converted to Judaism (as did Nebuzaradan; see b.Gittin 57b and b.Sanhedrin 96b).

49. See Silverstein, "Unmasking Maskh" (with sources).

50. Those who rejected Pharaoh's repentance based themselves on, among other things, Q 4:18, which states that, "repentance is not accepted from those who knowingly persist in sin until they start dying and then cry, 'Now I repent!'" On attitudes to Pharaoh's conversion in Abrahamic traditions, see Sinai, "Pharaoh's Submission to God," and Atzmon, "Did Pharaoh Repent?"

51. Nebuchadnezzar was (impossibly) said to have been the grandson of Nimrod (b.Ḥagigah 13a and b.Pesaḥim 94b), as was (even more impossibly) the Roman emperor Titus (b.Gittin 56b). Similarly, the rabbis who reviled Vashti held that she was the granddaughter of Nebuchadnezzar (b.Megillah 10b).

52. Although not a case of a villain's direct offspring converting, the rabbis held that Titus's nephew converted to Judaism (b.Gittin 56b-57a), which accrues significance when one considers that immediately preceding this is a description of Titus's torture and death caused by a mosquito, which brings him into line with such villains as Nebuchadnezzar and Nimrod (Lowin, "Narratives of Villainy").

53. To this list we may add Shaddād ibn ʿĀd (one son), who was the infamous opponent of the pre-Islamic Arabian prophet Hūd.

54. Jer 14:3–4.

55. Haman's daughter's name is unclear, but it appears to be a compound that relates to her "casting" (either from Hebrew: *sh-l-ḥ* or *sh-m-ṭ*, which is used in the Jezebel context) a "pot" (perhaps related to the Aramaic *ṭ-n-ʾ*, "basket").

56. Tg I 6:11 (trans. Grossfeld, *Two Targums*, 72). An equally-detailed version of the account, from the Sasanid side of the late antique divide, may be found in b.Megillah 16a.

57. In Grossfeld, *Two Targums*, 72 n 18.

58. Ibid., 63. Esther's prayer occurs precisely where her (and Mordecai's) prayers feature in the Greek versions (Addition C). In those versions, however, Haman's daughter is not mentioned.

59. For other versions of this midrash, see Glickman, *Haman and the Jews*, 38–39 and nn. 60–61. That Haman's actions caused his daughter to be "defiled with excrement" may have generated the midrash in which she eventually covers him with excrement, in the sort of reversal that is typical of *Esther*.

60. In Carruthers, *Esther through the Centuries*, 86.

61. Clines, *Esther Scroll*, 125 and 143, and Segal, *Babylonian Esther Midrash*, 3:250, among others.

62. Al-Ṭabarī, *Taʾrīkh*, 1:653. See *Pirqe de Rabbi Eliezer* 49:13 (trans. 395) for a similar tradition, in which God invested Esther with beauty in order to make her attractive to those who saw her.

63. The Pentateuch includes numerous narrative cycles that pivot around fraternal tensions. One wonders why the exegetes did not consider whether Haman had an upright sibling such as Abel, Shem, Isaac, Jacob, or Joseph, to balance out his villainy.

64. For a detailed treatment of this topic, see Silverstein, *Veiling Esther*, 79–91, especially 84–90 (with sources).

65. *Mujmal al-tawārīkh wa al-qiṣaṣ*, 190. Interestingly, according to medieval Jewish and Islamic traditions, both Haman and Haran were astrologers (Haran: Lowin, *Making of a Forefather*, 118 n 71, and 201; Haman: *Pirqe de Rabbi Eliezer*, 50:6 (trans. 399), and Carruthers, *Esther through the Centuries*, 144).

66. Deh Khodā, *Lughat Nāma*, s.v.v "Hāmān" and "Hāmān-sūz." It should be noted that in these entries Deh Khodā states that he is relying on Mirẓā 'Alī Akbarkhān Nafīsī's (d. 1964) dictionary, albeit without providing details. The point here is not the provenance of Deh Khodā's information, but rather that the prestige the *Lughat Nāma* holds in Iran makes its entry on "Haman" significant.

67. Al-Ṭabarī, *Ta'rīkh*, 1:252. This is the first of two options that al-Ṭabarī provides, the second being the expected Iraq.

68. On Nimrod's widespread association with the Tower of Babel, see Kiel, "Abraham and Nimrod."

69. Ginzberg (*Legends of the Jews*, 1:197–198) cites a midrash in which Nimrod is vexed by the challenge of Abraham and, in order to determine how to deal with him, Nimrod holds a seven-day feast at which he consults his advisors. This vignette echoes Ahashwerosh's behavior in the Esther story.

70. It should be admitted, nonetheless, that some Muslim exegetes, drawing on Jewish and Christian sources, specifically associate the Tower of Babel with Nimrod.

71. Jub 12:9–14, and Kugel, *Traditions of the Bible*, 267. Gen 11:28 merely says: "And Haran died in the presence of his father Terah in the land of his nativity, in Ur of the Chaldees." Exegetes have read "Ur of the Chaldees" not as a place name but as an event—"the Chaldean Fire."

72. *Genesis Rabba* 38:11, and see Kiel, "Abraham and Nimrod," 36ff.

73. The earliest source for this is pseudo-Philo from the second century CE (Kiel, "Abraham and Nimrod," 42).

74. Spicehadler, "Shahin's Influence," 162.

75. Another important piece of the Haran-Haman death-by-fire puzzle is the account in Dan 3. Here, three Jews refused to bow to Nebuchadnezzar's idol, for which they were threatened with being cast into a blazing furnace (only for their ill-wishers to suffer this fate in their stead).

76. The relatively succinct AT does not mention Haman's wealth.

77. Another, equally negative verdict on wealth attributed to Jesus may be found in Matt 6:19–21, where serving God and serving Mammon (wealth) are contrasted and deemed mutually exclusive.

78. The rabbis' version of the eye of a needle metaphor stresses the high improbability of an elephant (sic!) fitting through the eye of a needle (b.Berachot 55b and b.Baba Meṣi'a 38b). See n 121 above.

79. The Qur'ān's replacement of wealth with arrogance and denial of revelation may relate to the fact that Muḥammad's first wife, Khadijah, is said to have been wealthy.

80. b.Pesachim 119a: Korah took one third of the treasures that Joseph had buried in Egypt. Q 28:78: Qārūn attributed his success to his own wisdom. That both the Talmud (b.Sanhedrin 110a) and the Qur'ān (28:76) refer to the excessive weight of the keys of Korah's treasure indicates a relationship between the Korah lore in these respective traditions.

81. In Glickman, *Haman and the Jews*, 97 and the sources in n 29.

82. *Pirqe de Rabbi Eliezer* 50:5 (trans. 398), and *Esther Rabba* 7:5.

83. See above, Ch 9, n 18.

84. Charles ("Chiliarchs of Achaemenid Persia") has challenged the tendency to refer to Achaemenid "viziers" by the term "chiliarch" (derived from Greek *khiliarkhos*, and literally meaning "a commander of a thousand [soldiers]," like the biblical Hebrew *alūph* or the Old Persian *hazarapatiš*).

85. Other examples of the connection between wisdom and architecture include the reference to Jesus—who is "wise" in Rom 16:27 and Josephus's *Antiquities*, XVIII.3.3—as *ardēkhlâ* ("the architect") in late antique Syriac sources. Similarly, Ephrem the Syrian states that Jesus

is expected to descend to earth and erect a tower reaching up to heaven (in Kronholm, *Motifs from Genesis 1–11*, 211–212). Moreover, in Manichean psalms from this period the equivalent term *bān rabbâ* (literally, "great builder") is used for God (Murray, *Symbols of Church and Kingdom*, 223–224).

86. See above, Ch 5, n 20.

87. Recall, for instance, Ibn 'Abd al-Ḥakam's report that Haman funded the building of the Gulf of Sardūs by extorting the local population (see above, Ch 5, n 41).

88. b.Megilla 15a (end)—15b. The full back-story may be found in *Yalqut Shim'oni* §1056 (see above, Ch 6, n 244).

89. *Pirqe de Rabbi Eliezer* 50:5 (trans. 398). Friedlander renders *kotevīm ve-notarīn* as "keeping guard before [Haman]," but it is more likely that *notarīn* is a gloss on *kotevīm* (or vice versa), as the Byzantine bureaucracy in late antiquity was staffed with *notarioi*, ("scribes") of various sorts.

90. What follows is based on Silverstein, *Veiling Esther*, 127–145.

91. Al-Maqdisī, *al-Bad' wa al-ta'rīkh*, 3:81–82.

92. Al-Kisā'ī, *Qiṣaṣ al-anbiyā'*, 1:196–199 (trans. Thackston, 210–11).

93. Al-Bīrūnī, *al-Āthār al-bāqiya*, 280–81 (translation adapted from Sachau, *Chronology of Ancient Nations*, 273–274).

94. Diodorus Siculus, XVI:51.2.

95. In Boeschoten and O'Kane, *Al-Rabghūzī*, 2:253–54.

96. Sibṭ ibn al-Jawzī, *Mir'at al-zamān*, 2:30.

97. Bearing in mind the context here (as well as in Gen 39, where the title is also used), it is clear that the title indicates a functionary of a much higher standing than "chief cook."

98. The mishnah (m.Baba Meṣi'a 2:1) refers to "bakers' loaves," using the Hebrew phrase *kikkarot shel naḥtom*, recalling the "talents" (Hebrew: *kikkar*, which may also mean "loaves") of silver that Haman offers the king in *Esther* 3:9.

99. *Sefer ha-Yashar*, 40–42. The earliest manuscript of this work is from 1552. For an analysis of this text as it relates to al-Rabghūzī's, see Silverstein, *Veiling Esther*, 141–145.

100. The number twenty-two may well be topological: In Judg 10:3 Yair judged Israel for twenty-two years; in 1 Kgs 14:20 Jeroboam (a negative figure) reigned for twenty-two years; and in 1 Kgs 16:29, Ahab (whose father Omri was particularly evil) ruled Samaria for twenty-two years; among other examples.

101. *Leviticus Rabba* (28:6), a midrashic compilation that probably dates from the seventh century CE, describes Haman as having been *comes (rerum) privatarum* and *comes calator*, these being high ranking imperial positions. TgII 5:2 also associated Haman with a Byzantine profession, referring to him as a *speculator* (a special agent of sorts; see above, Ch 6, n 167). *Esther Rabba* 10:4 also suggests that it was Haman's father who had served in these capacities.

102. *Esther Rabba* 10:7.

103. Lieber, *Jewish Aramaic Poetry*, 119 (*piyyuṭ* 33, l. 39) and 120 *ad* line 49 for bath attendant.

104. Tanḥum ha-Yerushalmi, in Wechsler, *Strangers in the Land*, 312–313 *ad* Esth 6:11; and TgII 6:12 (Grossfeld, *Two Targums*, 176 and n 39).

105. Stable boy: Sabar, "The Purim Panel at Dura;" Roman chariot racer: Levit-Tawil, "The Purim Panel."

106. In support of this theory are the facts that in the Talmud (b.Megillah 16a) Mordecai refers to Haman only as a barber, and that "barber" is the only profession common to all traditions in this complex of midrashim.

107. See above, Ch 6, n 33 and Ch 9, n 65.

108. Note the debate on the influence of astrology in b.Shabbat 156a and the diversity of opinion regarding Haman's astrology in Walfish, *Esther in Medieval Garb*, 55ff.

109. Ibid., 57.

110. See Carruthers, *Esther through the Centuries*, 144. Hints of an association between Haman and gambling appeared centuries earlier when, as seen above, al-Kisāʾī's version of the Haman back-story included the fact that the villain (in this case, Pharaoh) had gambled all of his money away.

111. See Crone and Silverstein, "The Ancient Near East and Islam."

112. On the fraught yet fascinating question whether "the rabbis" actually believed their midrashim to be historically accurate, see Milikowsky, "Midrash as Fiction and Midrash as History," where the author argues that the rabbis did not hold their traditions to be accurate reflections of the past.

Chapter Ten: Haman's Death

1. The miracle of Pharaoh's well-preserved body features, unsurprisingly, in popular contexts. See, for instance: https://seekingoftruth.com/2013/03/19/pharaohs-body-preserved-as-predicted-by-the-Qur'ān-1400-years-ago/. Related to this are the reports (here, too, by and for popular consumption), that Haman's tower has been discovered. See, for instance: https://www.youtube.com/watch?app=desktop&v=zDNiHsio5zg.

2. Some Muslim exegetes (e.g., al-Samʿānī, *Tafsīr*, 1:79) do assume that Haman was drowned together with Pharaoh.

3. Sibṭ Ibn al-Jawzī, *Mirʾat al-zamān*, 2:59, Al-Nuwayrī, *Nihāyat al-arab*, 13:196, and al-Thaʿlabī, *al-Kashf*, 20:57.

4. As seen, Haman is described as having been crucified in the LXX, Vulgate, Josephus, Rhabanus Maurus, *Genesis Rabba*, and other sources.

5. Although it is not an example of poetic justice, the reference to the chief baker in the Joseph cycle being hanged from a tree (Gen 40:19) employs the same vocabulary found in MT *Esther* regarding Haman.

6. Note also the description in Deut 21:22–23, where it is stated (in language echoed in *Esther*) that hanging a criminal from a tree overnight is associated with disrespecting God and defiling the land that He is allocating to the Israelites. See above, Ch 3, n 8, for Paul's use of these verses with reference to Jesus in Gal 3:13.

7. See Shemesh, "How shall we kill him?" for an analysis of rabbinic discussions concerning Haman's execution. For midrashic elaboration on the tree chosen for Haman's gallows, see e.g., *Esther Rabba* 9:2. Haman's pleading with Mordecai for clemency moments before his execution is found in TgII 7:9, and it has an interesting parallel in modern Iranian practices, an example of which may be found in Maghen, *Reading Revolutionary Iran*, 646.

8. Important studies of this topic include: Horowitz, *Reckless Rites*; Goodman, *Purim Anthology*; Lewinsky, *Smiting Haman in the Diaspora*; Shamir, "The Smiting of Haman"; and Cohen, "Cursed Be Haman?".

9. *Genesis Rabba* 49:1.

10. The halakhic obligation to curse Haman and his sons is attributed to Rav (d. 247) in y.Megilla 3:7. A similar statement is found in *Massekhet Soferim* 14:6. Note that in the *Shulḥan Arukh*, the leading compendium of orthodox Jewish law, it is stated that one is commanded to get so drunk on Purim that he cannot distinguish between "cursed be Haman" and "blessed be Mordecai" (*Orakh Ḥayyīm*, 695:2, based on b.Megilla 7b).

11. Rubenstein, "Purim, Liminality, and Communitas," 265–272. Building on Bakhtinian theories of carnivalesque, Umberto Eco has made the salient point that temporarily upending the existing order actually serves to highlight the contours of that order (see Fisch, "Reading and Carnival").

12. For a useful summary of this enormous topic, see Kitz, "Curses and Cursing."

13. Silverstein, "Original Meaning," *passim*, especially 23–24.

14. See above, Ch 6, n 199, for Yefet ben 'Eli's use of this term, following his Karaite predecessor Salmon ben Yeruḥam.

15. Lewinsky, *Smiting Haman in the Diaspora*, 70 (Tunisia) and 75 (Tashkent, where Zeresh was cursed too), among a multitude of other examples. Related to this is the fact that in an early-fourteenth century parody of the *Esther* story, Zeresh, Amalek, and Haman repeatedly leveled curses against each other (Cohen, "Cursed be Haman?" 482–485).

16. To the far better-known verse in Deut 25:19 that is adduced in Haman-effacing contexts we may add *Proverbs* 10:7 ("the name of the wicked shall rot"), which was associated with Haman despite its not containing any direct instruction to efface a villain's name.

17. Curiously, the laws concerning the placing of holy texts in a pile are discussed in b.Megillah 27a.

18. On the miraculous nature of Qur'ānic texts, see Zadeh, "'Fire Cannot Harm It,'" and Silverstein, "Who are the *Aṣḥāb al-Ukhdūd*?" 302–305.

19. Such practices were not limited to Purim: A seventeenth century scribe is said to have tested his new quills by writing "Haman," "Amalek," or "Zeresh," only to erase them immediately (in Horowitz, *Reckless Rites*, 109).

20. See the various examples recorded in Lewinsky, *Smiting Haman in the Diaspora*, 25ff. And see Shamir, "The Smiting of Haman," for a study of the noisemakers used in medieval Europe to drown out Haman's name.

21. Sperber, "Effacing Haman's Name," 205–206.

22. The Hebrew phrase *yemaḥ shemo ve-zikhro* ("may his name and remembrance be erased") has popularly been appended to the names of hated figures for centuries, and it appears to originate in customs related to the punishment of Haman.

23. Ron, "Tattenai and Haman," 257.

24. On crucifixion and impalement in Achaemenid Persia, see Llewellyn-Jones, *Ancient Persia and the Book of Esther*, 160–162, and Shemesh, *Punishment and Sins*, 27–34.

25. Josephus (*Antiquities*, XI.6.11) specifies that Haman was killed by the act of hanging.

26. The chief baker in the Joseph cycle (Gen 40:19) is also described as having been killed and thereafter hanged from a tree, and it is this sort of treatment that is referred to in Deut 21:22–23 and in Gal 3:13.

27. Lewinsky, *Smiting Haman in the Diaspora*, 82.

28. Ibid., 74.

29. See Ibn Manẓūr, *Mukhtaṣar ta'rīkh dimashq*, 14:9, where we are told that God will punish the followers of the *Murji'a* (a theological trend in early Islam) "together with Haman."

30. Lewinsky, *Smiting Haman in the Diaspora*, 52 (citing an example from Iran). This idea may be distantly related to the tradition (in b.Megillah 16a and b.Menaḥot 65a) that Mordecai was a member of the Sanhedrin, which was entrusted with judgments involving capital punishment.

31. In some communities, Jews produced mock *ashkava* ("laying to rest") prayers to be said over Haman, with comedic contents (Lewinsky, *Smiting Haman in the Diaspora*, 40). According to Jewish law, such prayers were only to be said for Jews, a fact that did not appear to concern Jews celebrating Purim. Alternatively, it is the ironic application of Jewish law to the leading anti-Jew that was intended in these contexts.

32. For fire ordeals in the judicial systems of ancient Iran, see Boyce, "Ātaš," 3:1–5, and eadem, "On Mithra, Lord of Fire," 70–72. See also Shaki, "Judicial and Legal Systems," 15:177–180.

33. See Silverstein, "Who are the *Aṣḥāb al-Ukhdūd*?" 291–302 (with sources).

34. Examples of Haman-burning in Persianate societies may be found in Lewinsky, *Smiting Haman in the Diaspora*, 53–54 (Tehran), 75 (Tashkent), 75–76 (Mashhad), among others.

Ginzberg ("Genizah Studies," 650–652) quotes Gaonic descriptions of children in Babylonia and Persia ("Elam") making a Haman effigy, exposing it on a rooftop for four to five days, and then burning it on Purim. This practice is related there to a Purim custom whereby children would leap over a fiery pit (b.Sanhedrin 64b). The latter custom strikes me as a variation on the Iranian *Chāhārshanbe-Sūrī* (Red Wednesday) festival, which takes place on the final Wednesday of the solar year and has as its central feature men, women, and children jumping over bonfires (see Kasheff and Sīrjānī, "Čahāršanba-Sūrī").

35. Lewinsky, *Smiting Haman in the Diaspora*, 18–19 (Yemen), 70 (Tunisia), and 82–83 (Libya). That Jewish children in Tunisia were exempted from Torah study to prepare the Haman effigy illustrates how important the custom was taken to be.

36. Ibid., 69 (Hungary).

37. Recall also that in the late antique *Megillat Antiochus*, the story's Hamanic character, Bacchides, is executed by burning (MA, v. 59).

38. Thornton, "Crucifixion of Haman," 424, and Horowitz, *Reckless Rites*, 158.

39. Horowitz, *Reckless Rites*, 272, and see above, Ch 6, n 147.

40. Brauer and Patai, *Jews of Kurdistan*, 358.

41. See b.Mo'ed Qatan 15a, for an equivalent, rabbinic custom of stoning the burial site of an outcast.

42. Silverstein, "Original Meaning," 21–23 (with sources).

43. It would seem that adulterers might be subjected to either corporal punishment or execution by stoning: the Qur'ān prescribes one hundred lashes (Q 24:1–2), while the ḥadīth literature specifies that adulterers are to be stoned to death. (https://sunnah.com/shahwaliullah40:23, https://sunnah.com/tirmidhi:1432, https://sunnah.com/ibnmajah:2553, and others).

44. For example, Lewinsky (*Smiting Haman in the Diaspora*, 57) describes a Spanish community's custom of stoning Haman in effigy.

45. Ibid., 48.

46. For this custom, common in thirteenth- to fifteenth-century Italian communities, see Horowitz, *Reckless Rites*, 272–272, and n 88. The verse that accompanied the action of breaking the jar is Isa 30:14, which refers to the smashing of a potter's vessel.

47. A particularly (in)famous example of exocannibalism in Islamic history is Hind bint 'Utba's attempt to eat the liver of Muḥammad's uncle, Ḥamza, during the battle of Uḥud (625).

48. Lewinsky, *Smiting Haman in the Diaspora*, 57. For a description of an entire Purim-scene constructed of sugar, which was displayed at a Purim festival in Amsterdam in 1778, see Shamir, "The Smiting of Haman," 148.

49. Ibid., 148–149.

50. Shulḥan Arukh, *Orakh Ḥayyīm*, 695:2. Perhaps it is relevant here that some midrashic sources identify Hatakh (Esth 4) with Daniel. In other sources, Esther herself is described as having survived at the Persian court on a diet of seeds (though not specifically poppyseeds; b.Megillah 13a).

51. Lewinsky, *Sefer ha-Mo'adim*, 6:153–154.

52. https://www.oed.com/dictionary/jews-ear_n?tab=etymology and https://www.oed.com/dictionary/judass-ear_n?tab=meaning_and_use#289512353.

53. Lewinsky (*Sefer ha-Mo'adim*, 6:130–131) relates that Jews in Afghanistan hold egg-painting competitions on Purim, which brings to mind Easter practices.

54. Shamir, "The Smiting of Haman," 150. The cropping of criminals' ears is an ancient practice, known from Hittite, Ancient Egyptian, late antique, medieval, and other contexts (see Geltner, *Flogging Others*, 35, 39, 56, 60, and 65).

55. Wilk, "Abuse of Nicanor's Corpse," 56.

56. Accounts of Purim celebrations in a number of Kurdish communities include descriptions of sporting events held on Purim in which a ball representing Haman's head was smacked around in games that resemble hockey or baseball (Brauer and Patai, *Jews of Kurdistan*, 357). While some chose to eat Haman's body parts, others chose to beat them.

57. Benko, *Virgin Goddess*, 185–186, and Pope, *Song of Songs*, 222 and 378–379.

58. Sivan, *Palestine in Late Antiquity*, 155.

59. See above, Ch 7, n 7.

60. Bauer and Patai, *Jews of Kurdistan*, 357.

61. Harel, "Likhvod ha-Umah," 21–22.

62. See, e.g., Haupt, *Purim*, 3 and 25–26 n 11; Horowitz, *Reckless Rites*, 224; and Rubenstein, "Purim, Liminality, and Communitas," 248–249. Late antique Jews themselves appear to have been aware of similarities between Purim and ancient pagan holidays, specifically the Roman Saturnalia (*Esther Rabba* 7:12).

63. Less well-received was Frazer's theory that Jesus's death by crucifixion was part of just such a festival. For a rebuttal of Frazer's theories, see Leach, "Kingship and Divinity."

64. Frankfort, *Kingship and the Gods*, 328.

65. See above, Ch 8, n 131. The reception of the Magophonia in late antiquity and the transformation of the holiday to one in which a national hero (such as the *ShāhNāma*'s Fereydūn) defeats an exemplary villain (such as the *ShāhNāma*'s Zahhāk), are discussed in Cristoforetti, "Mehragān." See Shahbazi, "Hōmān," for the idea that Hōmān's defeat in the *ShāhNāma* negatively reoriented Ṭūrānian history, in a way that recalls interpretations of Haman's defeat and Amalekite fortunes.

66. Sivan, *Palestine in Late Antiquity*, 170. Interestingly, *piyyuṭim* from late antique Palestine refer to Haman as a native of Scythopolis (see above, Ch 6, n 129 and Ch 8, n 20).

67. The custom of burning effigies of Romans is described by Abū l-Fatḥ in Stenhouse, *Kitāb al-Ta'rīkh*, 186.

68. Carruthers, *Esther through the Centuries*, 273.

69. Frazer, *Golden Bough*, 120–146.

70. Lewinsky, *Smiting Haman in the Diaspora*, 44–45. Other comparisons between Judas and Haman have been explored earlier.

71. Fraser, *Gunpowder Plots*.

72. Oddly, Davies ("Haman the Victim," 137) states that "the Jewish Guy Fawkes is called Haman," thereby ignoring both that the Protestant Haman is Guy Fawkes and that Jews in England may also celebrate Guy Fawkes Night.

73. It worth noting that the leader of the Gunpower Plot, Robert Catesby, sought to have his daughter enthroned as queen, which brings to mind midrashim about Haman's plot to have his daughter replace Vashti.

74. Bradley-Birt, *Through Persia*, 114 (describing Omar Koshan in Shiraz, 1909). Before him, writing in 1845–1847, Binning (*A Journal of Travel in Persia, Ceylon*, 1:428–429) also compared Omar Koshan to Guy Fawkes Night.

75. See Floor, *History of Theatre in Iran*, 124–199. A limited number of *Ta'ziyah* descriptions exist from the earlier, Buyid period of Shī'a rule in Iran-Iraq (r. 945–1055).

76. Daryaee, and Malekzadeh, "Performance of Pain and Remembrance."

77. While *'Āshūrā'* is undoubtedly a day of mourning for Shī'a Muslims, the theological interpretation of Ḥusayn's martyrdom as being premeditated (for, as an infallible Imām, he will have been aware of the eventual outcome of his rebellion) brings to mind Christian interpretations of Jesus's crucifixion, which was seen as a moment of suffering, but one that was theologically essential for mankind's salvation.

78. Horowtiz, *Reckless Rites*, 269. The author was Pablo de Santa Maria (d. 1435), an apostate from Judaism born as "Solomon ha-Levi." That he converted to Christianity a year or two after composing this poem renders its accuracy questionable.

79. Note that in rural Iranian communities, villagers who were questioned about the nature of the carnivalesque Omar Koshan celebrations (to which we turn shortly), thought that they were commemorating Ḥusayn's martyrdom (Floor, *History of Theatre in Iran*, 211).

80. Ibid., 206.

81. Ibid., 205.

82. General treatments may be found in ibid., 203–212, Gaffary, "Evolution of Rituals and Theatre in Iran," and Torab, *Performing Islam*, 194–222.

83. Stewart, "Popular Shiism in Medieval Egypt," 46–48. As seen (Ch 8, n 79), already in the ninth century, this 'Umar was equated with Haman in Shīʿa sources.

84. Gaffary, "Evolution of Rituals and Theatre in Iran," 366.

85. For instance, Wills (*Persia As It Is*, 217–222), describes an Omar Koshan in 1880s Shiraz at which Jews played music and acted as buffoons.

86. Alternatively, the festival could be held on the twenty-sixth day of Dhū al-Ḥijjah.

87. b.Megillah 13b.

88. Wilson, *Persian Life and Customs*, 201. Writing in the 1890s, Wilson describes the Omar Koshan as "an occasion of great joy and cursing."

89. Stewart, "Popular Shiism in Medieval Egypt," 47 (Omar cookies oozing syrup-blood); Floor, *History of Theatre in Iran*, 203 (burning an effigy of Omar); 206, and 210 (intensification of cursing Omar, abusing effigies of Omar).

90. Shiel, *Glimpses of Life and Manners in Persia*, 139–140.

91. Floor, *History of Theatre in Iran*, 208.

92. For examples of Omarophobia in modern Iran, see: https://sonsofsunnah.com/2013/01/19/omar-koshan-9th-rabi-the-celebration-of-omars-ra-death-a-shia-majoosi-fetish/.

93. Horowitz, *Reckless Rites*, 95, and Narkis and Cohen-Mushlin, "Illumination of the Worms Maḥzor," 82.

94. Sisyphus, like Haman, was a hubristic tyrant, whose punishment, like Haman's, is repeated eternally. Also comparable to Haman's repeated deaths at Purim is the punishment promised in Sunnī Islam to those who take their own life: According to trustworthy (*ṣaḥīḥ*) ḥadīths, the Prophet stated that whoever commits suicide will be made to repeat the action in Hell for eternity. Examples of such ḥadīths (preserved by al-Bukhārī) may be found here: https://sunnah.com/bukhari:1365; https://sunnah.com/bukhari:6652; and https://sunnah.com/bukhari:1363.

Conclusions

1. As Lacocque ("Haman in the Book of Esther," 213) put it: "It is clear that Haman may ostensibly belong to any nation or group which happens to be inimical to the Jews at a given time." As seen throughout this book, Lacocque's statement must be expanded to take in Christian and Muslim conceptions of Haman.

2. The distinction between the ruler and his representative was not lost on late antique rabbis. In b.Ḥullin 89a, Haman is excluded from a list of hubristic rulers that includes Nimrod, Pharaoh, Sennacherib, Nebuchadnezzar, and Hiram. By contrast, Haman is included in a list of villains and other sinners in history who "desired that which they did not deserve," alongside Korah, Doeg, Balaam, and others (b.Sotah 9b).

3. Ibn Taghribirdī's *al-Nujūm al-zāhira*, 1:56.

4. A good example of the (Sunnī) schematization of leading villains in history is 'Abd al-Ḥakīm Murād's sermon, delivered August 12, 2022, in which he mentions Pharaoh, Nimrod,

and Abū Lahab as the respective opponents of Moses, Abraham, and Muḥammad (see: https://www.youtube.com/watch?app=desktop&v=G071PoICo9E).

5. For a discussion of this ḥadīth, see: https://islamonline.net/هذا-فرعون-هذه-الأمة/#:~:text=فرعون%20هذه%20الأمة%20عمرو%20بن,ذاته،%20لا%20يأبه%20برأي%20الآخرين, and https://www.islamweb.net/ar/fatwa/15606/فرعون-أمة-محمد-عليه-الصلاة-والسلام. See also Yasir Qadhi's remarks on Abū Jahl as the Pharaoh of the *ummah*, and on Yazīd I (r. 680–683), as "worse than Pharaoh," which may be found at: https://m.youtube.com/watch?v=BUYD_xv5xQ8.

6. Horowitz, *Reckless Rites*, 13 (Michaelis), and 253 (Reform Jews).

7. Bill Burr's sketch, broadcast on February 21, 2016, may be found at: https://www.youtube.com/watch?app=desktop&v=OG0rlDIqoeQ. Burr's reference to Attila as a "retired" name is inaccurate as the name is still used in Hungary and Turkey.

8. *Genesis Rabba* 49:1. Immediately following Shmuel ben Naḥman's statement we are told that Rav (d. 247) would curse Haman and his sons.

9. See Rosenthal, "With the Help of ha-Shem." It is worth noting that names such as Nimrod, Hagar, and Ishmael—all of which have negative connotations in Jewish tradition—are in common use in modern Israel. The use of Nimrod is especially interesting for its combination of negative cultural connotations with an etymology that means "we shall rebel." It was adopted in modern Israeli society in the context of the Canaanism movement (see Ohana, "Myth of Nimrod").

BIBLIOGRAPHY

Adali, S. Ferruh. *The Scourge of God: The Umman-Manda and Its Significance in the First Millennium B.C.*, Winona Lake, 2011.

Adang, C. "The Chronology of the Israelites According to Hamza al-Isfahani," *JSAI* 32 (2006), 286–310.

Aelian. *Claudius Aelianus His Various History* (Th. Stanley trans.), London, 1665.

Agapius of Manbīj. *Kitāb al-'unvān*, ed./trans. A. A. Vasiliev, Paris, 1912.

Agostini, D. "The Perception of the Romans (*hromayig*) in the Sasanian and Zoroastrian Traditions," *Mediterranean Historical Review* 37i (2022), 1–18.

Allepo Megillah: *Megillat Esther: Le-fi minhag yahadut aram-ṣoba (Ḥalab)*, Tel Aviv, 2005.

Alexander, Ph. "3 Maccabees, Hanukkah, and Purim," in A. Rapoport-Albert and G. Greenberg (eds.), *Biblical Hebrew, Biblical Texts: Essays in memory of Michael P. Weitzman*, London, 2001, 321–339.

Allepo Megillah: *Megillat Esther: Le-fi minhag yahadut aram-ṣoba (Ḥalab)*, Tel Aviv, 2005.

Amit, Y. "The Saul Polemic in the Persian Period," in O. Lipschits and M. Oeming (eds.), *Judah and the Judeans in the Persian Period*, Winona Lake, 2006, 647–661.

Anderson, B. W. "The Place of the Book of Esther in the Christian Bible," *Journal of Religion* 30 (1950), 32–43.

Anderson, G. and M. Stone, *A Synopsis of the Books of Adam and Eve*, Atlanta, 1999.

Antrim, Z. *Routes and Realms: The Power of Place in the Early Islamic World*, Oxford, 2012.

Asmussen, J. P. "Judeo-Persica I: Shahin-i Shirazi's Ardashir-Nama," *Acta Orientalia* 28 (1965), 245–261.

Atzmon A. "Did Pharaoh Repent? On the Development and Transformation of an Aggadic Motif," *European Journal of Jewish Studies* 13 (2019), 3–27.

Augustine of Hippo, *The City of God* (trans. W. Babcock), Hyde Park, NY, 2012.

Aus, R. *Water into Wine and the Beheading of John the Baptist*, Providence, 1988.

Badawi, A. "Le problème de Haman," in R. Traini (ed.), *Studi in onore di Francesco Gabrieli*, Rome, 1984, 29–33.

Bailyn, B. *The Ideological Origins of the American Revolution*, Cambridge, Mass., 1967.

Baumgarten, A. "Sacred Scriptures Defile the Hands," *JJS* 67i (2016), 46–67.

Beal, T. *Book of Hiding: Gender, Ethnicity, Annihilation and Esther*. London, 1997.

Beaulieu, P. A. *The Pantheon of Uruk during the Neo-Babylonian Period*, Leiden, 2003.

Beck, D. *Evolution of the Qur'ān: From Anonymous Apocalypse to Charismatic Prophet*, New York, 2018.

Bellmann, S. "The Theological Character of the Old Latin Version of Esther," *Journal for the Study of the Pseudepigrapha* 27i (2017), 3–24.

Bellmann, S. and A. Portier-Young, "The Old Latin book of Esther: An English Translation," *Journal for the Study of the Pseudepigrapha* 28iv (2019), 267–289.

Benjamin of Tudela (trans. N. A. Adler), *The Itinerary of Benjamin of Tudela*, Oxford, 1907.

Benko, S. *The Virgin Goddess: Studies in the Pagan and Christian Roots of Mariology*, Leiden, 2004.

Benson, M. "Violence in the Behistun Monument," Unpublished Ph.D. thesis, U.C.L., 2020.

Berkovitz, A. J. "Jewish and Christian Exegetical Controversy in Late Antiquity: The Case of Psalm 22 and the Esther Narrative," in G. Allen and J. A. Dunne (eds.), *Ancient Readers and Their Scriptures: Engaging the Hebrew Bible in Early Judaism and Christianity*, Leiden, 2019, 222–239.

Berlin, A. "The Book of Esther and Ancient Storytelling," *JBL* 120i (2001), 3–14.

Berman, J. "Aggadah and Anti-Semitism: The Midrashim to Esther 3:8," *Judaism* 38ii (1989), 185–196.

Bickerman, E. *Four Strange Books of the Bible: Jonah, Daniel, Koheleth, Esther*, New York, 1967.

Bidmean, J. *The Akītu Festival: Religious Continuity and Royal Legitimation in Mesopotamia*, Piscataway, 2004.

Binning, R. M. A *Journal of Two Years' Travel in Persia, Ceylon, Etc.*, London, 1857.

Bīrūnī, Abū Rayḥān al-, *al-Āthār al-Bāqiya min al-qurūn al-khāliya*, Leipzig, 1923; translation: E. Sachau, *The Chronology of Ancient Nations*, London, 1879.

Black S. A. (et al.), *A Concise Dictionary of Akkadian*, Wiesbaden, 2000.

Bledsoe, S. *The Wisdom of the Aramaic Book of Ahiqar: Unravelling a Discourse of Uncertainty and Distress*, Leiden, 2022.

Bloom, J. *Paper before Print: The History and Impact of Paper in the Islamic World*, New Haven, 2001.

Boeschoten, H. E. and J. O'Kane. *Al-Rabghūzī: The Stories of the Prophets. Qiṣaṣ al-Anbiyā': An Eastern Turkish Version* (Second Edition), Leiden, 2015.

Börner-Klein, D. and E. Hollender. *Die Midraschim zu Ester: Rabbinische Kommentare zum Buch Ester*, Leiden, 2000 (2 vols.).

Bowman, J. (ed./trans.), *Samaritan Documents Relating to Their History, Religion, and Life*, Pittsburgh, 1977.

Boyce, M. "On Mithra, Lord of Fire," *Monumentum H. S. Nyberg I, Acta Iranica* 4 (1975), 70–72.

———. s.v. 'Ātaš' in *EIr*, 3:1–5.

Bradley-Birt, F. *Through Persia, from the Gulf to the Caspian*, London, 1909.

Brauer, E. and R. Patai, *The Jews of Kurdistan*, Detroit, 1993.

Brody, R. "On the Sources for the Chronology of the Talmudic Period," *Tarbiz* 70 (2000), 75–107.

Brown, D. *Mesopotamian Planetary Astronomy-Astrology*, Leiden, 2000.

Brown, P. *The World of Late Antiquity: AD 150–750*, London 1971.

Bush, F. W. "The Book of Esther: *Opus non gratum* in the Christian Canon," *Bulletin for Biblical Research* 8 (1998), 39–54.

Cairns, E. C. *Esther in Early Modern Iberia and the Sephardic Diaspora: Queen of the Conversas*, London, 2017.

Carruthers, J. *Esther through the Centuries*, Oxford: Blackwell, 2008.

———. "Esther and Hitler: A Second Triumphant Purim," in M. Lieb et al. (eds.), *The Oxford Handbook of the Reception History of the Bible*, Oxford, 2011, 515–528.

Cassell, P. *An Explanatory Commentary on Esther*, Edinburgh, 1888.

Chalupa, P. "The Book of Esther in Josephus: Authority of Conflict-causing Laws," in J. Dušek and J. Roskovec (eds.), *The Process of Authority: The Dynamics in Transmission and Reception of Canonical Texts*, Berlin, 2016, 139–150.

Chapman, D. W. *Ancient Jewish and Christian Perceptions of Crucifixion*, Tübingen, 2008.

Charles, M. "The Chiliarchs of Achaemenid Persia: Towards a Revised Understanding of the Office," *Phoenix* 69iii-iv (2015), 279–303.

Charlesworth, J. H. *The Old Testament Pseudepigrapha*, New York, 1983.
Clines D. J. *The Esther Scroll: The Story of the Story*, Atlanta, 1984.
———. "In Quest of the Historical Mordecai," *VT* 41iii (1991), 129–136.
Codoñer, J. S. *The Emperor Theophilos and the East 829–842: Court and Frontier during the Last Phase of Iconoclasm*, New York, 2016.
Cogan, M. "Achaemenid Inscriptions: Cyrus Cylinder," in W. H. Hallo and K. L. Younger (eds.), *The Context of Scripture. Vol. II: Monumental Inscriptions from the Biblical World*, Leiden, 2003.
Cohen, M. *The Martyrs: Luis de Carvajal: A Secret Jew in Sixteenth-Century Mexico*, Philadelphia, 1973.
Cohen, M. R. *Under Crescent and Cross: The Jews in the Middle Ages*, Princeton, 1994.
Cohen, M. Z. *The Rule of Peshat: Jewish Constructions of the Plain Sense of Scripture and Their Christian and Muslim Contexts*, Philadelphia, 2020.
Cohen, R. "'Cursed be Haman?': Haman as a Victim in the 14th Century Pardoy *Massekheth Purim*," in R. Sterman Sabbath (ed.), *Troubling Topics, Sacred Texts: Readings in the Hebrew Bible, the New Testament, and the Qur'an*, Berlin, 2021, 469–493.
Cowe, S. Peter, "Scribe, Translator, Redactor: Writing and Rewriting Scripture in the Armenian Versions of Esther, Judith, and Tobit," in A. Aejmalaeus and D. Longacre (eds.), *From Scribal Error to Rewriting: How Ancient Texts Could and Could Not Be Changed*, Göttingen, 2020, 247–280.
Cowley, A. *Aramaic Documents of the Fifth Century B.C.*, Oxford, 1923.
Cristoforetti, S. s.v. "MEHRAGĀN" in *EIr*, available at: https://iranicaonline.org/articles/mehragan
Crone, P. and A. Silverstein. "The Ancient Near East and Islam: The Case of Lot-Casting," *Journal of Semitic Studies* 55ii (2010), 423–450.
Crown, A.D., R. Pummer, and A. Tal (eds.), *Companion to Samaritan Studies*, Tübingen, 1993.
Curtis, V. "The Iranian Revival in the Parthian Period," in V.S. Curtis and S. Stewart (eds.), *The Age of the Parthians: The Idea of Iran, Volume II*, London, 2007, 7–25.
Dalley, S. *Esther's Revenge at Susa*, Oxford, 2008.
Damascelli, A. "Cross, Curse, and Redemption: An Echo of Purim in Galatians 3:13," *Henoch* 23 (2001), 227–241.
Damsma, A. "The Targums to Esther," *European Judaism* 47i (2014), 127–136.
Dandanmaev, M. A. s.v. "Magophonia" in *EIr*, available at: https://www.iranicaonline.org/articles/magophonia
Daryaee, T. and S. Malekzadeh, "The Performance of Pain and Remembrance in Late Ancient Iran," *The Silk Road* 12 (2014), 57–74.
Davidson, O. M. "Traces of Poetic Traditions about Cyrus the Great and his Dynasty in the *Šāhnāme* of Ferdowsi and the Cyrus Cylinder," in M. R. Shayegan (ed.), *Cyrus the Great: Life and Lore*, Boston, 2018, 232–241.
Davies, Ph. R. "Haman the Victim," in idem (ed.), *First Person: Essays in Biblical Autobiography*, Sheffield, 2002.
Davis, D. *Panthea's Children: Hellenistic Novels and Medieval Persian Romances*, New York, 2002.
Day, L. *Three Faces of a Queen: Characterization in the Book of Esther*, Sheffield, 1995.
Deh Khodā, 'Alī Akbar, *Lughat Nāma*, Tehran, 1946-
De Jong, A. *Traditions of the Magi: Zoroastrianism in Greek and Latin Literature*, Leiden, 1997.
Delgado, J. Pinto, *The Poem of Queen Esther* (trans. D. Slavitt), New York, 1999.
De Smet, D. "The Demon in Potentiality and the Devil in Actuality: Two Principles of Evil according to 4th/10th Century Ismailism," *Arabica* 69 (2022), 601–625.

De Troyer, K. "Cosmic Events in the First and Last Additions to the Greek Text of the Book of Esther," in M. W. Duggan, R. Egger-Wenzel, and S.C. Reif (eds.), *Cosmos and Creation: Second Temple Perspectives*, Boston, 2020, 77–90.

De Troyer, K. and T. Smith, "The Additions of the Greek Book(s) of Esther," in G. Oegema (ed.), *The Oxford Handbook of the Apocrypha*, Oxford, 2021, 387–396.

Diodorus Siculus: *Diodorus of Sicily in Twelve Volumes with an English Translation by C. H. Oldfather. Vol. 4–8*, London, 1989.

Domazakis, N. "On the date of composition of Additions B and E to LXX Esther," *Journal for the Study of Judaism* 52 (2021), 330–358.

Dönitz, S. "*Sefer Yosippon* (Josippon)," in H. H. Chapman and Z. Rodgers (eds.), *A Companion to Josephus*, Oxford, 2016, 382–389.

EI1: *Encyclopaedia of Islam, First Edition*, Leiden, 1913–1936.

EI2: *Encyclopaedia of Islam, Second Edition*, Leiden, 1960–2003.

EI3: *Encyclopaedia of Islam, THREE* (online only). Available at: https://referenceworks.brillonline.com/browse/encyclopaedia-of-islam-3

EQ: *Encyclopaedia of the Qur'ān*, Leiden, 2002–2006.

Erder, Y. "Mourners of Zion: The Karaites in Jerusalem in the Tenth and Eleventh Centuries," in M. Polliack (ed.), *Karaite Judaism: A Guide to its History and Literary Sources*, Leiden, 2003, 213–235.

Eusebius, *Church History* (trans. G. A. Williamson), London, 1989.

Fausett, L. C. "Evidence for a Typology of Christ in the Book of Esther," unpublished M.A. thesis, Brigham Young University, 2020.

Feldman, L. "Hellenizations in Josephus' Version of Esther," *Transactions and Proceedings of the American Philological Association* 101 (1970), 143–170.

———. "Some Observations on the Rabbinic Reaction to Roman Rule in Third Century Palestine," *HUCA* 63 (1992), 39–81.

———. *Studies in Josephus's Rewritten Bible*, Leiden, 1998.

Finkel, I. "The Cyrus Cylinder: The Babylonian Perspective," in I. Finkel (ed.), *The Cyrus Cylinder: The King of Persia's Proclamation from Ancient Babylon*, London, 2013, 4–34.

Fisch, H. "Reading and Carnival: On the Semiotics of Purim," *Poetics Today* 15i (1994), 55–74.

Floor, W. *The History of Theatre in Iran*, Washington, 2005.

Fox, M. V. *Redaction of the Books of Esther: On Reading Composite Texts*, Atlanta, 1991.

———. "Three Esthers," in L. Greenspoon and S. W. Crawford (eds.), *The Book of Esther in Modern Research*, London, 2003, 50–60.

Frankel, J. "'Ritual Murder' in the Modern Era: The Damascus Affair of 1840," *Jewish Social Studies* 3ii (1997), 1–16.

Frankfort, H. *Kingship and the Gods*, Chicago, 1948.

Fraser, A., B. Buchanan, D. Cannadine, D. Cressy, J. Champion, M. Jay, and P. Croft, *Gunpowder Plots: A Celebration of 400 Years of Bonfire Night*, London, 2005.

Frazer, J. *The Golden Bough, Volume 10*, Cambridge, 1913.

Frazer, M. "Heads and Beds: On the Origin of the Akkadian Term for Eunuch or Courtier," *Journal of Ancient Near Eastern History* 9i (2022), 95–112.

Freigburg, A. D. "A New Clue in the Dating of the Composition of the Book of Esther," *VT* 50iv (2000), 561–565.

Frenkel, Y. "Al-Maqrizi on the Jewish Fesitvals," in M. Gruber et al., *Teshura le-Zafrira: Studies in the Bible, the History of Israel, and the Ancient Near East presented to Zafrira Ben-Barak*, Beersheba, 2012, 325–343.

Freymer-Kensky, T. "The Tribulations of Marduk: The So-Called 'Marduk Ordeal text'," *JAOS* 103i (1983), 131–141

Friedenreich, D. "The Use of Islamic Sources in Saadiah Gaon's 'Tafsīr' of the Torah," *Jewish Quarterly Review* 93iii/iv (2003), 353–395.

Gaffary, F. "Evolution of Rituals and Theatre in Iran," *Iranian Studies* 17iv (1984), 361–389.

Gane, R. E. and C. E. Gane, "Cosmic Conflict and Divine Kingship in Babylonian Religion and Biblical Apocalypses," in J. Moskala (ed.), *Meeting with God on the Mountains: Essays in Honor of Richard M. Davidson*, Berrien Springs, 2016, 279–305.

Garrison, M. "By the Favor of Ahuramazda: Kingship and the Divine in the Early Achaemenid Period," in P. P. Iosiff et al (eds.), *More than Men, Less than Gods: Studies in Royal Cult and Imperial Culture*, Leuven, 2011, 15–104.

Gaspa, S. "State theology and Royal Ideology of the Neo-Assyrian Empire as a Structuring Model for the Achaemenid Imperial Religion," in W. Henkelman and C. Redard, *Persian Religion in the Achaemenid Period*, Wiesbaden, 2017, 125–184.

Gaster, T. *Purim and Hanukkah*, New York, 1950.

Gehman, H. S. "Notes on the Persian Words in the Book of Esther," *JBL* 43 (1924), 321–328.

Geltner, G. *Flogging Others: Corporal Punishment and Cultural Identity from Antiquity to the Present*, Amsterdam, 2014.

Gerleman, G. *Esther*, Neukirchen-Vluyen, 1970.

Gertoux, G. *Queen Esther, Wife of Xerxes: Chronological, Historical, and Archeological Evidence*, n.p., 2015.

Gignoux, Ph. "La démonisation d'Alexandre le Grand d'après la littérature pehlevie," in M. Macuch, M. Maggi, and W. Sunderman (eds.), *Iranian Languages and Texts from Iran and Turan: Ronald E. Emmerick memorial volume*. Wiesbaden, 2007, 87–97.

Gilbert, M. *The Holocaust: The Jewish Tragedy*, New York, 1986.

Gilitz, D. M. *Secrecy and Deceit: The Religion of the Crypto-Jews*, Albuquerque, 2002.

Gindin, T. E. "Wordplay in the Scroll of Esther," in C. Cereti et al. (eds.), *Iranian Identity in the Course of History*, Rome, 2010, 153–161.

———. *The Book of Esther Unmasked*, Los Angeles, 2016.

Ginzberg, L. "Genizah Studies. First Article: Geonic Responsa," *JQR* 16iv (1904), 650–667.

———. *Legends of the Jews* (trans. H. Szold), Baltimore, 1909–1913.

Glaser, A.M. "Introduction," in eadem, *Stories of Khmelnytsky: Competing Literary Legacies of the 1648 Ukranian Cossak Uprising*, Stanford, 2015, 1–22.

Glickman, E. *Haman and the Jews: A Portrait from Rabbinic Literature*, Northvale, 1999.

Goitein, S. D. *A Mediterranean Society, Volume II: The Community*, Berkeley, 1971.

———. *A Mediterranean Society, Volume III: The Family*, Berkeley, 1978.

Goldberg, D. M. *The Curse of Ham: Race and Slavery in early Judaism, Christianity, and Islam*, Princeton, 2005.

Goodman, P. (ed.) *The Purim Anthology*, Philadelphia, 1949.

Granerød, G. "By the Favour of Ahuramazda I Am King: On the Promulgation of a Persian Propaganda Text among Babylonians and Judaeans," *Journal for the Study of Judaism* 44 (2013), 455–480.

Gribetz, S. Kattan. "Hanged and Crucified: The Book of Esther and *Toledot Yeshu*," in P. Schäfer, M. Meerson, and Y. Deutsch (eds.), *Toledot Yeshu ("The Life Story of Jesus") Revisited*, Tübingen, 2011, 159–180.

Gross, S. "The Curious Case of the Jewish Sasanian Queen Šīšīn-duxt: Exilarchal Propaganda and Zoroastrians in tenth- to eleventh-century Baghdad," *JAOS* 141ii (2021), 365–380.

Grossfeld, B. *Two Targums of Esther: Translated with Apparatus and Notes* (Aramaic Bible 18), Collegeville, 1991.

Grossman, E. "Three Aramaic Piyyutim for Purim: Text, Context, and Interpretation," *Aramaic Studies* 17 (2019), 198–255.

Grossman, J. "'Dynamic Analogies' in the Book of Esther," *VT* 59iii (2009), 394–414.

——. *Esther: The Outer Narrative and the Hidden Reading*, Winona Lake, 2011.
Gunkel, H. *Genesis: translated and interpreted by Hermann Gunkel*, trans. M. E. Biddle and E. W. Nicholson, Macon, 1997.
Hacham, N. "3 Maccabees and Esther: Parallels, Intertextuality, and Diaspora Identity," *JBL* 126 (2007), 765–785.
Haelewyck, J-C. (ed.), *Hester*, Freiburg, 2003–2008.
——. "Le Canon de l'Ancien Testament Dans la Tradition Syriaque (Manuscrits Bibliques, Listes Canoniques, Auteurs)," in F. Briquel Chatonnet and P. Le Moigne (eds.), *L'Ancien Testament en Syriaque: Études Syriaques* 5, Paris 2008, 141–171.
Hämeen-Anttila, J. *The Last Pagans of Iraq: Ibn Waḥshiyyah and His Nabatean Agriculture*, Leiden, 2006.
Harel, Y. "'Likhvod Ha-Umah ve Likhvod Elohey Yisrael': Hashpa'at ha-Reformot ha-Osmaniyot 'al Bitul Minhag Hakaat Haman ve-'Amalek," *Ladinaar* 3 (2004), 9–30.
Hary, B. *Multiglossia in Judeo-Arabic: With an Addition, Translation, and Grammatical Study of the Cairene Purim Scroll*, Leiden, 2000.
Haupt, P. *Purim*, Leipzig, 1906.
——. "The Cuneiform Name of the Second Adar," *JBL* 32iii (1913), 139–145.
Haynes, S. R. *Noah's Curse: The Biblical Justification of American Slavery*, Oxford, 2002.
Hayward, R. "Targum a Misnomer for Midrash? Towards a typology for the Targum Sheni of Esther," *Aramaic Studies* 9i (2011), 47–63.
Henkelman, W. *The Other Gods Who Are: Studies in Elamite-Iranian Acculturation based on the Persepolis Fortification Texts*, Leiden, 2008.
——. s.v. "Šimut" in *Reallexikon der Assyriologie* 12.7/8 2011, 511–512.
——. "Humban & Auramazdā: Royal Gods in a Persian landscape," in idem and C. Redard (eds.), *Persian Religion in the Achaemenid Period*, Wiesbaden, 2017, 273–346.
Henning, W. B. "The Murder of the Magi," *JRAS* 2 (1944), 133–44.
Herman, G. "Persia, Rome, and the Four Kingdoms Motif in the Babylonian Talmud," in G. Herman (ed.), *Four Kingdom Motifs before and beyond the Book of Daniel*, Leiden, 2020, 191–204.
Himmelfarb, M. *Jewish Messiahs in a Christian Empire*, Cambridge Mass., 2017.
Hintze, A. "The Greek and Hebrew versions of the Book of Esther and its Iranian Background," in Sh. Shaked and A. Netzer (eds.), *Irano-Judaica III*, Jerusalem, 1994, 34–39.
Hodgson, M.G.S., *The Venture of Islam: Conscience and History in a World Civilization*, Chicago, 1974.
Horowitz, E. *Reckless Rites: Purim and the Legacy of Jewish Violence*, Princeton, 2006.
——. "Esther (Book and Person) III.A Patristics and Western Christianity," in *Encyclopedia of the Bible and Its Reception*, Berlin, 2014, 8:30–34.
Hoschander, J. "The Book of Esther in the Light of History," *JQR* 9i (1918), pp. 1–41.
Hoyland, R. G. "Agapius of Manbiǧ, Qusṭā ibn Lūqā and the Graeco-Roman Past: The beginnings of Christian Arabic and Muslim Historiography," *Quaderni di Studi Arabi* 16 (2021), 7–41.
——. "Eutychius of Alexandria Vindicated: Muslim Sources and Christian Arabic Historiography in the Early Islamic Empire," in M. van Berkel and L. Osti (eds.), *The Historian of Islam at Work: Essays in Honor of Hugh N. Kennedy*, Leiden, 2022, 384–404.
——. *Theophilus of Edessa's Chronicle and the Circulation of Historical Knowledge in Late Antiquity and Early Islam*, Liverpool, 2011.
Ibn 'Abd al-Ḥakam, Abū al-Qāsim 'Abd al-Raḥmān. *Futūḥ miṣr*, Cairo, 1410 AH.
Ibn al-Jawzī, Sibṭ. *Mir'at al-zamān fī tawārīkh al-a'yān*, Damascus, 2013.
Ibn Kathīr, Abū al-Fidā'. *al-Bidāya wa al-nihāya*, Cairo, 2003.

Ibn Khaldūn, 'Abd al-Raḥmān. *Muqaddima* (ed. S. Zakkar), Beirut, 1988, trans. F. Rosenthal, *The Muqaddimah: An Introduction to History*, Princeton, 1967.
Ibn Manẓūr, Muḥammad ibn Mukarram. *Mukhtaṣar ta'rīkh dimashq*, Damascus, 1984.
Ibn Taghribirdī, Jamāl al-Dīn. *al-Nujūm al-zāhira*, Cairo, n.d.
Iṣfahānī, Ḥamza, al-. *Ta'rīkh sinī mulūk al-arḍ wa l-anbiyā'*, Leipzig, 1844.
Isidore of Seville, *The Etymologies of Isidore of Seville: Translation with introduction and notes by S.A. Barney, W.J. Lewis, J.A. Beach, and O. Berghof*, Cambridge, 2006.
Izbicki, T. M. "Juan de Torquemada's defense of the 'Conversos,'" *Catholic Historical Review* 85ii (1999), 195–207.
Jāḥiẓ, Abū 'Uthmān, al-. *al-Mukhtār fī al-radd 'alā al-naṣārā, Beirut, 1991.*
———. *Rasā'il* (ed. M. Harun), Cairo: n.d.
Jamzadeh, P. "A Shahnama Passage in an Achaemenid Context," *Iranica Antiqua* 39 (2004), 383–388.
Jastrow, M. "Signs and Names of the Planet Mars," *AJSL* 27i (1910), 64–83.
Jensen, P. "Elamitische Eigennamen. Ein Beitrag der elamitischen Inschriften," *WZKM* 6 (1892), 47–70.
Johns, A. s.v. "Haman," in *EQ*, 2:399.
Johnson, E. D. "Time and Again: Marduk's Travels," in L. Feliu, J. Llop, A. Millet-Alba, and J. Sanmartin (eds.), *Time and History in the Ancient Near East: Proceedings of the 56 Rencontre Assyriologique International at Barcelona, 26–30 July, 2010*, Winona Lake, 2013, 113–116.
Josephus, *Against Apion* (trans. H. St. J. Thackeray), Cambridge, Mass., 2014.
———. *Jewish Antiquities, Books IX-XI* (trans. R. Marcus), Cambridge, Mass., 1937.
JSAI: *Jerusalem Studies in Arabic and Islam.*
JTS: *Journal of Theological Studies.*
Kaddari, M. Z. "In what form of Aramaic was the Scroll of Antiochus written?," *Lešonenu* 23iii (1959), 129–145 (in Hebrew).
Kaldellis, A. *Hellenism in Byzantium: The Transformations of Greek Identity and the Reception of the Classical Tradition*, Cambridge, 2009.
Kalimi, I. *The Book of Esther between Judaism and Christianity*, Cambridge, 2023.
Kasheff, M. and 'Alī-Akbar Sa'īdī Sīrjānī, s.v. "ČAHĀRŠANBA-SŪRĪ" in *EIr* 4:630–634, available at: https://www.iranicaonline.org/articles/caharsanba-suri.
Khalidi, T. *Arabic Historical Thought in the Classical Period*, Cambridge, 1994.
Kiel, Y. "Abraham and Nimrod in the Shadow of Zarathustra," *The Journal of Religion* 95i (2015), 35–50.
Kisā'ī, Muḥammad ibn 'Abdallāh, al-. *Qiṣaṣ al-Anbiyā'* (ed. I. Eisenberg), Leiden, 1922, trans. Wh. Thackston, *Tales of the Prophets of al-Kisā'ī*, Boston, 1978.
Kister, M. J. "Ḥaddithū 'an banī isrā'īla wa-lā ḥaraja: A Study of an early tradition," *Israel Oriental Studies* 2 (1972), 215–239.
Kitz, A. M. "Curses and Cursing in the Ancient Near East," *Religion Compass* 1vi (2007), 615–627.
Kohlberg, E. *In Praise of the Few: Studies in Shi'i Thought and History*, Leiden, 2020.
Koller, A. *Esther in Ancient Jewish Thought*, Cambridge, 2014.
Kosmin, P. "A New Hypothesis: The Behistun Inscription as Imperial Calendar," *Iran* 57ii (2018), 1–10.
Krey, A. C. *The First Crusade: The Accounts of Eyewitnesses and Participants*, Princeton, 1921.
Kronholm, T. *Motifs from Genesis 1–11 in the Genuine Hymns of Ephrem the Syrian*, Lund, 1978.
Kruger, P. A. "A World Turned on Its Head in Ancient Near Eastern Prophetic Literature: A Powerful Strategy to Depict Chaotic Scenarios," *VT* 62 (2012), 58–76.

Kugel, J. *Traditions of the Bible: A guide to the Bible as it was at the start of the Common Era*, Cambridge Mass., 1998.

Kuhrt A. and S. M. Sherwin-White, "Xerxes' destruction of Babylonian temples," in H.W.A.M. Sancisi-Weerdenburg and A. Kuhrt (eds.), *Achaemenid History II. The Greek Sources*, Leiden, 1987, 69–78.

Kutsko, J. F. *Between Heaven and Earth: Divine Presence and Absence in the Book of Ezekiel*, Winona Lake, 2000.

Lacocque, A. "Haman in the Book of Esther," *HAR* 11 (1987), 207–222.

———. "Haman dans le livre d'Esther," *Revue de Théologie et de Philosophie* 121iii (1989), 307–322.

———. *Esther Regina: A Bakhtinian Reading*, Evanston, 2008.

Lambert, W. "Enmeduranki and Related Matters," *Journal of Cuneiform Studies* 21 (1967), 126–138.

———. *Babylonian Creation Myths*, Winona Lake, 2013.

Langdon, S. "The Babylonian and Persian Sacaea," *JRAS* 1 (1924), 65–72.

Laniak, T. *Shame and Honor in the Book of Esther*, Atlanta, 1998.

Lazarus-Yafeh, H. "Queen Esther—One of the Marranos?," *Tarbiz* 27 (1988), 121–122.

Leach, E. R. "Kingship and Divinity: The unpublished Frazer Lecture," *HAU: Journal of Ethnographic Theory* 1 (2011), 279–298.

Lee, L. "Reflections on the Scholarly Imaginations of Good and Evil in the Book of Esther," *Biblical Interpretation* 28 (2020), 273–302.

Lees, D. M. "Intertextual Ripples of the Book of Esther," unpublished PhD, University of Amsterdam, 2018.

Leiman, S. A. *The Canonization of Hebrew Scripture: The Talmudic and Midrashic Evidence*, Hamden, 1976.

Levenson, J. D. *Esther: A Commentary*, Louisville, 1997.

Levine, D. B. "Hubris in Josephus' 'Jewish Antiquities,' 1–4," *HUCA* 64 (1993), 51–87.

Levit Tawil, D. "The Purim Panel at Dura in the Light of Parthian and Sasanian Art," *JNES* 38ii (1979), 93–109.

———. "Queen Esther at Dura: Her Imagery in Light of Third-Century CE Oriental Syncretism," *Judaeo-Iranica* 4 (1999), 274–297.

Lewinsky Y. T., *Smiting Haman in the Diaspora*, Tel Aviv, 1946 (in Hebrew).

———. *Sefer ha-Mo'adim: Volume 6*, Tel Aviv, 1959.

Lewis, B. *The Jews of Islam*, Princeton, 1981.

Lewis, J. P. "Jamnia Revisited," in L. M. McDonald and J. A. Sanders (eds.), *The Canon Debate*, Peabody, 2002, 146–162.

Lewy, J. "The Feast of the 14th Day of Adar," *HUCA* 14 (1939), 127–151.

Lieber, L. S. "Stages of Grief: Enacting Lamentation in Late Ancient Hymnography," *AJS Review* 40i (2016), 101–124.

———. *Jewish Aramaic Poetry from Late Antiquity: Translations and Commentaries*, Leiden, 2018.

Lim, T. "The Defilement of the Hands as a Principle Determining the Holiness of Scriptures," *JTS* 61.2 (2010), 501–515.

Littman, R. J. "The Religious Policy of Xerxes and the 'Book of Esther,'" *JQR* 65iii (1975), 145–155.

Llewellyn-Jones, L. *Ancient Persia and the Book of Esther: Achaemenid Court Culture in the Hebrew Bible*, London, 2023.

Loader, J. A. *Esther*, Nijkerk, 1980.

Lowin, S. *The Making of a Forefather: Abraham in Islamic and Jewish Exegetical Narratives*, Leiden, 2006.

———. "Narratives of Villainy: Titus, Nebuchadnezzar, and Nimrod in the *ḥadīth* and the *midrash aggadah*," in P. M. Cobb (ed.), *The Lineaments of Islam: Essays in Honor of Fred McGraw Donner*, Leiden, 2012, 261–296.

Luria, D. *Josephus on the Book of Esther: Sources, Intentions, and Virtues*, Tel Aviv, 2015 (in Hebrew).

Macchi, J.-D. "Haman l'orgueilleux dans les livres d'Esther," in D. Böhler, I. Himbaza, and P. Hugo (eds.), *L'Ecrit et l'Esprit. Etudes d'histoire du texte et de théologie biblique en homage à Adrian Schenker*, Fribourg, 2005, 198–214.

Machinist P. and J. M. Sasson, "Rest and Violence in the poem of Erra," *JAOS* 103i (1983), 221–226.

Mackey, D. "'Nadin' [Nadab] of Tobit is the 'Holofernes' of Judith," unpublished paper available at: https://www.academia.edu/36576110/_Nadin_Nadab_of_Tobit_is_the_Holofernes_of_Judith

Maghen, Z. *Reading Revolutionary Iran: The Worldview of the Islamic Republic's Religio-Political Elite*, Berlin, 2023.

Maier, J. "Amalek in the Writings of Josephus," in E. Parente and J. Sievers (eds.), *Josephus and the History of the Greco-Roman Period: Essays in Memory of Morton Smith*, Leiden, 1994, 109–126.

Mampieri, M. *Living Under the Evil Pope*, Leiden, 2020.

Maqdisī, Muṭahhar ibn Ṭāhir, al-. *Kitāb al-bad' wa l-ta'rīkh*, Paris, 1903.

Maqrīzī, Aḥmad ibn 'Alī, al-. *Kitāb al-Mawā 'iẓ wa'l-i 'tibār fī dhikr al-khiṭaṭ wa'l-āthār*, Beirut, 1998.

Mas'ūdī, 'Alī ibn al-Ḥusayn, al-. *Murūj al-dhahab wa ma'ādin al-jawhar*, Paris, 1861–1877.

Maurus, Rhabanus, *Commentary of Rabanus Maurus on the Book of Esther*, trans. P Wyetzner: http://www.yoramhazony.org/wp-content/uploads/2015/12/Rabanus-Maurus-Esther-Commentary-English-v.-1.1-Dec-1-2015.pdf

Mazuz, H. "Al-Waṭwāṭ's description of Jewish Festivals—probing the sources of his knowledge," *Acta Orientalia Academiae Scientarium Hungaricae* 71iv (2018), 443–453.

McKane, W. "A Note on Esther IX and 1 Samuel XV," *JTS* 12ii (1961), 260–261.

Meinhold, A. *Das Buch Esther*, Zurich, 1983.

Meyerson, M. D. *A Jewish Renaissance in Fifteenth-Century Spain*, Princeton, 2010.

Milikowsky, Ch. "Midrash as Fiction and Midrash as History: What Did the Rabbis Mean?," in J-A.A. Brant, Ch. W. Hedrick, and Ch. Shea (eds.), *Ancient Fiction: The Matrix of Early Christian and Jewish Narrative*, Atlanta, 2005, 117–127.

———. *Seder Olam: Critical Edition, Commentary, and Introduction* (2 vols.), Jerusalem, 2013.

Millard, A. R. "The Persian Names in Esther and the Reliability of the Hebrew Text," *JBL* 96 (1977), 481–488.

Minov, S. "Satan's Refusal to Worship Adam: A Jewish Motif and Its Reception in Syriac Christian Tradition," in M. Kister et al. (eds.), *Tradition, Transmission, and Transformation from Second Temple Literature through Judaism and Christianity in Late Antiquity*, Leiden, 2015, 230–271.

Mishaly, A. and M. A. Zipor. *Abraham Ibn Ezra's Two Commentaries on Megilat Esther: An Annotated Critical Edition*, Ramat Gan, 2019.

Mitchell, T. C. "Biblical Archaeology in the Persian Period," in J. Curtis (ed.), *Studies in Ancient Persia and the Achaemenid Period*, London, 2020, 51–157.

Moore, C. A. *Esther*, Garden City, 1971.

———. "Esther, Book of," in D. N. Freedman (ed.), *The Anchor Bible Dictionary, Volume 2: D-G*, New York, 1992, 633–643.

Moreen, V. B. *Iranian Jewry's Hour of Peril and Heroism: A Study of Babai ibn Lutf's Chronicle (1617–1662)*, New York, 1987.

———. "The Iranization of Biblical Heroes in Judeo-Persian Epics: Shahin's Ardashir-nāmah and 'Ezra-nāmah," *Iranian Studies* 29 (1996), 321–338.

———. *In Queen Esther's Garden: An Anthology of Judeo-Persian Literature*, New Haven, 2000.

Mujmal al-tawārīkh wa al-qiṣaṣ (ed. "Malik al-Shu'arā'" Bahār), Tehran, 1317 A.H.

Münz-Manor, O. "Other Voices: Haman, Jesus, and the Representation of the Other in Purim Poems from Byzantine Palestine," in Y. Shapira, O. Herzog, and T. Hess (eds.), *Popular and Canonical: Literary Dialogues*, Tel Aviv, 2007, 69–79, 211–217.

———. "Carnivalesque Ambivalence and the Christian Other in Aramaic Poems from Byzantine Palestine," in R. Bonfil, O. Irshai, G. Stroumsa, and R. Talgam (eds.), *Jews in Byzantium: Dialectics of Minority and Majority Cultures*, Leiden, 2012, 829–843.

Murray, R. *Symbols of Church and Kingdom: A Study in Early Syriac Tradition*, Cambridge, 1977.

Narkis, B. and A. Cohen-Mushlin. "The Illumination of the Worms Maḥzor," in M. Beit-Arie (ed.), *Worms Maḥzor*, Vaduz, 1985, 79–89.

do Nascimento, R. N. "From Blessed to Accursed: The Demonization of Alexander in Persian Apocalyptic Literature," unpublished M.A. thesis, University of Brasilia 2015.

Nilsen, T. D. "Creation in Collision? Isaiah 40–48 and Zoroastrianism, Babylonian Religion, and Genesis 1," *Journal of Hebrew Scriptures* 13 (2013), 1–19.

Nir, S. "The Development of the Literary Character from Late Midrash Literature to Medieval Exegesis, as exemplified in the characters of Balaam, Jeremiah, and Esther," unpublished PhD thesis, Tel Aviv University, 2019.

Noam, V. *Shifting Images of the Hasmoneans: Second Temple Legends and Their Reception in Josephus and Rabbinic Literature*, Oxford, 2018.

Noegel, S. B. (ed.), *Puns and Pundits: Word-Play in the Hebrew Bible and Ancient Near Eastern Literature*, Bethesda, 2000.

Novick, T. *Piyyuṭ and Midrash: Form, Genre, and History*, Göttingen, 2019.

Nuwayrī, Shihāb al-Dīn, al-. *Nihāyat al-arab fī funūn al-adab*, Cairo, 1423 A.H.

Ohana, D. "The Myth of Nimrod: Between Canaanism and Zionism," in idem, *Modernism and Zionism*, London, 2012, 122–178.

Olmstead, A. T. "Tattenai, Governor of 'Across the River,'" *JNES* 3 (1944), 46.

Ophir, A. and I. Rosen-Zvi, *Goy: Israel's Multiple Others and the Birth of the Gentile*, Oxford, 2018.

Owens, R. J. *The Genesis and Exodus Citations of Aphrahat the Persian Sage*, Leiden, 1983.

Paton, L. B. *Critical and Exegetical Commentary on the Book of Esther*, London, 1908.

Peels, E. "God's Throne in Elam: The Historical Background and Literary Context of Jeremiah 49, 34–39," in J. de Moor and H. F. Van Rooy (eds.), *Past, Present and Future: The Deuteronomistic History and the Prophets*, Leiden, 2000, 216–229.

Perry, M., *Eldad's Travels: A Journey from the Lost Tribes to the Present*, London, 2019.

pseudo-Philo, *The Biblical Antiquities of Philo* (trans. M. R. James), London, 1917.

Polliack, M. "The Emergence of Karaite Bible Exegesis," *Sefunot* 22 (1999), 299–311 (in Hebrew).

Pope, M. *Song of Songs*, New York, 1977.

Quintana, E. "Elamite Religion and Ritual," in J. Alvarez-Mon (ed.), *The Elamite World*, London, 2018, 729–740.

Rabghūzī, Nāṣir al-Dīn, al-, H. E. Boeschoten, and J. O'Kane (eds.), *Al-Rabghūzī: The Stories of the Prophets. Qiṣaṣ al-Anbiyā': An Eastern Turkish Version (Second Edition)*, Leiden, 2015.

Raine, S. "Why Jihadis are Drawn to Khorasan," available here: https://engelsbergideas.com/notebook/why-jihadis-are-drawn-to-khorasan/

Rajak, T. "The Angry Tyrant," in T. Rajak, S. Pearce, J. Aitken, and J. Dines (eds.), *Jewish Perspectives on Hellenistic Rulers*, Berkeley 2007, 110–127.

Refael, Sh. (ed.) and M. Blum (trans.), *La vida de Adolf Hitler: el Haman moderno*, Salonika, 1933.

Reiner, E. "Inscription from a Royal Elamite Tomb," *AO* 24 (1973), 87–102.

———. "Astral Magic in Babylonia," *Transactions of the American Philosophical Society* 85iv (1995), 1–150.

Reynolds, F. "Unpropitious Titles of Mars in Mesopotamian Scholarly Tradition," in J. Prosecký (ed.), *Intellectual Life in the Ancient Near East*, Prague, 1998, 347–358.

———. "Stellar representations of Tiamat and Qingu in a learned Calendar Text," in K. van Lerberghe and G. Voet (eds.), *Languages and Cultures in Contact*, Leuven 1999, 369–378.

Rivlin, Y. Y. (trans.), *Perush Megillat Esther/ leha-nesher ha-gadol rabenu ha-Rambam*, Jerusalem, 1952.

Roaf, M. "Aššur in Esther," *N.A.B.U* (2023), 72–73.

Robinson, Ch. F. *Islamic Historiography*, Cambridge, 2003.

Ron, Z. "Tattenai and Haman," *Jewish Bible Review* 47iv (2019), 254–259.

Root, M. C. "Defining the divine in Achaemenid Persian Kingship: The View from Bisitun," in L. Mitchell and C. Melville (eds.), *Every Inch a King: Comparative Studies on Kings and Kingship in the Ancient and Medieval Worlds*, Leiden, 2013, 23–65.

Rosenthal, R. "With the Help of ha-Shem" *Makkor Rishon* 24/03/2011, available at: https://www.makorrishon.co.il/nrg/online/47/ART2/225/594.html.

Roth, C. "The Religion of the Marranos," *Jewish Quarterly Review* 22i (1931), 1–33.

———. "The Feast of Purim and the Origins of the Blood Accusation," *Speculum* 8iv (1933), 520–526.

Rubenstein, J. "Purim, Liminality, and Communitas," *AJS Review* 17ii (1992), 247–277.

Ruiz-Ortiz, F. J. *Dynamics of Violence and Revenge in the Hebrew Book of Esther*, Leiden, 2017.

Russell, J. R. "Zoroastrian Elements in the Book of Esther," *Irano-Judaica II* (1990), 33–40.

———. *Armenian and Iranian Studies*, Cambridge Mass., 2004.

Rustow, M. "Karaites Real and Imagined: Three Cases of Jewish Heresy," *Past and Present* 197i (2007), 35–74.

———. *Heresy and the Politics of Community: The Jews of the Fatimid Caliphate*, Ithaca, 2008.

Sabar, Sh. "The Purim Panel at Dura: A Socio-historical Interpretation," in L. I. Levine and Z. Weiss (eds.), *From Dura to Sephoris: Studies in Jewish Art and Society in Late Antiquity*, Portsmouth, 2000, 154–163.

Samʿānī, Abū l-Muẓaffar Manṣūr, al-. *Kitāb tafsīr al-qur'ān*, Riyadh, 1997.

Sanders, J. H. (trans.), *Tamerlane or Timur the Great Amir: Life of Tīmūr*, London, 1936.

Sapperstein, M. *Jewish Preaching, 1200–1800: An Anthology*, New Haven, 1989.

Sarbanani, M. Arabzadeh. "Revisiting the *Book of Esther*: Assessing the Historical Significance of the Masoretic Version for the (sic!) Achaemenian History," *Persica Antiqua* 3iv (2023), 19–32.

Schaudig, H. "The Magnanimous Heart of Cyrus: The Cyrus Cylinder and Its Literary Models," in M. R. Shayegan (ed.), *Cyrus the Great: Life and Lore*, Boston, 2018, 67–91.

Schwarzbaum, M. *Mi-maqor yisra'el ve-yishmaʿel*, Tel Aviv, 1974.

Sefer Yosippon, ed. D. Flusser, Jerusalem, 1981.

Segal, E. *The Babylonian Esther Midrash: A Critical Commentary* (3 vols), Atlanta, 1994.

———. "Esther and the Essenes," in E. Segal (ed.), *In Those Days, At This Time: Holiness and History in the Jewish Calendar*, Calgary, 2007, 139–145.

Seleznyov, N. N. "Al-Makīn Ibn al-ʿAmīd on Moses of Crete," *Scrinium* 15i (2019), 321–327.

Seri, A. "Borrowings to Create Anew: Intertextuality in the Babylonian Poem of "Creation" (*Enūma eliš*)," *JAOS* 134i (2014), 89–106.

Schrader, E. *Keilinschriften und das Alte Testament*, Berlin, 1903.

Schwenzner, W. "Gobryas," *Klio* 18 (1923), 41–58, 226–252.

———. Shäfer, P. *Judeophobia: Attitudes towards the Jews in the Ancient World*, Cambridge, Mass, 1998.

Shahbazi, A. Sh. s.v. HŌMĀN in *EIr*, 12:435–436, available at: https://www.iranicaonline.org/articles/homan-son-of-vesa

Shäfer, P. *Judeophobia: Attitudes towards the Jews in the Ancient World*, Cambridge Mass., 1998.

Shaked, Sh. "Iranian Functions in the Book of Esther," *Irano-Judaica* 1 (1982), 292–322.

Shaki, M. s.v. "Judicial and Legal Systems ii. Parthian and Sasanian Judicial Systems," in *EIr* 15:177–180, available at: https://www.iranicaonline.org/articles/judicial-and-legal-systems-ii-parthian-and-sasanian-judicial-systems

Shamir, Sh-M. "The Smiting of Haman in the Material Cultures of Ashkenazi Communities: Developments in Europe and the Revitalized Jewish Culture in Israel—Tradition and Innovation," unpublished PhD thesis, Hebrew University of Jerusalem, 2005 (in Hebrew).

Shapira, D. "Judeo-Persian translations of Old Persian lexica," in L. Paul (ed.), *Persian Origins—Early Judaeo-Persian and the Emergence of New Persian*, Wiesbaden, 2003, 221–242.

Sharon, M. *Black Banners from the East*, Leiden, 1983.

Shayegan, M. R. *Aspects of History and Epic in Ancient Iran*, Cambridge, Mass., 2012.

Shea, W. H. "Esther and History," *Concordia Journal* 13 (1987), 234–248.

Shemesh, A. *Punishments and Sins, from Scripture to Rabbinic Literature*, Jerusalem, 2004.

———. "How shall we kill him? By sword, fire, or lions? The Aramaic targum and the Midrashic narratives on Haman's gallows," *HTS Theological Studies* 74iv (2020), 1–11.

Shiel, M.L.W. *Glimpses of Life and Manners in Persia*, London, 1856.

Shinan, A. "The Late Midrashic, Paytanic, and Targumic Literature," in S. Katz (ed.), *The Cambridge History of Judaism, Volume IV: The Late Roman-Rabbinic Period*, Cambridge, 2006, 678–698.

Silverman, J. M. "Was there an Achaemenid 'Theology' of Kingship?" in D. Edelman, A. Fitzpatrick-McKinley, and Ph. Guillaume, *Religion in the Achaemenid Persian Empire*, Tübingen, 2016, 172–196.

Silverstein, A. J. "The Book of Esther and the *Enūma Elish*," *BSOAS* 69ii (2006), 209–223.

———. *Postal Systems in the Pre-Modern Islamic World*, Cambridge, 2007.

———. "The Qur'ānic Pharaoh," in G. S. Reynolds, (ed.), *New Perspectives on the Qur'ān*, London, 2011, 467–477.

———. "On the Original Meaning of the Qur'ānic Phrase *al-shayṭān al-rajīm*," JAOS 133i (2013), pp. 21–33.

———. *Veiling Esther, Unveiling Her Story: The Reception of a Biblical Book in Islamic Lands*, Oxford, 2018.

———. "Who are the *Aṣḥāb al-Ukhdūd*? Q 85:4–10 in Near Eastern Context," *Der Islam* 96ii (2019), 281–323.

———. "Q 30:2–5 in Near Eastern Context," *Der Islam* 97.1 (2020), 11–42.

———. "Unmasking Maskh: The Transformation of Jews into "Apes, Driven Away" (Qur'ān 7:166) in Near Eastern Context," *JSAI* 49 (2020), 177–216.

———. "Did Esther lose her *huile d'olive*? Bilingual puns in MT *Esther*," unpublished paper presented at the Hebrew University of Jerusalem, June 19, 2023.

Sinai, N. "Pharaoh's Submission to God in the Qur'an and in Rabbinic Literature: A case study in Qur'anic intertextuality," in H. Zellentin (ed.), *The Qur'an's Reformation of Judaism and Christianity: Return to the Origins*, Abingdon, 2019, 235–260.

Sivan, H. *Palestine in Late Antiquity*, Oxford, 2008.

Sivertsev, A. *Judaism and Imperial Ideology in Late Antiquity*, Cambridge, 2011.

Socrates Scholasticus, *Ecclesiastical History*, London, 1853.

Soudavar, A. *The Aura of Kings: Legitimacy and Divine Sanction in Iranian Kingship*, Costa Mesa, 2003.

———. *Mithraic Societies: From Brotherhood to Religion's Adversary*, n.p. 2014.

Sperber, D. "Effacing Haman's Name," in Y. Eisenberg, *Shanah be-Shanah: Yearbook for 2002*, Jerusalem, 2002, 203–211 (in Hebrew).

Spicehadler, E. "Shahin's Influence on Babai ben Lotf: The Abraham-Nimrod Legend," *Irano-Judaica* 2 (1990), 158–165.

Stal, J. I. "The End of Zeresh," *Ha-Paamon* 4 (2012), 74–80 (in Hebrew).

———. "On the identity of Shimshai the Scribe: Whether he was Haman or Haman's son," *Segullah* 1 (2019), 1–15 (in Hebrew).

Steinhaulf, E. "The Frescoes of the Dura Europos Synagogue: Multicultural Traits and Jewish Identity," unpublished M.A. thesis, McGill University, 2004.

Stenhouse, P. *The Kitāb al-Taʾrīkh of Abū ʾl-Fatḥ*, Sydney, 1985.

Stewart, D. "Popular Shiism in Medieval Egypt: Vestiges of Islamic Sectarian Polemics in Egyptian Arabic," *Studia Islamica* 84 (1996), 35–66.

Stolper, M. W. "Yet Another Iranian Loanword in Late Babylonian: Babyl. Mašaka < Ir. *važaka," *JAOS* 97 (1977), 547–549.

———. "A Paper Chase after the Aramaic on TCL 13 193," *JAOS* 116iii (1996), 517–521.

Stone, J. R. *The Essential Max Müller on Language, Mythology, and Religion*, New York, 2002.

Stone, M. E. *A History of the Literature of Adam and Eve*, Atlanta, 1992.

Stronach, D. "Cyrus and the Kingship of Anshan," *Iran* 51 (2013), 55–69.

Sulpicius Severus, *Sacred History*, trans. A. Roberts, *Nicene and Post-Nicene Fathers, Second Series*, Volume 11, ed. Ph. Schaff and H. Wace Buffalo, New York, 1894.

Swart, G. J. "Rahab and Esther in Josephus: An Intertextual Approach," *Acta Patristica et Byzantina* 17i (2006), 50–65.

Swain, J. W. "The Theory of the Four Monarchies: Opposition History under the Roman Empire," *CP* 35 (1940), 1–21.

Sweeny, M. A. "Contrasting Portrayals of the Achaemenid Monarchy in Isaiah and Zecharia," in M. R. Shayegan (ed.), *Cyrus the Great: Life and Lore*, Boston, Mass., 2018, 117–130.

Syed, Sh. M. "Historicity of Haman as mentioned in the Qur'ān," *Islamic Quarterly* 24i (1980), 48–59.

Ṭabarī, Abū Jaʿfar, al-. *Taʾrīkh al-rusul wa l-mulūk*, Leiden, 1879–1901, trans. W. M. Brinner, *The History of al-Ṭabarī: Volume III. The Children of Israel*, Albany, 1991, and M. Perlmann, *The History of al-Tabari: Volume IV, The Ancient Kingdoms*, Albany, 1987.

Tabory, J. "Yefet in the House of Shem: The Influence of the Septuagint Translation of the Scroll of Esther on Rabbinic Literature," *Sidra: A Journal for the Study of Rabbinic Literature* (2010), 485–502.

Tadmor, E. "Erudite Savagery: Intertextuality in Ashurbanipal's Account of the Siege of Babylon," *JNES* 82i (2023), 43–58.

Tafażżolī, A. s.v. "Arjāsp" in *EIr* 2:412, available at: https://www.iranicaonline.org/articles/arjasp

Talmon, S. "'Wisdom' in the Book of Esther," *VT* 13iv (1963), 419–455.

Tannous, R. "Negotiating the Nativity in Late Antiquity: The Qur'ān's Rereading of Mary's Preparation for the Conception of Jesus," unpublished PhD thesis, University of Toronto, 2019.

Tavernier, J. "An Achaemenid Royal Inscription: The Text of Paragraph 13 of the Aramaic Version of the Bisitun Inscription," *JNES* 60iii (2001), 161–176.

Taylor, D. "The Bodleian Letters: Text and Translation," in C. J. Tuplin and J. Ma (eds.), *Aršama and His World: The Bodleian Letters in Context. Volume I: The Bodleian Letters*, Oxford, 2020, 21–49.

Taylor, K. "The Erra Song: A Religious, Literary, and Comparative Analysis," unpublished PhD thesis, Harvard University, 2017.

Teter, M. *Jews and Heretics in Catholic Poland*, Cambridge, 2006.

Thaʿlabī, Aḥmad ibn Muḥammad, al-. *al-Kashf wa l-bayān ʿan tafsīr al-Qurʾān*, Jeddah, 2015.

Thackston, W. M. *Tales of the Prophets of al-Kisāʾī*, Boston, 1979.

Thambyrajah, J. "A Macedonian in the Persian Court: Addition E of Esther and the Vetus Latina," *VT* 71iv-v (2021), 743–50.

———. "'Other laws': Haman's accusation against the Jews in the book of Esther," *JSOT* 47i (2022), 43–55.

Thornton, T.C.G. "The Crucifixion of Haman and the Scandal of the Cross," *JTS* 37ii (1986), 419–426.

Tirosh-Becker, O. "The Use of Rabbinic Sources in Karaite Writings," in M. Polliack (ed.), *Karaite Judaism: A Guide to Its History and Literary Sources*, Leiden, 2003, 319–338.

Torab, A. *Performing Islam: Gender and Ritual in Iran*, Leiden, 2007.

Torrey, C. C. "The Older Book of Esther," *Harvard Theological Review* 37 (1944), 1–40.

Tottoli, R. s.v. "Haman" in *EI3*, available at: https://referenceworks.brillonline.com/entries/encyclopaedia-of-islam-3/haman-COM_30242?s.num=68&s.start=60.

Toumanoff, C. *Studies in Christian Caucasian History*, Washington DC, 1963.

———. s.v. "Amatuni," in *EIr* 1:928–929, available at: https://www.iranicaonline.org/articles/amatuni-armenian-dynastic-house-known-historically-after-the-4th-century-a.

Tuplin, C. J. "The Bodleian Letters: Commentary," in C. J. Tuplin and J. Ma (eds.), *Aršama and His World: The Bodleian Letters in Context. Volume I: The Bodleian Letters*, Oxford, 2020, 61–283.

Van Bekkum, W. "Anti-Christian Polemics in Hebrew Liturgical Poetry (Piyyuṭ) of the Sixth and Seventh Centuries," in J. den Boeft and A. Hilhorst (eds.), *Early Christian Poetry*, Leiden, 1993, 297–308.

VanderBurgh, F. A. "Babylonian Legends, BM Tablets 87535 and 87521, CT XV, Plates 1–6," *JAOS* 32 (1912), 21–32.

VT: *Vetus Testamentum*.

Wacholder, B.Z. "Pseudo-Eupolemus' Two Greek Fragments on the Life of Abraham," *HUCA* 34 (1963), 83–113.

Walfish, B. *Esther in Medieval Garb: Jewish Interpretation of the Book of Esther in the Middle Ages*, Albany, 1993.

———. "Kosher Adultery? The Esther-Mordecai-Ahasuerus Triangle," *Prooftexts: A Journal of Jewish Literary History* 22iii (2002), 305–33.

Walker, C. "Myth of Girra and Elamatum," *Anatolian Studies* 33 (1983), 145–152.

Waṭwāṭ, Jamāl al-Dīn, al-. *Mabāhij al-fikar wa-manāhij al-ʿibar, 2 vols*, Frankfurt am Main, 1990.

Wechsler, M. G. "Shadow and Fulfilment in the Book of Esther," *Bibliotheca Sacra* 154 (1997), 275–284.

———. "The Purim-Passover Connection: A Reflection of Jewish Exegetical Tradition in the Peshitta Book of Esther," *JBL* 117ii (1998), 321–335.

———. "Two Para-biblical Novellae from Qumran Cave 4: A Reevaluation of 4Q550," *Dead Sea Discoveries* 7ii (2000), 130–172.

———. "An Early Karaite Commentary on the Book of Esther," *HUCA* 72 (2001), 101–137.

———. "The Appellation βογγαιος and Ethnic Contextualization in the Greek Text of Esther," *VT* 51i (2001), 109–114.

———. *The Arabic Translation and Commentary of Yefet Ben ʿEli the Karaite on the Book of Esther*, Leiden, 2008.

———. *Strangers in the Land: The Judaeo-Arabic Exegesis of Tanḥum ha-Yerushalmi on the Books of Ruth and Esther*, Jerusalem, 2010

———. "Ten Newly Identified Fragments of Saadiah's Commentary on Esther: Introduction and Translation," in J. L. Kraemer and M. G. Wechsler (eds.), *Pesher Nahum: Texts and Studies in Jewish History and Literature from Antiquity through the Middle Ages Presented to Norman (Nahum) Golb*, Chicago, 2012, 237–292.

———. "Saadia's Seven Guidelines for 'Conviviality in Exile' (from His Commentary on Esther)," *Intellectual History of the Islamicate World* 1 (2013), 203–233.

———. "Medieval Judaism: Judeo-Arabic Commentary," in *Encyclopaedia of the Bible and Its Reception*, Berlin, 2013, 8:24–27.

———. "Dissimulation" in *Encyclopaedia of the Bible and Its Reception*, Berlin, 2013, 6:936–940.

———. "Esther (Book and Person) III.B Near Eastern Christianity," in *Encyclopaedia of the Bible and Its Reception*, Berlin, 2013, 8:34–38.

———. *The Book of Conviviality in Exile (Kitāb al-īnās bi-'l-jalwa): The Judaeo-Arabic Translation and Commentary of Saadia Gaon on the Book of Esther*, Leiden, 2015.

———. "Saʿadia Gaon on Esther's Invitation of Haman: A Case Study in Exegetical Innovation and Influence," in M. Polliack and A. Brenner-Idan (eds.), *Jewish Biblical Exegesis from Islamic Lands: The Medieval Period*, Atlanta, 2019, 321–338.

———. "The Reception of Saadia Gaon's Commentary on Esther in the Karate Tradition of Judaeo-Arabic Commentary on the Book," in G. Dye (ed.), *Perspectives sur l'histoire du karaïsme*, Brussels, 2022, 39–67.

Weitzman, S. "Plotting Antiochus's Persecution," *JBL* 123ii (2004), 219–234.

Wiggermann, F.A.M. s.v. "Nergal." In *Reallexikon der Assyriologie*: https://publikationen.badw.de/en/rla/index#8358

Wilk, R. "The Abuse of Nicanor's Corpse," *Sidra* (1992), 53–57 (in Hebrew).

Wills, C. J. *Persia as it is: Being Sketches of Modern Persian Life and Culture*, London, 1886.

Wills, L. M. *The Jew in the Court of the Foreign King: Ancient Jewish Court Legends*, Minneapolis, 1990.

———. *The Jewish Novel in the Ancient World*, Ithaca, 1995.

Wilson, S. G. *Persian Life and Customs*, Edinburgh, 1896.

Winitzer, A. "The Reversal of Fortune Theme in Esther: Israelite Historiography in its Ancient Near Eastern Context," *Journal of Ancient Near Eastern Religions* 11ii (2011), 170–218.

Wisnom, S. "Blood on the Wind and the Tablet of Destinies: Intertextuality in *Anzû*, *Enūma eliš*, and *Erra and Išum*," *JAOS* 139ii (2019), 269–286.

———. *Weapons of words: intertextual competition in Babylonian poetry:* A study of *Anzû*, *Enūma Eliš*, and *Erra and Išum*, Leiden, 2020.

Yahalom, Y. and Sokoloff, M. *Jewish Palestinian Aramaic Poetry from Late Antiquity*, Jerusalem, 1999.

Yalqut Shimʿoni, Jerusalem, 2004–2005.

Yamauchi, E. *Persia and the Bible*, Grand Rapids, 1990.

———. "Mordecai of the Persepolis Tablets and the Susa Excavations," *VT* 42 (1992), 272–275.

Yaʿqūbī, Aḥmad ibn Abī Yaʿqūb, al-. *Taʾrīkh al-yaʿqūbī*, Leiden, 1883.

Yāqūt al-Ḥamawī, *Muʿjam al-buldān*, Beirut, 1995.

Yerushalmi, Y. Y. *Zakhor: Jewish History and Jewish Memory*, Seattle, 1982.

Zadeh, T. "'Fire Cannot Harm It': Mediation, Temptation, and the Charismatic Power of the Qur'an," *Journal of Qur'anic Studies* 10ii (2008), 50–72.

Zadok, R. "On Five Biblical Names," *ZAW* 88 (1977), 266–268.

———. "On the Historical Background of the Book of Esther," *Biblische Notizen* 24 (1984), 18–23.

Zawanowska, M. "Islamic exegetical terms in Yefet ben 'Eli's commentaries on the Holy Scriptures," *JJS* 64ii (2013), 306–325.
Zimmern, H. "Zur Frage nach dem Ursprünge des Purimfestes," *ZAW* 11 (1891) 157–169.
———. *Zum Babylonischen Neujahrsfest*, Leipzig, 1918.
Zlotnick-Sivan, H. *Dinah's Daughters: Gender and Judaism from the Hebrew Bible to Late Antiquity*, Philadelphia, 2002.
———. "Moses the Persian? Exodus 2, the "Other," and Biblical 'Mnemohistory,'" *ZAW* 116 (2004), 189–205.

SCRIPTURAL INDEX

GENERAL INDEX

Aaron, 68, 250n4
Abbasid: Caliphate, 121–25, 127, 129, 131, 166, 167, 255n27, 266n202, 269n239; Revolution, 276n13
ʿAbdallāh ibn Salām, 156
Abraham, 77, 80, 89, 167, 188, 194, 199, 202–204, 222, 236, 284n6, 288n69, 295n4. *See also* Abram
Abrahamic religions, 1–3, 5, 7, 48, 64, 71, 77, 80, 81, 83, 101, 112, 127, 137, 167, 193, 205, 207, 213, 214, 237, 251n7, 272n35, 287n50
Abram, 203, 258n79. *See also* Abraham
Abū al-Fatḥ ibn Abī al-Ḥasan, 139–41, 271nn19 and 20
Abū al-Fidāʾ, 251n7, 288n26
Abū Bakr, 153
Abū Jahl, 200, 235, 295n5
Abū Lahab, 197, 200, 235, 295n4
Abū Righāl, 223
Achaemenid empire, 14, 16, 62, 67, 67, 77–82, 84, 88, 107, 109, 116, 123, 128, 129, 132, 133, 135, 155, 162, 165, 168–73, 175–77, 179–87, 192, 194, 195, 206, 209, 221, 225, 228, 244n43, 251n14, 253n37, 254nn2, 3 and 13, 255n19, 256n50, 269n46, 277n34, 277nn36 and 42, 280n100, 282nn121 and 126, 283nn136, 143 and 145, 288n84, 291n24
Adam, 29, 128, 162, 199, 248n22
Adar, 10, 64, 66, 85, 86, 93, 94, 134, 172, 184, 186, 189, 203, 231, 248n20, 278n52
Adrammelekh. *See* Arda-Mulissu
Aelia. *See* Jerusalem
Afghanistan, 164, 292n53
Agag/Agagite, 10, 11, 14–16, 18, 23, 24, 27, 28, 55, 64, 67, 86, 91, 107, 109, 118, 142, 162, 163, 165–68, 173–77, 225, 240n13, 243nn26 and 27, 244n48, 246n73, 260n102, 275n7, 278n60
Agapius (Maḥbūb) of Manbij, 125, 131, 135, 267n218, 268nn218–21
Ahab, 196, 289n100
Aharon ben Menaḥem. *See* Buonamici, Giovan Battista
Ahashwerosh, *passim*. *See also* Xerxes
Ahasuerus. *See* Ahashwerosh
Aḥiqar, 65, 169, 207, 252nn25 and 27, 257n68, 286n32
Aḥmad Pasha, 143
Ahriman, 79
Ahura-Mazda, 79, 180, 184–86, 282n128, 283n142
Akiba (rabbi), 89, 249n15
Akītu, 174, 181, 227, 281n109. *See also* New Year festival
Akkad/Akkadian, 10, 172, 173, 175, 176, 178, 179, 181–83, 186, 211, 221, 241n8, 278nn52 and 57, 279n81, 281n112, 282nn124 and 127, 283nn137 and 144
ʿĀl ha-Nissīm prayer, 11, 66, 116, 252n32, 261n117
Aleppo, 100
Alexander III (tsar), 146
Alexander the Great, 81, 84, 88, 92, 107, 108, 162, 184, 219, 228, 255n17, 259n89, 260n109, 261nn113, 116 and 119, 267n212, 282n131
Alexandria, 20, 21, 52, 57, 92, 98, 105, 162, 259n92
ʿAlī, 122, 153, 231, 266n203
Almoravids, 144
"Alpha Text," 21, 22, 25–34, 37, 40, 87, 163, 179, 207, 242nn21–23, 243nn24, 26 and 33–35, 244nn38, 42 and 45, 245nn54 and 55, 246n63, 268n33

Conversos, 139, 143–45, 157, 229, 272nn36 and 42, 273n65. *See also* crypto-Jews
Cooper, Thomas, 152
Coptic, 50, 54, 55, 256n43
crucifixion, 26, 45, 104, 108, 109, 125, 216, 220, 221, 225, 233, 247nn12, 16 and 17, 257n62, 261n122, 268n221, 280n100, 291n24, 293nn63 and 77
crypto-Jews, 143–45, 272n36. *See also* Conversos
Ctesias, 169
Cutha, 176
Cyril of Jerusalem, 55
Cyrus the Great, 14, 78, 79, 105, 122, 131, 135, 180–82, 184–86, 245n61, 253n57, 268n221, 270n251, 281nn107, 113, 114 and 116; cylinder of, 181, 182, 281nn113 and 114

Daivā, 185, 186, 197, 283nn141 and 142, 286n29
Dajjāl. *See* Antichrist
Dalley, S., 139, 276n27, 277nn38 and 45, 279n81
Damascus Affair (1840), 142
Damnatio Memoriae, 220
Daniel/*Daniel*, 15, 33, 77, 95, 96, 100, 104, 105, 115, 131, 187, 216, 222, 240n12, 244n39, 245n57, 259n88, 263n152, 264n165, 292n50
Dārāb/*DārābNāma*, 84, 88, 255nn17–19
Darius, 67, 84, 136, 169, 180, 182–86, 197, 221, 228, 244n43, 269n246, 271n20, 277nn36 and 37, 280n100, 282n130, 283n138
Davies, Phillip, 235, 236, 293n72
Day of Judgment, 56, 68, 205. *See also* End Times; Eschaton
De la Cavalleria, Pedro, 154
De Lagarde, Paul, 27
De Ratti Menton, Count, 142
Dead Sea Scrolls, 6, 44, 52, 71, 86, 90, 105, 258n79
Deh Khodā, ʿAlī Akbar, 202–4, 288n66. See also *Lughat Nāma*
Delgado, João Pinto, 144, 145, 272nn38 and 40
Della Valle, Piedro, 231
Demetrius, 94, 95
Diabolos. *See* Satan
Diaspora, 15, 21, 52–54, 79, 92–94, 97, 103, 106, 118, 123, 124, 171, 216, 232, 249n14, 263n152, 267nn205 and 214
Didascalia, 97
Diodorus Siculus, 209
Dionysus: rites of, 99, 245n52
Dositheus, 100
Dura Europos, 52, 81, 212, 244n44, 260n106, 269n245, 284n151

early modern period, 2, 111, 137, 146, 147, 151, 152, 157, 270n2
Easter, 226, 228, 229, 292n53
Eastern Roman empire. *See* Byzantium/Byzantine empire
Edom/Edomites, 18, 29, 38, 106, 108, 110, 116, 118, 141, 149, 165, 166, 179, 193, 205, 246n65, 259n99, 260n105, 262n135. *See also* Esau
Egypt/Egyptians, 15, 21, 42, 50, 62, 64, 65, 67, 69, 72, 81, 92, 93, 98–100, 105, 126, 128, 129, 142, 143, 153, 155, 156, 162–64, 167, 180, 182, 185, 188, 192, 208–10, 216, 226, 233, 242n12, 243n32, 251n7, 253n35, 256n42, 258n79, 259n92, 270n8, 275n85, 277n36, 283n138, 288n80, 292n54
Eisenberg, I., 154
Elam/Elamite, 50, 167, 171, 173–91, 195, 233, 275n1, 276n29, 278n53, 63 and 69, 279nn80, 83, 84 and 86, 280nn91, 92, 94, and 98, 281n114, 283nn136, 137 and 146, 284n148, 292n34. *See also* Neo-Elamite period/dynasty
Elephantine, 92
Eliezer (rabbi), 240n10
Elijah-cycle, 196
End Times, 105. *See also* Day of Judgment; Eschaton
Enlil, 173, 174
Enūma Eliš, 174, 175, 182, 227, 279n80
Ephrem the Syrian, 55, 288n85
Epic of Anzū, 173, 174
Epistle of Rabbi Sherirah Gaon, 124
Ereškigal, 176, 279n79
Eritrea, 163, 256n42
Erra/Erra Song, 175, 176
Esau, 13, 17, 18, 106, 107, 110, 141, 146, 162, 173, 179, 193, 204, 205, 241n20, 246n65, 259n99, 260nn103–5, 261nn117 and 124, 262nn135 and 138, 264n156, 275n7. *See also* Edom/Edomites